THE SURPRISING EFFECTS OF SYMPATHY

THE SURPRISING EFFECTS

O F

SYMPATHY

MARIVAUX, DIDEROT, ROUSSEAU,
A N D
MARY SHELLEY

DAVID MARSHALL

THE UNIVERSITY OF CHICAGO PRESS
CHICAGO AND LONDON

David Marshall is associate professor of
English and comparative literature at Yale
University. He is the author of *The Figure of
Theater: Shaftesbury, Defoe, Adam Smith, and
George Eliot.*

The University of Chicago Press, Chicago 60637
The University of Chicago Press, Ltd., London

© 1988 by The University of Chicago
All rights reserved. Published 1988
Printed in the United States of America
97 96 95 94 93 92 91 90 89 88   5 4 3 2 1

Frontispiece: Illustration by Jacob van den Schley,
from volume 1 of Marivaux's *La Vie de Marianne*
(The Hague: Jean Neaulme, 1736), reproduced by
permission of the Houghton Library,
Harvard University.

Chapter 5, "Rousseau and the State of Theater," has
been reprinted by permission of the Regents from
Representations, no. 13 (Winter 1986):84–114. © 1986
by The Regents of the University of California.

The University of Chicago Press gratefully acknowledges a subvention from the Frederick W.
Hilles Publication Fund of Yale University in partial
support of the costs of production of this volume.

Library of Congress Cataloging-in-Publication Data
Marshall, David, 1953 Dec. 20–
    The surprising effects of sympathy.

    Includes index.
        1. French fiction—18th century—History and
criticism. 2. Sympathy in literature. 3. Aesthetics,
French—18th century. 4. Marivaux, Pierre Carlet
de Chamblain de, 1688–1763—Fictional works. 5. Diderot,
Denis, 1713–1784. La Religieuse. 6. Rousseau, Jean
Jacques, 1712–1778. Lettre à d'Alembert sur les
spectacles. 7. Theater—Moral and ethical aspects.
8. Shelley, Mary Wollstonecraft, 1797–1851. Frankenstein.
9. Literature, Comparative—French and English.
10. Literature, Comparative—English and French.
    I. Title.
PQ637.S96M37   1988   843'.5'09353   87–19214
ISBN 0–226–50710–6

for Candace Waid

Contents

Acknowledgments

The acknowledgment of the participation and assistance of others is a complicated if necessary place to begin or end a book about sympathy, identification, and what it means to represent oneself or others before readers and spectators. I am nonetheless pleased to have the opportunity to express my gratitude for various contributions to my work.

I am grateful to Yale University for a Morse Fellowship; it provided me with the time to write a substantial portion of this book. I was also fortunate to begin writing while I was a fellow at the Whitney Humanities Center; the interest of the fellows and the director, Peter Brooks, was very much appreciated. A grant from the A. Whitney Griswold Fund facilitated preparation of the final manuscript. John Merriman, Master of Branford College, generously provided the office in which the book was completed.

Portions or versions of the following chapters were presented in lecture form on various occasions; my thanks to my hosts and audiences at Princeton University, the University of California at Berkeley, the University of Minnesota, Vanderbilt University, and the Eastern Comparative Literature Conference at New York University, as well as sessions of the Northeast Modern Language Association and the Modern Language Association. I was very fortunate to have had the opportunity to work out my interpretations in undergraduate and graduate courses at Yale. Such dialogues with colleagues and students inform the readings contained in this book. A version of Chapter Five appeared in *Representations*; I am grateful to the editors for their comments and permission to reprint.

April Alliston helped to prepare the translations provided in this book; without holding her responsible for any infelicities, I would like to acknowledge her thorough and creative work. Christopher Rivers and William Jewett provided careful assistance with the proofreading. As usual, I am grateful to Jean Edmunds for logistical and moral support.

I am especially grateful to numerous friends and colleagues for conversations, comments about particular chapters, and encouragement, particularly Jennifer Wicke, Michael Holquist, Norton Batkin, Peter Brooks, Margaret Ferguson, Patricia Meyer Spacks, Thomas Greene, David Hensley, Leslie Agnew, and Louis Marin. From the earliest stages of this book I have benefited from Michael Fried's generous advice and support, as well as his writing on Diderot and on eighteenth-, nineteenth-, and twentieth-century art. Jean-Christophe Agnew, whose work is also concerned with many of the issues treated here, and with whom I taught some texts of Rousseau and Diderot in an interdisciplinary seminar on theatricality, has been a crucial interlocutor; both his literary sympathies and his historical scepticism have contributed substantially to this book. Countless conversations with Candace Waid, who read various versions of this book, as well as a continuing dialogue with her work, are inscribed throughout these pages. As always, Arthur Marshall, Helene Marshall, Cindy Marshall, and Karen Marshall provided confidence and sustenance.

Introduction

The title of this book is borrowed from the title of Marivaux's first novel, *Les Aventures de *** ou Les Effets surprenants de la sympathie*, a strange, picaresque narrative filled with bloody spectacles, desperate lovers, kidnapped heroines, and Turkish sultans. I became interested in this obscure example of Marivaux's *oeuvres de jeunesse* some years ago at about the same time I became intrigued by a strange passage in book five of Rousseau's *Confessions* in which the most accident-prone figure of the Enlightenment describes a disastrous attempt to make *l'encre de sympathie*. As he tries to make a kind of invisible ink, Rousseau accidentally corks a bottle and the solution he is concocting explodes in his face, blinding him for several weeks. I was struck by the idea that sympathetic ink—the ink of sympathy—might play a role in the writing or reading of Rousseau's autobiography. The "Avis au lecteur" that prefaces *Les Effets surprenants de la sympathie* insists that a novel should be judged by its ability to move or touch its reader, and it repeatedly compares the reader to the witness of a bloody accident. Marivaux, it seemed, also wanted *l'encre de sympathie*.

What joins the uses of the word *sympathie* in Rousseau's ink and Marivaux's title is ostensibly the polyvalent sense of elective affinities that would allow Goethe to unite chemistry and sentiment in his title, *Die Wahlverwandtschaften*. At the same time, however, eighteenth-century works of fiction, autobiography, autobiographical fiction, aesthetics, and moral philosophy often turn and return to the question of the effects of sympathy: the question of what happens when readers of novels, beholders of paintings, audiences in the theater, or people in the world are faced with the spectacle of an accident, suffering, or danger. Both Rousseau and Marivaux are often preoccupied with experiences of compassion, commiseration, pity, and identification—in other words, sympathy—in the realms of both "life" and "art." I began to realize that this preoccupation with the effects of sympathy was more than a gesture toward sentiment and sensibility, especially in the context of the recurrent problem of theatricality in eighteenth-century narratives.

In my book, *The Figure of Theater: Shaftesbury, Defoe, Adam Smith, and George Eliot,* I focused on the metaphor of theater in certain key texts in the English tradition that are concerned with the theatrical roles and relations enacted *outside* of the playhouse.[1] I discussed critical reflections on books, authors, readers, and identity by Shaftesbury and fiction by Defoe and Eliot; my example of a work of moral philosophy that was concerned with theatrical relations was Smith's *Theory of Moral Sentiments,* a treatise about the dynamics and indeed the possibility of sympathy. I included Smith in the book because his treatise on sympathy seemed to me to be about the problem of theatricality, but I began to sense that texts which reflected or reflected on the problem of theatricality might also be addressing the question of sympathy. I crossed the threshold into the nineteenth-century novel and included a chapter on Eliot in part because I realized that *Daniel Deronda,* Eliot's novel about theater and theatricality, also was a philosophical investigation of the problem of sympathy. By the time I returned to Marivaux and Rousseau, as well as to Diderot, Du Bos, and other eighteenth-century French authors, I knew that my subject had become the interplay of theater and sympathy.

This focus became more clear as I considered discussions of the institution of the theater and the art of acting as well as works in which the *figure* of theater played a major role. Theories of acting as well as debates about the morality and effects of plays turn upon questions of identification, distance, and the ability of both actors and audience to perform acts of sympathy—just as discussions of sympathy turn on the theatrical relations that make the possibility of fellow feeling a problem of representation and aesthetic experience as well as a problem of moral philosophy. These are questions that are addressed by eighteenth-century novels, many of which are preoccupied with the theater of everyday life in which characters appear as actors and spectators, the status of the novel as a spectacle before readers who are pictured as spectators, and the problem of how to move, touch, and secure the sympathy of readers.

For Du Bos, Marivaux, Rousseau, Diderot, and Mary Shelley (and in general in eighteenth-century fiction and aesthetics), theatricality and sympathy are closely related problems. It is well known that the transition from classical aesthetics (with its emphasis on a priori rules and principles) to the pre-Romantic aesthetics of the eighteenth century (with its emphasis on subjectivity and affect) centered on the question of the *effects* that a work of art had on its reader or beholder.

I am concerned both with the effects of sympathy and the status of sympathy as a particularly desired effect in eighteenth-century reflections on the experience of the work of art. I suggest that a consideration of the problem of sympathy can help make sense of the deep analogies at work within eighteenth-century fiction and aesthetics between the acts of reading a novel, beholding a painting, and watching a play—as well as parallels between fiction, aesthetics, epistemology, and moral philosophy. These analogies also can help to explain why theater was so important to Marivaux, Rousseau, and Diderot.

Insofar as this introduction is my "Avis au lecteur," I should note that I use the words *sympathy* and *sympathie* here in the context of the network of associations in eighteenth-century France and England that linked such words and concepts as "sensation," "sentiment," "sentimental," "sensibilité," "sensibility," and "sensible."[2] *Sympathy* is, as it were, a subset of this network that suggests not just feeling or the capacity for feeling but more specifically the capacity to feel the sentiments of someone else. As I suggested earlier, taken in its most extended sense, *sympathie* implies a correspondence of feelings between people such as a mutual attraction or affinity; yet even in this sense it contains both an etymology and a network of eighteenth-century associations that suggest the act of entering into the sentiments of another person.

Departing from their original Greek sense of participation in the suffering of another, *sympathy* and *sympathie* acquire a general sense of fellow feeling. Adam Smith writes in *The Theory of Moral Sentiments*: "Pity and compassion are words appropriated to signify our fellow-feeling with the sorrow of others. Sympathy, though its meaning was, perhaps, originally the same, may now, however, without much impropriety, be made use of to denote our fellow-feeling with any passion whatever."[3] In the eighteenth century, the word suggests putting oneself in the place of someone else, taking someone else's part—a general condition or act, related to the modern word "empathy," of which pity, compassion, and commiseration are only specific examples. In my own discourse I prefer the word *sympathy* to the more modern word *empathy* because I would like to evoke the particularly eighteenth-century resonance of the word *sympathy* in English (which includes its associations with the experiences of pity, compassion, and commiseration) at the same time I would prefer to avoid the vaguely psychologistic connotations of the word *empathy*.

Having outlined these senses of sympathy, however, I should emphasize that I am concerned here with the category, concept, and conditions of sympathy in certain key eighteenth-century texts, not with particular words. For example, if I take the presence of the word *sympathie* in the title *Les Effets surprenants de la sympathie* as at least an indication of what Marivaux might think his novel is about, I do not consider the word in itself to be an authorization for my argument. (At the same time, however, if *sympathie* and *sympathy* are not precise cognates in eighteenth-century usage, it is nonetheless significant that *attendrir*, *émouvoir*, and *toucher* are crucial verbs in both the novel and its "Avis au lecteur.") I am concerned with textual representations and allegories of acts and experiences that I will describe under the general category of *sympathy*. I will argue that the specific experience and effects of sympathy are central preoccupations of Marivaux, Du Bos, Diderot, Rousseau, and Mary Shelley in the texts I am examining. In the course of my readings, I will attempt to articulate and interpret each author's particular understanding of the structure and dynamics of sympathy as it emerges in specific texts, and I will attend to the ambivalent and often contradictory forms such understandings usually take. Since I am generally interested in these authors' concern with the experience of entering into someone else's thoughts and feelings, particularly the experience of transporting oneself to the place and person of someone else when faced with either a work of art or the spectacle of someone suffering, I neither presuppose nor depend on a universal definition of the word *sympathy*.

Adam Smith's descriptions of the problem of sympathy (and following Smith, I will insist that sympathy is a problem) provide a useful tableau of the roles and relations enacted in a scene of sympathy. On the first page of *The Theory of Moral Sentiments,* in the opening chapter called "Of Sympathy," Smith writes:

> As we have no immediate experience of what other men feel, we can form no idea of the manner in which they are affected, but by conceiving what we ourselves should feel in the like situation. Though our brother is upon the rack, as long as we ourselves are at our ease, our senses will never inform us of what he suffers. They never did, and never can, carry us beyond our own person, and it is by the imagination only that we can form any conception of what are his sensations. Neither can that faculty help us to this any other way, than by representing to us what would be our own, if we were in his case. It is the impressions of our own senses only, not those of his, which our imaginations copy. By the imagination we place ourselves in his situation, we conceive ourselves enduring all the same torments, we enter as it were into his body, and become in some measure the same person with him, and thence form some idea of his sensations, and

even feel something which, though weaker in degree, is not altogether unlike them. His agonies, when they are thus brought home to ourselves, when we have thus adopted and made them our own, begin at last to affect us, and we then tremble and shudder at the thought of what he feels.[4]

I cite this remarkably unsentimental description of sympathy at length because it represents the experience of sympathy as an epistemological and an aesthetic problem: since we cannot know the experience or sentiments of another person, we must represent in our imagination copies of the sentiments that we ourselves feel as we imagine ourselves in someone else's place and person. Smith goes on to complicate this situation further by depicting a mirror of sympathy in which the person suffering tries to represent his spectators' point of view, representing to himself in his imagination what they feel as they represent to themselves in their imaginations what he feels. For Smith, acts of sympathy are structured by theatrical dynamics that (because of the impossibility of really knowing or entering into someone else's sentiments) depend on people's ability to represent themselves as tableaux, spectacles, and texts before others.[5]

Although Marivaux, Diderot, Rousseau, and Mary Shelley each display at times an investment in the concept of sympathy as a transport that would transcend the distance and difference between people, allowing an exchange between parts, characters, and persons, each recognizes sympathy as a problem: a problem that is both caused and responded to by the theatrical conditions in which people face each other as spectators and spectacles. Each of these authors displays considerable ambivalence in imagining the possibility of sympathy and in picturing the consequences it has for both the self and others. In the chapters that follow I will explore their critical reflections on the conditions and effects of sympathy.

The book begins with a discussion of the demands placed on the work of art (particularly the novel) at the beginning of the eighteenth century to achieve certain effects on its reader. I argue that *Les Effets surprenants de la sympathie* dramatizes the ways in which works of fiction of the period can be read as philosophical meditations on both the effects of sympathy and what was seen as the problematic experience of reading novels. The first chapter juxtaposes the remarkable theoretical preface about novels and aesthetic experience that begins Marivaux's first novel with a seminal work of eighteenth-century French aesthetics, the *Réflexions critiques sur la poésie et sur la peinture* by the abbé Du Bos. After discussing the demands placed on the work of art to *toucher, attendrir,* and *émouvoir* its readers or spectators—and the parallels between the experiences of reading a novel, watching a play, beholding a painting, and witnessing the spectacle of someone suffering or in danger—I argue that the tableau of someone witnessing an accident becomes Marivaux's figure for the experience of reading a novel. In tracing how Marivaux's preoccupation with this figure gets acted out in the bizarre plot of *Les Effets surprenants de la sympathie,* I suggest that the novel is about the preface as much as the preface is about the novel.

Chapter two, "*La Vie de Marianne,* or the Accidents of Autobiography," argues that Marivaux's most famous novel has its origins in the tableau of someone beholding a bloody or dangerous accident that figures so importantly in *Les Effets surprenants de la sympathie.* This reading explores the relation between the scene of sympathy and the scene of theater in the novel, as well as Marivaux's obsessive dramatization of what I call a primal scene scenario. The chapter offers an interpretation of the figure of the accident in *La Vie de Marianne* that considers the significance of autobiographical acts in the novel; and it ends by placing sympathy as an epistemological and linguistic problem as well as an aesthetic problem.

In the next chapter, "*La Religieuse:* Sympathy and Seduction," I again trace the interplay between the scene of theater and the scene of sympathy in a work of fiction posing as a woman's autobiography. I argue that Diderot is ambivalent about the effects of sympathy, despite his desire to move and touch his reader. In *La Religieuse,* a fiction which began as a practical joke that was too successful in securing the pity and compassion of its reader, sympathy is increasingly seen as deception, fraud, and seduction. Chapter three also suggests that the transport of sympathy has disconcerting effects when it leads to a seemingly dangerous eroticism and a loss or a forgetting of self.

The problem of sympathy and self-forgetting is reconsidered in chapter four, "Forgetting Theater," which discusses Diderot's writing about acting and the stage, particularly *Le Paradoxe sur le comédien.* I consider the question of the place of the beholder as it is articulated in Diderot's writing about the stage; and I focus on Diderot's demands that the effects of the work of art cause readers or spectators to forget themselves, as well as his insistence that actors should not forget themselves while on the stage. Both the question of the audience's sympathy and the question of the actor's sympathy are considered in the context of Diderot's fictions about the experience of the theater; these tableaux reveal Diderot's ambivalent attitude toward sympathy and the radical, almost Brechtian, position he insists on for the experience of both novels and plays.

These issues also are explored in chapter five, which presents a reading of Rousseau's famous antitheatrical polemic, the *Lettre á M. d'Alembert sur les spectacles*. Attempting to temporarily dislocate the *Lettre* from the antitheatrical tradition, I consider the work in the context of Rousseau's critique of theatrical relations in society as well as his critique of the institution of the theater. Both critiques, I suggest, depend on his belief that society and the stage result in the failure of sympathy; however, what is most threatening about actors (as well as women) for Rousseau is precisely their ability to perform acts of sympathy that seem to result in self-annihilation. Once again I address the role of theatricality and sympathy in autobiographical acts (including Rousseau's accounts of his experiment with *l'encre de sympathie*). The chapter closes with a discussion of the ideological implications of the acts of sympathy and theater advocated by Rousseau in the *Lettre à d'Alembert*.

In my last chapter, I venture once again into the territory of the nineteenth-century English novel to argue that *Frankenstein* is about Rousseau; I suggest that in her first novel Mary Shelley presents detailed and complex readings of both the figure of Rousseau and Rousseau's writing about the problem of sympathy. Reading *Frankenstein* next to Rousseau's *Rêveries, Confessions,* and the *Essai sur l'origine des langues,* I argue that Mary Shelley's first novel is itself in many ways a philosophical investigation of eighteenth-century French fiction and philosophy that focuses on the problems of representation, theatrical relations, and the failure of sympathy. Looking back to both Diderot and Marivaux, I examine the threatening sexual dynamics of sympathy suggested in *Frankenstein* and the obsession with primal scenes that recurs both in the story of the monster and in Mary Shelley's inscription of her parents in the novel. This reading of *Frankenstein* concludes the book by considering the problem of the theatrical dynamics of sympathy and the dilemma of representation that sympathy poses to authors and readers as well as actors and spectators.

In presenting interpretations of various kinds of texts by Marivaux, Diderot, Rousseau, and Mary Shelley, *The Surprising Effects of Sympathy* places in juxtaposition novels, theoretical reflections, and polemical arguments—all of which, I argue, are concerned with the effects of sympathy, the problem of theatricality, and the power of fiction. By recognizing these texts as philosophical investigations of the dual problems of theater and sympathy, we can help add to our understanding of the relation between the novel and the theater in the eighteenth century; indeed, this recognition should make us aware of the "blurred genres" that make distinctions between aesthetics, fiction, moral philosophy, and even autobiography artificial and anachronistic.[6] Finally, we might begin to make sense of what it meant for these authors to be readers and spectators—as well as what it meant for them to imagine the readers and spectators before whom they represented themselves.

ONE

The Surprising Effects
of Sympathy

Miranda: O, I have suffered
With those that I saw suffer!
. . . .
Prospero: Wipe thine eyes; have comfort.
The direful spectacle of the wrack, which touched
The very virtue of compassion in thee,
I have with such provision in mine art
So safely ordered that there is no soul—
No, not so much perdition as an hair
Betid to any creature in the vessel
Which thou heard'st cry, which thou saw'st sink.

Shakespeare, The Tempest

Marivaux's first novel, a bizarre and lengthy narrative filled with exotic characters, violent emotions, bloody spectacles, and *coups de théâtre,* begins with a double title: *Les Adventures de *** ou les Effets surprenants de la sympathie.* Appearing on the title page of a book published in 1713 and 1714, the first half of the title signals the narrative's novelistic and specifically picaresque characteristics.[1] Substituting the typographical characters of the printing press for the name of a title character, the title conforms to the eighteenth-century novel's aura of anonymity; it may warn that the book will have no consistent hero or heroine, and indeed perhaps *** is the most appropriate name for the protagonist of a novel in which the autobiographical and biographical subjects of the text appear to be almost interchangeable, shifting as if absentmindedly in a succession of overlapping stories and stories within stories.

The second half of the title, *Les Effets surprenants de la sympathie,* is more difficult to characterize. The novel's many scenes of love at first sight, its matches and mismatches between lovers with confusingly similar characteristics and names, dramatize the senses of secret correspondences and elective affinities contained within the word *sympathie.*[2] In this sense the title (and the place of the word *sympathie* in the vocabulary of the language of the heart) seems to announce an early example of a novel of sensibility and sentiment. The double title, then, might propose a marriage between the sentimental novel and the picaresque or adventure novel. To begin to understand the meaning of the title, however, to begin to understand the effects of *sympathie* in the novel, we need to consider the warning or advice contained in the "Avis au lecteur" ("Notice to the Reader") which prefaces both the narrative and, indeed, Marivaux's oeuvre.[3]

The preface begins by noting that it is not really the preface: "L'Avant-propos que l'auteur de ces Aventures fait lui-même en parlant à une dame pourrait leur servir de préface" ("The Preliminary Remarks that the author of these Adventures makes himself in speaking to a lady could serve as a preface" [*OJ,* p. 3]). This *avant-propos,* which follows the "Avis au lecteur" and leads into the narrative, contains the usual claims and disclaimers of eighteenth-century novels: the denial of authorship, the fiction that the fiction is true, the story of how the manuscript found its way into the hands of the "editor" and finally the reader. The "Avis," then, serves a different purpose. To begin with, it goes out of its way to inform the reader of the addressee inscribed in the role of the book's reader. The "editor" insists that the author addresses his narrative to a woman; this assertion takes place within the context of a dialogue between the "editor" and certain critics who are identified only as "pédants." These critics seem to write themselves into the text by suddenly objecting to the "bold writer of Prefaces" who wants to write them out of the text, to write them off as readers. Their presence turns the "Avis" into a polemical debate about the novel.

Although less threatened by a Puritan tradition than its English counterpart, in 1713 the eighteenth-century French novel also must begin by denying its status as a novel or justifying its existence, generally taking the cues for its defense from the polemical debate about the theater.[4] If, however, the "Avis au lecteur" can be seen as a defense of the novel, it is not necessarily as a defense that it is most interesting or revealing. I would argue that despite its polemical tone and dialogue—indeed, because of the anxiety with which it addresses certain issues—the preface can be seen as a series of critical reflections on the key terms and figures at play for Marivaux in writing a novel. The preface suggests the questions that Marivaux had to come to terms with in 1713 in order to write his first novel. It suggests the significance of the title and why *les effets surprenants de la sympathie* were a fundamental concern of novel writing and indeed aesthetics at the beginning of the eighteenth century.

In order to examine the theoretical implications of the issues Marivaux must address in beginning his first novel, I will read the "Avis au lecteur" next to a work that is often considered to have inaugurated eighteenth-century aesthetics, the *Réflexions critiques sur la poésie et sur la peinture* by the abbé Du Bos, published in 1719.[5] Frédéric Deloffre has written of the "Avis": "In 1731, Marivaux's views would have been merely lucid; in 1713, they are prophetic" (*OJ*, p. 1092); and in many ways Marivaux's text seems to prefigure some of the major concerns of Du Bos.[6] We could read the "Avis" not only as a preface for Marivaux's future work but also as a preface for the century to come. Furthermore, by opening up the theoretical and aesthetic issues that in effect necessitate the preface, we will be able to read the "Avis au lecteur" next to the narrative of *Les Effets surprenants de la sympathie*. This will help us to understand the patterns and repetitions and obsessions of the novel, its bizarre turns of plot and language. It also will suggest the relation between theory and fiction for Marivaux by allowing us to see the narrative not as the illustration or fulfillment of certain theoretical demands but rather as a series of figures and narrative scenes that act out the preoccupations of theory. We will see that in speaking of *Les Effets surprenants de la sympathie* it would be more appropriate to say that the novel is about the preface than to say that the preface is about the novel.

Throughout this chapter, I will be concerned with the importance of theater as a figure and a frame of reference for Marivaux. It is well known that Marivaux, a prolific playwright and the author of the *Spectateur français,* had (in Jean Rousset's words) "a theatrical view [une vue théâtrale] of man and life in society." Rousset argues persuasively in *Forme et signification* that Marivaux's work is structured by a "double registre du récit et du regard sur le récit" ("a double register comprised of the narrative and reflection on the narrative"), a critical self-consciousness acted out through the reflexivity and temporal *dédoublement* of Marivaux's autobiographical fiction, through the dramatization of spectator-spectacle relations in his plays, and through a lifelong preoccupation with masks, mirrors, roles, and *le regard*.[7] Assuming Rousset's observations as a point of departure, I will be concerned less with the structure of a theatrical self-consciousness in Marivaux's work than with Marivaux's interest and investment in theatrical relations: the relations formed between spectators and spectacles. Rather than examine Marivaux's actual writing for the stage, I will consider scenes from his fiction in which the theatrical relations of everyday life are reflected on and dramatized. We will see the significance of these relations for Marivaux's critical reflections on the effects of a work of art; from the preface of *Les Effets surprenants de la sympathie* to *La Vie de Marianne* Marivaux is preoccupied with the parallels (and differences) between the experience of becoming a spectator to the spectacle of another person and the experiences of beholding a painting, watching a play, and reading a novel. In particular, we will see that the experience of sympathy becomes in Marivaux's work both a figure for and a paradigmatic example of theatrical relations, marking a key intersection between eighteenth-century moral philosophy and aesthetics.

Before the "Avis au lecteur" of *Les Effets surprenants de la sympathie* can offer notice, warning, or advice to the reader, it must first establish who the reader is—or at least, who will be cast in the role of the reader. Playing the role of an editor who claims to speak for the author of the *Aventures,* Marivaux attempts to both prescribe and proscribe readers. This means that as much as the preface will be about the book or even novels in general, it will also be about the reader. The claim that the novel is addressed to a particular woman is modified to include "all the fair sex" who have a "secret sentiment [sentiment secret], independent of the sterile laws of art" and finally those readers who know as much as the "beaux esprits qui ne lisent un livre, pour ainsi dire, qu'avec la règle et le compas dans l'esprit" ("fine minds who only read a book, so to speak, with the rule and compass in mind") but who do not let rules interfere with taste and feeling (*OJ,* p. 4). *Les Effets surprenants de la sympathie,* warns the "Avis," is a work with "des beautés naturelles, et moins régulières" and "la délicatesse du sentiment" ("natural and less regular beauties . . . delicacy of sentiment" [*OJ,* p. 4]). If it is not addressed exclusively to women, it is addressed to those who are represented by women: readers with "beaucoup de goût sans art, et beaucoup de sentiment" ("a great deal of taste without artfulness, and a great deal of feeling" [*OJ,* p. 3]).[8] The aim of the fiction of the text's address is not to inscribe a particular reader or even a particular type of reader in front of the text; rather, it suggests the type of reading that the author expects: how the text is meant to be read. When Marivaux personates the "pédants" who represent the rule and rules of reason, he turns the preface into a debate about how the novel should be judged.

What is at stake is not just the form of the novel and its legitimacy as a genre but also the criteria that should be used to determine its value. Marivaux, playing the role of the "bold writer of Prefaces," appeals to the experience of the reader in order to justify his work. "Quand un roman attendrit les dames," he writes, "en vain on crie qu'il ne vaut rien; le coeur est gagné, il est persuadé ... et puisque le roman n'est fait que pour le coeur, quand il le touche, doit-on s'en plaindre?" ("When a novel moves the ladies, the cry that it is worthless is raised in vain; the heart is won, it is persuaded ... and since the novel is written only for the heart, should anyone complain when the heart is touched?" [*OJ*, p. 5]). Insisting that the heart is not subject to mere capriciousness, the author of the "Avis" claims that if women reading the novel are "attendries" ("moved"), then the work must not be bad: "l'intérêt secret qu'elles y prennent ne peut être que l'effet de quelque chose de touchant qui s'insinue dans le coeur" ("the secret interest which they take in it can only be the effect of something touching which insinuates itself into the heart" [*OJ*, p. 6]). The criteria Marivaux describes in defending the work imply what should be expected from the experience of reading a novel: what the experience and the effects of a novel should be.

Six years after Marivaux published his "Avis au lecteur," the abbé Du Bos prefaced the *Réflexions critiques sur la poésie et sur la peinture* with the suggestion that his book about art would really be about the reader. The book will meet with approval, writes Du Bos, only if he can "faire reconnoître au Lecteur dans mon Livre ce qui se passe en lui-même, en un mot les mouvemens les plus intimes de son coeur" ("make the reader recognize in my book that which occurs within himself, in a word the most intimate movements of his heart" [*RC*, I:3]). His reflections are meant to be "a mirror" (*RC*, I:3) in which individual readers will recognize themselves; but the book is also meant to be about readers in general, about the experience of being a reader (or the beholder of a painting, or the spectator of a play). Rejecting the claims and authority of a "Legislator" (*RC*, I:5), Du Bos will try to focus criticism on what he calls (in his well-known formulation) the sixth sense: "la portion de nous-mêmes qui juge sur l'impression qu'elle ressent et qui, pour me servir des termes de Platon, prononce, sans consulter la règle et le compas. C'est enfin ce qu'on appelle communément le sentiment" ("that portion of ourselves which judges the impressions that it feels, and which, to use Plato's terms, pronounces without consulting the rule and the compass. This is what we commonly call sentiment" [*RC*, II:326]).

Du Bos is not interested in the a priori rules that have governed classical aesthetics. "Chacun a chez lui," he writes, "la règle ou le compas applicable à mes raisonnemens" ("Everyone possesses the rule or the compass applicable to my reasonings" [*RC*, I:3]). If the *Réflexions critiques* will be useful for artists and writers, it is not because Du Bos intends to prescribe rules, but rather because Du Bos will "examiner en Philosophe comment il arrive que leurs productions fassent tant d'effet sur les hommes" ("examine as a philosopher how it comes about that their productions have such effect on men"). His goal is to show "l'effet general" of works of art, to display "le coeur humain dans l'instant ou il est attendri par un poème, ou touché par un tableau" ("the human heart at the moment that it is moved by a poem or touched by a painting" [*RC*, I:4]). The result of this philosophical investigation is finally neither phenomenology nor subjectivism. Du Bos is interested in understanding the *effects* of works of art in order to articulate criteria for judging and creating art.[9]

In describing the surprising effects of art (and, as we shall see, the effects of related experiences) the *Réflexions critiques* put forth a series of demands. Du Bos both describes and prescribes what it is we expect from the experiences of reading literature, beholding a painting, and watching a play. The public, he writes, judges a work of art "par la voie du sentiment et suivant l'impression que le poème ou le tableau font sur lui" ("by the path of sentiment, following the impressions which the poem or painting makes on him"). It follows, therefore, that since "le premier but de la poésie et de la peinture est de nous toucher, les poèmes et les tableaux ne sont bons ouvrages qu'à proportion qu'ils nous émeuvent et qu'ils nous attachent" ("the primary aim of poetry and painting is to touch us, poems and paintings are good works of art only in proportion to their ability to move and attach us" [*RC*, II:323]). For Du Bos, then, criticism will seek to understand "the language of the heart" in order to evaluate the experience and power of art and thereby provide instruction in "l'art d'émouvoir les hommes" ("the art of moving men" [*RC*, I:272, 276]).[10]

Du Bos and Marivaux both assert that the artist must speak the language of the heart and move the reader or beholder. Both appeal to the experience of a work of art: Du Bos seeks to provide an anatomy of reading or beholding by framing the very moment in which the heart of the reader or beholder is moved; Marivaux evokes the experience of the reader in order to establish the merit of his work. What interests me here in juxtaposing these texts of Marivaux and Du Bos is not that one defends his work by evoking criteria that the other takes as a point of departure. My point is that both authors insist that the value of a work of art is determined by its ability to move and to touch: *émouvoir, attendrir,* and *toucher;* these are the effects which a book or tableau must produce in the heart of the reader. In other words, both Marivaux and Du Bos describe the experience of art (and the criteria for judging works of art) in terms of the effects of sympathy.

I am suggesting that the specific experience and effects of sympathy are central preoccupations of both Marivaux and Du Bos in the texts we are examining. Not only could the first volume of the *Réflexions critiques sur la poésie et sur la peinture* have been appropriately subtitled *Les Effets surprenants de la sympathie;* the critical and practical reflections on art contained in Marivaux's preface and novel go beyond a general concern with *sentiment* to a particular interest in the characteristics of both *effets* and *sympathie.* At the heart of the question of how the novel should be read (what is expected from a work of art) are questions concerning both the effects of sympathy and the status of sympathy as an effect of the work of art.

The author of the "Avis au lecteur" offers to his imagined critics an example (actually a series of examples) to support his claims that if readers are "attendries" by *Les Effets surprenants de la sympathie* (which asks to be judged according to its ability to move its readers) then it must be the effect of something touching in the novel.

> Dira-t-on, par exemple, que le coeur n'a qu'une pitié déraisonnable et capricieuse? Quand nous sommes émus à l'aspect d'un accident qui blesse ou qui tue quelqu'un, reçoit-on mal à propos une impression d'inquiétude? Quand on regarde une personne exposée à quelque danger, sera-t-on bien venu d'assurer que le coeur a tort de frémir pour elle? (*OJ,* p. 6)

> Shall we say, for example, that the heart has only an unreasonable and capricious pity? When we are moved at the sight of an accident that wounds or kills someone, is it inappropriate to receive an impression of alarm? When we see a person exposed to danger, is it acceptable to declare that the heart is wrong to tremble for that person?

With the casual gesture of a "par exemple," Marivaux suddenly shifts the focus of his discussion from the scene of the novel to the spectacle of a person. Having made certain claims about the effects and experience of reading and a novel's need to move its reader, he imagines an actual situation of suffering or danger which evokes pity in a sympathetic spectator.

Through the objections of the critics personated in the preface, Marivaux seems to acknowledge that he has shifted the ground of his discussion:

Belle comparaison! répondront ces messieurs. Non sans doute, on n'a pas tort d'être ému à la vue des objets que vous dites, parce que ces objets sont présents, qu'ils sont effectivement vrais, le danger menace, le sang coule; le rapport que les yeux font à l'âme est certain ... (*OJ,* p. 6)

A fine comparison! these gentlemen will reply. No, to be sure, one is not wrong to be moved by the sight of the objects you mention, because those objects are present, they are in effect true; danger threatens, blood flows; the report that the eyes make to the soul is certain ...

Maintaining the bizarrely graphic and dramatic details of the author's examples, the critics object that there is a difference between being moved by objects that are present and true and objects that are absent or represented. The author responds by again shifting the terms and scene of the experience in question, insisting that "at that moment the soul" doesn't need the "report of its eyes" in order to be moved; he argues that a narrative can awaken the memory of a scene—if "nous *avons été* témoins des accidents" ("if we *have been* witnesses of accidents") and if the representation of the scene "figure un portrait fidèle de ce que nous *avons vu*" ("figures a faithful portrait of what we *have seen*" [*OJ*, p. 6; my emphasis]).

The critics that Marivaux writes into the text might have objected that a novel about bloody swordfights, Turkish sultans, kidnapped princesses, and near drownings is not likely to provide readers with faithful portraits of accidents they actually have seen. However, they simply object that such memories could be evoked by a badly painted representation and thus would not be proof of "une peinture naturelle" ("a natural painting" [*OJ*, p. 6]). At this point the author of the "Avis" claims that those sorts of sentiments were not what he had in mind; but he goes on to admit the basic premise of the critics' initial objection: that one could "distinguish the interest" that the soul might have in reading from "that which the thing itself [la chose effective] would excite." He continues: "La pitié que nous ressentons à la vue d'un objet vrai n'est pas la même que nous ressentons au récit d'un malheur feint" ("The pity that we feel at the sight of a real object is not the same as the pity that we feel at the narration of a pretended misfortune" [*OJ*, p. 7]).

Marivaux allows this point to be developed in some detail but it should be clear by now that the "Avis au lecteur" is not solely (indeed, not primarily) concerned with defending either the novel as a genre or the particular novel it prefaces; nor is it finally important who wins the debate. The dialogue of the preface seems designed to consider the differences, similarities, and analogies between the experiences of reading a novel and becoming a sympathetic spectator to a moving spectacle. As he begins his first novel, Marivaux considers—and asks his reader to consider—a series of differences: between readers and spectators, between the effects of a thing and the effects of a representation of the thing, between the pity that we feel when reading a book and the pity that we feel when faced with what we might call a scene from real life. In the course of the argument about how the book should be read, Marivaux offers a series of strange tableaux (all of which portray spectators, spectacles, and situations of sympathy) through which and with which he figures the act of reading his novel.

If we return to the *Réflexions critiques*, we can observe Du Bos elaborating the theoretical context of the questions about reading and beholding that are figured in the tableaux of Marivaux's "Avis au lecteur." Like many eighteenth-century writers, Du Bos is interested in the moral and aesthetic implications of Aristotle's comment that we delight in realistic representations of objects which themselves would be painful to see.[11] He begins his examination of the passions a work of art produces and reproduces by considering what happens when we become spectators to spectacles of suffering. Noting that poetry and painting "are never more applauded than when they succeed in afflicting us," Du Bos asks why the "moving representation [repré-sentation pathéthique] of the sacrifice of Jephthah's daughter set in a frame [enchassée dans une bordure] makes the most beautiful ornament in a room" or why a poem "of which the principal subject is the violent death of a young princess, is included in the arrange-ments for a celebration [l'ordonnance d'une fête]" (*RC*, I:1–2). Du Bos promises to "attempt to illuminate this paradox" that we applaud works of art that cause a "frémissement intérieur" ("inner shudder-ing" [*RC*, I:2–3]), that the border of a frame can change our view of a girl sacrificed, or lines of verse a violent death. As part of his examination of the effects of art, Du Bos will seek to understand the sentiments of sympathy that do or do not occur when we are faced with spectacles of suffering.

Like many of his contemporaries, Du Bos asserts that sympathy is natural. Anticipating Rousseau, he argues that nature, in order to counter the "amour-propre" that evolves from "amour de soi" ("love of self"), constructed people so that "the emotions [l'agitation] of everyone who comes near to us would have a powerful sway over us." This "natural sensibility [sensibilité naturelle] of the human heart" which works independently of "the ways of reasoning" is for Du Bos "the primary foundation of society" (*RC*, I:38–39). As if following the example of the author of the "Avis au lecteur," Du Bos presents a series of tableaux that depict sympathetic responses:

> Les larmes d'un inconnu nous émeuvent même avant que nous sachions le sujet qui le fait pleurer. Les cris d'un homme qui ne tient à nous que par l'humanité, nous font voler à son secours par un mouvement machinal qui précede toute déliberation (*RC*, I:39)

> The tears of someone we don't know move us even before we know the subject which makes him weep. The cries of a man to whom we are attached only by humanity make us fly to his aid with an automatic movement which precedes all deliberation.

Later in the *Réflexions critiques*, Du Bos revises these portrayals of what takes place in the heart of the reader when he insists that such spectacles of suffering are most capable of moving us if they are really spectacles—if we actually see them. "Par exemple," writes Du Bos, as he introduces another tableau,

> les cris d'un homme blessé que nous ne voïons point, ne nous affectent pas, bien que nous aïons connoissance du sujet qui lui fait jetter les cris que nous entendons, comme nous affecteroit la vûë de son sang & de sa blessure. (*RC*, I:387)

> the cries of a wounded man whom we do not see do not affect us (even if we are aware of the subject which makes him bring forth the cries we hear) in the same way as the sight of his blood and his wound would affect us.

Du Bos would seem to agree here with the critics characterized in the "Avis au lecteur" who object to the author's *exemple* of an "accident funeste qui blesse ou qui tue quelqu'un" ("a deadly accident which wounds or kills someone") that one is moved only "à la vue des objets" ("by the sight of objects"). Faced with the sight of objects which are "present" and "actually true," they insist, "le danger menace, le sang coule; le rapport que les yeux font à l'âme est certain" ("danger threatens, blood flows; the report that the eyes make to the soul is certain" [*OJ*, p. 6]). Du Bos asserts that "la vue a plus d'empire sur l'âme que les autres sens," that "l'oeil est plus près de l'âme que l'oreille" ("sight has more power over the soul than the other senses have . . . the eye is nearer to the soul than is the ear" [*RC*, I:387]).

This belief is the basis for the doctrine of *ut pictura poesis*—the words that stand as an epigraph for Du Bos's book and govern his unsystematic system of aesthetics.[12] If the work of art, according to Du Bos, must speak the language of the heart and move us, if it must "create in the heart a sentiment that approaches" the sentiment about which one is reading, then the most effective way to *émouvoir, attendrir,* and *toucher* is to appeal to our sense of sight. Even the most austere writer, claims Du Bos, must "pour nous émouvoir, mettre sous nos yeux par des peintures, les objets dont il nous parle" ("in order to move us, put before our eyes by means of paintings the objects he speaks to us about" [*RC,* I:278]). Poetry, then, in order to move us, must present images and tableaux to our imagination: "Il faut donc que nous croïions voir, pour ainsi dire, en écoutant des Vers" ("Thus we must believe that we see, so to speak, in listening to verse" [*RC,* I:275]). The author of the "Avis au lecteur" seems to accept this premise, at least implicitly; at the same time he denies that "in order to be moved" the soul needs the "report of its eyes," he bases his argument on the claim that we could read a narrative which "figures a faithful portrait of what we have seen"—what his interlocutors call "a natural painting" (*OJ,* p. 6).[13]

Both Du Bos and Marivaux try to imagine an experience of reading that would be the same as or at least analogous to the experience of becoming a spectator to a moving spectacle. For Du Bos, painting is more powerful than poetry because "it is nature itself which painting puts before our eyes" (*RC,* I:388). The belief that a text could in some sense present tableaux and images to the reader's imagination allows the possibility of a translation through which, in the words of Lord Kames, a later follower of Du Bos, the reader is transformed into a spectator. Such an illusion of sight is supposed to bring with it an illusion of presence, as if it could erase the distinction between reading a narrative about an accident and actually witnessing an accident as a spectator. "A lively and accurate description," writes Kames, "raises in me ideas not less distinct than if I had been originally an eye-witness: I am insensibly transformed into a spectator; and have an impression that every incident is passing in my presence."[14]

However, the possibility that works of art could move us in the ways that we are moved by the tears of a stranger, the cries of a wounded man, or the spectacle of someone in distress or danger or pain returns us to the paradox with which Du Bos begins his *Réflexions critiques sur la poésie et sur la peinture.* Du Bos must reconcile his notions of natural and automatic sympathy (and the tableaux he presents so we can imagine becoming sympathetic spectators to spectacles of suffering) with the pleasure that people appear to take in witnessing such spectacles. One explanation of the paradox that "men find even more pleasure crying than laughing when they are at the theater" (*RC,* I:2) is suggested by Du Bos's sense of the limits of the effects of art. "L'imitation," writes Du Bos, "agit toujours plus foiblement que l'objet imité" ("The imitation always acts more feebly than the object imitated" [*RC*, I:51]).

The imitation of an object produces imitations of the effects that the object itself would have produced; reading a text or beholding a painting, we find reproduced inside us "passions artificielles" or "phantômes de passions" ("artificial passions ... phantoms of passions" [*RC*, I:26]). Du Bos continues:

> Comme l'impression que ces imitations font sur nous est du même genre que l'impression que l'objet imité ... feroit sur nous: comme l'impression que l'imitation fait n'est différente de l'impression que l'objet feroit, qu'en ce qu'elle est moins forte, elle doit exciter dans notre ame une passion qui ressemble à celle que l'objet imité y auroit pû exciter. La copie de l'objet doit, pour ainsi dire, exciter en nous une copie de la passion que l'objet y auroit excitée. (*RC*, I:26)

> Since the impression which such imitations make on us is of the same kind as the impression which the imitated object ... would make on us; since the impression which the imitation makes is no different from the impression which the object would make, except in that it is less strong, it must excite a passion in our soul that resembles that which the imitated object might have excited. The copy of the object must, so to speak, excite in us a copy of the passion which the object would have excited.

We are faced with a chain of mimetic acts: the sympathetic feeling we are supposed to feel when faced with a spectacle of suffering is already in some sense a copy of the feeling of the person we witness.

According to Adam Smith, one of the most important eighteenth-century theoreticians of sympathy, in an act of sympathy we must represent to ourselves in our imagination the sentiments of the other person (whose feelings we cannot really know or share).[15] For Du Bos, the sympathetic passion that we experience when faced with an artistic representation is the artificial reproduction of a representation; this phantom passion duplicates the representation and reproduction of an "original" passion which would have occurred in us had we been faced with an actual person or object. The real effects produced by these imitations and reproductions provide us with what Du Bos calls "un plaisir pur" ("a pure pleasure"); since our sympathy takes place at several removes, we are able to "[jouir] de notre emotion" ("enjoy our emotion") without losing our reason (*RC*, I:28–29). A tableau imitating a tragic event, explains Du Bos, "nous émeut & nous attendrit" ("moves and touches us") but it excites "notre compassion, sans nous affliger réellement" ("our compassion without really afflicting us" [*RC,* I:29]). Our sympathy, like the work of art that moves us, takes place within the realm of fiction, mimesis, representation, and reproduction. If the success of a novel, play, or painting depends on acts of sympathy, our experience of sympathy depends on an aesthetic experience. Sympathy in this sense is always already an aesthetic experience.

Despite the claims Du Bos makes for the power and effects of a work of art, despite the faith in illusion he displays by insisting that texts should present us with tableaux and images that we think we see, Du Bos suggests that reason prevails over sentiment and safeguards us from the pain we would expect to feel when faced with real suffering. After insisting through the "author" of the "Avis au lecteur" on the parallels between witnessing a bloody accident and beholding or reading a representation of one, Marivaux also admits that the pity we feel "at the sight of a real object" is not the same as the pity we feel "at the narration of a pretended misfortune." When faced with an object that is actually present, he explains, our soul is afflicted and feels pity: "Elle est attendrie: mais elle souffre réellement. Le sentiment est triste" ("It is moved: but it really suffers. The sentiment is sorrowful"). However, he continues, no matter how terrible a narrative might be, "s'il excite la pitié, [il] ne porte dans l'âme qu'un intérêt compatissant sans douleur. On gémit avec ceux qui nous paraissent gémir: mais comme leurs maux ne sont que feints, l'âme émue se fait un plaisir de sa sensibilité, en se garantissant par la raison d'une tristesse véritable" ("if it excites pity, it brings to the soul only a compassionate interest without pain. We lament with those who seem to lament; but as their ills are only pretended, the soul, being moved, finds pleasure in its own sensibility, while protecting itself through reason from any real sorrow" [*OJ,* p. 7]).

In describing the sympathy we feel without really suffering, the sentiment of pain that reason allows us to experience as pleasure, Marivaux might be translating Miranda's famous line in act 1, scene 2 of *The Tempest,* where she describes her response to the "direful spectacle of the wrack, which touched / the very virtue of compassion" in her, and she declares: "I have suffered / with those that I saw suffer!" Of course Miranda appears in Shakespeare's play as a figure for a naive spectator, unaware that the spectacle of suffering she witnesses is only a stage illusion created by Prospero's "art."[16] Marivaux's "On gémit avec ceux qui nous paraissent gémir" contains the acknowledgment that those we see only appear to suffer. Indeed, at this point in the "Avis" the author's examples of sympathetic acts switch from spectacles of actual blood, danger, and suffering to spectacles that are in fact scenes from plays: theatrical illusions.

He describes, for example, the tragedy about the sacrifice of Iphigenia (just as Du Bos offers the example of the "sacrifice of the daughter of Jephthah"). Although this tragedy makes us "share with her the horror of her situation," according to the author of the "Avis" we find her misfortune touching rather than horrible: "we weep with her," but as we represent to ourselves her affliction "the degree of her misfortune determines the degree of our feeling and of our pleasure" (OJ, p. 7). The theater provides the frame that translates suffering into pleasure. Du Bos writes: "tout ce que nous voïons au théatre, concourt à nous émouvoir, mais rien n'y fait illusion à nos sens, car tout s'y montre comme imitation" ("everything that we see in the theater converges to move us, but nothing there deceives our senses, for everything reveals itself as imitation" [RC, I:422]). However, the explanation of (what Marivaux calls) the "secret remembrance" that reminds us of our place as spectators to a play (OJ, p. 8) also raises questions about our position as spectators to spectacles of real suffering.

The problem is not what we see *in* the theater but rather what we see *as* theater. This problem is suggested not only by both authors' emphasis on the analogies between the experience of sympathy and the experiences of watching a play, beholding a painting, and reading a novel—analogies that might suggest the theatrical aspects of sympathy as well as the capacity of plays or novels to move us. In addition, both Marivaux and Du Bos repeatedly describe the experience of sympathy in terms of spectator-spectacle relations. The same frame of theater that secures us from real affliction when faced with representations on the stage might also produce in us mere phantoms of sympathy when we are faced with the representations of other people.

In the second chapter of the *Réflexions critiques* we find Du Bos evoking another famous example of the experience of beholding the spectacle of a shipwreck: he cites the observation of Lucretius that there is pleasure in witnessing danger, suffering, or violence. Du Bos translates: "Il est touchant, dit Lucrèce, de voir du rivage un vaisseau luter contre les vagues qui le veulent engloutir, comme de regarder une bataille d'une hauteur d'où l'on voit en sûreté la melée" ("It is touching, says Lucretius, to watch from the shore a vessel struggling against the waves that seek to engulf it, as it is to watch a battle from a height where one can see the melee in safety" [RC, I:13]).[17] That Du

Bos should use "touchant" to translate the Latin "suave" suggests that he would rather imagine Shakespeare's version of this moment— tearful, compassionate Miranda suffering with those she sees suffering in the spectacle of a shipwreck—than Lucretius's description of the "sweetness" of watching danger while assured of one's own safety.

The example, however, is meant to illustrate a problem that worries Du Bos from the outset of his discussion. Indeed, although he claims that a natural sympathy protects society from *amour-propre* and our self-interested tendency to be "too harsh towards others" (*RC*, I:38), he acknowledges that people are strangely attracted to spectacles of real suffering or misfortune. He speculates that it may not be sympathy (or not sympathy alone) that "makes people run toward the objects most fit to break their hearts" (*RC*, I:12). He suggests that "ennui" compels us to seek out objects and emotions that will stir and occupy our souls: "Cette émotion naturelle qui s'excite en nous machinalement, quand nous voïons nos semblables dans le danger ou dans le malheur, n'a d'autre attrait que celui d'être une passion dont les mouvemens remuënt l'âme & la tiennent occupée" ("This natural emotion which arises in us automatically when we see our fellow beings in danger or misfortune attracts us only because it is a passion whose movements stir and occupy the soul" [*RC*, I:12]).

Despite the apparent blandness of this pre-Baudelairean psychol- ogy, Du Bos seems somewhat troubled as he depicts vivid tableaux of spectators flocking to see direful spectacles which are not imitations and do not produce phantoms of passions. "On va voir en foule," he writes, "un spectacle des plus affreux que les hommes puissent regarder, je veux dire le supplice d'un autre homme qui subit la rigeur des loix sur un échaffaut" ("We go in crowds to watch one of the most atrocious spectacles men can see: I mean the torture of another man who suffers the severity of the law upon the scaffold"). Marivaux uses the example of a public execution in a discussion of curiosity and sympathy in his *Lettres sur les habitants de Paris* (published in 1717). The people of Paris, he writes, "courait à ce triste spectacle avec une avidité curieuse, qui se joignait à un sentiment de compassion pour ces malheureux" ("run to this sad spectacle with an avid curiosity, joined with a feeling of compassion for these unfortunates"). Marivaux describes the Parisian people as "un vrai caméléon qui reçoit toutes les impressions des objets qui l'environnent" ("a real chameleon, which receives all the impressions of the objects surrounding it"); they have a soul "comme une espèce de machine incapable de penser par elle-même, et comme esclave de tous les objets qui la frappent" ("like a kind of machine incapable of thinking for itself, like a slave of all the objects which strike it").[18] This "stupid and brutal curiosity" is denounced in the second part of *La Vie de Marianne* (published in 1734) in the famous scene of Mme Dutour's argument with the coachman. Marivaux writes: "Ce sont des émotions d'âme que ce peuple demande" ("it is the emotions of the soul that this people wants"); the people of Paris seek to "s'attendrir pour vous si on vous blesse, à frémir pour votre vie si on la menace" ("be touched for you if you are wounded, to tremble for your life if it is threatened"), all for a fright that "stirs the soul" and thus causes "pleasure" (*VM*, pp. 95–96).

Both Marivaux and Du Bos are troubled that (in Du Bos's words) "the attraction of emotion makes us forget the first principles of humanity," that there is "in the cruelest spectacles an attraction capable of making the most humane peoples love them" (*RC*, I:20–21). However, I suggest that what is most troubling about the examples of beholding shipwrecks, battles, accidents, and public executions is that they feel like theater. The spectators behold these spectacles—and both Marivaux and Du Bos emphasize the status of these events as spectacles—as if they were watching a play. Marivaux and Du Bos describe the sentiments and responses of these spectators as if they were describing the emotions of an audience; it is no coincidence that the spectacle of the public execution is performed for the eyes of the world on an *échaffaud:* a platform, scaffold, or stage.

The most extensive and vividly depicted example of the problematic interplay of theater and sympathy occurs in the *Réflexions critiques* in Du Bos's discussions of the Roman "spectacles de l'amphithéâtre" (*RC*, I:14). Du Bos describes at length the calculated and bloody destruction of the gladiators, a combat that has been designed as a performance meant to please spectators. Referring to the groups of gladiators as "quadrilles"—a term that evokes dancing—Du Bos sets the scene:

> On les nourrissoit mêmes avec des pâtes & des alimens propres à les tenir dans l'embonpoint, afin que le sang s'écoulât plus lentement par les blessures qu'ils recevroient, & que le spectateur pût joüir ainsi plus long-tems des horreurs de leur agonie. La profession d'instuire les Gladiateurs étoit devenuë un art: le goût les Romains avoient pour ces combats, leur avoit fait rechercher de la délicatesse, & introduire des agrémens dans un spectacle que nous ne sçaurions imaginer aujourd-'hui sans horreur. (*RC*, I:15)

> They were even fed grain-pastes and other foods suitable to keep them stout, so that the blood would flow more slowly through the wounds

they would receive, and so that the spectator could thus enjoy for a longer time the horrors of their agony. The profession of instructing the gladiators had become an art: the taste which the Romans had for these combats made them seek out delicacies and introduce charms into a spectacle which we could not imagine today without horror.

Part of the horror of the description lies in the peculiar inappropriateness of the language of aesthetics here: "art," "goût," "délicatesse," "jouir," "spectateur," and "spectacle." Du Bos goes on to describe how "Fencing Masters" (like the ubiquitous eighteenth-century dancing masters) instructed gladiators "in which attitude one should lie down, and what bearing one should maintain when one was mortally wounded"; following this choreography, the gladiators could "expire gracefully" (*RC*, I:15).

What finally horrifies Du Bos the most is not the sight of battles where blood flows and danger threatens, where wounded men face death and a bloodthirsty audience. What Du Bos pictures and recoils from is the pure theatricality of these "spectacles de l'amphithéâtre": the art that arranges the stage effects of wounds, that designs poses and attitudes which affect dying even as death really occurs. The gladiators become actors who die for the pleasure of their spectators, and what seems worse, who must perform their own deaths with broad, theatrical strokes. Du Bos does not speculate about whether the effects of real suffering are inadequate to move an audience accustomed to the Roman amphitheater; or whether the gladiators are given an air of artifice in order to mask the reality in which they actually are engaged. Du Bos makes it clear, however, that the imitation and representation of the gladiators do not make their suffering any less real. The only illusion in this spectacle of overwhelming theatricality seems to be the sympathy of the spectators.

In the spectrum of experiences that interest Du Bos and Marivaux in their critical reflections on the effects of spectacles, the example of the gladiators at first seems to occupy a middle ground between the experience of witnessing a battle or a bloody accident and the experience of watching a tragedy performed in a theater.[19] What seems troubling about this example, however, is that it conflates those two experiences and thereby threatens to erase certain distinctions that both Marivaux and Du Bos depend on (despite their investment in the parallels between such experiences). Here the frame of theater signals the pleasure of the audience in beholding a spectacle of suffering, yet it does not signal the secret awareness that the spectacle is false. If the audience watches the spectacle at several removes, it is because of the self-interested sense of distance and safety that Lucretius describes, not because of the effects of mimesis. The problem is no longer the paradox that spectators feel pleasure beholding representations of things which, if present and seen, would cause them pain; the problem is that they do not seem to experience sympathetic sentiments when faced with a spectacle of real suffering. They may feel enough sympathy to stir their souls but the positions and relations of theater appear to allow them to behold a spectacle in real life as if it were a play (or a painting or a novel).

In the context of their general aesthetic reflections, both Du Bos and Marivaux seem to repress the possibility that the power and effects of sympathy might be limited in what we call real life as well as in the realm of art. Indeed, if they were to pursue the implications of their discussions of sympathy in the theater, they might find themselves in territory staked out by the antitheatrical tradition.[20] Du Bos's tableau of the spectacle of the gladiators even approaches Rousseau's indictment of the theater for teaching people a false sympathy, as well as a theatrical distance from others that destroys sympathy. However, Du Bos and Marivaux are primarily interested in positing an ideal experience of sympathy which will allow them to formulate claims and demands for the work of art: to delineate its power, effects, and capacity to speak to the sentiments of readers and spectators. They want to imagine an experience of reading or beholding that would be the same as or at least analogous to the experience of becoming a sympathetic spectator to a moving spectacle. Sympathy thus must be maintained or recuperated; and Marivaux and Du Bos finally must ignore suggestions that their own examples might undermine not only the moral but also the epistemological basis for their aesthetics.

What is not repressed, however—indeed, what becomes a preoccupation for Marivaux—is that the analogies in question have reversed directions, so to speak. In tracing Marivaux's and Du Bos's efforts to elaborate the necessary effects of the work of art in terms of its power to *attendrir, émouvoir,* and *toucher,* we began by considering ways in which reading a novel, watching a play, or beholding a painting might be analogous to beholding a moving spectacle in real life. Yet having witnessed Marivaux and Du Bos describe the effects of art in terms of the effects of sympathy, we arrive at an example that shows the experience of beholding a spectacle of real and present suffering to be analogous to (indeed the same as) the experience of beholding an artistic performance and representation.

The experience of sympathy may be presented as a figure for the ideal experience of (for example) reading a novel; but sympathy itself finally must be seen as a theatrical relation formed between a spectacle and a spectator, enacted in the realm of mimesis and representation. The gladiators in the Roman amphitheater represent an extreme example of both spectacles of suffering and spectacles of theatricality, but the conflation of these two spectacles suggests the theatrical conditions of sympathy that underwrite all of Du Bos's and Marivaux's examples. I suggest that *Les Effets surprenants de la sympathie* is about this troubling aspect of the effects of sympathy: not only must works of art touch or move their readers or beholders; people in the world must regard each other as spectators and spectacles, readers and representations. At the same time that the experience of novels and plays and paintings is transported into the realm of affect, sentiment, and sympathy, the experience of sympathy itself seems to be uncomfortably like the experience of watching a play. Furthermore, the violence of the examples that Marivaux and Du Bos use to figure their principles of aesthetics suggests that people who become spectacles might face more threatening prospects than a lack of sympathy.

After considering the claims made in Marivaux's "Avis au lecteur" for the experience of reading *Les Effets surprenants de la sympathie,* and after exploring the theoretical context and implications of those claims as they are elaborated in the *Réflexions critiques sur la poésie et sur la peinture,* one might approach the narrative of the novel itself with certain expectations—if not about one's individual experience of reading, at least about the design, aims, and look of the novel. One might expect the narrative to be filled with pathetic tableaux that present to the eyes of the reader moving spectacles of danger, suffering, or misfortune: scenes that speak in the language of the heart to address the sympathy of the reader represented by a woman of sensibility. Marivaux's preface might prepare us for *La Vie de Marianne,* or later novels such as *La Religieuse* and *La Nouvelle Héloïse.* Reading *Les Effets surprenants de la sympathie,* we do find violent passions, bloody duels, kidnappings, rescues, Turkish sultans, reunions with long-lost relatives, love at first sight, and unrequited love; however, as episodes of excess, portrayed with hyperbole and strung together in a rambling and repetitive narrative, these scenes seem more at home in the conventionally *romanesque Les Aventures de* *** than in the pre-Romantic novel promised by the manifesto-like preface. Deloffre notes that "as is normal in a young author," *Les Effets surprenants de la sympathie* reveals "a certain lack of correspondence [un certain décalage]" between the novel itself and "the program sketched out by the Preface" (*OJ,* pp. 1092–93).[21]

However, if the narrative of the novel does not fulfill the program of the preface, this does not mean that the novel is unrelated to the preface. Indeed, what we find when we read the narrative of *Les Effets surprenants de la sympathie* is a series of scenes in which characters become spectators to bloody accidents, deadly battles, people in distress, and other moving spectacles which evoke their sympathy and compassion. The novel dramatizes scenes in which the spectacles of people (usually suffering or in danger) act to *attendrir, toucher,* or *émouvoir* those who become spectators to them. These scenes are framed by a narrative that opens up to include numerous stories within stories within stories—at one point the reader is at six removes from the original narrator—which themselves dramatize acts of telling moving stories about love, danger, and suffering to listeners who respond with sympathetic sentiments.

If we find, then, in reading *Les Effets surprenants de la sympathie,* an illustration of the "Avis au lecteur," it is not in the sense that the narrative acts like (or looks like) the ideal novel defended in the preface. The narrative, rather, illustrates the preoccupations and theoretical concerns of the "Avis." In particular, it reproduces the tableaux that stand as examples in the "Avis" and expands them into actual episodes of the narrative; the comparisons or analogies that appear in the preface to represent the experience of reading the novel are translated into narrative fiction, dramatized in the novel's play of plot and characters. Woven, so to speak, into the fabric of the narrative, the tableaux which have appeared as analogies and comparisons turn scenes from the novel into allegories for the experience of reading the novel. These tableaux extend and elaborate the critical reflections on (and of) the situations and questions addressed in the preface.

Despite its comic and picaresque aspects, Marivaux's first novel becomes an informal philosophical investigation of the conditions of reading and beholding which is no less serious than the more systematic and premeditated examinations of the abbé Du Bos. As the rambling and repetitive picaresque narrative unfolds and reveals the pattern of its preoccupations, we can recognize a dramatization of the "Avis au lecteur" that reflects on the experience of becoming a spectator to a moving spectacle; the novel considers the differences between reading a text, beholding a painting, watching a play, and becoming a spectator to the spectacle of other people, repeatedly asking what it means to behold people as if they were spectacles, texts, or representations. It is this investigation of the effects of sympathy that makes the narrative of *Les Effets surprenants de la sympathie* about the preface as much as the preface is about the novel.

For example: in one of the first adventures of Clorante (who is ostensibly the hero of the novel, despite the frequent eclipsing of his story by the stories of five different narrators and several other major and minor characters) Clorante is attacked by three men in a forest. He is rescued by some passing horsemen at the moment that, having lost "so much blood," he is in danger of being killed. However, rather than present a vivid painting of Clorante's dangerous battle and subsequent wounds in a description that would elicit the reader's sympathy, the narrator reports that a near-by witness was moved to help Clorante in his distress: "Sa jeunesse, un certain air charmant frappa la personne qui était dans la chaise. C'était une jeune dame. . . . Une tendre compassion s'empara de son âme: elle ne put voir couler le sang de Clorante sans frémir" ("His youth, a certain charming air, struck the person who was in the coach. It was a young lady. . . . A tender compassion took hold of her soul: she could not see the blood of Clorante flow without shuddering" [*OJ*, p. 24]). In reading this scene, we see come to life (or rather, come to fiction) the tableaux in the "Avis" which asks us to imagine the sensibility of women and the experience of witnessing scenes where "blood flows" and "danger threatens" with pity and compassion: "Quand nous sommes émus à l'aspect d'un accident funeste qui blesse ou qui tue quelqu'un, reçoit-on mal à propos une impression d'inquiétude? Quand on regarde une personne exposée à quelque danger, sera-t-on bien venu d'assurer que le coeur a tort de frémir pour elle?" ("When we are moved at the sight of an accident that wounds or kills someone, is it inappropriate to receive an impression of alarm? When we see a person exposed to danger, is it acceptable to declare that the heart is wrong to tremble for that person?" [*OJ*, p. 6]).

There are many such accidents and duels throughout the novel which act as a "sad spectacle" and leave witnesses "truly touched" (*OJ*, p. 162). At the end of the novel, Clarice (who beholds Clorante being wounded in the passage just cited and falls in hopelessly unrequited love) is killed in a bloody struggle with a kidnapper which forms a "spectacle of violence." She tells Clorante, who is "truly touched," "I am losing all my blood, and I am dying; . . . I no longer need anything but compassion." Clorante, we are told, "received her last looks [regards] and paled at this moving spectacle [ce spectacle attendrissant]" while Caliste (Clarice's rival for Clorante's love) exclaims, "how touching is this death! [que cette mort est touchante!]" (*OJ*, pp.

300–301). Clorante and Clarice's relationship thus begins and ends with scenes in which one becomes the sympathetic spectator to the bloody and moving spectacle of the other being wounded.

The moving spectacle that ends the book recalls Clarice's reproach to Clorante early in his adventures when he decides to follow the "invincible sympathie" which leads him to seek out Caliste. After Clorante rejects the love of the woman who saved him and turns away from the "spectacle" of her pain, Clarice complains, "quand il se ressouviendrait de moi, que peut sur un coeur un impuissant et faible souvenir, quand la vue de l'objet mourant n'a point été capable de le toucher?" ("even if he were to remember me, what effect can a weak and feeble memory have upon such a heart, which could not be touched by the sight of the dying object?" [*OJ*, pp. 30–32]). This question could fit easily into the dialogue of the "Avis au lecteur" in the debate about the effects of "the sight of an object" as compared to the effects of a memory (*OJ*, pp. 6–7); or into Du Bos's discussions about the effects of representations: "Comment serons-nous touchez par la copie d'un original incapable de nous affecter?" ("How would we be touched by the copy of an original which is incapable of affecting us?" [*RC*, I:51]). The examples we considered in the discussions of Du Bos and Marivaux are also evoked by the various metaphorical and literal shipwrecks that take place in *Les Effets surprenants de la sympathie*. At the end of the novel, the narrator sums up the adventures of Clorante and Caliste with this image: "I compare Caliste and Clorante, arrived at the height of their felicity, to two unfortunates who are shipwrecked [qui font naufrage]. They struggle against the waves and against death ..." (*OJ*, p. 306).

There have been actual incidents of shipwrecks recounted in the course of the narrative, such as the "shipwreck" in which Clorante and Clarice almost drown in a river and the "shipwreck" in which a "tempest" casts away Merville on an island populated by savages (*OJ*, pp. 68, 246). However, this self-conscious comparison, appearing almost as an epilogue to the novel, suggests that our position in reading about all of the characters' adventures has been like the position of the spectator watching a ship in danger at sea in the famous passage from *De Rerum Natura*. As we have seen, this figure may subvert the presupposition of sympathy which Marivaux depends on in the "Avis au lecteur." At the least, it opens the question of how spectators respond to spectacles of danger or distress.

Indeed, the question of our sympathy as we behold the various spectacles of danger, suffering, and violence the novel presents is raised by a recurring joke about the response of the woman who is supposedly addressed by the author. The narrator playing the role of the author of *Les Effets surprenants de la sympathie* from time to time interrupts the narrative to suggest that the woman figured as the paragon of sensibility and sentiment in the preface is not responding to the language of the heart with an abundance of sympathy. For example, when Clarice encounters her rival for Clorante's love ("tears flowed from her eyes, she was engulfed in a profound sorrow") and feels "a sentiment of pity," the narrator feels called upon to defend Clarice's sympathetic reaction. Insisting that lovers might be "moved with compassion for those that they hate," he protests to his apparently skeptical reader: "cette pitié, que vous trouvez si chimérique, on la verrait en vous, s'il était possible que vous fussiez jamais à la place de Clarice" ("this pity, which you find so fantastical, would be seen in you if you were ever in Clarice's place" [*OJ*, pp. 112–13]).

Whether or not this reader could ever put herself in the place of Clarice—that is, take her place, take her part, feel pity or compassion for her—is left in doubt. At the end of the novel, the narrator complains to his reader about her indifference to love and rejects her as a "judge," suggesting that she displays more of the distance ("éloignement") Lucretius ascribes to spectators of moving spectacles than the sympathy evoked in the "Avis au lecteur" (*OJ*, p. 307). However, this ironic undermining of the terms of the novel by Marivaux is consistent with the sense that the novel itself is less invested in actually moving its readers than in presenting scenes and tableaux that dramatize and illustrate acts of sympathy. For the most part, the sympathetic spectators of *Les Effets surprenants de la sympathie* are the characters themselves responding to the moving spectacles of each other; and indeed, as the novel progresses, its representations of sympathy seem less and less likely to inspire analogous experiences on the part of the reader.

One of the most astonishing representations of the effects of sympathy in the novel reads almost like a parody of the scenes we have been considering (although despite its extreme character, it is finally no more a parody than Du Bos's example of the amphitheater of the gladiators). In the third volume of the narrative Mériante enters a room to see his beloved Parménie; he does not know that she has been bled for medicinal purposes, that in her sleep she has accidentally reopened her wound, and that she has been moved to another room. Parménie, who is recounting the scene in the course of her own first-person narrative, describes the spectacle that presented itself to Mériante: "quel spectacle pour lui! le sang que j'avais répandu ruisselait jusqu'à terre, les draps du lit en étaient baignés; j'y avais laissé un mouchoir ensanglanté. A cet aspect . . . il se jette d'abord à terre dans mon sang" ("what a spectacle for him! the blood which I had shed flowed in streams to the ground, the bed-sheets were bathed in it; I had left a bloody handkerchief there. At this sight . . . he first throws himself to the ground in my blood"). We learn that those witnessing this scene were "émus de compassion pour ce qu'il souffrait, et versant presque des larmes au triste spectacle dont gémissait Mériante, voulurent l'arracher de cette chambre" ("moved with compassion for what he suffered, and almost shedding tears at the sad spectacle which Mériante lamented, they wanted to pull him from the room"). The sad spectacle that these onlookers witness with compassion, suffering with someone they see suffer, is the spectacle of Mériante being moved by the aspect of a bloody spectacle: the scene of an accident where someone has been wounded and apparently killed.

Mériante responds to this sight by wounding himself with a piece of glass that had been used to bleed Parménie, thus adding his blood to hers: "Déjà la plaie est faite," narrates Parménie, "son sang qui coule augmente les ruisseaux du mien; les ruisseaux en inondent la chambre" ("The wound is already made . . . his flowing blood augments the streams of my own; these streams flood the room"). Eventually Mériante is informed that "ce sang répandu dont la vue vous a si fort attristé, est l'effet, dit-on, d'une saignée qui s'est rouverte" ("this bloodshed, the sight of which has saddened you so much, is the effect, we are told, of a blood-letting wound which has reopened" [*OJ*, pp. 185–88]). His gory gesture might be described by a phrase the narrator uses elsewhere to describe Clarice's unexpected sentiment of pity: "a hyperbolic nobility of soul" (*OJ*, p. 113). What it represents in this scene, however, is the literalization of an act of sympathy. Faced with the spectacle of Parménie's suffering, Mériante tries to literally share her pain: to take her part and place by inflicting her wounds on himself. The aspect of his "transports" of sympathy as he seems to drown in the waves and rivers of blood then forms a moving spectacle for others, for whom his bloody clothes and face "presented a frightening object"—all of which present a rather bloody spectacle for the reader. The effect of the scene is to present tableaux within tableaux which double and redouble acts of sympathy in response to moving spectacles of bloody accidents, suffering, and danger. As the comparisons that figure as examples in the "Avis au lecteur" seem to become both more literal and more obsessive, the scene of reading which is the referent of the comparisons seems more and more to carry the trauma of some primal scene.

I would like to return to this primal scene and Marivaux's apparent compulsion to repeat it; but first we should consider what it means that the episode of Mériante's hyperbolic sympathy represents the misinterpretation of a spectacle. The scene suggests the possibility that in viewing the people and events to which we become spectators—indeed, in the very act of viewing them as spectacles, as if they were paintings or scenes from a play—we might be misconstruing what we see. The spectacle of Parménie's bloody accident is not a false representation in the way that a representation on the stage of the sacrifice of Iphigenia would be false; nor is it a dramatic representation of real suffering like the spectacle of the gladiators. Despite the reality of what Mériante sees, however, the "sad spectacle" which moves him is in some sense a fiction. The scene is not what it appears to be; what Mériante represents to himself in his act of sympathy is an illusion. It is as if Mériante has stumbled upon a stage set and imagined that the bloody spectacle it represented was a scene from real life, or as if he burst into a theater, thought he recognized the scene on stage, and then realized that he was at the wrong play. Or rather: in beholding the spectacle of the bloody accident, Mériante—acting as a spectator—has turned a scene from real life into a play or a fiction, as if he has read too many novels.

We are aware of the status of characters as real and imagined representations (not just as spectacles) for each other from the outset of *Les Effets surprenants de la sympathie*. In the first pages of the novel the narrator tells us that when Clorante's father departs for England ("tearing himself from a place which offered to his view [à ses regards] only a spectacle of sorrow") he leaves his wife with both a portrait and a son who seems to act as a portrait. "Only the sight of this dear son could console her for the absence of her husband," writes the narrator; "she saw in him her husband's features; it seemed to her that she saw her husband himself." She is said to "deceive herself with this resemblance." The father later instructs her, "imagine, when you look at him, that it is another me [un autre moi-même]" and the mother herself shows the actual portrait to Clorante, sighing at the thought of her husband's "absence," and tells her son: "Your features resemble his. . . . Try, my son, to resemble him in everything."

The ostensible hero of the novel is thus introduced as a representation, an actor in a tableau vivant who stands for someone else. Deluded by an illusion of resemblance, Clorante's mother speaks to her absent husband, as if Clorante were a compellingly realistic work of art that she mistook for a real person. She confronts the figurative portrait with the literal portrait, showing the copy that is her son one illustration of imitation and resemblance and demanding that he imitate his "original" in another sense to the point of resembling it in everything. She wills the person she has turned into a representation to become a real person, as if he could render present the absent person he represents.

Marivaux then presents us with the text of a letter written by Clorante's absent father from an English prison where he awaits his death. The letter explains that he has been betrayed by his friends and will be executed. As we read, we witness Clorante's mother reading the letter in which her husband sympathetically imagines her response in reading of his execution:

> Je pense avec douleur à la triste surprise où vous jettera la nouvelle de ma mort. Il me semble que vous êtes gémissante, que rien ne vous peut consoler. Je vous vois baignée de larmes, cette idée fait couler les miennes. L'état funeste où je vous vois m'arrache des soupirs. . . . je meurs, je me représente votre affliction, je la vois avec douceur. (*OJ*, pp. 13-15)

> I think with pain of the state of sad surprise into which you will be thrown by the news of my death. It seems to me that you are moaning, that nothing can console you. I see you bathed in tears; that idea makes my own tears flow. The deadly state in which I see you makes me sigh. . . . I die, I represent to myself your affliction, it is sweet for me to see it.

As the absent author of the text presents his own death, he represents to himself the tears and the affliction of his reader, who suffers at the image of his suffering and death, and as he does so, he is moved by her misfortunes. Like the mother speaking to the absent husband whom she thinks she sees, the father imagines that he sees his wife and speaks to her, joining his tears to hers, responding with pity and compassion to her sympathetic response. The reader of the narrative and the reader of the text within the narrative witness the author of the text being moved by a representation of his reader being moved. Clorante's mother, like Mériante when faced with the bloody spectacle of Parménie's accident, is moved to join her own death to her husband's death and she says farewell to her son. "This spectacle moved those who were present" (*OJ*, p. 23)—especially Clorante, who, we are told, felt "compassion for the misfortunes which he saw suffered" (*OJ*, p. 13).

These melodramatic details help to motivate and prepare for the romantic, *romanesque,* and romance in the plot of the novel (Clorante sets out to avenge his father's death and thus begins the adventures promised in the title), but they also introduce a series of frames in which characters turn each other into moving spectacles and representations. What is most striking here is not the dramatization of acts of sympathy, or the metaphors in which the narrative pictures characters as spectacles or representations, or even the metaphors used by characters themselves to describe others as spectacles and representations. Marivaux places in literal and figurative juxtaposition a series of different types of representations: a portrait, a written text, a person who acts as and like a portrait, scenes represented in the imagination, and the spectacles which people present to each other in everyday life.

As the novel begins, it asks us to consider the major questions that have been raised by the "Avis au lecteur": in addition to being faced with acts of sympathy which take place between spectators and spectacles, as well as imagined representations of acts of sympathy which take place between an author and a (female) reader, we are asked to consider the differences between reading a text, writing a text, beholding a painting, beholding a spectacle, looking at a person, looking at a person who (like an actor) stands for someone else, imagining a person, and looking at a person as if he or she were a spectacle or representation. Marivaux does not act as if these experiences are interchangeable or even necessarily analogous. The adventures of the novel take place, so to speak, in the interstices between these juxtaposed experiences, asking us to reflect on our own as well as the characters' experiences of reading and beholding. *Les Effets surprenants de la sympathie* repeatedly interrogates the analogies and comparisons which (in the "Avis au lecteur") set the stage for Marivaux's first novel.

Marivaux presents us with a particularly emblematic dramatization of these questions in a story that Caliste tells about her father, Frédelingue. While riding in the country, Frédelingue is forced by a storm to take shelter in a garden by the side of a house. Caliste describes what Frédelingue sees when he approaches the pavilion:

> Quel spectacle s'offrit à ses yeux! Il y vit la plus aimable femme qu'on puisse voir, couchée sur un lit de repos semé de fleurs. Cette personne était endormie; la manière dont elle était couchée se joignant à sa beauté naturelle la rendait encore plus touchante: elle était penchée; elle soutenait sa tête d'une de ses mains, et laissait voir le plus beau bras du monde. L'éclat de son teint éblouissait; le sommeil augmentait ses couleurs naturelles de l'incarnat le plus vif . . .

> What a spectacle offered itself to his eyes! He saw the most charming woman one could see, lying on a divan strewn with flowers. She was

asleep; the manner in which she was lying there, adding to her natural beauty, made her even more touching. She was leaning to one side; she supported her head with one of her hands, revealing the most beautiful arm in the world. The lustrous hue of her complexion was dazzling; sleep augmented her natural color with the most vivid flush ...

Up to this point Marivaux's description of this spectacle works as an eighteenth-century novel set piece: it carefully presents the reader with a tableau, as if the sentences themselves composed a painting. Indeed, the scene described appears to belong to that category of eighteenth-century French painting that Michael Fried has described in terms of its depiction of absorption: a painting in which the figures are so engrossed in an activity or meditative state that they appear to be oblivious of all beholders, especially the beholders who actually view the painting. In Fried's terms, the figure of a person sleeping often operates as a synecdoche of absorption, guaranteeing a lack of self-consciousness through the depiction of unconsciousness.[22]

Furthermore, although the narrative presents itself as if it were a painting (trying, so to speak, to make the words on the page look like a painting) it quickly leaves *ut pictura poesis* behind and describes the spectacle of the woman as if it were describing an actual painting, complete with attention to details of hue and color. Marivaux acknowledges this by having Caliste refer to her description as a "portrait" and by focusing on the *effects* of this spectacle on its beholder. Caliste continues:

> Ses yeux fermés faisaient un effet charmant dans tout son visage; ils avaient en cet état un attrait particulier; sa bouche semblait sourire; et malgré toute l'aimable douceur répandue dans sa physionomie, on remarquait dans ses traits je ne sais quoi de languissant qui inspirait en même temps et de la tendresse et de l'intérêt pour elle.... Mon père, en la voyant, fut frappé: il l'admira, et l'aima en même temps; saisi de ces deux mouvements à la fois, il s'arrêta presque sans force.

> Her closed eyes had a charming effect on her whole face; in that state they had a special attraction; her mouth seemed to smile, and in spite of all the charming sweetness spread over her physiognomy, one noticed in her features a certain languishment which inspired both tenderness and interest in her.... Seeing her, my father was struck; he admired her and loved her at the same time; seized with these two impulses in one moment, he stopped still, almost without strength.

Taken out of context, this description of the effects of a spectacle on its beholder might pass as an eighteenth-century description of someone seeing a painting for the first time in a salon. Later in the century, Diderot would write of the power of paintings to *arrêter, attirer, attacher,* and *absorber* the beholder; while others (including Du Bos and Marivaux himself) would talk about the quality of *je ne sais quoi* possessed by a work of art.[23] Caliste's account moves from an imitation of a painting to a description of a woman as if she were a painting to a description of the experience of viewing a work of art. Marivaux poses Frédelingue before a tableau vivant of a beautiful woman posed motionless on a kind of bed; faced with a spectacle that touches, charms, interests, attracts, moves, and arrests him, Frédelingue acts as if he has stumbled upon a particularly striking painting.

The spectacle that moves Frédelingue is, of course, a real person— at least up to this point. However, there is more to see. The narrative continues:

> Mon père, revenu de cette émotion qu'il avait sentie, jeta ses yeux partout: il vit sur une petite table de marbre un nombre de lettres qui semblaient être de l'écriture d'un homme. Parmi toutes ces lettres il aperçut quelque chose qui brillait; ... c'était une boîte de portrait: il l'ouvrit en tremblant, et il y vit le portrait de celle qui reposait sur le lit.

> Recovered from the emotion he had felt, my father cast his eyes about everywhere: he saw on a small marble table a number of letters which seemed to be in a man's handwriting. Amid all these letters, he noticed something shining; ... it was a portrait case: he opened it trembling, and he saw the portrait of the woman who was lying on the divan.

After beholding the woman as if she were a painting (in a description that at first tries to act like a painting in prose), Frédelingue discovers an actual, literal painting of the woman alongside a number of letters.

Suddenly the reader is presented with a new tableau: not just the tableau of a woman, presented like a painting; not just the tableau of a woman described as if she were a painting; not just the tableau of a beholder viewing a woman as if she were a painting, described as if it were taking place in a salon; but finally the tableau of a beholder posed between the spectacle of a woman, a painting of the woman, and several pages of text. It turns out that Frédelingue's interpretation of this juxtaposition of woman, painting, and text is wrong; he imagines that the author of the letters and the *destinataire* of the portrait is the woman's lover, whereas what Frédelingue witnesses is not a love scene but the signs of another abducted woman in need of a rescue. What is significant in this context, however, are not details of plot but rather the way in which these props and positions compose an emblem that juxtaposes the different types of representations and experiences we have been considering.

Frédelingue seems almost mesmerized by this sight: "Il se contenta de regarder les lettres. . . . Il tenait toujours son portrait; il jetait les yeux tantôt sur lui, tantôt sur elle. . . . Mais pouvait-il être dans cette posture, et si près d'un objet charmant, sans se laisser aller à quelques transports?" ("He contented himself with looking at the letters. . . . He still held her portrait; he cast his eyes now upon it, now upon her . . . But could he be in this position, so close to the charming object, without allowing himself to go into transports?" [*OJ,* pp. 116–17]). Stunned, it seems, the beholder stands as his eyes race back and forth between the three interrelated sights—the letters, the portrait, the woman—trying to make sense of the tableau that they together compose. There is a sense of vertigo here, a sense of *décalage,* as if our eyes in following the transports of the beholder were directed to the spaces between these three terms.

At the center of the tableau is the woman; but to situate her between the texts about her and the painting of her is also to identify her ontologically, so to speak: to underline her status as a written and painted representation, her roles as both text and spectacle. As we read the novel (ostensibly written as a series of love letters by a man to a woman) we encounter an emblem for the range of aesthetic experiences that frame and introduce Marivaux's first novel. Appearing as the climax of a scene in which the text both declares its desire to act like a painting and dramatizes its preoccupation with the experience of beholding written and painted representations, the tableau of Frédelingue posed between text, portrait, and woman offers a somewhat anxious illustration of the predicament of the novel at the beginning of the eighteenth century.

One way to understand the predicament of the novel in the eighteenth century is to imagine authors like Marivaux trying to design the experience of reading a novel while their eyes race back and forth between the experiences of beholding a painting, watching a play, and witnessing the spectacle of another person. If the novel is expected to reproduce these experiences, it is not simply because of the demands of nascent realism, aesthetic doctrines such as *ut pictura poesis,* or theories about universal principles and the parallels between the arts. The sort of demands articulated in the "Avis au lecteur" for the experience of reading a novel are part of a general set of demands and expectations expressed in the eighteenth century that call on the novel to provide its readers with what a written text must deny: voice, sight, and presence. This is partly because despite its roots in the epic and in early romance and picaresque narratives, the eighteenth-century novel grows out of the theater (the rival it ultimately surpasses as a popular narrative art form). It is no coincidence that in his career Marivaux moves back and forth between plays and novels; his novels are preoccupied with the scene of theater no less than his plays.

Although Du Bos does not seem to pay attention to narrative fiction, the *poésie* in the title *Réflexions critiques sur la poésie et sur la peinture* refers largely to *poésie dramatique,* which Du Bos praises for its ability to present "an infinity of tableaux" (*RC,* I:396). Whether or not he is actually speaking of drama when he discusses literature, Du Bos imagines texts that have the effect of plays produced on the stage. It is not a contradiction that Du Bos makes enormous claims for the effects and power of works of art at the same time that he insists that we are always aware that we are responding to an illusion; nor that he should make "ut pictura poesis" the epigraph and the governing principle for a book in which he remarks that reading is "a labor for our eyes" since we read "as we say, with our eyes upon the paper [l'oeil sur le papier]" (*RC,* I:402). The eyes may offer the most direct access to the soul but what we *see* when we read a book, Du Bos reminds us, are words on a page.

For both Du Bos and Marivaux, the demands that literary texts should produce illusions of sight and act like paintings or plays are accompanied by (indeed motivated by) an acknowledgement of the limitations of the effects of reading a novel. Although the eighteenth century would produce readers who described the experience of reading novels in hyperbolic, mystical, and mystified terms, the demands made on the experience of reading were, strictly speaking, impossible precisely because they focused on what the novel is not—on what the novel cannot do. If eighteenth-century writers searched for parallels and universal principles to unite the "sister" arts, this is at least in part because they were concerned with the *differences* between the experiences of novels, paintings, and plays. Marivaux's tableau of Frédelingue posed between pages of text, a painting, and a woman signals the key terms and experiences between which and about which the eighteenth-century novel takes place.

We have seen that *Les Effets surprenants de la sympathie* is also concerned with the effects and experience of theater because of the theatrical structure of sympathy—which Marivaux (like others in the eighteenth century) takes as a paradigm both for the ideal experience of the work of art and for the way that people in the world appear before each other as spectators or spectacles. In this context the novel's

concern with the effects and experience of art is finally not distin-
guishable from its concern with relations enacted between people in
the world. As we read the novel, the aesthetic and critical reflections
of *Les Effets surprenants de la sympathie* become less and less distinct
from the plot and characters of *Les Aventures de ***. Perhaps the most
extensive incorporation of Marivaux's aesthetic preoccupations into
the plot of the novel occurs in the story of Merville, a stranger who
recounts his adventures to Parménie (who reports them to Frédelingue, all within the story that Caliste tells to Clarice). For the
moment we need not concern ourselves with Merville's life story; the
episode in question takes place while Merville is a slave in a country
inhabited by Turks.

Merville recounts how the wife of his Turkish master sees him and
is moved by his condition as a slave: "by chance this young woman
cast her eyes upon me; she read my affliction; a tender compassion
took hold of her soul" (*OJ*, p. 215). The wife (whose name is Halila)
continues to be moved by his suffering and eventually her sympathy
turns to love: "Halila cast upon me eyes in which all imaginable
tenderness was painted. The state in which I found myself pierced her
to the heart" (*OJ*, pp. 216–17). In order to lessen his affliction and
increase their intimacy, Halila inquires what other work Merville is
capable of; and discovering that (in Merville's words) "je peignais un
peu en miniature" ("I did a little painting of miniatures") she engages
him to teach her how to paint. The next day, narrates Merville, the
master "ordered me to teach his wife to paint" (*OJ*, p. 219). Thus,
having posed Halila as a sympathetic spectator to the spectacle of
Merville's suffering, and having posed Merville as the beholder of the
signs of sympathy painted in Halila's eyes, Marivaux brings his
characters together for a painting lesson.

It should not surprise us that when Merville sits down to "tracer
quelques figures sur du papier" ("draw a few figures on paper"), he
draws a pair of eyes: "J'achevai cependant ce que j'avais à dessiner,
c'étaient des yeux" ("I finished, however, what I was drawing: it was
a pair of eyes" [*OJ*, p. 221]). Merville's choice for the figure he draws
becomes a figure for what is at stake in the entire scene: sight,
spectacles, looking, seeing, beholding. They stand for both the
beholder and the physiognomic canvas on which the soul tries to
represent itself. In order to understand how the figure of eyes is set in
play in this episode we need to note another detail of plot: since Halila
speaks no French and Merville speaks no Turkish, they depend on a
servant maid named Frosie to translate for them. This interpreter,
however, is also in love with Merville, and she becomes angry when

he does not respond to her advances. When Merville draws the eyes Frosie tells him, "Ne dessinez jamais des yeux, à moins que vous n'y peigniez vos regards, alors on pourra s'appliquer à les étudier" ("Never draw eyes, unless you paint your own gaze in them, for one might apply oneself to studying them"); but it turns out that he would be fortunate if this were possible since Frosie in her jealousy cannot be relied upon as an interpreter.

Halila draws a heart next to the eyes Merville has drawn and then tries, explains Merville, "de me faire entendre par signe que cela signifiait que son coeur avait, en me voyant, suivi ses yeux" ("to make me understand by signs that this signified that when she saw me her heart had followed her eyes" [OJ, p. 221]). Merville seems to understand this sign language in which Halila glosses the hieroglyphic translation she has provided of the account in Merville's own narrative; but when Halila asks Frosie to interpret the signification of these signs, Frosie quarrels with Merville and then provides Halila with a "translation" that makes her run from the room crying. Faced with this apparent mistranslation, Merville laments "our lack of power to make ourselves understood"; feeling "touched [attendri] by a movement of compassion" for Halila, he vows to "la détromper sur mon chapitre" ("undeceive her on my score" [OJ, p. 222]).

Merville tries to communicate with Halila in the only language available to them, the language of sight: "I approached her," he narrates, "and made a thousand gestures which marked my horror at Frosie's proceedings. . . . Halila watched my gestures with attention and surprise; she spoke to Frosie, who answered her; and I redoubled my signs to make Halila understand that Frosie had evil designs [mauvais desseins] against her" (OJ, p. 223). Confronted by the evil designs of Frosie, Merville stands in the "chambre au dessin" (literally the drawing room, where he has been teaching his most important beholder how to draw eyes) and speaks in sign language—only this time he communicates not through figures and hieroglyphs written on paper but through the language of gestures.

In order to make himself understood, he must turn himself into both text and drawing, present himself as a spectacle of signs for Halila to behold and interpret. Merville designs himself as he would trace figures on paper; he acts out a scene for his astonished spectator: "I raised my hands to heaven, as if to pray to the gods to turn away the blow that threatened this lady" (OJ, pp. 222–23). Unlike other tableaux in Les Effets surprenants de la sympathie, in this scene Merville is not described as if he were a spectacle or painting or even as if he were regarded as a spectacle or painting; here a drawing master literally becomes his own drawing, designed in the signs of gestures which mean to delineate the "funestes desseins" ("deadly designs"), the "mauvais desseins" ("evil designs"), the "desseins de vengeance" ("designs of vengeance") of his interpreter.

We have seen other scenes in the novel in which spectacles are misinterpreted; but here we see a crisis of interpretation that is initially brought about by conscious and willful misinterpretation but is then compounded by "the lack of power to make ourselves understood" and the ambiguity of visual signs. Although "anger is eloquent" and Merville finally is able to communicate enough to Halila to make her "look at Frosie with eyes of fury," Merville is unable to make himself clear; "it was practically impossible to distinguish with my gestures the anger which Frosie's actions inspired in me, and the alarm she caused me for this lady, from the equivocal marks [marques équivoques] of a tenderness that I did not feel" (OJ, p. 223). Dependant on equivocal signs to convey their inner sentiments, Merville and Halila return to the "chambre au dessin" without Frosie; Halila "en dessinant encore sur son papier" ("again drawing on her paper") offers Merville another picture of her feelings: "elle me montra deux coeurs unis, et qu'un soleil entourait, comme pour me faire connaître que deux coeurs bien unis lisaient tout ce qui se passait l'un dans l'autre, et qu'ils n'avaient pas besoin d'interprète" ("she showed me two united hearts surrounded by a sun, as if to make me understand that two united hearts read all that went on within each other, and that they had no need of an interpreter" [OJ, p. 223]).

Tracing figures on a piece of paper, Halila designs a complex metaphor in order to signify (according to Merville's interpretation) that two lovers can read each other like perfectly legible texts. Ironically, this declaration that in their transparency they have no need of an interpreter allows Merville to conceal his true feelings—which at this moment have to do with his love for another woman: "This manner of declaring our sentiments ... spared me the chagrin of having to tell Halila aloud that my heart could feel only gratitude" (OJ, pp. 223–24). The figure of illumination and communication in Halila's design ironically underlines the epistemological crisis that has been set in play by signs, figures, translations, metaphors, and spectacles throughout the episode. Furthermore, as Halila and Merville design "encore plusieurs figures" ("a few more figures") and as Halila gives a bracelet to Merville, they are themselves composing a simultaneously revealing and misleading spectacle for Halila's husband—who, having been told by the jealous Frosie, "you will be a better judge of things when your eyes are witnesses of them," is hiding in a closet watching them through "une porte vitrée" ("a door with a window" [*OJ*, pp. 224–25]). The husband would appear to have no need for an interpreter to understand the spectacle he witnesses, to read in the hearts of the figures before him. It is not self-evident, however, what the Turkish master actually sees.

Before considering this question, we should note that Merville has found himself in this position before. Earlier in his adventures, while a guest in the house of an Englishman named Hosbid, Merville falls in love with Hosbid's daughter (who happens to be engaged to someone else). Merville describes how one day, while he and Misrie were secretly planning an honorable marriage, the young man to whom Misrie had been promised "entra dans la chambre au moment qu'aux genoux de cette fille je lui baisais une main qu'elle abandonnait à mes caresses, pendant qu'elle appuyait l'autre sur ma tête" ("entered the room at the moment when I was at the knees of this girl, kissing the hand that she abandoned to my caresses, while she rested the other hand on my head"). The unfortunate beholder of this scene is killed in the struggle that follows this "vue" (*OJ*, p. 200). Shortly thereafter, Merville plays the same role in another tableau vivant; this time, he is discovered with Hosbid's wife, Guirlane, as she offers him tokens of love which will help him escape. The spectator this time is Hosbid: "quel spectacle pour Hosbid! il me vit assis, et Guirlane auprès de moi, qui venait d'entrer, fondante en larmes du chagrin de me voir partir; elle me disait les derniers adieux, et m'offrait des bijoux de prix" ("what a spectacle for Hosbid! he saw me seated, and next to me Guirlane, who had just come in, bursting into tears at the chagrin of seeing me leave; she was saying her last farewell, and she offered me valuable jewels" [*OJ*, p. 208]).

Each of these tableaux presents the same aspect to the unknowing spectator who happens to stumble into the room.[24] However, each "vue" (*OJ*, pp. 200, 208) requires a different interpretation or reading: Merville is guilty in the first tableau and innocent in the second, even if both tableaux look alike. Marivaux presents the same pair of ambiguous spectacles in *La Vie de Marianne:* first, M. de Climal discovers Marianne "à demi couchée sur un lit de repos, les yeux mouillés de larmes, et tête-à-tête avec un jeune homme" ("half reclining on a divan, eyes moist with tears, and in a tête-à-tête with a young man"). Marianne asks: "n'était-ce pas là un tableau bien amusant pour M. de Climal?" ("was this not an amusing tableau for M. de Climal?" [*VM*, p. 83]). Next Valville, who also suddenly enters a room, finds M. de Climal "dans la même posture où, deux heures auparavant, l'avait surpris M. de Climal" ("in the same position in which, two hours before, M. de Climal had surprised him" [*VM*, p. 120]). Once again, the two tableau vivants are effectively identical, although they have different meanings. The signs seem perfectly clear but they are in some sense equivocal or misleading; the spectator beholding them seems to need an interpreter if he is to read correctly the actions and sentiments of the actors in the tableau.

Judging by these examples and Merville's past experience, it would seem that the spectacle of "the fatal gift of the bracelet" witnessed by the Turkish master might not be as easy to read as it appears to be. Indeed, the husband does not know that Merville does not reciprocate Halila's love, or that nothing but the bracelet and some figures have passed between them. On the other hand, the husband is not exactly wrong in his interpretation of the scene when (according to Merville) the manner in which Halila put the bracelet on Merville "pierced him to the heart" (*OJ*, p. 225). However, like the intricate series of signs, symbols, figures, and hieroglyphs that have preceded it, the sight of the gift of the bracelet is actually much more complicated and equivocal than it appears to its distant beholder.

Halila puts the bracelet on Merville as they sit in the "chambre au dessin" and draw "figures"—presumably designs that act figuratively, such as the drawing of the hearts and the sun. Merville narrates how Halila took a bracelet from her hair and "took both my hands, which she pretended to chain together with the bracelet, showing me by this act that she wanted me to have no other chains than those of love" (*OJ*, p. 224). What the husband (and the reader) witness in this scene appears to be a continuation of the signing and designing that Merville and Halila have been performing both with figures on paper and with the signs of their bodies. According to Merville, Halila acts out a metaphor; she dramatizes and physically represents a figure of speech (which, when enacted literally, appears to function symbolically, as if it had ritual meaning). Strangely, this literal rendering of a figure of speech signifies to Merville (who is literally Halila's slave) that henceforth his enslavement will be figurative rather than literal; her pretending to chain him is supposed to represent the absence of chains. The husband, on the other hand, seems to take what he sees literally; but he would be just as enraged by this spectacle if he had arrived at Merville's interpretation and understood the metaphor that his wife was acting out. Ironically, the performance of this dialogue in the language of signs and figures—its status as pure spectacle—allows the husband to decipher the scene simply by spying on them from the closet.

Regardless of the correct interpretation of this scene (and in this case both the literal and the figurative readings of Halila's actions add up to essentially the same interpretation), what is clear is that, once again, the actors in this tableau have themselves become the texts and tableaux on which and with which their figures are designed. They are not just seen and described as spectacles, representations, paintings, or texts; they literally as well as figuratively turn themselves into texts and tableaux. In this sense the episode of the painting lesson itself becomes a miniature of the entire novel. The relations and situations in which the characters of the novel are repeatedly framed as spectacles, representations, paintings, tableaux, and texts (for each other and the reader) are here framed and displayed in a dizzying design of literal and figurative figures. Furthermore, Merville's adventures suggest that there might be risks in opening oneself to interpretation as well as misinterpretation.

At this point I would like to return to my suggestion that the scene of reading—which is figured in *Les Effets surprenants de la sympathie* in terms of spectators and spectacles—carries with it the trauma of some primal scene. In the tableaux we have been considering, a spectator unexpectedly finds himself a witness to an apparently erotic scene that he is not supposed to see. In Merville's narrative, the scene is more or less adultery: Misrie's fiancé discovers his bride-to-be, and Hosbid and the Turkish master both discover their wives, in compromising situations with Merville. In more general terms, each of these tableaux, like the tableaux in which Marianne is discovered with Valville and M. de Climal, appear to have an erotic content; to the beholders who are not supposed to view them, they appear to be scenes of erotic transgression, and each of them ends in bloodshed and violence.

Perhaps the most violent and sexually suggestive of these episodes turns on a spectacle in which the main characters are absent: the empty and bloody bed of Parménie. Ostensibly, when Mériante unexpectedly stumbles into this scene and finds the bed of his beloved soaked in blood, he fears that Parménie is dead. However, the gory details of the sheets bathed in blood and the "mouchoir ensanglanté" ("bloody handkerchief") add a sexual aspect to Mériante's anxiety in a narrative in which virtually all of the male characters feel threatened by the imminent violation of the abducted virgins they are in love with. The signs that Mériante beholds when he charges into Parménie's bedroom might be interpreted as the dreaded loss of Parménie's virginity—or merely as the signs of her womanhood, her maturity as a sexual being. What gives the entire tableau (including the role Mériante plays in it) the sense of a primal scene is the fact that the point of view in the description really belongs to Caliste, who is retelling the story of her mother, Parménie. In other words, it is Parménie's daughter who is picturing the scene of someone discovering the bloody sheets of her mother's bed.

Furthermore, this episode comes after the story about Frédelingue discovering the spectacle of Parménie sleeping on a bed in a garden—which is also recounted by Caliste, this time about both of her parents. The daughter of Parménie and Frédelingue imagines the moment her father discovers her mother on a bed. (One needn't be Tristram Shandy to imagine in this scene the "original" moment of Caliste's conception.) Within the story, Frédelingue supplies an explicitly erotic content to the scene by imagining a relationship between the woman on the bed and the author of the love letters beside her. When Frédelingue returns to the scene later, this fantasy is realized as he unexpectedly stumbles upon the prince threatening to force himself on Parménie, whom he rescues in yet another bloody struggle. Taken together, Caliste's stories about her mother's bed (which are stories about her mother's possible violation) feel like an imagined primal scene—including the punishment of the unexpected spectator represented by Mériante: mutilation, the shedding of his own blood, or castration.[25]

Obviously, I do not mean to claim that these episodes represent primal scenes in the strictly Freudian sense, or that they necessarily bear the trace of some real or imagined primal scene to which Marivaux was a spectator. My point is that the scene of writing, represented here as the scene of theater, seems to be charged with a degree of anxiety that exceeds the particular local details of plot and character. These spectacles all have the air of an illicit and a dangerous eroticism about them both for the actors in the scene and for the spectators who accidentally stumble upon them and see what they are not supposed to see. The transgression dramatized in these scenes often seems to be performed by those who compose the tableau (Merville, Misrie, Guirlane, Halila, Marianne, Valville, M. de Climal) but there is also a sense that the spectator of the scene (Mériante, Frédelingue, Caliste) is in some sense guilty. This might make us reflect on our own position as readers and spectators of *Les Effets surprenants de la sympathie* and remind us that the novel is supposed to have an erotic frame that casts the narrative in the language of seduction as well as the language of the heart.

As we have seen, the fiction that the novel is written to elicit the love of a rather unsympathetic woman ultimately becomes a joke on Marivaux's part; but nevertheless, this fiction serves to put us in the position we see acted out by characters throughout the narrative as they are cast in the role of *voyeur*. We might wonder if we are like the minor character who (with a friend) spies on a woman named Ostiane when she goes to bathe. He describes how they hid themselves "in a small room adjoining the bath; and there, through a small window, we could see Ostiane come in without her seeing us." The sight of Ostiane in the bathhouse overwhelms him ("what beauty struck my eyes . . . what became of me at this sight? . . . my eyes were fixed on Ostiane") but when he later tries to kidnap her he mistakenly abducts Misrie—tricked by the "ressemblance" between the two women. "Alas!" he exclaims later, "my eyes, deceived by love, are now cruelly disabused [détrompés]."

That he should be "trompé" by "ressemblance" might seem surprising after the view he has had of Ostiane—whose name might have its etymology in the Latin *ostendere:* to show. But he knows her only as a spectacle and indeed mostly as an image or representation; he first becomes acquainted with Ostiane when his friend "made me a charming portrait of her." After the sight which obsesses him, we learn, "je me représentai ce que je venais de voir. . . . tout me montrait Ostiane, je croyais la voir à chaque instant" ("I represented to myself what I had just seen. . . . everything showed me Ostiane, I thought I saw her every instant"). He describes what he sees at the bath as a "bel ouvrage" ("beautiful work") and he seems to imagine that this work is designed for his sight: "un corset . . . délacé à moitié par-devant avec un négligence qui semblait un ouvrage de l'amour, laissait entrevoir une gorge" ("a corset . . . half unlaced in front with a negligence which seemed to be a work of love, revealed a bosom" [*OJ*, pp. 241–45]). This *voyeur* is not just a spectator; he is the beholder of an *ouvrage.* He views a woman who is first introduced to him in a verbal "portrait" and then secretly beheld as a spectacle as if she were a work of art, then turns her into a representation in his mind's eye, and then mistakes a similitude for the "original" that he beheld. Although a minor character in the novel, this beholder, along with the other *voyeurs* portrayed in the narrative, stands in and for the position of the unseen readers and spectators of Marivaux's *ouvrage.*

The fictitious second person to whom the first-person narratives of the novel are addressed (either the woman for whom the novel supposedly is written or the various interlocutors for whom stories are recounted in the narrative) places the actual reader in the position of an unsuspected spectator. If this position is called into question, however, it is not exactly because the reader is guilty of voyeurism. There is a recurring sense in the novel that it is dangerous to turn someone into a spectacle—especially for the person who is beheld. We have seen that the person who is viewed as a spectacle risks being misinterpreted, misread, mistranslated, and mistaken. The prospect that sight is the key to sympathy, that the view of a spectacle will allow or even cause a beholder to enter into the thoughts and sentiments of the person who is seen, is undermined by the difficulty that spectators seem to have in reading the representations of other people. In the scenes we have considered, misinterpretation (although sometimes simply interpretation) of scenes threatens to turn spectacles into life or death situations.

Indeed, most of the scenes of theater we have considered seem to begin or end in violence. We may be *voyeurs* in reading *Les Effets surprenants de la sympathie,* but for us, as for Mériante, the scene of sexuality seems to have been replaced or displaced by scenes of violence. From the "Avis au lecteur" until the last pages of the narrative, the spectacles which evoke sympathy and love are usually spectacles of people wounded or in mortal danger. The novel contains scenes of idealized love at first sight, such as when Clorante sees Caliste framed by a window or when Frédelingue first regards Parménie in the garden as if she were a painting; but as the relations between this innocent spectacle of Parménie and the spectacle of her bloody sheets suggest, the spectacles of sympathy in *Les Effets surprenants de la sympathie* run the risk of becoming like the bloody "spectacles de l'amphithéâtre" which haunt the abbé Du Bos. Behind the scenes of theater in *Les Effets surprenants de la sympathie* are versions of primal scenes that bear the sense of a dangerous eroticism and translate into scenes of violence.

The spectacles of bloody accidents, danger, violence, and suffering that are dramatized first in the examples of the "Avis au lecteur" and then within the pages of the narrative are supposed to guarantee our sympathy; but they also suggest that our sympathy—and the pleasure we seem to take in it—depend on the violence and suffering inflicted on those who appear as spectacles before us. This is what informs the central paradox of Du Bos's *Réflexions critiques*—a paradox that begins in a double consciousness in which reason coexists with imitations or phantoms of emotions and ends in the frighteningly theatrical conditions of the gladiators' amphitheater. Such guilty pleasures—and such violent effects—threaten to eclipse the scenes and acts of sympathy which are supposed to characterize the experience of reading the novel.

Les Effets surprenants de la sympathie suggests that the act of viewing someone as a spectacle, and the situation of being turned into a spectacle, may have surprising and undesired effects. Indeed, Marivaux's insistent comparison of the experience of reading a novel with the experience of beholding "the aspect of a deadly accident that wounds or kills someone" or "a person exposed to some danger" or a "sight" in which "danger threatens" and "blood flows" (*OJ*, p. 6) suggests that authors and actors, as well as readers and beholders, may enter into situations that are both dangerous and difficult to control. I have argued that the plot of the novel—by translating example, comparison, analogy, and figure into dramatic scene and narrative event—reworks (and tries to work out) the theoretical reflections about the effects of sympathy and theatrical relations that preoccupy both Marivaux and Du Bos in their considerations of the complex interplay between "life" and "art." The novel depicts the effects that Marivaux expects for and from his art, as well as the unexpected effects that seem to be a source of anxiety.

I have suggested that the "Avis au lecteur" stands as a legend for *Les Effets surprenants de la sympathie;* however, I also have tried to convey that the reader must wander through hundreds of pages of the picaresque and somewhat random narrative in order to discover the patterns that display the preoccupations and concerns that Marivaux seemed to feel in writing his first novel. In *La Vie de Marianne,* the first part of which appeared in 1731, Marivaux constructs a narrative around the preoccupations that are central to the "Avis au lecteur" and somewhat off-center, if unmistakably recurrent, in the narrative of *Les Effets surprenants de la sympathie.* In the next chapter, I will argue that the scene of the accident that figures so importantly in Marivaux's *oeuvre de jeunesse* becomes the primal scene of the most famous novel of Marivaux's maturity. We will see that the scene of a moving accident in which the hero or heroine is wounded, placed in danger, or turned into a victim is once again a key figure for the experience of reading a novel, as Marivaux investigates the effects of sympathy in the context of autobiographical acts.

TWO

La Vie de Marianne, or the Accidents of Autobiography

> Quand nous sommes émus à l'aspect d'un accident funeste qui blesse ou qui tue quelqu'un, reçoit-on mal à propos une impression d'inquiétude? Quand on regarde une personne exposée à quelque danger, sera-t-on bien venu d'assurer que le coeur a tort de frémir pour elle?
>
> Marivaux, *Les Effets surprenants de la sympathie*

"Il y a quinze ans que je ne savais pas encore si le sang d'où je sortais était noble ou non, si j'étais batarde ou légitime. Ce début parait annoncer un roman" ("Fifteen years ago I still did not know whether the blood I came from was noble or not, whether I was a bastard or legitimate. This beginning seems to announce a novel" [*VM*, pp. 9–10]).[1] With this acknowledgment, Marianne begins the narration of her life story in *La Vie de Marianne*, starting with the known and unknown beginnings of her life. What is it about the beginnings of both her *vie* and her *Vie* that appears to announce a novel? The narrative of Marianne's life is prefaced by the usual assurances that we are reading a genuine autobiography rather than a novel, although it is unclear whether in 1731 such fictions were meant to guarantee the text's authority and authenticity or to signal its fictional status, or both. More specifically, Marianne's allusion to the early appearance of the *romanesque* in her narrative refers to the mysterious origins which leave her legitimacy and class status in doubt: a romantic beginning which she acknowledges she shares with the heroes and heroines of many novels. In raising questions about the nobility and legitimacy of her origins, Marianne—that is to say, Marivaux—also is gesturing toward the origins of the novel, a bastard and lower-class relative in the hierarchical family of eighteenth-century literary genres.[2] I would like to suggest, however, that the sign of the novel at the beginning of Marianne's *Vie* appears precisely in the blood that she comes from: "le sang d'où je sortais."

The paragraph immediately following Marianne's announcement that there is something *romanesque* about the beginning of her life makes it clear that the *sang* from which she emerges at the beginning of her story is both figurative and literal. Indeed, she describes in gory detail the first known episode in her life: the bloody attack on the coach in which all of her companions are killed or wounded; the infant who will become Marianne is pulled "toute sanglante" ("all bloody") from under a dead woman who, Marianne recounts, "m'avait baignée de son sang" ("had bathed me in her blood" [*VM*, p. 11]). I want to insist on the literal status of the blood Marianne comes from, but this is because it is the literalness of the bloody scene that should most alert us to its figurative status. To begin with, we can read this depiction of the accident that delivers Marianne into the world of the novel as a rather graphic fantasy of birth. By picturing the spectacle of "le sang d'où je sortais," Marianne inaugurates her life story with a version of a primal scene. J. Laplanche and J.-B. Pontalis relate primal scene scenarios to fantasies of origins, which provide "a representation of, and a solution to, the major enigmas which confront the child. Whatever appears to the subject as something needing an explanation or theory," they continue, "is dramatized as a moment of emergence, the beginning of a history. Fantasies of origins: the primal scene pictures the origin of the individual."[3] Introducing the autobiography of someone who doesn't know who she is, the scene of Marianne's deliverance both explains how her "birth became impenetrable" (*VM*, p. 13) and imagines her birth.

However, Marianne's personal primal scene also points to what might be considered the scene of origin of the novel itself. Frédéric Deloffre has noted that the story of Marianne's origins recalls the story told in *Les Effets surprenants de la sympathie* about the "accident" which delivers Dorine, who as an infant is saved from a similar attack and left without any clue to her identity except the assurance of a dying nurse that she comes from a noble family.[4] But the bloody spectacle that begins Marianne's life recalls less a particular scene from *Les Effets surprenants* than the examples that stand as figures for the experience of reading a novel in the "Avis au lecteur" which prefaces Marivaux's debut as a novelist. We saw that the "Avis au lecteur" compares the experience of reading a novel to the experience of becoming a spectator to a moving spectacle of a bloody accident where people are wounded, killed, or in danger: "Quand nous sommes émus à l'aspect d'un accident funeste qui blesse ou qui tue quelqu'un, reçoit-on mal à propos une impression d'inquiétude? Quand on regarde une personne exposée à quelque danger, sera-t-on bien venu d'assurer que le coeur a tort de frémir pour elle?" ("When we are moved at the sight of an accident that wounds or kills someone, is it inappropriate to receive an impression of alarm? When we see a person exposed to danger, is it acceptable to declare that the heart is wrong to tremble for that person?"[*OJ*, p. 6]).

We saw also that Marivaux's descriptions of the effects of becoming "witnesses of accidents" where "the danger threatens, the blood flows" (*OJ*, p. 6) can be located in the context of philosophical reflections in which the abbé Du Bos compares the effects of works of art to the effects of "the cries of a wounded man" and "the sight of his blood and his wound" (*RC*, I:387), as well as other spectacles of blood and violence. We saw as well that the scenes of violence to which characters accidentally become spectators are often related to erotic scenes which appear to reenact versions of a primal scene; this scene, which is not necessarily located in the psychological story of a particular character, appears to be behind the scene of writing as well as the scene of theater. The context of these reflections on the paradigmatic status of the experience of beholding the moving scenes of a bloody accident allows us to understand what is *romanesque* about the beginning of Marianne's life. The examples of the "Avis au lecteur," translated again into plot, provide a key for deciphering the accident as a figure for the experience of reading a novel.

Indeed, we can see that from the outset, in being described as a moving spectacle that inspires curiosity or compassion in its beholders, Marianne is regarded as if she were a novel. She recounts that having begun as a "terrible spectacle," she becomes "an object of curiosity"; the people from the neighboring villages came to see her, she explains, because "on se prenait pour moi d'un goût romanesque" ("they took to me with a taste for the romantic" [*VM*, p. 13]). It is no coincidence that in the "Avis au lecteur" Marivaux refers to readers who regard "un livre sans aveu comme un espèce d'enfant trouvé que quelque misérable auteur a fait perdre" ("an unacknowledged book as an orphaned baby which some miserable author has abandoned" [*OJ*, p. 8]). *La Vie de Marianne* tells the story of an *enfant trouvé* whose *vie romanesque* begins with the primal scene of a bloody accident which inaugurates her life as a spectacle. Furthermore, as an autobiography, it must tell the story of someone who turns herself into a spectacle.

Les Effets surprenants de la sympathie suggests that it is dangerous to turn someone into a spectacle. Not only are those characters who are framed as spectacles subject to misinterpretation and misreading; the scenes of reading and theater which seem designed to evoke love and sympathy from the reader or beholder also seem to depend on or at least end in violence (often the violence associated with primal scenes).

To understand Marianne's life as a spectacle, then—to understand her *Vie* as a novel—we need to understand how to read and behold her accidents. The *Avertissement* introduces Marianne's narrative by referring to "les accidents de sa vie" ("the accidents of her life" [*VM*, p. 5]) and Marianne herself in the very first sentence of her account describes the text as "le récit de quelques accidents de ma vie" ("the narrative of some accidents of my life" [*VM*, p. 8]). Following *Les Effets surprenants de la sympathie* and beginning with the terrible spectacle of the accident which delivers Marianne into the world, *La Vie de Marianne* might lead its reader to expect that the accidents it promises will be both literal and gory. If it turns out that Marianne's story is closer to a novel of manners than to the more baroque and picaresque genre of Marivaux's first novel, its preoccupation with accidents should seem all the more significant. In this chapter I will try to understand what is *romanesque* about Marianne's accidents by placing her autobiography within the overdetermined network of juxtapositions and superimpositions that we have viewed associating the scene of theater, the scene of writing, the scene of the novel, the scenes of accidents and moving spectacles, and the primal scene. Viewing Marianne within the frame of the scene of autobiography, we will consider what it means to become a victim in or of any of these scenes; this will involve once again tracing the effects of sympathy.

Reading the beginning of Marianne's life with the examples and preoccupations of *Les Effets surprenants de la sympathie* in mind, we can recognize the characters and characteristics that identify the scene of the novel. We read the details of the fatal attack, the aftermath of which is described as a "terrible spectacle." Marianne describes her "terrible cries, half smothered under the body of a wounded woman"; she describes witnesses who stop at the scene "either out of the curiosity we often have for things that have a certain horror, or to see what child was crying and to help it" (*VM*, pp. 10–11). The witnesses of this spectacle are divided in their response, like the people Marivaux describes in his *Lettres sur les habitants de Paris* as rushing to the "sad spectacle" of an execution with "an avid curiosity" and "a sentiment of compassion,"[5] or perhaps like those denounced later in the novel who possess a "stupid and brutish curiosity" and the desire to "s'attendrir pour vous si on vous blesse, à frémir pour votre vie si on la menace" ("be moved for you if you are wounded, to tremble for your life if it is threatened" [*VM*, p. 95]). Some want to flee, while another, "ému de compassion" ("moved to compassion"), rescues the bloody child. Marianne is eventually adopted by the curé's sister, "in whom I inspired so much pity" and becomes, as we saw, an "object of curiosity" for whom people have a "goût romanesque."

If the scene of this accident is to be read as both the locus of Marianne's fantasy of her origin and the primal scene of the novel itself, we must recognize that it represents a moment that is repeated throughout the narrative: Marianne ends the first volume by announcing, "J'approche ici d'un événement qui a été l'origine de toutes mes autres aventures, et je vais commencer par là la seconde partie de ma vie" ("Here I draw near to an event which was the origin of all my other adventures, and with it I shall begin the second part of my life" [*VM*, p. 52]). Once again, Marianne begins both her life and her life story by locating her origin, and once again she describes herself becoming both a spectacle and the victim of a moving and dangerous accident. The famous scene in which she displays herself at church at the beginning of the second volume of the novel marks the zenith of Marianne's theatrical exhibitionism, but it can be seen as the logical culmination of the events that begin with Marianne's debut as a part of a "terrible spectacle."

Since arriving in Paris, Marianne has resisted M. de Climal's attempts to seduce her but she has allowed herself to be seduced by his efforts to make a spectacle of her. He persuades her to accept his gifts of clothing by offering her an image of herself framed in a mirror: "go look at yourself in the mirror, and see if these linens are too fine for your face" (*VM*, p. 39). Eventually Marianne's *amour-propre* is not satisfied with the spectacle presented by "a little ungrateful mirror which only gave me back one half of my face [ma figure]" (*VM*, pp. 49–50), and she decides to view herself in the wider reflection of others' view of her: "I was impatient to show myself and to go to the church to see how much people would look at me" (*VM*, p. 52). "Quelle fête!" ("What a celebration!" [*VM*, p. 60]) Marianne exclaims as she describes her place at the front of the church before the crowd, suggesting that this "jour de fête" ("festival day" [*VM*, p. 49]) is more like a public festival than a day of religious observance.

Like Defoe's Roxana at the height of her masked ball, Marianne is the cynosure of all eyes and she carefully measures the exchange of regards of which she is the focal point.[6] She writes: "ma vanité voyait venir d'avance les regards qu'on allait jeter sur moi. . . . A peine étais-je placée, que je fixai les yeux de tous les hommes" ("my vanity saw in advance the glances that would be cast upon me. . . . I was hardly in my place before the eyes of all the men were fixed upon me" [*VM*, p. 60]). Even the other women watch her to see why they are no longer being watched. Aware of the *regards* of an audience, Marianne consciously manipulates the display of her charms:

> De temps en temps ... je les régalais d'une petite découverte sur mes charmes; je leur en apprenais quelque chose de nouveau, sans me mettre pourtant en grande dépense. Par exemple, il y avait dans cette église des tableaux qui étaient à une certaine hauteur: eh bien! j'y portais ma vue, sous prétexte de les regarder, parce que cette industrie-là me faisait le plus bel oeil du monde. (*VM*, p. 62)

> From time to time ... I regaled them with some small discovery of my charms; I taught them something new, however, without putting myself to any great expense. For example, in this church there were some paintings placed at a certain height: well! I lifted my gaze toward them, with the pretext of looking at them, because that labor gave me the most beautiful eye in the world.

The positions and reflections Marianne describes are almost vertiginous: as she regulates an economy of discovery and uncovering (in what Nancy K. Miller has called "an artful striptease"), she takes advantage of her status as a spectacle before beholders by posing herself as a beholder of tableaux.[7] This looking is only a pretext, yet as a vision of her vision it stages a tableau that mirrors and repeats the multiple acts of looking that frame Marianne as if she were a tableau. It dramatizes looking for her beholders, presenting them with an allegory of their gaze that seems to embody looking almost literally as Marianne presents herself to both reader and beholder as an eye. The surrealistic synecdoche which idiomatically images Marianne as the *oeil* that represents her mode of being in this scene is accompanied by the carefully exposed "main nue" ("naked hand" [*VM*, p. 62]) that substitutes for her body. It follows her insight that "a new dress is almost a beautiful face" (*VM*, p. 52), and it precedes the scene in which she erotically displays "le plus joli petit pied du monde" ("the prettiest little foot in the world" [*VM*, p. 67]) which is ceremoniously undressed before Valville. I want to suggest that the sexual displacement and fetishism enacted in these scenes—the fragmentation of Marianne's body—are effects of the framing of Marianne; it is not surprising that this scene of multiplying theatrical perspectives should end in violence.[8]

Valville is described as the most significant spectator Marianne encounters in the church. She does not seem to be able to control her performance and attitude before him in the way that she does before the other "young men whose looks [regards] I attracted"; "I loved the sight of him [J'aimais à le voir]," Marianne writes, adding, "I forgot to try to please him, and only thought of looking at him [ne songeais qu'à le regarder]" (*VM*, p. 63). Whereas others "openly applauded," Valville seems to feel her charms and, Marianne recounts, "his looks [regards] embarrassed me" (*VM*, p. 64). At the moment that Marianne is unable to regulate the economy of regards and indeed seems to forget about her own performance ("I neglected my face [ma figure], and no longer worried about showing it to my best advantage"), her scene of theater turns into the scene of an accident. She is so "rêveuse" ("pensive") as she leaves the church, she writes, "que je n'entendis pas le bruit d'un carrosse qui venait derrière moi, et qui allait me renverser, et dont le cocher s'enrouait à me crier: Gare! Son dernier cri me tira de ma rêverie; mais le danger où je me vis m'étourdit si fort que je tombai en voulant fuir, et me blessai le pied en tombant" ("that I didn't hear the noise of a carriage which, coming up behind me, was about to run me over; the coachman was making himself hoarse shouting: Watch out! His last cry drew me out of my reverie, but the danger in which I saw myself dazed me so much that I fell when I tried to get away, and I wounded my foot in falling" [*VM*, p. 64]).

This is the (second) moment of origin that Marianne has announced at the end of the first volume and in the tableau that it forms we can behold all of the components of what I have suggested is the primal scene of *La Vie de Marianne*: an accident, a coach, a person who is exposed to danger and wounded, a moving spectacle which is witnessed by sympathetic beholders. Valville later tells Marianne that "a thousand people were witnesses to your accident" (*VM*, p. 78) but he is the beholder who gives the scene its meaning. Marianne recounts that "il parut touché de mon accident" ("he seemed touched by my accident" [*VM*, p. 65]), and one could speculate that the love at first sight that sets their relationship in play really begins in this scene of violence as much as in the scene of theater enacted in the church. However, insofar as the scene of the accident repeats the dynamics of theater, sympathy, and violence that have been played out in the church, it reveals the deep analogies that have been present all along between the two scenes. Just as we have witnessed in *Les Effets surprenants de la sympathie*, a love scene is represented as the spectacle of a dangerous accident in which someone is wounded in the presence of a sympathetic beholder who is touched at the sight.

Of course the spectacle of blood and violence that we witnessed earlier in both *La Vie de Marianne* and *Les Effets surprenants de la sympathie* is here transformed into an almost comic scene in which the only *blessure* is Marianne's sprained foot. In this sense the scene might

be viewed as a parody of those earlier accidents or at least as a
domestication of them as the genteel novel of worldliness replaces the
more baroque atmosphere of Marivaux's *oeuvre de jeunesse*. Yet the
apparent translation and domestication of this scene—which is
referred to as an "accident" on six separate occasions[9] and is paired
with the bloody accident that stands as a moment of origin at the
beginning of the book—suggest the necessity of the scene for
Marivaux. We need to decipher the figures and configurations
described by the parts that Marianne and Valville play in the scene of
this accident.

One could read Marianne's accident as a punishment for the
exhibitionism she displays in the church; and indeed she feels guilty
about the pleasure she experiences after the accident in anticipating
the intimate view that Valville will have of her naked foot. As Valville
and the male doctor oversee the undressing of the foot, and Marianne
protests her innocence to herself while exchanging with Valville
"clandestine looks" (*VM*, p. 68), we again witness the concurrence of
theatrical perspectives, guilty eroticism, and (through the fetishism
which isolates Marianne's foot) a domesticated form of violence. This
scene, following the translation of her theatrical display into the scene
of an accident, further suggests that in *La Vie de Marianne* it is
dangerous to become a spectacle. It is no coincidence, then, that these
episodes should lead to the entry of M. de Climal onto the set of what
we have recognized as a version of a primal scene.

I introduced this scene in the preceding chapter in the context of
spectacles of dangerous or illicit eroticism which are discovered
accidentally by observers who are not supposed to see them. M. de
Climal unexpectedly enters a room and beholds "Marianne en face, à
demi couchée sur un lit de repos" ("Marianne facing him, half
reclining on a divan" [*VM*, p. 83]), just as Frédelingue stumbled upon
the "spectacle" of the beautiful Parménie "couchée sur un lit de repos"
("reclining on a divan" [*OJ*, p. 116]) next to the signs of his rival. As
in the "vue" and "spectacle" (*OJ*, pp. 200, 208) in which rivals discover
Merville with Misrie and Guirlane, and as in the scene between
Merville and Halila secretly witnessed by the Turkish master,
Marianne is discovered with her "eyes moist with tears, in a tête-à-tête
with a young man, whose tender and deferential posture led one to
believe that this conversation turned upon love"; Marianne sardoni-
cally sums up the scene: "Wasn't that an amusing tableau for M. de
Climal?" (*VM*, p. 83). In addition to the context of the scenes we have
considered in *Les Effets surprenants de la sympathie*, it is the subsequent
reenactment of this tableau that inscribes it within what I have called

a primal scene scenario. As I have noted, Valville soon arrives unexpectedly at Marianne's room and discovers Climal "in the same
posture in which, two hours before, M. de Climal had surprised him."
After describing this spectacle with precision, Marianne describes how
Climal is turned into a tableau vivant by the sight of Valville beholding him: "Jugez de ce qu'il devint à cette vision; elle le pétrifia,
la bouche ouverte; elle le fixa dans son attitude. Il était à genoux, il y
resta; plus d'action . . . plus de paroles" ("Imagine what became of him
when faced with this vision; it petrified him, mouth open; he was
fixed in this attitude. He was on his knees; he remained there; no
more action . . . no more words" [*VM*, p. 120]).

Marianne calls attention to her own framing of these scenes,
adding, "J'ai beau appuyer là-dessus, je ne peindrai pas ce qui en était"
("I can dwell upon this but I could not paint what it was like" [*VM*,
p. 120]), just as she called attention to her tableau in the previous scene
by describing Climal trying to control his face to "empêcher qu'on n'y
vît son désordre qui allait s'y peindre" ("prevent anyone from seeing
the confusion which was about to be painted there" [*VM*, p. 83]). Like
the description of Parménie in the garden, both of these tableaux are
described as if they were paintings—which is to say that the objects of
the descriptions more than the descriptions themselves seem like
paintings. However, it is the juxtaposition of these tableaux, carefully
framed for both the reader and a beholder within the scene of the
narrative, that allows us to read them as more than examples of *ut
pictura poesis*. In exchanging Valville and Climal in the set-piece love
scene played with Marianne, a sexual rivalry is given an explicitly
oedipal character. Although Valville turns out to be Climal's nephew,
there is no father on the scene and Valville is referred to as his uncle's
sole heir. The situation of the "son" stumbling upon the "father"
posed in an erotic tableau with the object of the "son's" love retrospectively reinvests the first tableau (a scene of guilty pleasure) with
oedipal anxiety.

Another version of this configuration is repeated later in *La Vie de
Marianne* in the story that Tervire tells about another uncle and
nephew. Tervire's planned marriage to the elderly M. de Sercour
would deprive her husband's nephew of his status as his uncle's sole
heir; so the nephew sabotages the marriage by staging a scene in
which the uncle discovers his fiancée and nephew alone in her
bedroom on the night before the wedding. The details of plot (to
which I will return) are different but the configuration of the tableau
and its roles repeats the oedipal scenario enacted in Marianne's scenes
with Valville and Climal.

These scenes (along with the scenes we have considered from *Les Effets surprenants de la sympathie* and other scenes we will consider in *La Vie de Marianne*) contribute to the sense that repetition with replacement, reversal, or displacement is one of the generating principles of narrative structure in Marivaux's fiction. Indeed, the tableau of Tervire discovered with the nephew by the uncle is immediately followed by an account of a character who is hurt in an "accident" with a "carriage" (*VM*, p. 480)—as if the narrative ingredients of the novel were circulating in the fixed economy of a Proppian folktale or dictated by the obsessive repetition of dream symbols in the unconscious. My point here, however, in discussing these particular scenarios of Marivaux's preoccupations, is to characterize the danger (or at least the anxiety) that seems to result when someone is turned into a spectacle. The spectacles of Marianne and Tervire in these episodes do not involve physical violence, like some of the spectacles we have seen; yet both of the young women at the center of these scenes describe themselves as having been victims. After the second tableau Marianne insists that Climal find Valville and explain to him what he has seen; she asks: "voulez-vous que je sois la victime de ceci?" ("do you want me to be the victim of this?" [*VM*, p. 121]). Explaining the tableau in which she has appeared, Tervire insists "que je n'y avais point d'autre part que d'en avoir été la victime" ("that I had no other part in it than that of having been victim" [*VM*, p. 480]). What does it mean to be a victim of or in these kinds of spectacles?

To begin with, it is to be a victim of misinterpretation, a victim of the possibility that two spectacles with different meanings might look alike to a beholder who knows no more than seeing.[10] Just as Merville is caught with Misrie, Guirlane, and Halila in compromising tableaux that falsely appear to represent the same story, Marianne discovers that the sight of her responding to a man's advances seems to look identical to the sight of her rejecting a man's advances; and Tervire finds herself an unwitting player in a scene that is staged to be misinterpreted. Yet we have seen that both Merville and Marianne find it dangerous to become spectacles even when they are correctly interpreted. In another scene, in comparing Marianne to a beautiful rival in her convent, someone says of Marianne "que ce serait là une belle victime à offrir au Seigneur" ("what a lovely victim this would be to offer to the Lord").

The "lovely sacrifice" (*VM*, p. 235) that would make a victim of Marianne alludes to the renunciation of the world by a beautiful young woman, but it depends on Marianne's status in the convent as "a kind of spectacle," an object of "curiosity" whose story and appearance attract everyone's attention: "I was, as they say, the talk of the town [la fable de l'armée]; my story [histoire] ran through the whole convent," recounts Marianne, describing nuns "who cast upon me the most indiscreet eyes in the world as soon as I appeared" (*VM*, pp. 232–33). The description of Marianne leading up to the characterization of her as a beautiful victim ("at my appearance [apparition], all eyes were fixed upon me" [*VM*, p. 235]) is very similiar to the description of her display in the church. In Tervire's narrative, a character who is the center of a deathbed scene à la Greuze (which is described as a staged theatrical performance) refers to himself as a "victim" (*VM*, p. 527).[11] Although these last two characterizations do not specifically refer to characters being victimized by their appearance in or as spectacles, the victims are nonetheless described extensively as objects of sight.

The most telling identification of a victim in the novel occurs in a passage in which Marianne pictures herself; this self-portrait refers both to Marianne's own autobiographical activity and to her status as the subject of an autobiographical text. In an intimate conversation in the convent with her new friend Varthon, Marianne tells the story of her life and in the version of her autobiography that is addressed to her reader, she writes: "Mon récit devint intéressant; je le fis, de la meilleure foi du monde, dans un goût aussi noble que tragique; je parlai en déplorable victime du sort, en héroïne de roman" ("My narrative became interesting; I told it, in the best possible faith, with a taste for nobility as well as tragedy; I spoke as a pitiable victim of fate, as a heroine in a novel" [*VM*, p. 356]). In writing these lines, Marianne is ironically alluding to the "ton romanesque" with which she renders herself "touchante" (*VM*, p. 356) as she recounts the events which, she has acknowledged many times, might seem "romanesque" to readers of novels. Yet in a context in which novels, spectacles, and accidents seem closely related—in which the protagonist in a dramatic scene or the focus of a spectacle is pictured as a victim—the apposition of "victime" and "héroïne de roman" is especially striking.

What is the relation in *La Vie de Marianne* between a victim and the heroine of a novel; or more specifically, how is speaking as a victim related to speaking as the heroine of a novel? *La Vie de Marianne*, a narrative about accidents which begins by picturing its heroine as a victim in an accident that is both spectacular and *romanesque*, suggests that one risks becoming a victim by becoming the subject of a spectacle or the character in a scene or story. To address the question of whether *victime* and *heroine de roman* might function as synonyms in this novel, we need to trace what happens to Marianne in the various accidents of her life. Another way to formulate the question is to ask what Marianne means when she hears a story that presents her with a picture of herself and remarks: "me voici comme dans mon cadre" ("here I am, as if in a frame" [*VM*, p. 177]). We will consider what it means in *La Vie de Marianne* to be framed.

After Marianne is the victim of the tableau in which she is framed with Climal, she tries to renounce the theatricality that she reveled in only a few pages earlier. She risks making a "scene" and a "spectacle" (*VM*, p. 124) of herself by insisting on returning Climal's gifts, even the dress which has been the costume and metonymic focus of her theatrical display in the church. After having become the victim of a second spectacular accident and the two spectacles with Valville and Climal, and after witnessing the behavior of "the people" who flock to "open their stupidly avid eyes" with a "stupid and brutal curiosity" (*VM*, p. 95), Marianne seems uncomfortable with her exposure before the eyes of the world. She describes how a neighbor "who until that point had not looked at me very much, then opened her eyes upon me," and although the woman says "that's a pity [cela fait compassion]" there is no more pleasure in this kind of sympathy than in that of the crowd; the woman considers her "with a vulgar curiosity" (*VM*, p. 134). When Marianne first walked to the church in her new dress she was pleased to note that "many passers-by looked at me a great deal"; now, she writes, "Many people look at me in passing; I note it without applauding myself" (*VM*, pp. 52, 135). Whereas earlier she went to a church in search of spectators and applause, now she enters the church of a convent to "hide the tears which were fixing the attention of passers-by on me" (*VM*, p. 145). It is in this convent that Marianne finds refuge under the protection of Mme de Miran.

It is with Mme de Miran, however, that Marianne once again finds herself the subject of a story and spectacle. Mme de Miran unsuspectingly tells Marianne a story about her son falling in love; her son, of course, turns out to be Valville, which means that she recounts Marianne's own narrative in the third person. It is when Marianne recounts her realization that she is the heroine in the story told by Mme de Miran that she writes: "me voici comme dans mon cadre" ("Here I am, as if in a frame"). Once again, Marianne finds herself framed in a tableau. She exclaims to herself "c'est donc moi" ("but this is me") as the scene of the accident seems to flash before her eyes: "I thought that I was coming out of the church, that I saw myself again in that street where I fell in that cursed dress. . . ." Seeing herself framed, presented with images of herself as a spectacle beheld by a thousand witnesses, becoming a spectator and a listener to the scenes of her story that she has just narrated, Marianne refers to herself in the third person, as if she were talking about someone else. Commenting on the detail of plot that convinced her that she was hearing her own adventures, Marianne writes: "A l'article du pied, figurez-vous la pauvre petite orpheline anéantie" ("At the detail of the foot, picture the poor little orphan girl annihilated" [*VM*, p. 177]). On the next page, she follows this command to the reader to picture her with a command to sympathize, once again rendered as if she were talking about someone else: "mettez-vous à la place de l'orpheline" ("put yourself in the place of the orphan" [*VM*, p. 178]). Of course Marianne is again lapsing into a *ton romanesque* to describe the uncanny experience of hearing a story about oneself in the third person. But what is the effect of the third-person narration that she herself adopts as she frames herself for her reader in trying to describe what it is like to become a reader to oneself? What does it mean that she feels annihilated when she is confronted with herself as a spectacle, when she is placed, as it were, in a frame?

Later in the novel Marianne is again presented with a third-person narration of her adventures which recapitulates the scenes we have been reading. In an effort to make Marianne socially acceptable, Mme de Miran plans to place her in a convent where, she says, "no one will know anything about the accidents of your life [accidents de votre vie]" (*VM*, p. 206), and although this plan is not immediately carried out, Marianne is presented to the world as the daughter of a friend of Mme de Miran from the provinces. Although Marianne might still be inclined to "look at myself in the mirror from time to time" (*VM*, p. 209), in this new stage of her life she continues to feel uncomfortable when she finds herself appearing before someone for whom she is "an engaging spectacle . . . a new object of curiosity" (*VM*, p. 254). The spectator described here is Mme de Fare (a friend of Mme de Miran who is told the new fiction of Marianne's identity), and the description of her closely resembles the description of the people of Paris: she has "eyes that are always moving around, always occupied with looking, eyes that are searching for something to provide amusement for an empty and idle soul." Comparing such a person to "a man who would spend his life standing by a window," Marianne remarks that "such looks [regards] are such a burden!" (*VM*, p. 254).

It is no accident that this portrait evokes the portrait of the crowd presented in the scene with Mme Dutour and the coachman in which

Marivaux offers his Du Bosian explanation of the attraction of dangerous or violent spectacles. In the next episode Mme Dutour unexpectedly appears at Mme de Fare's house (Marianne and Valville are guests of Mlle de Fare) and it is she who once again turns Marianne into story and spectacle. Just as Mme de Miran presented Marianne with scenes from her life story narrated in the third person, Mme Dutour insists on identifying her as "la pauvre orpheline" ("the poor orphan girl") by offering what amounts to a plot summary of the novel up to that point. Beginning with "Isn't that you, Marianne?" she ends with a third-person account which names Marianne as Marianne: "it's Marianne; and what more? Marianne" (*VM*, pp. 263–64). Just as Marianne described herself as "la pauvre petite orpheline anéantie" ("the poor little orphan girl annihilated") when she found herself "comme dans mon cadre" ("as if in a frame") in hearing Mme de Miran's version of her story, in listening to Mme Dutour's characterizations of her as "la pauvre orpheline" ("the poor orphan girl") Marianne recounts: "A ce discours, . . . j'étais anéantie" ("At this speech, . . . I was annihilated" [*VM*, p. 263]).

What annihilates Marianne in this scene is not simply the destruction of her false identity and the exposure of her true identity—the revelation that she has no true identity since she doesn't know who she is. Marianne is once again "anéantie" by being framed, presented to herself in a third-person narrative, turned into a spectacle that is analogous to the representations of her own autobiographical text. This encounter (which exposes Marianne to that disconcerting spectator, Mme de Fare) is referred to on three occasions as an "accident" (*VM*, pp. 279, 280, 282). Here Marianne becomes a victim of her own story; she is turned into a victim by being forced to confront herself as a *héroïne de roman*. This accident leads eventually to another encounter in which a strange woman visits Marianne at the convent and again frames her in her own story. Upon seeing the woman, Marianne writes, "I thought there must be some mistake, that the ghost had wanted another Marianne," just as Mlle de Fare insisted to Mme Dutour, "Mademoiselle is not the Marianne that you take her for" (*VM*, pp. 288–89, 264). But the woman is able to provide a third-person précis of the story of "a young orphan girl," and once again finding herself as if in her frame Marianne is compelled to say: "c'est moi-même" ("this is me" [*VM*, p. 289]). Marianne characterizes this encounter as "ce nouvel accident" ("a new accident" [*VM*, p. 289]).

To be placed in a frame, to be turned into the heroine of a story, to be mirrored (through narrative reflections and reflexivity) as the heroine of the novel we are reading: in Marianne's descriptions these experiences seem to coincide with the experiences of becoming a victim, having an accident, or feeling annihilated. The dangers of becoming a spectacle seem to extend to narratives which can place one in a frame. However, the most important episode in this series of scenes occurs when Marianne hears a story that is ostensibly about someone else. Following the scenes we have examined in which Marianne encounters herself as a heroine in both her own and other people's stories, this account is narrated by her friend Varthon; Marianne says of the effect of this story: "ce récit me tuait" ("this narrative killed me" [*VM*, p. 369]). What about this story seems to be fatal? In terms of plot, Marianne is referring to Varthon's account of Valville's infidelity, his attentions to Varthon while Marianne has been ill. But in order to understand the surprising effects of this story (as well as the other stories we have considered) we need to understand the relation between Marianne and Varthon and the relation between the stories that they relate.

It is clear from the outset that Marianne regards Varthon almost as a double; she is, like Marianne, "so to speak, a foreigner [étrangère]" and practically an "orphan." Marianne writes: "Je songeais donc que son sort pourrait avoir bientôt quelque ressemblance avec le mien, et cette réflexion m'attachait encore plus à elle; il me semblait voir en elle une personne qui était plus réellement ma compagne qu'une autre" ("I imagined therefore that her fate might well have some resemblance to mine, and this reflection attached me to her still more; I seemed to see in her a person who was more truly my companion than anyone else" [*VM*, p. 355]).[12] Marianne's reflection on the ways that their lives seem to mirror one another is supported by the exchange of sympathy that is the effect of their exchange of stories. "Elle me confiait son affliction," relates Marianne, "et dans l'attendrissement où nous étions toutes deux, dans cette effusion de sentiments tendres et généreux à laquelle nos coeurs s'abandonnaient, comme elle m'entretenait des malheurs de sa famille, je lui racontai aussi les miens" ("She confided her affliction to me . . . and being both moved in that effusion of tender and generous sentiments to which our hearts abandoned themselves, while she was telling me the misfortunes of her family, I recounted my own to her" [*VM*, p. 355]). It is at this point, as the two become sympathetic readers to each other's moving stories of suffering, that Marianne, assuming a "ton romanesque," tells her story as if she were writing a novel and speaks "en déplorable victime du sort, en héroïne de roman" ("as a pitiable victim of fate, as a heroine in a novel")—by which she means that she "ornait la vérité de tout ce qui pouvait la rendre touchante" ("embellished the truth with all that might render it touching" [*VM*, p. 356]). Marianne's descriptions of her techniques in designing a moving story and the effects of her and Varthon's narratives on their respective female audiences sound like the claims made in the preface to *Les Effets surprenants de la sympathie* for the experience of reading novels written in the language of the heart for female readers. Indeed, as Marianne describes her story both as a novel and as if it were a novel, she provides a summary of the plot of the narrative we have been reading; Varthon, "mingling her tears with mine" (*VM*, p. 356), stands as a figure for the ideal sympathetic reader to whom *La Vie de Marianne* is addressed.

This double exchange of sympathy which occurs when Marianne and Varthon identify with each other, abandoning themselves to tears of compassion as they exchange their touching stories of affliction, is logically followed by a scene in which each becomes subject to accidents in which danger threatens and blood flows. These accidents take the form of illnesses: first, after Marianne's story is interrupted, Varthon becomes ill and is "saignée" ("bled"); Marianne is moved to tears, and the next day (as she reaches for her "work [ouvrage] which was on the table") she also becomes ill and is also "saignée" (*VM*, p. 357). Although Varthon recovers quickly, and, writes Marianne, "this little illness to which I had been so sensitive only served to prove my tenderness for her, and to redouble hers [redoubler la sienne]" (*VM*, p. 357), Marianne seems to become ill as a result of sensibility and redoubling compassion. She seems afflicted with a sympathetic illness, as if Varthon's illness were contagious—not in the medical sense, but in the etymological sense which relates *contagion* to *touching*.[13]

A fever is followed by "un redoublement" ("a relapse") which, writes Marianne, "joint à d' autres accidents compliqués, fit désespérer de ma vie. J'eus le transport au cerveau" ("combined with some other complicated accidents, made them fear for my life. I had transports of delirium" [*VM*, p. 358]). What she describes is the transport and *redoublement* of sympathy which cause her to move from compassionate beholder of dangerous and bloody accidents to the subject of those accidents herself. She resembles Mériante, who (as we saw in *Les Effets surprenants de la sympathie*) is faced with the spectacular effects of the bloody accident which follows Parménie's *saignée*, and in a physical act of sympathy tries to add his blood to hers. Marianne calls for "a pen and some paper" in order to write her will but finally, after being bled, "the accidents decreased" (*VM*, p. 359). Once again Marianne becomes the victim of bloody accidents which are inseparable from an exchange of sympathy; and once again these accidents are associated with the acts of telling and listening to stories and writing and reading novels.

In the midst of the transports, doubling, and redoubling of these sympathetic exchanges, Marianne remarks: "I no longer recognized anyone" (*VM*, p. 358). Ostensibly she is referring to her delirium, but I have been suggesting that the stakes of recognition (at least recognition of oneself) are high in *La Vie de Marianne*. To understand the implications of Marianne's remark, we need to recall Marianne's first sight of Varthon: she appears for the first time in Marianne's life and in her life story as the victim of an *accident funeste*. The configuration of persons, props, and sentiments—an accident, a "carriage," a moving spectacle, and sympathetic beholders—should alert us to another version of the novel's primal scene. The scene takes place as Marianne, Valville, and Mme de Miran arrive at the convent in their coach as Varthon, a new *pensionnaire*, is parting from her mother. Suddenly Varthon faints and Marianne and her party become "witnesses" of an "accident" in which it is believed that the young woman "is dying." As one might expect by now, the narrative emphasizes the status of this accident as a "spectacle" (*VM*, pp. 349, 350).

Marianne asks her reader to picture a sight which focuses on eyes: "Imagine eyes [Figurez-vous des yeux] which have a special beauty when closed." She goes on to describe her sentiments as a beholder of what she pictures as a painted image: "Je n'ai rien vu de si touchant que ce visage-là, sur lequel cependent l' image de la mort était peinte; mais c'en était une image qui attendrissait" ("I have never seen anything so touching as that face, although the image of death was painted upon it; but it was an image that moved one"). As she describes the spectacle that moves her as if it were a representation, Marianne seems to stop to reflect on her own medium of representation in presenting the image for her reader. She writes:

> En voyant cette jeune personne, on eût plutôt dit: Elle ne vit plus, qu'on n'eût dit: Elle est morte. Je ne puis vous représenter l'impression qu'elle faisait, qu'en vous priant de distinguer ces deux façons de parler, qui paraissent signifier la même chose, et qui dans le sentiment pourtant en signifient de différentes. Cette expression, elle ne vit plus, ne lui ôtait que la vie, et ne lui donnait pas les laideurs de la mort. (*VM*, p. 350)

> Upon seeing this young woman, one would have rather said, "She lives no longer" than one would have said, "She is dead." I cannot represent for you the impression she made except by asking you to distinguish between two manners of speaking which seem to signify the same thing but which signify different things in terms of sentiment. This expression, "she lives no longer," took away only her life, without giving her the ugliness of death.

The only way she can convey the impression made by the expression on a face is to call attention to the expressions or "façons de parler" that are used to distinguish meanings as language seeks to represent with figures of speech what the figure of a face looks like. As we saw in *Les Effets surprenants de la sympathie*, the description of an accident focuses on the effects it produces—as event, as sight, and as verbal description.

However, despite Marianne's concern for the effect on her reader of her description of the effect that the sight of Varthon's face had on her, it is the effect of Varthon's accident on Valville that is most important in the scene; and we will see that it is this relation that gives particular significance to Marianne's unusually explicit self-consciousness as a stylist in the passage we have been reading. The narrative depicts Valville as the most moved beholder of Varthon's accident: "Valville, ému de ce spectacle qu'il avait vu aussi bien que nous du carrosse où il était resté, oubliant qu'il ne devait pas se montrer, en sortit sans aucune réflexion" ("Moved by this spectacle, which he had seen from where he had remained inside the carriage, and forgetting that he must not show himself, Valville left the carriage without a moment's reflection"). It is Valville's gaze that gives the accident special meaning as he sees from an unauthorized point of view and runs to assist the woman in danger—like those spectators that Diderot imagines who forget their positions as *témoins ignorés* ("unsuspected witnesses") in an audience and seek to join the actors on stage.[14]

Placed unconscious on a bed, "with that body unlaced, with that lovely head leaning over, . . . with those beautiful closed eyes" (*VM*, pp. 350–51), Varthon recalls the tableau of Parménie asleep on her *lit de repos* in *Les Effets surprenants de la sympathie*. Like Frédelingue poised before the erotic tableau of the sleeping woman, Valville stands absorbed as he beholds what has become an erotically charged scene. Marianne describes the tableau of beholding that she witnesses: "Valville was behind us, and his gaze was fixed upon her; I looked at him several times, and he did not notice at all" (*VM*, p. 351). When Varthon regains consciousness, Marianne becomes the spectator to an exchange of regards enacted between Varthon and Valville in a description that obviously recalls the looks Marianne and Valville give each other after Marianne's accident in front of the church: Varthon "half opened her eyes, and looked Valville up and down languishingly"; she has "her eyes fixed on him" as he is "still on his knees before her . . . still in the same posture . . . without taking his eyes off of her" (*VM*, pp. 351–52).

What we see, then, is not only another primal scene scenario in which Marianne observes an erotic tableau enacted between her lover and her rival, not only another version of the primal scene of the novel which stands as the originary story of Marianne's adventures and of her narrative. We see Marianne become the spectator of these scenes, the beholder of spectacles that mirror her own adventures. A young woman whom Marianne will come to regard as her double has an "accident"—this characterization appears four separate times (*VM*, pp. 349, 351, 354, 370)—which presents a moving spectacle to numerous beholders and most of all to Valville; he seems to immediately fall in love with the victim of this accident, and he ends up posed in a tableau at her bedside which is similar to the tableau of Valville and Marianne witnessed by M. de Climal. Marivaux's narratives often repeat turns of plot numerous times, but here we see Marianne become a spectator to a reenactment of her own story—only this time with Varthon playing the role of Marianne. This is the most graphic version of the scenes we have considered in which Marianne is presented with third-person narratives which dramatize her story and confront her with images of herself as if she were someone else. Rather than seeing herself in a description or picturing herself in her imagination, she is almost literally placed in a frame by being shown to herself as a touching spectacle.

What is surprising, however, is that Marianne does not at first recognize herself in these tableaux. It is only after she exchanges sympathy, stories, illnesses, and bloody accidents with Varthon that she is able to recognize this "third-person" narrative as her own; and this seems possible only when she encounters the story in the form of an autobiography. When Marianne recovers from her illness, the two young women resume their storytelling and Marianne learns of Valville's attentions to Varthon. Varthon recounts an autobiographical story that is, as it were, practically plagiarized from Marianne's autobiography: "As soon as I came to [dès que je fus revenue à moi], the first object which struck me was him, at my feet. He held my hand. I do not know if you noticed the looks he gave me." Like Marianne, Varthon emphasizes the effects of the sight of her accident on Valville: "He told me that my fainting had made him tremble, that he had never in his life been so moved [attendri] as by the state in which he saw me." It is at this point that Marianne remarks that "son récit me tuait" ("her narrative killed me" [*VM*, pp. 368–69]).

In case there is any doubt about the uncanny scenario that Marianne is faced with, Varthon shows her a letter from Valville; the text of this autobiographical document begins: "Depuis le jour de votre accident, mademoiselle, je ne suis plus à moi" ("Since the day of your accident, mademoiselle, I have not been myself"). Marianne prefaces this text by lamenting that these words are addressed to Varthon rather than herself: "Il écrit, mais ce n'est plus à moi, dis-je, mais ce n'est plus à moi! Je fus si penetrée de cette réflexion" ("He writes, but no longer to me, I say, no longer to me. I was penetrated by this reflection" [*VM*, p. 370]). What kills Marianne is precisely this reflection: the realization that she has been supplanted by a double rather than a rival. As she recognizes herself in the mirror of her own story, her insistent "ce n'est plus à moi" is really her way of saying, "Depuis le jour de votre accident, mademoiselle, je ne suis plus à moi." Varthon herself makes this explicit by explaining that it is in her accident that she most doubles Marianne; Varthon offers a comprehensive interpretation both of Valville's sentiments and of the narrative structure, so to speak, that makes their accidents identical:

D'où lui est venue cette fantaisie de m'aimer dans de pareilles circonstances? Hélas! je vais vous dire: c'est qu'il m'a vue mourante. Cela a remué cette petite âme faible, qui ne tient à rien, qui est le jouet de tout ce qu'elle voit d'un peu singulier. Si j'avais été en bonne santé, il n'aurait pas pris garde à moi; c'est mon évanouissement qui en a fait un infidèle. Et vous qui êtes si aimable, si capable de faire des passions, peut-être avez-vous eu besoin d'être infortunée, et d'être dangereusement tombée à sa porte, pour le fixer quelques mois.... il ne vous aurait peut-être pas aimé sans votre situation et sans votre chute. (*VM*, p. 378)

Where did he get this fantastic idea of falling in love with me under such circumstances? Alas! I will tell you: he saw me dying. This stirred his weak little soul, which fixes on nothing, which is the plaything of anything it sees that is a bit unusual. If I had been in good health, he would have paid no attention to me; my fainting is what made him unfaithful. Even you who are so charming, and so capable of inspiring passions, perhaps even you needed to be unfortunate, to have dangerously fallen at his door, in order to attach him for a few months.... perhaps he would not have loved you without your situation and your fall.

Speaking as if she has read the abbé Du Bos, or at least Marivaux's own critical reflections on the attraction of spectacles of violence or danger, Varthon describes Valville's sentiments in terms of the behavior of crowds and audiences. Identifying the connections between the scene of an accident, a moving spectacle, and an erotic tableau, she explains that Marianne has mistaken for love what was only the transitory sympathy of theatrical relations; the sentiments she has evoked she shares with actors and victims of accidents or public executions. Marianne is also confronted with an image of herself as an actress because Varthon makes it clear that they both have played the same role in the same scenario.

Varthon's *récit* thus kills Marianne both by taking away her identity (effacing and replacing her as the subject of her own story) and by identifying her. It identifies Marianne in the same way as the stories told by Mme de Miran and Mme Dutour which were said to annihilate her; she realizes that she has been turned into a spectacle, placed in a frame. After Varthon tells Marianne, "your story [histoire] has come out" and recites all the obstacles to her marriage, Marianne writes, "I had endured the tale [récit] of my woes"; but Marianne already has been forced to endure her own narrative by becoming witness to Varthon's story (*VM*, pp. 391, 392). It is the recognition that Varthon's story is really about herself that seems to kill Marianne.

It is no accident, then, that the story that forces Marianne to identify herself presents her with a scene of death: she recognizes the scene of her own death as she retrospectively recognizes herself in the spectacle of Varthon dying. We saw that this accident (which she learns to see as a dramatization of her own accident) is followed by a symbolic death that mirrors Varthon's symbolic death and leads Marianne to author her will, only to come back to life and find that she is no longer herself. (Indeed, Marianne vows to herself that Valville "me reverra, pour ainsi dire, sous une figure qu'il ne connaît pas encore.... Ce ne sera plus la même Marianne" ["will see me again, so to speak, in a shape that he hasn't yet known.... It will no longer be the same Marianne" (*VM*, p. 377)].) In realizing that she is the victim in Varthon's accident Marianne recognizes herself as the *héroïne de roman*—and in recognizing herself as heroine, she recognizes herself as victim. When Tervire reads the love letter written by Valville to Varthon which, as it were, tells the whole story, she refers to "the accident that happened to you . . . the most frequent accident in the world" and says, sympathetically, "j'entre dans votre douleur" ("I enter into your pain" [*VM*, p. 381]). Varthon's *récit* is not only about an accident and its surprising effects; it is itself an accident, and by turning Marianne into spectacle, heroine, and victim, it is the most dangerous accident that Marianne faces.

There are two scenes in the novel in which Marianne is the subject of a spectacle and an exchange of sympathy and yet still appears to avoid the role of victim. The first takes place when she is discovered by Mme de Miran after taking refuge from the eyes of the crowd in a convent church. Marianne places herself "in a confessional"—which one might read as the place of autobiography—and she presents a touching spectacle of affliction for the eyes of Mme de Miran: "Là, je m'abandonnai à mon affliction, et je ne gênai ni mes gémissements ni mes sanglots" ("There I abandoned myself to my affliction, and I held back neither my groans nor my sobs"). Marianne carefully pictures the tableau for her reader: "J'étais alors assise, la tête penchée, laissant aller mes bras qui retombaient sur moi, et si absorbée dans mes pensées, que j'en oubliais en quel lieu je me trouvais" ("I was seated with my head leaning to one side, letting my arms fall, and I was so absorbed in my thoughts that I forgot what place I was in"). Mme de Miran plays the role of intent spectator that her son played in the previous scene in the church—one might speculate that her name shares with *miroir* an etymology in *mirer*: "regarder avec attention"[5]—and although she doesn't witness an accident she is pictured as a sympathetic beholder of Marianne's suffering. Marianne writes: "Mon affliction, qui lui parût extrême, la toucha; ma jeunesse, ma bonne façon, peut-être aussi ma parure, l'attendrirent pour moi" ("My affliction, which appeared to her extreme, touched her; my youth, my manner, perhaps also my adornment, moved her on my behalf" [*VM*, pp. 145–46]).

Marianne emphasizes her "jeune et jolie figure" ("young and pretty aspect") and her ability to "plaire un peu aux yeux" ("please the eyes a little"), but she makes it clear that if this is a scene of voyeurism, it is not a scene of exhibitionism. Marianne has no idea that she is being watched; absorbed in her thoughts and self-forgetting, she is unaware of Mme de Miran's presence; like the subjects of those eighteenth-century French paintings that Michael Fried has described as tableaux of absorption, she is oblivious of any beholder.[16] When finally their "eyes met," Marianne writes, "Seeing her, I blushed to have been surprised in my lamentations." She adds again that "my affliction touched her," but she provides a reading of their "regards" that suggests that this sympathy involves a mutual correspondence between them. Marianne explains: "car les âmes se répondent" ("for souls answer one another" [*VM*, pp. 146–47]). Deloffre notes that this formula illustrates Marivaux's concept of "a social life founded upon elective affinities" and cites Mme de Lambert: "Il y a des amitiés d'étoile et de sympathie" (*VM*, p. 147n).[17] (In this sense one could also read the name of the woman who will call herself Marianne's mother as an abbreviated anagram for Marianne's name.) The scene in the confessional eventually leads to one of Marianne's numerous recitals of her life story up to that point; but the tableau of her absorption and self-forgetting, and the sympathy that seems to make Mme de Miran more of a doubling mirror than a distant spectator, appear to guarantee Marianne from the dangerous theatricality of finding herself a spectacle.

Marianne's sympathetic exchange with Tervire also takes place in the framework of a spectacle that evokes compassion without exhibitionism. "Il y a des afflictions où l'on s'oublie," writes Marianne, "où l'âme n'a plus la discrétion de faire aucun mystère de l'état où elle est. Vienne qui voudra, on ne s'embarrasse guère de servir de spectacle, on est dans un entier abandon de soi-même" ("There are afflictions in which one forgets oneself . . . in which the soul has no longer enough discretion to make any mystery about the state it is in. No matter who comes along, one is hardly embarrassed to serve as a spectacle, one is in a state of complete self-abandon" [*VM*, p. 380]). It is in this state of self-forgetting that Marianne becomes a spectacle to Tervire, who, like Mme de Miran, is pictured as the most sympathetic of beholders. She guesses "the subject" of Marianne's "affliction" and is "touched" as she says to Marianne: "j'entre dans votre douleur. . . . je connais votre situation, je l'ai éprouvée, je m'y suis vue, et je fus d'abord aussi affligée que vous" ("I enter into your pain. . . . I know your situation, I have experienced it, I have seen myself in it, and at first I was as afflicted as you are" [*VM*, p. 381]). Tervire's compassion, identification, and mirroring resembles the *redoublement* that takes place between Marianne and Varthon and it begins with a kind of self-exposure; but this transport of sympathy does not lead to Marianne assuming the role of an autobiographical subject. Indeed, this exchange has the opposite effect. Whereas the sympathetic doubling between Marianne and Varthon turned on Marianne recounting her life story in a *ton romanesque* and casting herself as a *héroïne de roman*, in this scene the mirror of sympathy leads to Tervire's—not Marianne's—autobiographical narrative: the first-person story that casts Tervire as both heroine and victim and literally takes over *La Vie de Marianne*, never to return to Marianne's story again.

In both of these scenes of sympathy, Marianne seems to undergo a loss of self, an abandoning and forgetting of the self, that saves her from making a spectacle of herself at the moment she is framed for a beholder. This lack of self-consciousness resembles the literal unconsciousness of Varthon in her accident and Parménie asleep in the garden; and indeed the tableau of Marianne in the confessional with "la tête penchée, laissant aller mes bras qui retombaient sur moi" ("my head leaning to one side, letting my arms fall") anticipates the tableau of the unconscious Varthon ("Sa tête penchait sur le chevet; un de ses bras pendait hors du lit" ["Her head was leaning on the bolster; one of her arms hung out of the bed" (*VM*, p. 350)]). It also recalls the spectacle of Parménie ("elle était penchée; elle soutenait sa tête d'une de ses mains, et laissait voir le plus beau bras du monde" ["she was leaning to one side; she supported her head with one of her hands, revealing the most beautiful arm in the world" (*OJ*, p. 117)]).[18] Paradoxically, however, in these scenes loss of self is what saves Marianne from the more dangerous theater of the confessional—from the framing spectacle of autobiography. What Marianne accomplishes through her exchange with Tervire is in fact the abandonment of herself; the spectacle of her oblivious to her beholder allows her to stop being a spectacle. Tervire becomes the subject who is framed in spectacle, story, and autobiography. Although her story may resemble Marianne's in some ways, it finally eclipses Marianne. Rather than framing Marianne, it allows Marianne to disappear.

This turning point in Marianne's narrative illuminates a central paradox in the scenes about Varthon that we have examined. We saw that Marianne's encounter with Varthon was dangerous because it turns her into a *héroïne de roman*; but we must recognize what it means that at this point Marianne also becomes an author. She turns herself into a heroine by reciting her life story in a *ton romanesque*, presenting a version of the autobiography we are reading to a sympathetic reader who is moved to tears by what Marianne elsewhere calls "le pathétique de mon aventure" ("the pathos of my adventure" [*VM*, p. 377]). We saw that this reader doubles Marianne both through the *redoublement* and *dédoublement* of sympathy and through the recital of a moving story of affliction in which Marianne sees herself. However, Varthon does more than mirror Marianne's self; she presents Marianne with an image of her autobiography. She acts out Marianne's own story, performs before her eyes a dramatization or reenactment of Marianne's own adventures—as if Marianne had gone to the theater to see *La Vie de Marianne* performed. Varthon is a figure for the double that Marianne creates in telling her autobiography, in creating an image of herself as a character in a story; she is a reflection of the character created through the mirroring act of autobiography.

The paradox is that although Varthon's spectacles and *récit* present Marianne with an image of herself as the victim of an accident, although they seem to annihilate and kill her by framing her in story and spectacle, this same doubling also allows Marianne to stop being the heroine of her novel. Varthon takes Marianne's place not only as the object of Valville's affections but also, more importantly, as heroine and victim. It is as if Varthon substitutes for Marianne in the sacrifice of the *belle victime* that is required in the arena of the novel's theatrical relations. These doublings allow us to read the "death" of Marianne in another way: although the *récit* of Varthon may kill Marianne by turning her into a spectacle and framing her as the heroine of a story that identifies her as a victim, in killing her it also allows her to stop being a victim, to disappear as the heroine of the novel. By becoming an author, Marianne can cease being a character.

This, as we saw, is where Tervire enters the scene. It is not coincidental that Marianne is the victim of the near-fatal accident of her sympathetic illness just as she is reaching for her "work [ouvrage]" and that in the midst of her "transport" and "redoubling [redoublement]" she calls for "a pen and paper" and her "writing desk [écritoire]" (*VM*, pp. 357, 358, 360). Nor is it a coincidence that the scenes containing the *récit* of Varthon which explain her reenactment of Marianne's accident are interrupted by a disclaimer—that is to say a reminder—about the status of the text as a novel. Playing the role of author rather than character, Marianne appears in the brief introduction to part 8 to insist: "you think you have been reading a novel [roman] rather than a true story [histoire véritable]. You have forgotten that I was telling you my life [c'était ma vie que je vous racontais]" (*VM*, p. 376). A few pages after this reminder of her position as author, following Varthon's Marivaudian metanarrative interpretation of Valville's response to their accidents, Tervire appears as Marianne's sympathetic double. At the end of part 8 she announces "un petit récit des accidents de ma vie" ("a short narrative of the accidents of my life" [*VM*, p. 425]), just as Marianne began her narrative by referring to "le récit de quelques accidents de ma vie" ("the narrative of some accidents of my life"). A few sentences later part 9 begins the autobiographical narrative of Tervire that will replace and displace Marianne's life story.

Furthermore, within the last three parts of *La Vie de Marianne* (which might more accurately be called *La Vie de Tervire*) the same movement from heroine/victim to author emerges. We saw that Tervire, who is called "a touching spectacle," becomes the "victim" of a tableau which is used to frame her (*VM*, pp. 454, 480). In the course of the narrative, however, Tervire gains authority and eventually becomes the author of a scenario which sets up "an equally touching [attendrissant] spectacle" in which someone else is framed as a "victim" (*VM*, pp. 510, 527). As Tervire schemes to reunite and re-concile Mme Dursan with her disowned and dying son, she creates a deathbed scene designed to move the most hardened beholder. She says of her call for a priest to administer last rites, "my design [dessein] was to place the moment of recognition between mother and son in the midst of this august and frightening ceremony"; and indeed she strives so much to create the effects of the pathetic in her scene that she worries that "Mme Dursan might have regarded this whole adventure as a fabrication [un tissu de faits concertés], and the illness of her son as a game played to touch her [un jeu joué pour la toucher]" (*VM*, p. 521). Later she says, "the *coup* which must have struck them was my work [ouvrage]" (*VM*, p. 526). Mme Dursan is said to be "immobile at this new spectacle" when her daughter-in-law is revealed but it is the tableau of her dying son, framed by "the curtains of the bed," which touches her the most. It is as the center of this spectacle that he identifies himself to his mother as a "victim" (*VM*, pp. 529, 526, 527).

Toward the end of the novel, it is Tervire's mother and not Tervire who repeats Marianne's uncanny experience of becoming a witness to a third-person representation of her life story; reversing the positions we saw in the scene between Mme de Miran and Marianne, it is Tervire who acts as the author of someone else's story, framing her mother in her *récit*. Like Marianne, Tervire moves from being victim and spectacle to being an author: the *metteur en scène* of spectacles in which someone else figures as subject and victim. Within her own narrative Tervire repeats the same structure that placed Marianne behind the scenes, in the wings, so to speak, of her dramatization of Tervire's life story. In this sense Tervire stands as a figure for the Marianne who plays novelist but not heroine—which is to say, she stands for the absent Marivaux. *La Vie de Marianne* suggests that if one is to enter the confessional and represent oneself in the exhibitionism of autobiography, to dramatize the accidents in which one is framed as spectacle and victim, either one should negate exhibitionism by representing oneself in the mirror of sympathy, or one should try to frame someone else in the tableaux that expose one to the dangerous gaze of even sympathetic beholders.

Following the pattern of scenes that we have traced in *Les Effets surprenants de la sympathie* and *La Vie de Marianne*, Tervire's trajectory from victim of a spectacle to author and stage manager of a spectacle in which someone else plays the victim places two striking tableaux in juxtaposition and asks us to consider the differences and similarities between them. On the level of plot, the pairing of these scenes emphasizes Tervire's newly gained authority over plots, the power that comes with being an author as opposed to the heroine of someone else's scene. Obviously, the two spectacles also differ in that the first (Tervire framed with the abbé the night before her wedding) is "false" while the second (the deathbed scene of Mme Dursan's son) is "true." However, I want to suggest that there are disturbing similarities between these spectacles. Both are fabricated, staged, artificial, and theatrical scenes consciously designed to have a certain effect on their audiences. The second tableau is just as much a dramatic fiction as the first. Indeed, we saw that Tervire acknowledges that the deathbed drama she sets up for Mme Dursan might be regarded as "un tissu de faits concertés . . . comme un jeu joué pour la toucher" ("a tissue of contrived facts . . . as a game played in order to touch her" [*VM*, p. 521]). Earlier she refers to an act of impersonation designed to trick Mme Dursan as "une petite supercherie qui n'est que louable . . . qu'elle trouvera touchante, qui l'est en effet, qui ne manquera pas de l'attendrir" ("a little hoax which is only praiseworthy . . . which she will find touching, which is indeed touching, and which will not fail to move her" [*VM*, p. 512]). Tervire acts as if she has read the "Avis au lecteur" or the *Réflexions critiques* before staging scenes designed to have powerful effects on their beholders.

What is most disturbing in these scenes, however, is not that innocent dramatic fiction uses the same techniques as malicious dramatic fiction (although the fraudulent character of all fiction and drama is a consistent source of anxiety for many eighteenth-century French writers, including Rousseau and Diderot).[19] In calling attention to the staging of her spectacles, Tervire leads us to realize that her deathbed drama would have looked exactly the same if it *were* a contrived fraud playacted in order to manipulate its audience—just as the tableau that M. de Sercour discovers on the night before his wedding would have looked exactly the same if it *were* a late-night tryst revealing a secret infidelity. We saw that the spectacle of Tervire discovered with a nephew by an uncle recalls the spectacles of Marianne discovered with a nephew by an uncle and with an uncle by a nephew; all of these scenes return us to the problem raised by the tableaux of Merville with Misrie and Guirlane and Halila: two spectacles which have different and even opposite meanings can appear identical to the spectators who behold them. We saw that it was dangerous to become the object of a spectacle because one risked falling victim to the accident of misinterpretation.

But is it *misinterpretation* that is an accident? Tervire's tableau with the abbé is designed to be misinterpreted, just as Frosie purposely provides mistranslations when she acts as interpreter between Halila and Merville. In both of these scenes we are faced with a problem of interpretation which turns on a problem of language: here the staged spectacle that frames Tervire is textual as well as visual, centering on a text that is both true and false. As part of the "conspiracy [complot]" (*VM*, p. 482) between Mme de Sainte-Hermières and the abbé to prevent the marriage between Tervire and the abbé's uncle, M. de Sercour, Mme de Sainte-Hermières asks Tervire to write a note to a friend to remind her that she is expected for dinner. Tervire narrates:

> Mademoiselle, ajouta-t-elle, j'ai depuis hier une douleur dans la main; j'aurais de la peine à tenir ma plume; voulez-vous bien écrire pour moi? Volontiers, lui dis-je; vous n'avez qu'à dicter. Il ne s'agit que d'un mot, reprit-elle, et le voici: "Vous savez que je vous attends ce soir; ne me manquez pas." Je lui demandai si elle voulait signer. Non, me dit-elle, il n'est pas nécessaire; elle saura bien ce que cela signifie. (*VM*, pp. 474–75)

> "Mademoiselle," she added, "since yesterday I have had a pain in my hand; it would be hard for me to hold my pen; would you please write for me?" "Gladly," I said, "you just have to dictate." "It is only a word," she replied, "and this is it: 'You know that I shall await you this evening; do not fail me.'" I asked her if she wanted to sign it. "No," she said, "it is not necessary; she will know perfectly well what this signifies."

Of course, when the abbé secretly enters Tervire's bedroom and M. de Sercour is led to discover them together, the note in Tervire's hand seeming to request and authorize the abbé's presence adds to the "incomprehensible fact" which, Tervire says, "mettait l'apparence contre moi, mais que je n'y avais point d'autre part que d'en avoir été la victime" ("made appearances go against me, but I had no other part in it than to have been the victim" [*VM*, p. 480]).

It is appropriate that Tervire's fall should be set up by Mme de Sainte-Hermières. Hermes is indeed the patron saint of this trick: as the messenger god, the god of eloquence and duplicity, Hermes might be said to preside over this exchange in which a message is the vehicle for misinformation and misinterpretation.[20] Paradoxically, however, the writing at the center of this "false" spectacle is not in itself fradulent; neither a forgery nor a fabrication, the message is altered by the frame that transforms it from an autobiographical fiction in which Tervire assumes the first person of Mme de Sainte-Hermières to an autobiographical fiction in which Tervire is assumed to be the subject of first-person statements which, as it were, have been put into her mouth. Nor is it accurate to say that this writing is misinterpreted. The context which allows the reader to know "ce que cela signifie"

(*VM*, p. 475) has been changed, but the content of the message itself remains the same in both contexts.

Tervire's predicament here recalls the problem of expression that Marianne articulated in describing the spectacle of Varthon during her accident. Marianne asks her reader to distinguish "deux façons de parler, qui paraissent signifier la même chose, et qui dans le sentiment pourtant en signifient de différentes" ("two manners of speaking which seem to signify the same thing but which signify different things in terms of sentiment" [*VM*, p. 350]). Tervire's problem is not two different expressions which seem to mean the same thing; in her case two identical sentences give the false appearance of meaning the same thing. "Il ne s'agit que d'un mot" ("It is only a word"), says Mme de Sainte-Hermières before dictating words which she refuses to "sign" because their reader "will know perfectly well what this signifies." The issue here is the signification of identical words or signs: the problem is how to distinguish between two texts which appear to mean the same thing and yet really mean different things. This is precisely the predicament presented to Tervire by the spectacle in which she unexpectedly finds herself: the tableau that poses her with the abbé looks identical to the tableau that a beholder would have seen if she really had been surprised in an illicit late-night tryst. She is condemned because her beholders cannot distinguish between tableaux with different meanings—texts with identical signs which, contrary to their appearance, have different significations.

In reading *Les Effets surprenants de la sympathie* and *La Vie de Marianne*, we have encountered the problem of two spectacles with opposite meanings which appear to mean the same thing—whether (as in the scenes with Marianne caught in tableaux with Valville and M. de Climal) two contrary scenes are actually juxtaposed, or whether (as in the scene that Tervire stages for Mme Dursan or the one in which she is framed with the abbé) we are shown that a tableau would appear the same even if its meaning were opposite. Part of the danger of becoming framed as a spectacle is that it seems difficult for beholders to distinguish between signs which look alike yet mean different things. We have seen that the misinterpretation inscribed in Tervire's accident is not exactly an accident; in the context of a variety of spectacles and accidents which all in some way raise the problem of distinguishing between appearances, we might ask what the relation is between interpretation itself and accidents. In speculating about the appearances of accidents and the accidents of appearances—the difficulty of discerning and distinguishing meaning in and from appearances—we must consider the place of meaning in a spectacle, a tableau, a text, or an expression. To do this we must consider the meaning of accidents.

The *Dictionnaire de l'Académie Française* in the late seventeenth and early eighteenth centuries defines *accident* as a philosophical term: "Ce qui se trouve dans un sujet & qui n'en fait point l'essence, ce qui peut estre ou n'estre pas, sans que le sujet périsse, comme la blancheur, la couleur, l'odeur, la chaleur, la froideur, etc." ("That which is found in a subject but which does not constitute its essence, that which may either exist or not exist without the subject itself perishing, such as whiteness, color, odor, heat, coldness, etc.").[21] This sense of *accident* as an attribute or mode of being which can be distinguished from substance or essence derives from Aristotle's discussion of being and appearances in book 4 of the *Metaphysics*, but in Marivaux's time the most accessible discussion of the logical sense of *accidents* probably would have been the Port Royal *Logique, ou l'Art de Penser*, published and augmented between 1662 and 1683 (and republished eighteen times between 1684 and 1800).[22] Differentiating "substance" from "accidens ou qualitez qui nous frappent les sens" ("accidents or qualities that strike the senses"), Arnauld and Nicole write that a term such as "prudent" or "round" is given the name of "accident, parce qu'il n'est pas essentiel à la chose à qui l'on attribue" ("accident, because it is not essential to the thing to which we attribute it"). Ideas are called "*accidens communs*, quand leur objet est un vray mode qui peut être separé au moins par l'esprit de la chose dont il est dit accident; sans que l'idée de cette chose soit détruite dans notre esprit, comme rond, dur, juste, prudent" ("common accidents, when their subject is truly a mode of being that can be separated, at least in the mind, from the thing of which it is said to be an accident, without the idea of the thing being destroyed in our mind—such as round, hard, just, prudent").[23]

In tracing Marivaux's preoccupations in this chapter, I have been suggesting that the term and situation of *accident* represents an overdetermined network of associations which include what I have called scenes of theater and the novel as well as versions of primal scenes. It should be clear, then, that I am not suggesting that Marivaux's many descriptions of accidents and his over thirty-five references to *accident* in *La Vie de Marianne* have one particular meaning. I believe, however, that the well-known logical sense of *accident* must be seen as relevant in a novel in which descriptions of various types of accidents raise questions about appearances and meaning, attributes or modes of being and essences, interpretation and truth. As an autobiography about someone who doesn't know who she is, someone who must convince the world that her essential nobility should be more important than her nonaristocratic attributes, *La Vie de Marianne* must try to compose a self through attributes and external characteristics in order to pose the question of what constitutes a woman or a man. As an investigation of theatrical relations and the experience of sympathy, *La Vie de Marianne* also must confront the epistemological dilemma that, in the words of the Port Royal *Logique*, "la vérité interieure des choses est souvent assez cachée; que les esprits des hommes sont ordinairement foibles & obscurs, plein de nuages & de faux jours; au lieu que les marques exterieures sont claires & sensibles. De sort que comme les hommes se portent aisément à ce qui leur est le plus facile, ils se rangent presque toujours du côté où ils voyent ces marques exterieures qu'ils discernent facilement" ("the inner truth of things is often rather hidden, and the minds of men are ordinarily weak and obscure, full of clouds and false lights; whereas the exterior marks are clear and perceptible. So that, since men more readily approach that which offers them the least difficulty, they almost always place themselves on that side where they can see the exterior marks that are easily discerned").[24]

Arnauld and Nicole warn that "si l'on ne juge du fond des choses que par ces manieres exterieures & sensibles, il est impossible qu'on n'y soit souvent trompé" ("if one judges the depths of things only by their exterior and perceptible manners, it is impossible not to be deceived often").[25] The issue here is not hypocrisy; although M. de Climal may sound like Tartuffe, he is seen through fairly easily. If exterior appearances obscure a hidden truth, it is not necessarily because they were meant to be deceptive. Arnauld and Nicole, like Marivaux, are concerned with those who are deceived by reading too quickly or carelessly, by attributing a cause, for example, to an effect that was produced only "par accident." However, in the theater of Marivaux's novels, in order to judge *du fond des choses*, one must decipher *marques extérieures*; and, as Arnauld and Nicole write: "Toutes ces choses exterieures ne sont que des signes équivoques, c'est-à-dire, qui peuvent signifier plusieurs choses" ("All these exterior things are only equivocal signs, which is to say that they may signify several things").[26] Equivocal signs seem dangerous in the scenes that Marivaux describes because they are not recognized as equivocal; indeed they are not even recognized as signs. Accidents are taken for substances—appearances for essential meaning—rather than signs that speak with different voices: verbal and visual expressions whose meanings must be distinguished despite their apparent similarities. *La Vie de Marianne* suggests that appearances are in some sense accidents that must be separated from an essential meaning; the most dangerous accident might be the mistaking of accidents for essences, *marques extérieures* for *la vérité intérieure*. Such a mistake would turn on a failure to distinguish between the different meanings signified with *signes équivoques*.[27]

At this point I should note that a reader or student in the late seventeenth and early eighteenth centuries also might have recognized *accident* as a term from grammar. The Port Royal *Grammaire générale et raisonnée* (first published by Arnauld and Lancelot in 1660) uses the terms *accident* and *substance* to distinguish between "les choses, comme *la terre, le soleil, l'eau*" and "la manière des choses, comme d'être *rond*, d'être *rouge*, d'être *dur*, d'être *savant*" ("things, such as the earth, the sun, the water" and "the manner of things, such as being round, being red, being hard, being knowledgeable"). It explains that "les substances subsistent par elles-mêmes, au lieu que les accidents ne sont que par les substances. C'est ce qui a fait la principale différence entre les mots qui signifient les objets des pensées: car ceux qui signifient les substances ont été appelés *noms substantifs*, et ceux qui signifient les accidents, en marquant le sujet auquel ces accidents conviennent, *noms adjectifs*" ("substances exist by themselves, whereas accidents only exist through substances. That is the principle difference between words which signify the objects of thought: for those which signify substances are called *substantive nouns*, and those which signify accidents, marking the subject to which these accidents apply, are called *adjectival nouns*").[28] By the time Du Marsais wrote his then authoritative articles on grammar for the first volumes of the *Encyclopédie*, the grammatical sense of *accident* overshadowed the logical sense from which it seems to have been translated. Du Marsais seems to follow the Port Royal *Grammaire* in defining *accident* as "une propriété, qui, à la vérité, est attachée au mot, mais qui n'entre point dans la définition essentielle du mot" ("a property which, in truth, is attached to the word, but which does not partake of the essential definition of the word"), but the first example given by this author of a famous treatise on tropes describes another dimension of meaning:

1. Toute diction ou mot peut avoir un sens propre ou un sens figuré. Un mot est au propre, quand il signifie ce pourquoi il a été premièrement établi: le mot *Lion* a été d'abord destiné à signifier cet animal qu'on appelle *Lion* . . . mais si en parlant d'un homme emporté je dis que c'est un *lion*, *lion* est alors dans un sens figuré. Quand par comparaison ou analogie un mot se prend en quelque sens autre que celui de sa premiere destination, cet accident peut être appellé *l'acception du mot*.[29]

1. Every expression or word can have a literal sense or a figurative sense. A word is used in the literal sense when it signifies that for which it was originally established. The word *Lion* was first intended to signify that animal which we call *Lion* ... but if, in speaking of an impassioned man, I say that he is a *lion*, *lion* is then used in a figurative sense. When in a comparison or analogy a word lends itself to some other sense than that for which it was originally intended, this accident can be called the *acceptation* of the word.

A 1767 dictionary offers virtually the same example and explains that in the use of a word "par figure" the new meaning arrived at "sera un *accident*" ("will be an *accident*").[30]

Contemporary dictionaries and grammars do not suggest that *accident* as a term of grammar generally referred to the figurative usage of a word before the middle of the eighteenth century; but whether or not the signification of *accident* for Marivaux would have included the sense of a figure of speech, its traditional logical and grammatical senses still suggest an expression that requires interpretation. As a property that is attached to a word or substance yet is not proper to it, an *accident* describes, figures, or represents the mode of being of a substance. As attribute and adjective, as mode of being and appearance, an *accident* is an exterior mark that must be read as an equivocal sign; it stands for or in the place of an essential meaning that must be represented in order to be seen.

Even in their literal manifestations in the plots of Marivaux's texts, accidents raise questions of representation and interpretation; in positing and even demanding acts of sympathy on the part of readers or beholders, these spectacles of danger or suffering raise the epistemological question that all eighteenth-century discussions of sympathy must confront: how can one know the hidden *vérite intérieure* of a person from the *marques extérieures* that appear as *signes équivoques*? Marivaux's accidents remind us that we are all victims of interpretation. If it is dangerous to become the subject of a spectacle or a story, it is not only because we risk the accident of misinterpretation; interpretation itself must depend on accidents as we present and represent appearances to others, allow ourselves to be named and identified by the accidents that describe our aspects. In becoming the heroine or hero of a story or scene, one risks appearing before beholders whose lack of sympathy will turn one into a spectacle of equivocal signs: signs which might be misread by readers who cannot distinguish between similar signs with different meanings or by readers who do not even recognize the signs of an accident as they confuse essences and appearances.

Autobiography, at least as it is represented in and by the eighteenth-century novel, is supposed to provide the inner truth and essence of a character; but to do so it must produce the adjectives and aspects of character, the attributes and appearances that will signify the self in textual form. Autobiography, then, as it represents the textual form of the self, is also an accident: an appearance that would pass for an essence, a figure for a self that through the transports of writing has taken a new turn, a series of adjectives that would pass for a proper noun (a first-person singular). If there is violence in being framed, in being turned into the subject of a story or scene, this is also because any expression of the self must take the form of an accident. *La Vie de Marianne* suggests that it is safer to become the author of someone else's story, the *metteur en scène* of someone else's spectacle. Otherwise one must hope for readers and beholders who will regard one's self-display with enough sympathy to interpret equivocal signs, or at least to acknowledge the accidental character that makes us all victims of appearances.

THREE

La Religieuse:
Sympathy and Seduction

Je partage, madame, avec une vraie sensibilité, votre inquiétude sur la maladie de Mlle Simonin. Son état infortuné m'avait toujours infiniment touché ...

Response of M. le Marquis de Croismare to Madame Madin
(Préface-Annexe to La Religieuse)

There is some undigested, unrefined, unassuaged sensuality in Diderot that allows him to abuse the privilege of an author. And if we think that we get this impression of Diderot's enjoyment through the words of the nun herself, we must realize that this creature of Diderot's is made to appear conscious of her own seductive powers; that she has been infected by her creator's sensuality.

Leo Spitzer, Linguistics and Literary History

In 1760 Diderot entered into a "horrible plot [complot]" to lure the marquis de Croismare back to Paris by sending him a series of letters supposedly written by a persecuted nun who had fled her convent; *and* he became deeply engaged by the novels of Samuel Richardson (perhaps for the first time in English).[1] It may be a coincidence that these two moments in the overdetermined narrative of literary history overlapped, but one result of their coinciding is the Richardsonian character of the pseudoepistolary fiction that emerged from Diderot's *mystification*.[2] Diderot himself seems to have been aware of this connection. His *Éloge de Richardson* (written in 1761) refers to Richardson as a painter and praises the tableaux of his work and in his work; it instructs painters as well as poets to read Richardson "constantly [sans cesse]" (*OE*, p. 35). Some twenty years later Diderot described *La Religieuse* as "filled with pathetic pictures [tableaux pathétiques]," adding: "This is a work that painters should leaf through constantly [sans cesse]; and if vanity did not stand in the way, its true epigraph would be: I too am a painter" (*OR*, pp. 868–69).

In a now famous passage, the *Éloge* praises Richardson not only for moving his readers but also for actually drawing them into dialogue with his characters and texts: "O Richardson!" Diderot apostrophizes, "on prend, malgré qu'on en ait, un rôle dans tes ouvrages, on se mêle à la conversation, on approuve, on blame, on admire, on s'irrite, on s'indigne" ("despite oneself, one takes a role in your works; one enters into the conversation, one approves, one blames, one admires, one becomes annoyed, one becomes indignant" [*OE,* p. 30]).[3] Characteristically, Diderot's Richardsonian novel began as an actual correspondence written in dialogue with a specific reader who, in spite of himself or perhaps too willingly, played the role that had been written for him. (In his account of the plot, Grimm notes of the marquis that "le rôle qu'il joue dans cette correspondance n'est pas le moins touchant du roman" ["the role which he plays in this correspondence is not the least touching one in the novel" (*OR,* p. 867)].)

"Monsieur," writes "Suzanne Simonin" to the marquis—who, like the reader of Richardson Diderot describes, has begun to treat fictitious events and characters as "real events" and "living characters [personnages vivants]" (*OE,* p. 37)—"may my present situation touch you, may it awaken in your heart some sentiment of pity!" (*OR,* p. 852). "Her unfortunate state had always touched me infinitely" writes Croismare to Mme Madin; "her misfortunes had touched me deeply" (*OR,* pp. 865, 867). Croismare plays the role of the moved, sympathetic reader; and although the voice of this interlocutor disappears from the text when the correspondence becomes *La Religieuse,* Croismare (or the character he becomes) still stands as and for the ideal reader: the sympathetic spectator of pathetic scenes who is so transported by compassion that like the reader of Richardson he lacks the strength to restrain his tears and say to himself: "*Mais peut-être que cela n'est pas vrai*" ("But perhaps this isn't true" [*OE,* p. 35]).

Of course if the marquis de Croismare had thought to question the truth of the epistolary narrative he found himself engaged in, the text of *La Religieuse* might never have evolved. As it stands, however, the novel is inscribed under the double sign of sentiment and fraud. Although it is not a satire in the genre of Swift's *Modest Proposal* or Defoe's *Shortest Way with the Dissenters, La Religieuse* is like those eighteenth-century impersonations in that its fiction proved too convincing, deceiving a reader with whom the author meant ultimately to share a joke. It is not surprising, then, that the text of Suzanne's memoirs is framed by somewhat anxious reflections about narrative truth and artifice. Suzanne begins by claiming that she paints her misfortunes "sans talent et sans art, avec la naïveté d'un enfant de mon âge et la franchise de mon caractère" ("without talent and without artfulness, with the naïveté of a child of my age and the frankness of my character" [*OR*, p. 235]). The last words of her text insist that if she is "un peu coquette" ("a bit coquettish"), it is "naturellement et sans artifice" ("naturally and without artifice"; [*OR*, p. 393]). To some extent such demurrals reflect a common eighteenth-century anxiety about the status of fiction in a time when novels often claimed the status of historical truth; Richardson himself displays this anxiety in his ambiguous and ambivalent representations of the innocence and artfulness of both *Pamela* and "Pamela."4 However, if such contradictions are already implicit in Richardson's fiction, they achieve a critical articulation in *La Religieuse*, a Richardsonian novel of sentiment and sensibility with origins in deceit and deception.

Suzanne Simonin herself poses the problem in the postscript with which she ends her story. To the reader she addresses because she has heard "l'éloge de sa sensibilité" ("praise of his sensibility" [*OR*, p. 235]), she writes, "Monsieur, ayez pitié de moi" ("have pity on me" [*OR*, p. 392]), but then she worries that she has shown herself truthfully yet too "aimable"; and she wonders: "Serait-ce que nous croyons les hommes moins sensible à la peinture de nos peines qu' à l'image de nos charmes? et nous promettrions-nous encore plus de facilité à les séduire qu' à les toucher?" ("Might it be that we believe men to be less sensible to the painting of our woes than to the image of our charms? And would we assure ourselves that it would be easier to seduce them than to touch them?" [*OR*, p. 392]). In an age when tableaux of affliction were all but guaranteed to evoke the sympathy of readers and spectators, Suzanne worries whether she has counted on seduction rather than sympathy to have the greatest effect on the sensibility of her reader.

The narrator's retrospective glance at the reading prescribed in the narrative might seem appropriate in a novel in which (or through which) a young woman recounts pseudopornographic scenes of seduction to an older male reader—all within the voyeuristic frame of a fantasy about female sexuality shared between men.5 What interests me here, however, is not the opposition but rather the apposition that the text suggests between *séduire* and *toucher*. *La Religieuse* raises the possibility that the effects of sympathy might be disturbingly similar to the effects of seduction—indeed, that the Richardsonian novel of sensibility designed to move and touch its reader might be dangerous as well as deceptive. In reflecting on its own status not only as artifice but also as seduction, *La Religieuse* interrogates the conditions of sympathy that (according to Englightenment theories of art) are supposed to govern the experience of works of art.6

*

La Religieuse is well known for the rather explicit scenes which recount the seduction of Suzanne by the mother superior at Saint-Eutrope. The question of seduction, however, is present throughout the novel, operating from the outset as a kind of masterplot. The Richardsonian model, as evolved in *Pamela* and *Clarissa* and in some sense anticipated in *La Vie de Marianne*, generates its plot through the resistance of an innocent young woman to repeated threats of seduction.[7] In *Pamela* (and to a limited extent in *La Vie de Marianne*), marriage is presented as the institution which can reform men and save the heroine/victim from seduction. In *Clarissa*, the heroine is threatened with an unwanted marriage and violation as well as seduction. In Marivaux's novel, Marianne finds the convent a refuge when she is threatened with seduction, and she thinks about taking vows when she is faced with an unwanted marriage and when she sees her fiancé acting like a seducer.

Diderot utilizes and plays on all of these elements in *La Religieuse*. At the beginning of the narrative Suzanne's head is filled with "projets séduisants" ("seductive plans") in anticipation of a marriage like her sisters'; but other types of seduction await her. She discovers that she is an unwitting character in a previous story of seduction (an unknown story in which her mother was the heroine/victim) and, like Clarissa, she is imprisoned in her room until she consents to take her vows. In contrast to the Richardsonian plot, however, Suzanne's family and persecutors want to seduce her into the marriage of a monastic life. Rather than offering an alternative to unwanted marriage or protection against seduction, the convent becomes the scene of seduction: Suzanne describes her novitiate as "un cours de séduction" ("a course of seduction" [*OR*, p. 240]) in which "la douceur et la séduction" ("gentleness and seduction" [*OR*, p. 280]) are used to persuade her to take her vows. There is an unspoken threat of violence, but when she accedes to her family's demands she finds "les caresses revenues avec toutes les flatteries et toute la séduction" ("the caresses returned, along with all the flattery and all the seduction" [*OR*, p. 244]). In the second half of the novel, Suzanne falls prey to the seduction of her mother superior and finally to the seduction of a man as she tries to save herself from her vows and monastic life. After she escapes from the convent and is destitute and hurt she is exposed to dangers "from both men and women" in the form of "séductions grossières" ("gross seductions" [*OR*, pp. 389–390]). These later seductions are only literalizations of the various forms of seduction that threaten Suzanne throughout her narrative.

Indeed, very few of the central characters of *La Religieuse* seem to escape the contagion of seduction. In recasting the family romances of Richardson's plots of seduction, Diderot creates a series of good and bad parents—including (in addition to M. and Mme Simonin and various more or less absent fathers) the "good" mother Mme de Moni, the "bad" mother Sainte-Christine, and the mother whose name Suzanne dares not speak, who is presented as both "good" and "bad." Yet it is not so clear what the difference finally is between these good and bad mothers. Mme de Moni, for example, Suzanne's "good mother superior" (*OR*, p. 282) at Longchamps, is described as a spiritually inspiring prophetess: "Ses pensées, ses expressions, ses images pénétraient jusqu'au fond du coeur; d'abord on l'écoutait; peu à peu on était entrainé, on s'unissait à elle; l'âme tressaillait, et l'on partageait ses transports" ("Her thoughts, her expressions, her images, penetrated one to the heart; at first one listened; little by little one was carried away and was united with her; the soul thrilled, and one shared her transports" [*OR*, p. 259]). Readers of eighteenth-century moral philosophy and aesthetics will recognize in Suzanne's descriptions the standard characteristics of sympathy. Not only does the mother superior's "enthusiasm" (*OR*, p. 260) transport the nuns to take her place and share her feelings, like an actor who inspires the audience with sympathetic sentiments; Suzanne notes that her own sensibilities make her especially sympathetic in regard to Mme de Moni's transports: "j'éprouvais une facilité extrême à partager son extase" ("I felt a great facility for sharing her ecstasy" [*OR*, p. 282]). Furthermore, in uniting her audience to herself and communicating to them her feelings, Mme de Moni can also enter into their feelings: for example, Suzanne writes, "apparently she read in my eyes, in my whole person, that the profound sentiment I bore within me was beyond her strength" (*OR*, p. 260). At the same time, however, Suzanne writes of Mme de Moni's powers to evoke and practice sympathy, her ability to share sentiments in an apparent exchange of persons and places: "Her intention was not to seduce [Son dessein n'était pas de séduire]; but that is certainly what she did" (*OR*, p. 259).

In the light of this characterization of the mother superior's transports, the spiritual and emotionalist terms of Suzanne's descriptions begin to take on an erotic tone: "peu à peu on était entrainé, on s'unissait à elle; l'âme tressaillait, et l'on partageait ses transports ... on sortait de chez elle avec un coeur ardent, la joie et l'extase étaient peintes sur le visage" ("little by little one was carried away, and was united with her; the soul thrilled, and one shared her transports ... one left her with a burning heart, joy and ecstasy painted on one's face"). Just as the mother superior at Saint-Eutrope seems to experience "the greatest pleasure" in her moments of ecstasy with Suzanne, the nuns at Longchamps feel "the need to be consoled" by Mme de Moni "like the need for a very great pleasure" (*OR*, pp. 343, 259). Suzanne, who has a special ability to share her mother superior's "ecstasy" adds: "I think I lacked only a little practice to get to that point" (*OR*, pp. 282, 259).⁸

It may not be surprising that these scenes of sympathy should be described as seduction; insofar as *sympathie* in the eighteenth century is related to the elective affinities experienced between lovers, fellow feeling always has the potential to pass from the transport of compassion to the transports of eroticism (or at least love). Indeed, even the *Encyclopédie* article on the physiological senses of sympathy begins with a digression about "that deep understanding of hearts" in which "two kindred souls seek each other out, love each other, attach themselves to one another, and merge together"—a description which in some ways recalls Diderot's entry on *jouissance*.⁹ What is most remarkable in *La Religieuse*, however, is not the erotic resonance of the sympathetic transports of the mother superior at Longchamps, but rather the evocation of the experience of sympathy in the erotic scenes with the mother superior at Saint-Eutrope.

Leo Spitzer has described the seduction scene in which the mother superior at Saint-Eutrope recapitulates the story Suzanne has told her of her sufferings at Longchamps, kissing and caressing Suzanne where she imagines her being injured, as a perversion of "the religious practice of the *exercitum spirituale* which requires the believer to visualize every stage of Christ's bodily suffering."¹⁰ I would like to suggest further that the seduction scenes represent a literalization and almost a parody of the ecstasy and transports Suzanne shares in her scenes of sympathy with Mme de Moni. When Suzanne describes the caresses of the mother superior at Saint-Eutrope and writes, "she came even closer to me, so that she was touching me, and I was touching her" (*OR*, p. 347), she is describing both the literal and the figurative touching that cast these scenes simultaneously as scenes of seduction and sympathy. When Suzanne first witnesses the mother superior's sexual transports she thinks that "she was ill"; later she suspects that "her illness was contagious" and eventually she tells the superior: "I thought that you had a contagious disease [maladie contagieuse], the effects of which were beginning to work in me" (*OR*, pp. 344, 348, 371–72). *Contagion* is etymologically related to the Latin *tangere*—to touch—and indeed what Suzanne is experiencing in these

scenes as she finds herself mirroring the mother superior's strange
symptoms appears to be the surprising effect of sympathy.[11] *Toucher*
has come to mean *séduire*.

The very next lines after Suzanne's account of the positions in
which "she was touching me and ... I was touching her" cite the
mother superior's pretext for touching: "Raconte, mon enfant, dit-
elle; j'attends, je me sens les dispositions les plus pressantes à
m'attendrir; je ne pense pas avoir eu de ma vie un jour plus
compatissant et plus affectueux" ("Tell, my child, she said; I am
waiting; I feel myself most urgently disposed to be moved; I do not
think that I have had a more compassionating and affecting day in my
life" [*OR*, p. 347]). Suzanne's moving story (and the mother superior's
apparent need to exercise her compassion and pity) may serve as a
pretext or at least a prelude for seduction; but the passage suggests
that the erotic communion enacted between them in some sense is
indistinguishable from the sympathetic exchange. In a similar manner
Suzanne explains the mother superior's caresses and transports as
Suzanne plays the piano in terms of the woman's "incredible
sensibility" and "a most ardent taste for music." We may respond to
Suzanne's naïveté or Diderot's joke when Suzanne says, "I never
knew anyone else upon whom [music] produced such singular effects"
(*OR*, p. 341), but here as well we see the seduction as the result or
effect of sensibility. "Are there not certain people," asks Suzanne,
"upon whom music makes a most violent impression?" (*OR*, pp.
368–69)—just as she spoke of the "impression" (*OR*, p. 259) made by
Mme de Moni's transports on both the mother superior herself and
her nuns.

In eliciting Suzanne's moving story the mother superior at Saint-
Eutrope says, "tu essuieras mes larmes, j'essuierai les tiennes, et
peut-être nous serons heureuses au milieu du récit de tes souffrances;
qui sait jusqu'où l'attendrissement peut nous mêner?" ("You will
wipe my tears, I will wipe yours, and perhaps we will be happy in the
middle of the tale of your sufferings; who knows where this emotion
may lead us?" [*OR*, p. 347]). We know that such *attendrissement* and
compassion lead to the misleading inscribed in the etymology of
seduction; but it is these experiences of sympathy that Suzanne must
evoke in trying to justify the behavior of her mother superior.
Insisting late in the novel that her superior was "one of the most
sensitive [sensibles] women in the world," she recalls: "Elle ne pouvait
entendre un récit un peu touchant sans fondre en larmes; quand je lui
racontai mon histoire, je la mis dans un état à faire pitié" ("She could
not hear any story that was slightly touching without dissolving into

tears; when I told her my story, I put her into a pitiable state"). Even at this point in the narrative Suzanne must commiserate with the mother superior's commiseration. Even after the mother superior's sympathy has been revealed to her as seduction, Suzanne still presents seduction as sympathy. She asks of her confessor's suggestion that the mother superior's behavior was not innocent: "Que ne lui faisait-il un crime aussi de sa commisération?" ("Shouldn't he also have made a crime of her commiseration?" [*OR*, p. 369]). This is the question that frames Suzanne's encounters with the mother superior at Saint-Eutrope and, indeed, the epistolary dialogue with the marquis de Croismare, and finally the novel itself. Could commiseration be a crime? To pose this question is also to ask: could *toucher* lead to a *maladie contagieuse*? Could the effect of sympathy be seduction?

These questions have consequences for our reading of *La Religieuse* (as well as the reading Suzanne herself imagines for her narrative) since they determine how one sees Suzanne's role in the scenes of her story. The question of Suzanne's innocence is repeatedly at issue in the narrative—in the suggestion that she must atone for some originary guilt of her mother, in the accusations made against her at Long-champs, in both her acquiescence and resistance at Saint-Eutrope, and especially in the narrative technique through which Diderot has Suzanne describe scenes of seduction which she appears not to understand not only at the moment they occur but even in the more informed retrospective view of her autobiographical memoir. However, whether or not Suzanne is aware of the erotic content of the sensibility and sympathy of the mother superior at Saint-Eutrope, the narrative suggests that it is Suzanne who is in some way responsible for evoking those dangerous transports. This may be blaming the victim; but if it is commiseration that is a crime, if sympathy is a contagious disease which results in seduction, it must be acknowledged that in the scenes we have been examining Suzanne is the one who moves and touches the mother superior. Furthermore, the effects of sympathy are repeatedly produced by Suzanne's art: not only her performance at the piano but (especially) her story telling.[12]

The mother superior responds to Suzanne's recital of her misfortunes (the "narrative [récit] of your sufferings" which narrates the same scenes and events we have been reading up to this point in the novel) in the way that a sympathetic reader might respond to a particularly moving novel. She tells Suzanne afterward: "the pains you have suffered retrace themselves in my imagination; I see you in the clutches of these inhuman women, I see your disheveled hair in your face, I see you with bloody feet ..." (*OR*, p. 354). This response, which leads to the mother superior getting into bed with Suzanne in the middle of the night, recalls Diderot's description of the effect of reading Richardson. He writes in the *Eloge* that Richardson's "phantoms wander in my imagination constantly; ... I hear the laments of Clementine; the shade of Clarissa appears to me; I see Grandisson walking before me" (*OE*, p. 48). Just as Diderot compares the reader of Richardson to "children who have been brought to the theater [au spectacle] for the first time, crying: *Don't believe him, he's deceiving you* ..." (*OE*, p. 30), the mother superior describes her reaction to her "troublesome dreams": "I think they are going to do away with your life: I shiver.... I want to come to your aid; I cry out ..." (*OR*, p. 354). As in the piano scene and the scene in which Suzanne first tells her story, this sympathetic response may again represent a pretext for the mother superior's seduction, but it is also once again a prelude for an erotic exchange.

Suzanne's story has a similar effect in its written form: just as the mother superior acts like the moved reader of Richardson when she hears a recital of the scenes and sentiments which have made up the first half of the novel, Suzanne's friend Soeur Ursule actually becomes a reader of the "original" version of the narrative that we read. Like Pamela, Suzanne has obtained ink and paper under false pretenses to write a secret memoir which she thinks about hiding in her clothes and burying in the garden. She finally gives it to Ursule, who responds to the "packet of papers" like the reader of Richardson who, "weakened with grief [douleur]," lacks the strength to "hold back the tears which are ready to flow" (*OE*, p. 35). She tells Suzanne: "I could never resolve to part with them; ... no matter how much pain [douleur] I feel at reading them; alas! they are almost blotted out by my tears" (*OR*, p. 323). Ursule is dangerously ill when she says this and in the next paragraph of the narrative Suzanne persuades herself "her illness [maladie] was a result either of my own or of the pain that it had caused her" (*OR*, p. 323). Ursule had nursed Suzanne when she was ill, but Suzanne's fear that she has somehow caused Ursule's "maladie" anticipates her fear of the mother superior's "maladie contagieuse, dont l'effet commençait à s'opérer en moi" ("contagious disease, the effects of which were beginning to operate in me" [*OR*, p. 372]). What is at stake here is not a sympathetic disease but rather a disease of sympathy—a contagious illness which is preceded (and in some sense perhaps caused) by a sympathetic reading of Suzanne's story.

Suzanne's role in producing these effects through her artistic powers anticipates her apprehensions about the art and artifice of her narrative and the question of whether she has seduced rather than touched (or seduced as well as touched) the reader of her autobiographical memoir. We might recall at this point one of Suzanne's first experiences in the convent when she accidentally sees a deranged nun who has escaped from the cell in which she is imprisoned. Noting her horror, Suzanne writes: "I saw my own fate in that of this unfortunate" (*OR*, p. 241). The description of the nun—chained, in disarray, "dishevelled and almost without clothing," apparently mad—does indeed prefigure the state to which Suzanne will be reduced at Longchamps; but the tableau of a madwoman who "courait" ("ran") and "hurlait" ("screamed") and "se chargeait elle-même, et les autres, des plus terribles imprécations" and who "ne voyait plus que des démons, l'enfer et des gouffres de feu" ("loaded herself and others with the most horrible imprecations ... no longer saw anything but demons, hell, and gulfs of fire" [*OR*, p. 241]) just as strongly anticipates the fate of the mother superior at Saint-Eutrope who, by the end of the novel, becomes mad and must be sequestered when she is found "pieds nus, en chemise, échevelée, hurlant, écumant et courant autour de sa cellule" shouting "Eloignez-vous de ce gouffre; ... Ce sont les enfers; il s'élève de cet abîme profond des feux que je vois" ("barefoot in her shift, dishevelled, screaming, foaming at the mouth, and running around her cell ... Stay away from this chasm; ... There's hell; it is rising up out of this deep abyss and out of the fires I see" [*OR*, pp. 385–86]).

One of the stories that Suzanne is told about the mad nun at Longchamps is that "She had done some pernicious reading [des lectures pernicieuses] which had spoiled her spirit" (*OR*, p. 241). The striking parallels between the descriptions of this deranged nun and the mother superior at Saint-Eutrope suggest the possibility that these sorts of readings (at least among other things) have led to the downfall of Suzanne's sympathetic listener. Obviously, at the level of plot in *La Religieuse*, Suzanne is not to be blamed if the mother superior's response to the "reading" of Suzanne's story contributes to her erotic transgressions, damnation, and madness; it is the mother superior who threatens Suzanne's morals and innocence. However, at the level of the associations we have been examining which suggest that sympathy is a contagious disease that can be brought about by hearing or reading a moving story—in the light of Suzanne's fears that her graphic story about homosexuality and seduction might work to seduce the man she imagines as her reader—we must wonder whether Suzanne's own narrative might be classified in the genre of "lectures pernicieuses."

The potentially pernicious and dangerous consequences of Suzanne's story are displayed again at the end of the novel when (Suzanne tells the reader) dom Morel "desired to know the events of my life" (*OR*, p. 377). Just as the mother superior had insisted, "I want to know your whole life.... I want to know everything that has occurred in that dear little soul" (*OR*, p. 345), dom Morel makes Suzanne recount "the most minute details" of her life and character, as if she were writing her *Confessions* rather than making her confession. Just as Suzanne described Mme de Moni's ability to read her deepest sentiments in her eyes and "my whole person," she says to dom Morel: "you read the depths of my heart" (*OR*, pp. 260, 381). Furthermore, the recital of the narrative of Suzanne's life once again leads to sympathy: dom Morel tells Suzanne his story and they discover "so many points of contact and resemblance" between their lives as well as "a resemblance of our characters." Suzanne writes: "l'histoire de ses moments, c'était l'histoire des miens; l'histoire de ses sentiments, c'était l'histoire des miens; l'histoire de son âme, c'était l'histoire de la mienne" ("the story of his moments was the story of my own; the story of his sentiments was the story of my own, the story of his soul was the story of my own" [*OR*, p. 379]). Suzanne's story leads to perceptions of resemblance, mutual acts of identification in which they are able to mirror each other's sentiments and take each other's part. Finally, of course, this transport and transfer of sympathy once again lead to seduction: Suzanne soon finds herself compromised, abducted, and taken to a house of ill repute by her sympathetic reader—now a "perfidious ravisher" (*OR*, p. 389).

Once again, we see a seducer taking advantage of Suzanne. However, in the context of these scenes Suzanne's role in producing the effects of sympathy suggests that she, too, might be cast as a seducer in the novel, not (or not only) as the seduced. Suzanne compares herself to Mme de Moni specifically in terms of her ability to move others through transports of sympathy. She describes a scene in which three other nuns witness her praying: "je fus un spectacle bien touchant ... elles étaient toutes les trois placées derrière moi et fondant en larmes ... elles attendaient que je sortisse de moi-même de l'état de transport et d'effusion où elles me voyaient.... Je ressemblais alors à notre ancienne supérieure, lorsqu'elle nous consolait, et ... ma vue leur avait causé le même tressaillement" ("I was quite a touching spectacle ... all three of them were behind me, melting in tears ... they were waiting for me to by myself come out of the state of transport and effusion in which they saw me ... I resembled then our former mother superior when she would console us, and ... the sight of me had given them the same thrill" [*OR*, p. 281]). She goes on to say that she had a special facility for sharing the ecstasy of the mother superior whose effect if not design was seduction; and she remarks that with these powers she would have been able to "jouer un rôle dans la maison" ("play a role in the house" [*OR*, p. 282]). We have seen the association of "plaisir" ("pleasure") with the "tressaillement" ("thrill") Suzanne describes, as well as the similarities between Mme de Moni in the scene that Suzanne evokes here and the mother superior at Saint-Eutrope in the transports of her sympathy and ecstasy. It is not surprising that Suzanne is accused of seduction at Longchamps by the second mother superior, who refers to "those whom you have seduced" (*OR*, p. 274), and by the nuns who imagine some sort of lesbian assault by Suzanne on a young sister. Although these accusations are part of the persecution of Suzanne at Longchamps, the narrative suggests that Suzanne might be implicated in the seduction that is both dramatized in and enacted by the novel specifically through her evocation of sympathy—and in particular through the role she plays as a moving author, performer, and spectacle.

Throughout *La Religieuse*, Suzanne is aware of her status as a spectacle, both before other people in the events represented in her narrative, and before her reader in and through the memoir itself. In the retrospective dramatization of the narrative and often at the time of her various scenes of suffering, Suzanne represents herself as a spectacle designed (sometimes consciously) to move or touch its beholders. "I have an interesting face [figure]; . . . I have a touching voice," she explains in describing how she made "a strong impression of pity on the young acolytes of the archdiocese" (*OR*, p. 303) during the investigation of her case. The "acts" (of faith, love, charity, and so on) that she performs at the direction of the archdeacon are said to be "full of pathos [pathétiques]; for I drew sobs from several nuns, and the young clerics were pouring forth tears" (*OR*, p. 304).

This moving spectacle recalls the scene at the beginning of the narrative in which Suzanne refuses to take her vows before the unexpectedly large "assembly" that she arranges to witness the ceremony. The night before, she explains, "I represented to myself my role at the foot of the altar," and on the day of the ceremony she appears to play the role of the sacrificed daughter that eighteenth-century theoreticians of sympathy such as Du Bos and Marivaux saw as a paradigmatic moving spectacle.[13] "I do not know what was going on in the soul of the audience [l'âme des assistants]," writes Suzanne, "but they saw a young dying victim [jeune victime mourante] being led to the altar, and sighs and sobs escaped from all quarters" (*OR*, p. 246). Suzanne's "tears and the blood which flowed from my nose" (*OR*, p. 247) complete the tableau of suffering. Later, after the scandals she has caused, she hesitates to "se donner encore une fois en spectacle" ("make a spectacle of myself yet one more time" [*OR*, p. 363]). She refers to the "spectacle of my suffering" and is aware of herself as "quite a touching spectacle" which often "would have touched souls of bronze" (*OR*, pp. 314, 281, 276).

Unfortunately for Suzanne, despite the frequent spectacle of her misfortunes and suffering, she does not always succeed in touching the souls of those who behold her. She writes of her parents, for example, "I spared myself no effort in order to touch them, and ... I found them inflexible" (*OR*, pp. 238–39). However, this particular failure to achieve the effects of sympathy suggests that Suzanne is aware not only *when* she is moving, but also *how* to move others. She explains that the memoir M. de Manouri writes to represent her case must move the public in order to have any effect; it fails, she suggests, because it does not evoke sympathy: "M. de Manouri published a first memoir, which made little sensation; there was too much wit, and not enough of the pathetic [pas assez de pathétique]" (*OR*, p. 309). Her own memoir is designed to have greater effect. As if imitating the technique Diderot praises in his *Éloge de Richardson*, Suzanne repeatedly pictures the events of her narrative as scenes and tableaux to be visualized by her reader; and we have seen in the responses of the mother superior, Ursule, and dom Morel that both the spoken *récit* and the written text of Suzanne's story are touching and compelling. The memoir that we read, which is addressed to the marquis de Croismare, is designed (among other things) to "increase" the "commiseration" of its reader (*OR*, p. 383).

Suzanne, then, like the actor Diderot praises in his *Paradoxe sur le comédien*, does not expect to invariably or necessarily compose a touching spectacle of the suffering she feels; she understands the need to display her sentiments so they will have "assez de pathétique" ("enough of the pathetic") to create the effects of sympathy. She presents herself as an accomplished performer: at Longchamps, writes Suzanne, "I sang, I played the organ [je touchai de l'orgue], I was applauded" (*OR*, p. 282). On another occasion she compares herself to an actor: "Je chantai assez bien pour exciter avec tumulte ces scandaleux applaudissements que l'on donne à vos comédiens dans leurs salles de spectacle" ("I sang well enough to elicit tumultously the scandalous applause that is given to your actors in their playhouses" [*OR*, p. 279]). This comparison suggests that Suzanne is conscious of her role as an artist or performer; and in the preceding paragraph, she describes another musical performance in which she and Ursule have a surreptitious conversation while singing: she explains to her reader that "I sang while she spoke to me, and she sang while I replied; our conversation was interspersed with snatches of song" (*OR*, p. 278). Although this is not a performance of the sort that an actor in the theater gives for the applause of an audience, it is a kind of act or show or masquerade; but what is perhaps most revealing is that it recalls the "double scène" with which Diderot illustrates his theory of the actor's art in his *Paradoxe sur le comédien.*

In this scene a husband and wife acting team performs "two simultaneous scenes": one in which they represent a love scene before the public watching them, and another in which they surreptitiously trade insults. In another double scene provided by the "first interlocutor" of the dialogue to prove that cold and tranquil actors do not need to feel their parts in order to present the exterior signs and effects of sentiments to their audience, we read: "While the lover is speaking, the actress says of her husband: 'he is vile . . .' While she is replying, her lover replies to her . . . And so on, from couplet to couplet" (*OE*, pp. 326–27). Although Suzanne and Ursule are concerned with deceiving a different kind of audience in a somewhat different way, the similarities between Diderot's representations of these double scenes—in addition to the juxtaposition of this musical performance with the one Suzanne compares to that of actors in "salles de spectacles"—suggest that Suzanne is engaged in theater.

Indeed, this textual resonance between *La Religieuse* and the *Paradoxe sur le comédien* might lead us to remark that Suzanne in some ways is not unlike the actor that Diderot compares to "un séducteur aux genoux d'une femme qu'il n'aime pas, mais qu'il veut tromper" ("a seducer at the knees of a woman he does not love but whom he wants to deceive")—whose talent consists "non pas à sentir, comme vous le supposez, mais à rendre si scrupuleusement les signes extérieurs du sentiment, que vous vous y trompiez" ("not in feeling, as you suppose, but in rendering so scrupulously the exterior signs of sentiment, that you are deceived" [*OE*, pp. 312–13]). Suzanne (unlike Diderot) may not intend to deceive anyone, but the description of her that emerges in one of her conversations with the mother superior recalls some aspects of the actor who is praised by the first interlocutor for being "a cold and tranquil spectator" with "no sensibility" (*OE*, p. 306). "What!" exclaims the mother superior in questioning Suzanne about her passions and sentiments, "your heart never felt anything?" "Nothing," answers Suzanne. The mother superior describes Suzanne as having "a tranquil character. . . . Even cold." When she asks a few lines later, "is your heart tranquil?" Suzanne responds: "Up until now, it has been without any emotion" (*OR*, pp. 349–50). The actor praised in the *Paradoxe* is of course in practice as well as in etymology a hypocrite as he imitates the exterior signs and symptoms of feeling; we saw that Suzanne remarks that if she had "any penchant for hypocrisy . . . and if I had wanted to play a role in the house, I do not doubt that I would have succeeded" (*OR*, pp. 281–82).

This same passage, however, refers to Suzanne's sensibilities, sympathy, and ability to achieve a "state of transport and effusion" which resembles the moving transports and ecstasy of Mme de Moni. After describing the "very touching spectacle" which she composed, Suzanne comments: "Mon âme s'allume facilement, s'exalte, se touche" ("My soul is easily inflamed, exalted, and touched" [*OR*, pp. 281–82]). In this description of Suzanne's moving prayers—during which, she says, "I forgot in an instant everything around me. . . . I thought I was alone" (*OR*, p. 281)—as well as in Suzanne's description of what happens sometimes when she sings—"when I was completely beside myself [hors de moi], I almost did not know what had become of me [ce que je devenais]" (*OR*, p. 369)—she seems to resemble the *comédien sensible* praised by the "second interlocutor" in the *Paradoxe* for his extreme sensibilities and his ability to feel his part and lose himself in his role. This actor, with his "natural sensibility," is said to achieve "ces moments rares où sa tête se perd, où il ne voit plus le spectateur, où il a oublié qu'il est sur un théâtre, où il s'est oublié lui-même" ("those rare moments when he loses his head, he no longer sees the spectator, he has forgotten that he is in a theater, he has forgotten himself" [*OE*, pp. 368–69]). Suzanne also experiences these moments of self-forgetting, "these moments of alienation" (*OE*, p. 369) as they are called in the *Paradoxe*, and not only in the transports of artistic performance or spiritual sympathy. She describes herself in the scene in which she is forced to take her vows as "reduced to the state of an automaton" and "physically alienated" in a "profound forgetfulness" (*OR*, pp. 262, 264). Later in the narrative, she again speaks of her "alienation" at that moment and insists: "J'étais si peu à moi, que je ne me rappelle pas même d'y avoir assisté" ("I was so little myself that I do not even remember having been there" [*OR*, pp. 283–84]). Suzanne is not exactly playing a dramatic role here, but she is sacrificing her own identity in a ceremony which she previously described in explicitly theatrical terms.[14]

I am not interested here in the apparent paradox or contradiction that Diderot's descriptions of Suzanne evoke both types of actor opposed in the *Paradoxe*. I have been suggesting that in the course of *La Religieuse* the distinctions between artifice and natural sensibility, like the distinctions between seduction and sympathy, tend to break down. In either case, however—in both cases—Suzanne seems to be associated with the actor's art. We saw that Suzanne herself raises the question of her art and artifice, framing her narrative with protests that she writes "sans art" ("without artfulness" [*OR*, p. 235]) and "sans artifice" ("without artifice" [*OR*, p. 393]). We saw also that Suzanne's insistence that she writes naturally and without artifice follows her acknowledgement that her narrative may have relied on seduction more than on sympathy. We might note also that the *Encyclopédie* defines *séducteur* as someone who "dans la seule vue de volupté, tâche *avec art* de corrompre la vertu, d'abuser de la foiblesse, ou de l'ignorance d'une jeune personne" ("with a view solely to sensual pleasure artfully tries to corrupt virtue, to take advantage of the weakness or ignorance of a young person") and that *séduction* is defined as "une *tromperie artificieuse*, que l'on emploie pour abuser quelqu'un" ("an artful deception used to take advantage of someone").[15]

Once again it is clear that on the level of plot Suzanne does not, like the mother superior at Saint-Eutrope or dom Morel, abuse anyone's virtue or take advantage of anyone's ignorance—although we should not forget that this is precisely the effect of the "tromperie artificieuse" ("artful deception") with which Diderot, playing the role of Suzanne Simonin, deceives the marquis de Croismare. My point is that whether she is a cold and tranquil spectator of the scenes of her life who can dramatize her story in moving autobiography, whether she is an accomplished performer who can win applause and play double scenes, whether she is a touching spectacle and a paragon of sensibility capable of transports of enthusiasm and sympathy, or whether she is a victim of artifice who unwillingly plays a role in scenes of alienation, Suzanne is presented as an actor who is engaged in acts of both sympathy and seduction. Furthermore, the introduction of the scene of theater (particularly as it is described in the *Paradoxe sur le comédien*) can help us to understand why sympathy has the effect of seduction. I suggest that the moments of alienation that are said to characterize the acting of the *comédien sensible* point to the real danger of sympathy as it is portrayed in *La Religieuse*: the danger of losing oneself.

We have seen that in *La Religieuse* Diderot dramatizes sympathy in different aspects and from different points of view. In the course of the novel we witness acts of sympathy in the form of the transports of spiritual ecstasy and erotic ecstasy, both of which involve a mirroring and sharing of sentiments between individuals who seem to lose themselves in the transports of another. We behold characters both evoking the pity of others through touching spectacles or moving stories and experiencing compassion in the face of *tableaux pathétiques* that seem to compel fellow feeling. Sympathy is presented as if it were the effect of seduction, just as seduction is presented as if it were the effect of sympathy; both sympathy and seduction seem to act like a contagious disease which touches and thereby infects someone with someone else's feelings. At the center of all of these experiences there seems to be an act of identification that structures the exchange of sentiments that occurs when someone takes the part and person of someone else and shares that person's sentiments. This is most explicit in Suzanne's description of the scenes of sympathy and seduction that take place between herself and dom Morel:

> Il acheva de me confier de sa vie, moi de la mienne, une infinité de circonstances qui formaient entre lui et moi autant de points de contact et de ressemblance; ... C'est ainsi que la ressemblance des caractères se joignant à celle des événements, plus nous nous revoyions, plus nous nous plaisions l'un à l'autre; l'histoire de ses moments, c'était l'histoire des miens; l'histoire de ses sentiments, c'était l'histoire des miens; l'histoire de son âme, c'était l'histoire de la mienne. (*OR*, p. 379)

> He finished confiding in me, and I in him, an infinite number of circumstances in our lives which formed so many points of contact and resemblance; ... The resemblance between our characters thus being added to that of events, the more we saw each other, the more we pleased each other; the story of his moments was the story of my own; the story of his sentiments was the story of my own; the story of his soul was the story of my own.

The reciprocal mirroring between Suzanne and dom Morel is reflected in the repetition and mirroring of language here—as the difference between Suzanne and Morel seems reduced to the initial difference between the "s" and the "m" in possessive pronouns such as "son" and "mon" or "ses" and "mes." These reflections of stories and selves and language are underlined by the doubling of the reflexive "nous nous" which doubly points to an already doubled *moi* at the moment that seeing again and seeing each other again and seeing the self in the other again are in question. One resemblance joins itself to another as two individuals exchange stories and sentiments in a double sense as they not only trade but share auto-biographies.

I suggest that the description of the sympathy and seduction exchanged between Suzanne and dom Morel spells out the identification and subsequent merging of selves that structure all acts of sympathy in the novel: from the transports of Mme de Moni that the nuns liked to "share" as "one was united with her" (*OR*, p. 259) to the erotic exchanges in which Suzanne redoubled the caresses of her compassionate mother superior and began to experience her contagious sentiments. We saw that the *Encyclopédie* describes sympathy as a "deep understanding of hearts" in which "two kindred souls seek each other out, love each other, attach themselves to one another, and merge together"; but this merging, mixing, and uniting of selves that is seen in the *Encyclopédie* as an "heureuse liaison" ("happy bond")[16] is presented in *La Religieuse* as a dangerous communion. This communion is dangerous, I suggest, not so much because it leads to illicit sexuality but rather because it threatens to dissolve the boundaries that separate self from other. In the course of the novel both sympathy and seduction come to represent acts of dangerous overidentification. Suzanne's self-portrait of her mirroring experience with dom Morel—and her seduction at the very moment that he is explaining to her that the mother superior took advantage of her innocence—suggest the loss of self that is implied by the descriptions of sympathy and seduction throughout the novel, even at the moment that the self seems doubled or extended or projected onto another.[17]

At this point we should recall that Suzanne's encounter with dom Morel is the only example of heterosexual eroticism in *La Religieuse* (excluding for the moment the possible seduction by Suzanne of the marquis de Croismare); and if this exchange of sympathy and sentiments is dangerous because it represents some form of overidentification, then the predominantly homoerotic exchanges that occur on various levels throughout the novel might be seen as particularly threatening. Some critics have taken pains to express their revulsion at the lesbian scenes in the novel, at the least citing Diderot's condemnation (through his characters) of the mother superior.[18] Dom Morel receives far less attention, although he apparently is willing to take advantage of Suzanne's innocence by rape as well as seduction. I would argue, however, that in the novel Diderot does not really single out homosexuality or present it as being very different from heterosexuality. Suzanne's seduction by dom Morel (her seduction of dom Morel?) recapitulates the rhetoric, the mirroring, and the dangerous sympathy that have been present in all of Suzanne's erotic or pseudoerotic experiences. I am suggesting that in *La Religieuse* homosexuality figures what is most threatening about sexuality itself.

Diderot represents sympathy almost entirely as homosexual seduction because, in *La Religieuse*, sympathy—which structures all the erotic exchanges in the novel—is, so to speak, homoerotic.[19]

Homosexuality seems to be a literal (as it were, a too physical) instance of sympathy. The homoerotic manifestations of both sympathy and seduction double the already doubling structure that seems to threaten the self with what Peter Brooks describes in another context as "too much sameness" and "the collapse of difference." Brooks uses these terms as he traces the complex interplay between incest and miscegenation in Faulkner's *Absalom, Absalom!* "Incest," he writes, "is that which overassimilates, denies difference, creates too much sameness" (as opposed to miscegenation, which in Faulkner's text "over-differentiates, creates too much difference").[20] I believe that Brooks' categories are relevant here not merely because one could use the terms of too much sameness and not enough difference to pose an analogy between incest and homoeroticism in Diderot's text. My point is that in *La Religieuse* homosexuality—which here only literalizes what is threatening about any erotic exchange—is presented as if it *were* incest.[21]

In making this argument I am taking seriously the situation that the characters in the novel relate to each other as sisters, mothers, children, or fathers: Suzanne is called "dear sister" by her rival Sainte-Thérèse; she is called "my child" by the mother superior at Saint-Eutrope, whom she calls "dear mother"; she is called "my sister" by dom Morel, whom she calls "my father."[22] To say that the erotic relations in the novel take place between mothers and children, fathers and children, and above all sisters, is not to take too literally the rhetoric or ritual symbolism of the convent. It doesn't explain anything to say that Diderot wrote erotic scenes between "sisters" (scenes that play no part in the original correspondence with the marquis de Croismare) because he happened to be writing about a convent; the point is that the convent appears to have been especially compelling or attractive to Diderot precisely because it allowed him to dramatize or figure certain relationships. It would be relevant here to recall that Georges May has shown that Diderot appears to have been obsessed, at the time he was first writing *La Religieuse*, with the idea that his mistress Sophie Volland was having an illicit relationship with her sister—in other words, a simultaneously incestuous and homosexual relationship; furthermore, as May has noted, in the first versions of the novel Diderot's heroine was called not Suzanne but rather Anne-Angélique—virtually the same name as Diderot's daughter Angélique, who was seven years old in 1760. It is well known also that Diderot's sister Catherine became a nun and died mad in a convent; parts of *La Religieuse* apparently allude to or at least attempt to imagine her fate.[23] Thus there are various reasons why the threat of incest may have entered Diderot's conscious or unconscious mind as he imagined the autobiography of Soeur Sainte-Suzanne. We should recall also at this point the dimension of homoerotic seduction through which Diderot, disguised as a woman who tells rather graphic stories about her seduction and then worries about the seductiveness of her narrative, tries to lure the marquis de Croismare back to Paris.

I am not recalling these details about Diderot's life in order to "explain" *La Religieuse* by translating its preoccupations onto a biographical or psychological level. My point is that the psychological associations which appear to have been operating in Diderot's mind as he began his novel confirm a series of metaphorical associations that are implicit in the narrative itself. Sympathy comes to mean seduction; seduction is presented (either literally or figuratively or somewhere in between) as being homoerotic and incestuous. Homoeroticism and incest are only two associations, two names, that could describe the relations enacted in the novel: two figures for the collapse of difference between self and other that occurs in the "too much sameness" of sympathy. Sympathy, as we have seen, despite the investment placed in it by the Richardsonian novel of sentiment and sensibility, seems to become dangerous or at least a source of anxiety because it is associated with artifice, fraud, and seduction; but in the end we are left with the sense that art, fiction, and eroticism may be dangerous or anxiety-producing precisely because they are contaminated with the contagious disease of self-forgetting or self-loss called sympathy.

This realization should return us to a consideration of the effects of the novel. We might recall at this point the famous self-portrait that Diderot inserted into Grimm's account in the "Préface-Annexe" of the writing of *La Religieuse*: he describes a scene in which a friend discovers him working on the novel, "plongé dans la douleur et le visage inondé de larmes" ("plunged into sorrow, his face flooded with tears"); Diderot explains to him: "je me désole d'un conte que je me fais" ("I'm upsetting myself with a story that I'm making up"). Grimm goes on to praise the novel as one of the most "pathétiques" ever written, adding: "On n'en pouvait pas lire une page sans verser des pleurs" ("One could not read a page of it without shedding tears" [*OR*, p. 850]); but the story raises the question of the effects of a moving work of art, the effects of sympathy, on the author or actor as well as on the reader or spectator. Diderot's story of being moved to tears by his own impersonation might be another fiction, another dramatization of the effect that Suzanne's narrative is supposed to have on its readers. Yet Grimm notes in the "Préface-Annexe" that in the course of the correspondence with the marquis de Croismare, Diderot "thought that he was being mocked [persiflé] by the marquis and his friends" (*OR*, p. 851), fearing that he (and not his reader) was the one being *trompé* by a moving performance.

Diderot describes a related moment after Suzanne escapes from the convent in which she almost gives herself away by acting like a nun in the gestures, attitudes, and forms of address that she maintains through force of habit. "My companions," she says, "think I find it amusing to imitate nuns [contrefaire la religieuse]" (*OR*, p. 391). After denying her identity as a nun throughout the narrative, and while disguised as a laundress, *la religieuse* is mistaken for an actress playing the part of a nun at the very moment that she seems to have become the part, at least in its outward signs and symptoms—at the moment that Diderot is engaged in counterfeiting a nun in a performance and role that have become too convincing, perhaps even for him. Suzanne, we have seen, worries about the effects of her narrative on its readers—and if we read the novel carefully, even without the knowledge of the fraud revealed in the "Préface-Annexe," we can find many *avertissements* about the risks of becoming a sympathetic reader to Suzanne's touching story. However, as the scene about Suzanne's counterfeiting reminds us, the novel continually dramatizes Suzanne's status both as an actor or performer and as a role that is played by Diderot. As they raise the question of the effects of art and the effects of sympathy on the performer as well as on the audience, they suggest that the problem of self-forgetting that is at stake in *La Religieuse* for both author and reader must be addressed in the context of the theater. This is my focus in the next chapter.

FOUR

Forgetting
Theater

Sans la supposition que l'aventure du *Fils naturel* était réelle, que
devenaient l'illusion de ce roman et toutes les observations répandues
dans les entretiens sur la différence qu'il y a entre un fait vrai et un fait
imaginé, des personnages réels et des personnages fictifs, des discours
tenus et des discours supposés; en un mot, toute la poétique où la vérité
est mise sans cesse en parallèle avec la fiction?

Diderot, *Discours sur la poésie dramatique*

As Michael Fried has demonstrated in his discussion of the relation
between eighteenth-century French painting and Diderot's writing
about painting and theater, Diderot believed that both paintings and
plays should advance the fiction that their beholders were absent.[1] In
the *Entretiens sur Le Fils naturel* and the *Discours sur la poésie
dramatique* (published with the texts of Diderot's plays in 1757 and
1758 respectively) Diderot presents the view that actors on the stage,
like the figures in a painting, must *act oblivious* to the spectators who
watch them. Rejecting attitudes, posing, posturing, and playing to the
audience, Diderot insists that actors must pretend that the spectators
are not there. He elaborates a crucial paradox: "quoiqu'un ouvrage
dramatique ait été fait pour être représenté, il fallait cependant que
l'auteur et l'acteur oubliassent le spectateur" ("although a dramatic
work is written to be represented, both the author and the actor must
forget the spectator" [*OE*, p. 230]). Implied in this and other declarations,
however, is an *as if*: the framework of an analogy. "Soit donc que vous
composiez," writes Diderot in the *Discours*, "soit donc que vous jouiez, ne
pensez non plus au spectateur que s'il n'existait pas. Imaginez sur le bord
du théâtre, un grand mur qui vous sépare du parterre; jouez comme
si la toile ne se levait pas" ("whether you compose or act, think no
more of the spectator than if he did not exist. Imagine at the edge of
the stage a large wall which separates you from the orchestra; act as
if the curtain never rose" [*OE*, p. 231]). The audience must be
forgotten—which is to say that as the actors act oblivious to the

105

audience, the spectators must feel as if they have been forgotten; they must feel ignored or even unsuspected, and never addressed.

Equally important as the theoretical statements that Diderot makes (in his own voice or through such characters as Dorval) is the narrative frame that enclosed *Le Fils naturel* when the text of the play and the text of the dialogues with the supposed author of the play were first published. Here Diderot creates a fiction that Dorval, both author and protagonist of the play, has allowed him to watch a performance of the drama—which is supposedly a reenactment of real events—by the characters themselves. Diderot describes his position hidden in a corner, where he can watch not only "sans être vu" ("without being seen") but also ignored or unknown by the actors, as that of a "spectateur ignoré" ("unsuspected, unknown spectator" [*OE*, p. 78]), which is precisely the position that Diderot assigns to the audience in the *Discours* when he insists: "Les spectateurs ne sont que des témoins ignorés de la chose" ("The spectators are only unsuspected witnesses of the thing" [*OE*, p. 226]).[2] This ideal scene of theater, as Fried has argued, is designed to defeat the *theatricality* of a theater in which spectators are continually reminded of their presence by affected actors who address and play to their audience. In this context, and especially when viewed next to the dialogues which accompany the play, Diderot's fiction also can be seen as an enactment of the ideal scene of the philosophical dialogue as it was represented by Shaftesbury. Describing this nontheatrical dramatic form, Diderot's precursor writes: "For here the author is annihilated, and the reader being no way applied to, stands for nobody. The self-interesting parties both vanish at once. The scene presents itself as by chance and undesigned."[3]

I have argued elsewhere that Shaftesbury was concerned with the theatrical aspects of the relations that joined authors and readers as if they were actors and spectators.[4] Although, like many English and French writers in the eighteenth century, Diderot was concerned with the theatricality of books and authors, in his writing about the stage he addressed the literal conditions that provided the terms of Shaftesbury's analogy. Writing at a time when the conventions of staging and performing seemed false, affected, and intolerably theatrical, Diderot imagined a reform of the stage that would translate Shaftesbury's nontheatrical dramatic form into the playhouse as well as onto his own pages. If, however, the audience must stand for nobody, if unaddressed and unapplied to it must enact the fiction that it is not there, does this mean that the actor is annihilated? Shaftesbury (at least in theory) advocated an author who would not exhibit himself on the stage of the world before the eyes of mankind; in this context he reiterated Aristotle's praise of Homer for not speaking *in propria persona*.[5] But what happens to the actor in Diderot's theories? In this chapter I would like to consider the question of the actor's annihilation as it is dramatized and debated in Diderot's writing about drama and theater. This question must be addressed in the context of the problem of forgetting theater. We must ask not only what happens when the actor—as well as the spectator—is forgotten; but also what happens when either the actor or the spectator forgets theater.

At first glance, *Le Paradoxe sur le comédien* (written in its first version in 1769 and revised and augmented at least twice in the 1770s) might seem to contradict the position advocated in the *Entretiens* and the *Discours*.[6] In the *Paradoxe*, Diderot seems to refute the argument that the ideal actor is a *comédien sensible* (an actor of sensibility) whose talent consists in his ability to "s'oublier et se distraire de lui-même" ("forget himself and become distracted from himself" [*OE*, p. 362]), who is said to give a great performance when "il ne voit plus le spectateur, où il a oublié qu'il est sur un théâtre, où il s'est oublié lui-même" ("he no longer sees the spectator, when he has forgotten that he is on a stage, when he has forgotten himself" [*OE*, pp. 368–69]). This argument, which is advanced in the dialogue by the *second interlocuteur,* is disputed by the *premier interlocuteur;* playing the part of Diderot (like the *Moi* in the *Entretiens*) he advocates an actor who is a "spectateur froid et tranquille" ("cold and tranquil spectator") able to "rendre si scrupuleusement les signes extérieurs du sentiment, que vous vous y trompiez" ("render the exterior signs of sentiment so scrupulously that you might be deceived" [*OE*, pp. 306, 312]). With such a knowledge of the exterior symptoms of feeling, rather than any special depth of feeling itself, this actor can "s'adresser à la sensation de ceux qui entendent, qui [le] voient" ("address himself to the sensations of those who are watching and listening to him" [*OE*, p. 358]). This cool, detached, and manipulative counterfeiter of feelings is not supposed to forget anything, least of all his effect on the audience.[7]

We must remember, however, that in the *Discours* it seems more important for the spectator to *feel* forgotten rather than literally *be* forgotten. Furthermore, it does not necessarily follow that an actor who loses himself and forgets the audience will be less theatrical—less histrionic—than the actor who designs his performance to achieve a certain effect on the audience. Indeed, one could argue that the cold and calculating actor is finally less theatrical in his performance than the emotive actor because the former never reveals himself or his sentiments to the audience. Whereas the *comédien sensible* makes a theatrical display of genuine, private emotions before the eyes of the world, the cold and tranquil spectator reverses positions with the audience and hides behind a mask; he is supposed to show the spectators themselves rather than his feelings. In this sense the actor advocated by the first interlocutor, like the author of the dialogue, is indeed annihilated; he speaks through a persona, never *in propria persona*.

One could argue that it is the second interlocutor's position that calls for the actor's annihilation. In the *Lettre à d'Alembert sur les spectacles*, Rousseau condemns the actor's art precisely because he takes the self-forgetting with which the actor is supposed to lose himself in his role to be an annihilation or annulment of the actor's self. Unlike the orator, who "ne représente que lui-même" ("represents only himself"), writes Rousseau, the actor must "oublier enfin sa propre place à force de prendre celle d'autrui" ("finally forget his own place by taking the place of someone else"); in what Rousseau calls an "oubli de l'homme" ("a forgetting of the man"), the actor "s'anéantit, pour ainsi dire, s'annule avec son héros" ("annihilates himself, so to speak, cancels himself with his hero" [*L*, p. 187]).[8] Diderot appears to be refuting both Rousseau and the generally accepted emotionalist school of acting by insisting that the actor must be self-possessed and not "hors de lui-même" ("outside of himself" [*OE*, 309]). However, one of the paradoxes of the dialogue is that the self-possessed actor advocated by the first interlocutor seems to lack a self to begin with. Shaftesbury condemned the "author who writes in his own person" and changes himself to please his audience because, "being who and what he pleases," he "is no certain man, nor has any geniune character." Paradoxically, it is this ubiquitous, theatrical, and protean author who refuses to be annihilated. Although Diderot's ideal actor does not "suit himself on every occasion to the fancy of his reader" or spectator, he lacks a certain or genuine character; he can act his character—if not become his character—precisely because he is no certain man.[9]

"A vous entendre," remarks the second interlocutor, "le grand comédien est tout et n'est rien" ("According to you, the great actor is everything and nothing"). The first answers: "Et peut-être est-ce parce qu'il n'est rien qu'il est tout par excellence" ("And perhaps it is because he is nothing that he is everything par excellence" [*OE*, p. 341]). Responding, perhaps, directly to Rousseau, he asserts: "On dit que les comédiens n'avaient aucun caractère, parce qu'en les jouant tous ils perdaient celui que la nature leur avait donné.... Je crois qu'on a pris la cause pour l'effet, et qu'ils ne sont propre à les jouer tous parce qu'ils n'en ont point" ("It is said that actors have no character because in playing all characters they lose that which nature had given them. . . . I think the cause has been taken for the effect, and that they are fit to play all characters only because they have no character of their own" [*OE*, p. 350]). The actor does not lose himself because he has no self—"aucun caractère," no certain character—to lose. In a sense, following Shaftesbury, Diderot suggests that the actor must disappear in order for the character to appear for the audience; and according to Diderot's semiotics of acting, the character will appear on the stage only if a master of the signs of sentiments can represent rather than present it. The first interlocutor makes the point that it is "impossible d'apprécier autrement ce qui se passe au dedans de nous" ("impossible to understand otherwise what goes on within us" [*OE*, p. 358]). Only the self-conscious actor without a self can present us with the character rather than an actor.

Insofar as the *Paradoxe*, like the *Entretiens* and the *Discours*, is concerned with a reform of dramatic conventions and the question of which actor or acting technique will deliver the best performances on the stage, it is clear that the second interlocutor plays the straight man to Diderot's Socrates and that his theory of acting is more or less demolished. However, in reading Diderot it is always necessary to remember the dramatic and dialogic structure of his texts; as dialogues, they belong to Shaftesbury's genre of *soliloquy*, in which the mind divides itself into parts and persons and apostrophizes itself. My point here is that despite their argument about acting technique, the two interlocutors in the *Paradoxe* have in common a concern with the actor's self-forgetting. Both believe in the annihilation of the actor's character.

The first believes that the actor must lack a self (or at the very least put aside his self) in order to coolly impersonate a character; the second believes that the actor (although always full of himself) must forget himself and lose himself in his part, leaving behind his identity in order to become his character. Both agree, however, that it is the character of the actor to somehow forget his identity. In saying this I do not mean to reduce these positions to identical points of view. The purpose of my discussion is not to reconcile Diderot's positions (either within the *Paradoxe* or between the *Paradoxe* and other texts) but rather to identify a continuing preoccupation on Diderot's part. I suggest that in considering these different positions together we can make sense of the experiences of forgetting that seem to be so important to Diderot's characterizations of both the actor's art in particular and, in general, the theater.

We saw in the preceding chapter that in *La Religieuse* Suzanne Simonin seems to possess the characteristics of both of the actors represented in the *Paradoxe sur le comédien*: the cold and tranquil observer who lacks emotion and has a talent for performing double scenes, and the *âme sensible* who is capable of moments of alienation and moments of enthusiasm in which she loses herself in various forms of ecstasy. The same doubleness of character, bringing together the two roles of the actor that are apparently opposed in the *Paradoxe*, can be seen in Diderot's portrayal of Rameau's nephew. Like Suzanne, he is an accomplished musician and performer who is aware of the spectacle he makes on different occasions; yet Rameau is, of course, Diderot's consummate actor. He claims to be the "best actor" in his circles, a descendant "in a direct line, apparently, from the famous Stentor" (*OR*, p. 437). In the course of the narrative we witness (through the descriptions of the *philosophe*) Rameau's dazzling performances, as well as his talents in pantomime, music, and imitation. *Le Neveu de Rameau* (which appears to have been composed and revised during the years between 1761 and 1776)[10] reads in many ways as a companion piece to *Le Paradoxe sur le comédien;* whereas the *Paradoxe* reflects on the conventions of the stage, *Le Neveu* considers the theatrical characters, acts, and relations which take place outside of the playhouse in the realm of everyday life.

If, however, Rameau appears to confine his performances to the realm of everyday life, he still corresponds closely to the actor who is advocated by the first interlocutor in the *Paradoxe*. He is not exactly a cold and tranquil spectator with no sensibility—although the *philosophe* is offended by the way in which he describes despicable acts "as a connoisseur of painting or poetry examines the beauties of a work of taste" (*OR*, p. 462)—but he is certainly (what the first interlocutor calls) a "rigorous copyist of himself or of what he studies, and a continual observer of our sensations" (*OE*, pp. 306–7). The *philosophe* is impressed by Rameau's "observations . . . on men and characters," and we learn that Rameau's favorite authors are "Theophrastus, La Bruyère and Molière" (*OR*, p. 447). Like the actor praised in the *Paradoxe*, who possesses that "spirit of observation [esprit observateur]" that Diderot elsewhere attributes to genius, Rameau performs the character book he has compiled in the course of his life. In his representations of the "different pantomimes of the human species,"

Rameau, reports the *philosophe,* "sketched the characters of the passions [les caractères des passions] with a surprising truth and finesse" (*OR,* pp. 486, 481). He is like the "great dramatic poets" whom the first interlocutor describes in the *Paradoxe* as "assiduous spectators of what goes on around them in the physical world and in the moral world" (*OE,* pp. 309–10).

Rameau's expertise in imitating the characters of others raises the question of the status of his own character. The beginning of *Le Neveu* describes him as being composed of contrary and contradictory characteristics: "Rien ne dissemble plus de lui que lui-même" ("Nothing resembles him less than himself" [*OR,* p. 396]). He fears being "pulled by two contrary forces . . . equally inept at good and evil" (*OR,* p. 474)—in some senses like the "great actors, and perhaps generally like all great imitators of nature" who are described in the *Paradoxe* as being "equally suited to too many things; they are too occupied with looking, recognizing, and imitating to be deeply affected within themselves" (*OE,* p. 310). The *philosophe* is especially disturbed by Rameau's expertise in and admiration for people who counterfeit exterior signs and symptoms and deceive others with representations of sentiments that are not really felt. It is no coincidence that Tartuffe plays an important role in both the *Paradoxe* and *Le Neveu de Rameau.*

Both texts are interested in the relation between the actor's art and hypocrisy. Although it is said that in terms of admitting his own vices Rameau "was no hypocrite" (*OR,* p. 477), he alarms the *philosophe* by translating the actor's knowledge of physiognomy, gesture, attitudes, and appearances—his deceiving imitation of the signs of feelings— onto the stage of everyday life.[11] "Je suis moi et je reste ce que je suis" ("I am myself and I remain that which I am"), remarks Rameau after alluding to Tartuffe and hypocrisy, "mais j'agis et je parle comme il convient" ("but I act and I speak in whatever way is appropriate" [*OR,* 448]). One of his heroes is the Renegade of Avignon, who is said to carry hypocrisy to sublime heights: the discrepancy between this villain's totally convincing exterior signs and his secret interior sentiments is presented as the proof of a superb performance. His other hero is Bouret, who in order to train a dog changes himself into two contrasting characters with the use of a mask and costume. Rameau particularly admires Bouret's mask, which is used to deceive a naive spectator in as literal and as symbolic a manner as the child with the mask in the *Paradoxe* who is called by the first interlocutor "le vrai symbole de l'acteur" ("the true symbol of the actor" [*OE,* p. 376]).

Rameau, then, in many ways personifies the actor who is advocated by the first interlocutor; to the dismay of the *philosophe*, he often appears to have read *Le Parodoxe sur le comédien* and applied its lessons to the realm of social relations. At the same time, however, at the very height of his dramatic performances before the *philosophe* Rameau seems most to resemble the *comédien sensible* who is praised in the *Paradoxe* by the second interlocutor. As Rameau prepares for his great pantomime and representation of the opera, singing (among other fragments of arias) the same lines from Pergolese's *La Serva padrona* which stand as the epigraph for *Le Paradoxe sur le comédien*, the *philosophe* says to himself: "voilà la tête qui se perd et quelque scène nouvelle qui se prépare" ("he is losing his head and preparing himself for some new scene" [*OR*, p. 468]). In the scene that follows, Rameau does seem to lose himself as he divides himself between "twenty different roles" (*OR*, p. 469)—not only characters from operas but all the instruments of the orchestra and even the shadows of the night. He is described as being "saisi d'une aliénation d'esprit, d'un enthousiasme si voisin de la folie qu'il est incertain qu'il en revienne" ("seized with an alienation of the mind, with an enthusiasm so close to madness that it is not certain that he will recover from it" [*OR*, p. 468]). Rameau is clearly described as experiencing what Diderot calls in the *Paradoxe* "moments d'aliénation," or, in the words of the second interlocutor, "ces moments rares où sa tête se perd, où il ne voit plus le spectateur, où il a oublié qu'il est sur un théâtre, où il s'est oublié lui-même, où il est dans Argos, dans Mycènes, où il est le personnage même qu'il joue" ("those rare moments when he loses his head, when he no longer sees the spectator, when he has forgotten that he is on a stage, when he has forgotten himself, when he is in Argos, in Mycene, when he is the very character that he plays" [*OE*, pp. 368–69]).

Rameau pushes the limits of the boundaries of the self as he seems to metamorphose himself into birds at sunset, water, a storm, a temple, shade, and silence, as well as different characters—which is to say that he seems less to forget his self than to forget that he has a self. As in the *Paradoxe*, Diderot focuses on the acts of forgetting that seem to be both cause and effect of the performance. He is particularly interested in the liminal moments that represent both the forgetting and the remembering of the self. The *philosophe* presents this tableau of Rameau at the end of his performance:

> Sa tête était tout à fait perdue. Epuisé de fatigue, tel qu'un homme qui sort d'un profond sommeil ou d'une longue distraction, il resta immobile, stupide, étonné. Il tournait ses regards autour de lui comme un homme égaré qui cherche à reconnaître le lieu ou il se trouve. . . .

Semblable à celui qui verrait à son reveil son lit environné d'un grand nombre de personnes, dans un entier oubli ou dans une profonde ignorance de ce qu'il a fait, il s'écria dans le premier moment: "Eh bien, messieurs, qu'est-ce qu'il y a?" (*OR*, pp. 469–70)

He had completely lost his head. Exhausted with the fatigue of a man who comes out of a deep sleep or a long period of distraction, he remained immobile, stunned, surprised. He cast his looks about him like a lost man who is trying to recognize the place in which he finds himself. . . . Like someone who awakens to find his bed surrounded by a large number of people, in complete forgetfulness or profound ignorance of what he has done, he immediately cried out: "Gentlemen, what's going on?"

I have quoted from this passage at length because the tableau described by Diderot writing in the character of the *philosophe* is remarkable for its detail. Unlike the other descriptions of Rameau's pantomimes or impersonations, this description takes place within the framework of an extended simile, or rather a series of similes. Rameau is figured as a man who wakes from a deep sleep, then a long distraction; then as a lost man trying to get his bearings; then again as a man who wakes to find his bed surrounded by people. As Diderot's metaphors repeat the sudden and successive metamorphoses that Rameau has just passed through, the narrative makes a Homeric gesture; like a passage from Donne, the description figures and refigures a moment in a series of extended or alternative similes that almost disrupt the progress of the narrative—as if Diderot had forgotten the scene he was describing and lost himself on a detour from the path of the plot.[12] Diderot is clearly *interested* in this moment, interested in defining its terms and conveying its conditons to the reader. We see the self-conscious manipulator of signs and appearances and masks, the observer of passions and characters who can deceive any spectator with his counterfeiting, in a sublime performance that is characterized by technical virtuosity but also—or especially—by "un entier oubli" ("complete forgetfulness"). What accounts for Diderot's investment in this moment?

In part, the forgetting Rameau displays in this scene would appear to guarantee him from theatricality. Despite Rameau's status as both a quintessential actor and Diderot's most theatrical character, the narrative makes it clear that he is oblivious to his spectators. "Outside, the windows of the cafe were filled by passers-by who had stopped at the noise," notes the *philosophe*; "They were laughing hard enough to bring down the ceiling. He noticed nothing" (*OR*, p. 468). Rameau's ignorance and forgetting of his spectators, his complete surprise at finding himself a spectacle of amusement, underline the nontheatrical character of his most dramatic performance. The *philosophe* appears to have been forgotten; the spectators at the window, to whom the scene has presented itself by chance and undesigned, watch as *témoins ignorés*. His audience unaddressed and unapplied to, Rameau in his moment of alienation seems almost annihilated.

In this moment Rameau also resembles Suzanne Simonin when she is in an "état de transport et d'effusion" ("state of transport and effusion"). Although she remarks in retrospect, "je fus un spectacle bien touchant" ("I was quite a touching spectacle"), she also recounts: "j'oubliai en un instant tout ce qui m'environnait" ("in a moment I forgot everything around me"). Suzanne is not giving a performance in this scene, but she describes how in a state of transport and *oubli* she becomes a moving spectacle for spectators she is completely unaware of: "Quand je me relevai, je crus être seule; je me trompais; elles [three other nuns] étaient toutes les trois placées derrière moi et fondant en larmes" ("When I awoke I thought I was alone; I was wrong; all three of them [the other nuns] were behind me, melting in tears" [*OR*, p. 281]). It is in this scene that Suzanne's transports are said to resemble the "enthousiasme" (*OR*, p. 260) of her first mother superior. The passage from this spiritual (if, as we saw, implicitly erotic) enthusiam to Rameau's artistic "enthousiasme si voisin à la folie" ("enthusiasm so close to madness") retraces Shaftesbury's reappropriation of enthusiasm for philosophy. After offering a skeptical if tolerant account of religious fanaticism in his *Letter Concerning Enthusiasm*, in *The Moralists* Shaftesbury tried to create an eighteenth-century version of the divinely inspired philosophical raptures and rhapsodies of the ancients; in doing so, he set the scene for Diderot's reinscription of enthusiasm as genius.[13]

The article "Génie" in the *Encyclopédie* (in which Diderot almost certainly had a hand) devotes considerable attention to the "enthousiasme" of the artist and genius: "il est transporté dans la situation des personnages qu'il fait agir; il a pris leur caractère" ("he is transported into the situation of the characters he causes to act; he takes on their character"); he is capable of being "porté jusqu'à l'oubli de soi-même ("carried to the point of forgetting himself"). The article on "Enthousiasme" also describes the self-forgetting of the enthusiast, who is pictured "tout à fait hors de lui-même" ("completely outside of himself"), experiencing "*un fureur, un transport*, c'est comme si l'on avoit dit qu'il eût un *redoublement de folie*" ("a furor, a transport; it is as if one had said he had a relapse [literally: a redoubling] into madness"). According to the author, "L'enthousiasme plonge les hommes privilégiés qui en sont susceptibles, dans un oubli presque continuel de tout ce qui est étranger aux arts qu'ils professent" ("Enthusiasm plunges the privileged men who are susceptible to it into an almost continual forgetfulness of everything foreign to the arts which they practice").[14] In his writing about the theater, Diderot clearly associates enthusiasm and genius with the negative capability—that is, the powers of sympathy—of the dramatic artist. In the *Discours sur la poésie dramatique*, in describing his difficulties writing *Le Pére de famille*, he asks: "comment se métamorphoser en différents caractères, lorsque le chagrin nous attache à nous-mêmes? Comment s'oublier lorsque l'ennui nous rappelle à notre existence? Comment échauffer, éclairer les autres, lorsque la lampe de l'enthousiasme est éteinte, et que la lampe du génie ne luit plus sur le front?" ("how can we metamorphose ourselves into different characters, when sorrow attaches us to ourselves? How can we forget ourselves, when vexation reminds us of our existence? How does one inflame and illuminate others when the lamp of enthusiasm is extinguished, and the lamp of genius no longer shines upon one's brow?" [*OE*, pp. 221–22]). In describing what he lacks here, Diderot uses terms that (although idealized) are almost identical to the ones he later uses to describe Rameau's enthusiasm and dramatic performance.

The same characteristics of enthusiasm, genius, dramatic imagination, and the ability to metamorphose and forget oneself are personified by Dorval. At the beginning of the second *Entretien*, the narrator playing the part of Diderot describes a proto-Romantic tableau, set at the foot of a hill in a spot that is "solitaire et sauvage" ("solitary and wild"), in which he encounters the character who plays the part of the protagonist, leading actor, and author of *Le Fils naturel*: "J'approchai de lui sans qu'il m'aperçut. Il s'était abandonné au spectacle de la nature. . . . Je suivais sur son visage les impressions diverses qu'il en éprouvait; et je commençais à partager son transport" ("I approached him without his noticing me. He had abandoned himself to the spectacle of nature. . . . I followed in his face the various impressions he experienced, and I began to share his transport" [*OE*, p. 97]). Like Suzanne and Rameau at the height of their enthusiasm, Dorval is said to be oblivious of any beholder as he is absorbed and abandoned in a spectacle of his own. As Dorval begins to speak of "le séjour sacré de l'enthousiasme" and "génie" ("the sacred abode of enthusiasm" and "genius" [*OE*, p. 97]), the narrator begins to share his transports—like the sympathetic audience of a touching spectacle, like the nuns who behold Mme de Moni and later Suzanne, and to some extent like the *philosophe* who in part feels "pitié" while watching Rameau's moving performance (*OR*, p. 469). Finally, just like Rameau after the moments of alienation and enthusiasm of his performance, Dorval asks, "comme un homme qui sortirait d'un sommeil profond: 'Qu'ai-je dit? Qu'avais-je à vous dire? Je ne m'en souviens plus'" ("like a man who awakens from a deep sleep: 'What have I said? What did I have to say to you? I don't remember anymore'" [*OE*, p. 98]). Then, ignoring Dorval's description and experience of the enthusiasm of genius, the Diderot figure abruptly picks up where they had left off at the end of the previous *Entretien* by recalling some ideas about "les passions, leur accent, la déclamation, la pantomime" (*OE*, p. 99)—exactly the subjects of Rameau's most important *entretiens*.

In his notes to the Garnier edition of Diderot's *Oeuvres esthétiques*, Paul Vernière remarks on the significance of this portrait of the artist as "an enthusiast, a sensitive soul [une âme sensible], an irrational force which expresses itself only in a state of mystical possession" and goes on to say: "Diderot will correct this romantic vision thirteen years later in the *Paradoxe sur le comédien*" (*OE*, p. 98n). It is true that Diderot offers other views of the poet and actor. His comments on the "esprit observateur" of the genius in the fragment "Sur le génie" resemble the views of the first rather than the second interlocutor in the *Paradoxe sur le comédien*;[15] and, of course, insofar as it stages a debate about acting technique and dramatic convention, the *Paradoxe* does argue against an "enthusiastic" school of acting and actors with *âmes sensibles*. However, I have been suggesting that Diderot does not abandon his investment in the forgetting of self and beholder that characterizes Dorval's transports. The points of resemblance between the positions of the two interlocutors in the *Paradoxe*, the presence of the characteristics of both types of actors in Suzanne and especially Rameau, the deep associations between *Le Neveu de Rameau* and the *Entretiens* and the *Discours* as well as the *Paradoxe*—all this suggests that Diderot did not simply correct or refute himself in the *Paradoxe sur le comédien*. The extent to which *Le Neveu de Rameau* seems to be (at least in part) an offstage dramatization of the terms and characters of the *Paradoxe* suggests that the *Paradoxe* should receive the sort of reading that *Le Neveu* usually receives: that is to say, a reading that is more dialectical and more open to the possibility of irony, play, and the interplay of positions.

For example, in the *Paradoxe sur le comédien*, a few pages after the two interlocutors discuss the compromise position offered by the second that would reserve "à la sensibilité naturelle de l'acteur ces moments rares où sa tête se perd, où il ne voit plus le spectateur, où il a oublié qu'il est sur un théâtre, où il a oublié lui-même" ("to the actor's natural sensibility those rare moments when he loses his head, when he no longer sees the spectator, when he has forgotten that he is on a stage, when he has forgotten himself" [*OE*, pp. 368–69]), a third-person narrative voice appears out of nowhere to describe the two characters walking in the Tuileries after they have tried unsuccessfully to attend the theater. As the scene and form of the dialogue suddenly shifts, we read: "They seemed to have forgotten that they were together, and each one conversed with himself as if he had been alone" [*OE*, p. 373]). After speaking a lengthy "soliloquy" (*OE*, p. 374), the first interlocutor suddenly realizes that the second hasn't heard a word he has said. "I was dreaming" he explains. "But then have I been talking by myself all this time?" asks the first. "That may be," responds the second, "for as long as I've been dreaming all by myself" (*OE*, p. 379). After writing virtually all of the text in a genre that resembles the text of a play, Diderot interrupts his dialogue to send his characters to the theater: which turns out to mean that they forget themselves in soliloquies and reveries and in their respective transports become oblivious to their interlocutor. Each, however, wakes from his dreamlike state somewhat disappointed to learn that the other has not been playing the role of sympathetic audience to a display of the transports of enthusiasm.[16]

One could explain this scene as Diderot's joke on the first interlocutor—that is, himself. One could argue also that the forgetting of self and other experienced by the first interlocutor does not in itself contradict the arguments he has made about the need for actors to be self-possessed and unemotional manipulators of the signs of characters and passions. Indeed, as the dialogue breaks down (both on the page and in the plot), we are reminded that the characters have not found a place "au spectacle" ("at the theater" [*OE*, p. 373]); they are not on the stage. However, the suggestion that the first interlocutor cannot leave the dialogue before finding himself in the position advocated by the second suggests that we need to reconsider the terms of the debate, the differences or similarities between the characters' points of view, and in general Diderot's investment in both of the actors characterized in the text. I argued earlier that both interlocutors share the belief that the actor's self should be annihilated. In the context of the outcome of the dialogue we need to reconsider the compromise position that is proposed by the second interlocutor; the terms in which the first interlocutor seems to refute it—and the fact that he does not exactly refute it—can help us to understand the stakes in the debate.

The second interlocutor, as we have seen, is more or less ready to relegate everything that happens on the stage to the calculations of the actor's art except those rare moments when the actor forgets himself and the audience and becomes the character he plays. The first suggests that if the actor and spectator really forget themselves, the spectacle would cease to be a pleasure and become a "supplice" ("torture"). He goes on to insist that "ce pathétique de fiction" ("this pathos of fiction") represented on the stage would not be as moving as the "spectacle domestique et réel" ("domestic and real spectacle") of a genuine deathbed scene, and he concludes: "Vous ne vous êtes donc pas, ni le comédien, ni vous, si parfaitement oubliés" ("Neither you nor the actor have completely so forgotten yourselves" [*OE*, p. 370]). He is, of course, following Du Bos, who found it the central paradox of the theater (and indeed of art) that watching tragedies was pleasurable, and explained this paradox in part by asserting that despite the power of dramatic illusion the audience never forgets that it is watching a play.[17] It is not clear, however, exactly what point the first interlocutor has gained here, even if the second tries to end the debate by suggesting that they go to the theater. Theater, the first interlocutor maintains, is not entirely forgotten, either by the actor or the audience; if it were really forgotten, it would be as moving as a real and domestic spectacle—for example, the scene of "the deathbed of a cherished father or an adored mother" (*OE*, p. 369)—and therefore it would make us suffer rather than give us pleasure. But does this mean that theater cannot or should not be forgotten? Does it mean that a spectacle on the stage cannot or should not ever be confused with a "spectacle domestique et réel"?

Earlier in the dialogue, in reflecting on "ce qu'on appelle au théâtre *être vrai*" ("what we call being true in the theater"), the first interlocutor insists that dramatic representation is necessary to move us not only on the stage but even in a scene of real suffering: "An unhappy woman, a truly unhappy woman, weeps without touching you at all: what is worse, some little disfigurement in her makes you laugh" (*OE*, p. 317). Once again recalling Du Bos, he evokes the paradigmatic yet complicated example of the gladiator, who dies "to applause ... in an elegant and picturesque attitude." Dramatic convention and the rules of representation that govern the difference between *vérité* (truth) and *vraisemblance* (verisimilitude) require that the gladiators *act* dying even as they actually die. "Le gladiateur ancien, comme un grand comédien, un grand comédien, ainsi que le gladiateur ancien, ne meurent pas comme on meurt sur un lit, mais sont tenus de nous jouer une autre mort pour nous plaire" ("The ancient gladiator, like a great actor, a great actor, like the ancient gladiator, does not die as one dies in a bed, but is there to perform another sort of death in order to please us" [*OE*, p. 318]). Whereas Du Bos is appalled by the theartricality of this scene, the interlocutor playing the part of Diderot is simply a cold and tranquil spectator of the effects of spectacles on their audience. The distinction between these "deathbed" scenes is crucial to his argument, which is based on the difference between the effects of genuine and imitated sentiments, the salon and the stage, a dramatic representation and a *spectacle domestique et réel*. The argument of the *Paradoxe* is based on the supposition that on the stage—and as we have seen, perhaps even off the stage—a real spectacle will be less moving than an imitated one. The spectacle of the gladiators represents for Diderot (as it did for Du Bos) an extreme and somewhat troubling demonstration of the principle that a real spectacle must be artificial in order to please and move its audience.

It should be obvious that my purpose in raising these questions is not to invalidate the argument of the first interlocutor by finding a problem or inconsistency in his rejection of the "compromise" (*OE*, p. 368) proposed by the second interlocutor. His most persuasive response to this proposal is his point that such rare "moments d'aliénation . . . dissoneront avec le reste d'autant plus fortement qu'ils seront plus beaux" ("moments of alienation . . . would be more incompatible with the rest the more they were beautiful" [*OE*, p. 369]). What is significant here is the first interlocutor's insistence on the effects of a *spectacle domestique et réel*—not only in the general context of his argument but precisely at the moment that the possibility of forgetting theater is at stake. We need to ask at this point what a real spectacle would be. (The scene of "the deathbed of a cherished father or an adored mother" described to illustrate the "spectacle domestique et réel" [*OE*, p. 369] sounds like a tableau painted by Greuze.) Could there be a real spectacle on stage? What would it take to make one forget that a spectacle was not real? What would happen in such a moment?

In his last attempt to argue his position in the *Paradoxe,* after the reveries and forgetting of both characters in the dialogue, the second interlocutor recounts the story of a Greek actor named Paulus who, while playing the role of Electra, "au lieu de se présenter sur la scène avec l'urne d'Oreste, parut en embrassant l'urne qui renfermait les cendres de son propre fils qu'il venait de perdre" ("instead of presenting himself upon the stage with the urn of Orestes, appeared embracing the urn which contained the ashes of his own son, whom he had just lost"). The conclusion he draws is that "ce ne fut point une vaine représentation, une petite douleur de spectacle, mais que la salle retentit de cris et de vrais gémissements" ("this was no vain representation, no little theatrical sorrow; rather the room echoed with cries and real laments" [OE, p. 379–80]). The first interlocutor responds on several grounds: he suggests that Paulus might not have been a good actor anyway, that he probably didn't speak "on stage" as he would have "in his home," and that the audience was reacting not to his portrayal of Electra but to "the sight of a despondent father who bathed the urn of his own son with his tears" (OE, p. 380). In other words, theater has not been forgotten in this scene; it only has been displaced or replaced for a moment by real emotions. It appears that the character has disappeared as the actor plays himself; the audience is moved by Paulus rather than Electra. The first interlocutor adds a story about an actor playing Atreus who, "étant hors de lui-même" ("being beside himself") in his representation of vengeance, kills a servant who just happens to walk by (OE, p. 380). Neither actor, according to the first interlocutor, shows signs of being particularly skilled or talented; but what exactly have the audiences to these performances witnessed? Once again (and in the last pages of the dialogue) we see Diderot returning to the question of the actor's loss of himself and identification with his part in a scene that might be represented as a real spectacle.

Even within the plot and debate of the Paradoxe, the first in-terlocutor is also interested in a version of this moment. Earlier in the dialogue, speaking as the author of Le Père de famille—that is, as Diderot—he tells the story of a royal production of his play in Naples where the play has been cast not with actors but with ordinary people found in society: "des personnages d'âge, de figure, de voix, de caractère propres à remplir ses rôles" ("persons of an age, face, voice, and character appropriate to their roles"). These people chosen for their resemblance to the characters in the play are made to rehearse for six months. Perfection, he continues, is approached only when "les acteurs sont épuisés de la fatigue de ces répétitions multipliées, ce que nous appelons blasés. De cet instant les progrès sont surprenants, chacun s'identifie avec son personnage" ("the actors are exhausted from the fatigue of these multiple rehearsals, what we would call blasé. From that moment on, the progress made is surprising; each one identifies with his character"); and after six more months of rehearsal the performance reaches the height of "illusion théâtrale" ("theatrical illusion" [OE, p. 364]). In an amazing anticipation of the techniques of Italian neo-realist cinema, the director chooses non-actors and relentlessly wears away all vestiges of affectation and overstatement that might make their performances theatrical. The first interlocutor introduces this story to insist that such a performance could not be "l'effet de la sensibilité" ("the effect of sensibility" [*OE*, p. 364]); yet it is somewhat surprising to find him praising a performance in which actors who are already like their characters— people chosen because they would not really have to *act*—are brought to the point where they *identify* with the parts they play.[18]

In a sense the character playing the part of Diderot sidesteps questions of imitation, counterfeiting, and sensibility by describing a familial group of ordinary people who appear to play themselves. The confusion of character and actor, part and person, is set up from the beginning by Diderot's use of the word "personnages" to describe the people found to perform the play. Although the word might simply refer to a person (usually it connotes a famous or distinguished person) it is also defined in the *Encyclopédie* as "un rôle qu'on fait sur la scène ou dans le monde" ("a role one plays on the stage or in the world").[19] In any case, Diderot himself uses the same word a few lines later to refer to the play's characters, not its actors, in the phrase "chacun s'identifie avec son personnage" ("each one identifies with his *personnage*"). This assertion, of course, is the source of the real conceptional and not merely verbal ambiguity in the passage. The same confusion is suggested in the word "caractère," which is used in the phrase "des caractères propres á remplir ses rôles" ("characters appropriate to fill their roles") to refer to the characters of the people rather than characters or roles who form the *dramatis personae*. (The *Discours sur la poésie dramatique*, originally published with *Le Père de famille*, contains a long and important chapter on "caractères" which uses the word to refer to the *personnages* created by a dramatist.)[20] In the scene described by the first interlocutor, the persons performing the drama, forced to repeat their roles for a year, seem to become the *personnages* they play, although they seem to almost be those *personnages* to begin with. We are faced with a performance that seems more like a "spectacle domestique et réel" ("domestic and real spectacle") rather than a "vaine représentation, une petite douleur de spectacle" ("vain representation, a little theatrical sorrow"). This situation—in conjunction with Diderot's naming of himself as the author of the domestic *drame bourgeois*—should remind us of the first performance that Diderot imagined for *Le Fils naturel*.

We saw that when he published the text of *Le Fils naturel* with the *Entretiens sur Le Fils naturel,* Diderot created a narrative frame that posed him as an ideal "spectateur ignoré" to whom the performers were oblivious. Depicting an ideal, nontheatrical performance of the play in Dorval's salon, this narrative fiction also insists on the status of the play and performance as a *spectacle domestique et réel.* The prologue or "Histoire véritable de la Pièce" (the "true story or history of the play") provides the fiction that just before he died, Dorval's father Lysimond commanded Dorval to write a play which would chronicle the unusual yet true history of the family. Lysimond suggests further that the members of the family represent the play themselves amongst themselves—"entre nous." He explains: "Il ne s'agit point d'élever ici des tréteaux, mais de conserver la mémoire d'un événement qui nous touche, et de le rendre comme il s'est passé. . . . Nous le renouvellerions nous-mêmes, tous les ans, dans cette maison, dans ce salon. Les choses que nous avons dites, nous les redirions" ("the point is not to build a stage here, but to conserve the memory of an event that touches us, and to render it as it happened. . . . Every year we would ourselves repeat and renew it, in this house, in this drawing room. What we once said, we would say again").[21]

Describing a sort of dramatic family portrait gallery, Lysimond imagines a ritual representation and reenactment of the originary story of the family that will be repeated for generations to come as if it were the founding myth of a religion or nation.[22] What the character playing the role of Diderot actually witnesses, however, is the first performance of the play in which the actors play themselves. In this performance the actors do not cease being themselves when they become the characters, nor do they cease representing the characters if they should suddenly act themselves. The *personnages* are already the *personnages*. More than ordinary people of appropriate ages, appearances, and characters who happen to resemble the characters they play, these actors already identify with their parts. There is no difference between actor and character; like the differences between theater and salon, representation and sentiment, performance and sensibility, the difference between actor and character seems to have disappeared.

Indeed, within the fiction of the performance, the play is brought to a halt when an actor appears on the scene. The Diderot figure explains that since Lysimond died before the first representation of the play, "one of his friends had been engaged to replace him in the play, a friend who was about his age and had the same build, voice, and white hair." When this elderly man actually enters the scene, "dressed in the clothes which his friend had brought with him from prison," Diderot recounts that "no one could hold back his tears"; this "moment of the action" is said to place again "before the eyes of the family a man it had just lost" (*OE*, p. 77). What has happened here? After almost an entire performance in which all the characters are represented by themselves, the play is brought to a halt by the intrusion of an actor who is not one with his part. Although, like the *personnages* who performed *Le Père de famille* in Naples, the actor playing the character of the father of the family is "d'âge, de figure, de voix, de caractère" appropriate to his role, the effect of his performance is not sublime theatrical illusion. The old man places again before the eyes of the family a person who is not and cannot be there; in doing so, his presence comes to stand for the absence of his character. In this domestic performance in which almost everything is "real" and "true," the actor replacing Lysimond represents the intrusion of the ultimate reality that must stop all theater dead: the fact that the characters are (and must be) absent. The realization that there can be no identification between actor and character here causes the scene of theater to break down.[23]

It is no coincidence that Diderot closes the narrative frame (the epilogue which closes the text of the play and introduces the text of the *Entretiens*) with an acknowledgement of the "difference between what Dorval said to me and what I am writing." He laments the lack of "the spectacle of nature and the presence of Dorval" and closes with this self-portrait: "I am alone, among the dust of books, in the shadows of a study ... and I write lines which are weak, sad, and cold" (*OE*, p. 78–79). It is as if within the frame of his fiction Diderot is acknowledging the ultimate character of the texts of both his play and his dramatic dialogues. The story of the performance of *Le Fils naturel* reveals the difference and absence inscribed in any representation of a character, whether personated by an actor or delineated by the lines of a book. Until the acknowledgment forced by the absence of the character (either Lysimond or Dorval), theater seems almost avoided or at least forgotten. This is what transforms the command performance in which the characters of *Le Fils naturel* play themselves in a ritualistic re-presentation of real events from Lysimond's fantasy about immortality to Diderot's fantasy about the theater.

A few paragraphs before the acknowledgment of the absence of Dorval and the spectacle of nature, describing his experience watching *Le Fils naturel* before the performance of the *spectacle domestique et réel* broke down, Diderot pictures himself enthralled by theatrical illusion. After the performance, he says, he tries to tell himself that the spectacle he saw was not real: "Il faut que je sois bien bon de m'affliger ainsi. Tout ceci n'est qu'une comédie" ("How can I afflict myself in this way? All this is only a play"). He recalls, however, that the history of Dorval was well known, and he recalls the *truth* of the representation as he was watching it: "La représentation en avait été si vraie, qu'oubliant en plusieurs endroits que j'étais spectateur, et spectateur ignoré, j'avais été sur le point de sortir de ma place, et d'ajouter un personnage réel á la scène" ("The representation was so true that, forgetting at several points that I was a spectator, and an unsuspected and unknown spectator, I had been about to leave my place and add a real character to the scene" [*OE*, p. 78]). In the context of the fiction of a performance in which the difference between actor and character seems to disappear, the terms of this passage are both crucial and perplexing.

What would it mean for the spectator of a truthful representation, a *spectacle domestique et réel*, to want to add "un personnage réel à la scène"? After all, what is peculiar about the representation to begin with, what lends the spectacle its truth, is that *all* of the characters are, as it were, *personnages réels*. The actors are, like the actors in the Naples production, "personnages" found "in society" (*OE*, p. 364); the characters (or *personnages*) are just as real as the actors. If, however, Dorval and the others represent real characters in the scene—that is to say, if they *are* real characters—then what is the old man who plays the part of Lysimond, if not a "personnage réel"? Is he a real person but not a real character? Finally, how is Dorval playing the role of Dorval different from the narrator who speaks the entire fiction while playing the character of Diderot? Is "Moi"—the character who is identified with the historical personage Diderot—more of a *personnage réel* than Dorval, the supposed author of *Le Fils naturel*?

Writing as himself in the *Discours sur la poésie dramatique,* while defending himself against the accusation that he plagiarized *Le Fils naturel* from Goldoni, Diderot describes the book containing his play and the *Entretiens* as "une espèce de roman" ("a kind of novel") and in a long rhetorical question he again confronts the ambiguous role of *personnages réels*:

> Sans la supposition que l'aventure du *Fils naturel* était réelle, que devenaient l'illusion de ce roman et toutes les observations répandues dans les entretiens sur la différence qu'il y a entre un fait vrai et un fait imaginé, des personnages réels et des personnages fictifs, des discours tenus et des discours supposés; en un mot, toute la poétique où la vérité est mise cesse en parallèle avec la fiction? (*OE*, p. 223)

> Without the supposition that the adventure of the *Fils naturel* was real, what would become of the illusion of that novel, and of all the observations spread throughout the dialogue on the difference between

a true fact and an imagined fact, between real characters and fictional characters, between actual discourses and supposed discourses; in a word, the entire poetics in which truth is constantly placed in parallel with fiction?

I do not have space in the course of this argument to elaborate fully the context and implications of this unanswered question, which interrupts the text like a non sequitur, as if it has forced its way onto the page from another discussion. Taken in itself, the passage provides an insight into Diderot's method in the *Entretiens*. It suggests that in order to write a poetics of truth and fiction, in order to discuss the relations between truth and verisimilitude, the difference between the salon and the stage, Diderot had to place himself at the crossing of truth and fiction. In order to write about theater he had to enter into theater—not only by writing a play but by dramatizing his poetics of theater through impersonation, acting, and dramatic dialogue.[24]

However, the fiction of *personnages réels* in many ways confuses and complicates the discussions between Dorval and "Moi" about "la différence d'un événement imaginaire et d'un événement réel" or "le monde imaginaire et le monde réel" ("the difference between an imaginary event and a real event" or "the imaginary world and the real world" [*OE*, pp. 130, 136]). It is true that Diderot is trying to stake out the ground for the conventions of a new genre that is meant to be faithful to a different kind of reality and to guarantee a new relation between actor and audience by taking place in a different kind of dramatic space. Yet when Dorval repeatedly defends his writing by claiming that his play is merely faithful to reality—"Il s'agit ici d'un fait, et non d'une fiction" ("we're concerned here with a fact, not a fiction")—or by evoking the proper realm of representation of his play—"laissez là les tréteaux; rentrez dans le salon. . . . C'est dans le salon qu'il faut juger mon ouvrage" ("Leave the stage alone, go back to the drawing room. . . . It is in the drawing room that my work should be judged" [*OE*, pp. 94, 85–86])—one might suspect Diderot of merely cheating in *his* defense of the play. After all, Dorval's real world and real events are in fact imaginary; it is only a fiction that he is a *personnage réel*. But the novel that is comprised of the play and the *Entretiens* together is in some sense about this confusion of the imaginary and the real: the confusion between characters and characters, *personnages* and *personnages*. Even in the explanation of his method offered in the *Discours*, Diderot neither specifies the difference between *personnages réels* and *personnages fictifs* nor identifies who the *personnages réels* really are.

At the very end of the novel, the narrator—whom Dorval has just named as the editor of the *Encyclopédie*—describes his meeting with Dorval's family: the characters and actors of *Le Fils naturel.* "Je reconnus toujours le caractère que Dorval avait donné à chacun de ses personnages" ("I always recognized the character that Dorval had given to each one of his personages"), he writes, and in noting the different characteristics he has learned to identify with each character ("Constance, the air of reason," and so on) he ends with himself: "moi, celui de la bonhomie" ("myself, that of good nature"). Once again, the words "personnages" and "caractère" should give us pause here, and once again the verbal ambiguity points to a basic ambiguity in the scene described. In the end, like the *dramatis personae* of *Le Fils naturel,* the character Diderot also has a character, and he includes himself in a list of the characters from the play. When he writes, "en un moment je fus de la famille" ("In a moment, I was one of the family" [*OE*, pp. 174–75]), Diderot is describing more than a particularly friendly cast party. This vaguely idyllic happy ending almost fulfils the narrator's earlier desire to "ajouter un personnage réel à la scène" ("add a real *personnage* to the scene"). On at least two levels real and fictive personages are placed in parallel as if there were no difference between them: within the fiction of the novel as Diderot compares the characters of the play with the characters of the personages who represented them; and in the fiction itself which juxtaposes the historical personage Diderot with the imaginary Dorval. Most important, however, in returning us to the scene in which Diderot forgot that he was the "spectateur ignoré" of a "spectacle domestique et réel," the reunion of the characters for both *Le Fils naturel* and the *Entretiens* rehearses this dream of a theater without alienation, difference, or distance, and refocuses this dream on the experience of the spectator.

Diderot's description of reading Richardson's novels in the *Éloge de Richardson* contains moments that are similar to the response of the spectator of *Le Fils naturel.* Just as Diderot describes his effort to console himself after watching the play by saying, "Tout ceci n'est qu'une comédie" ("All this is only a play"), he describes how in reading Richardson, "affaissé de douleur ou transporté de joie, vous n'aurez plus la force de retenir vos larmes prêtes à couler, et de vous dire à vous-même: *Mais peut-être que cela n'est pas vrai*" ("overwhelmed with grief or transported with joy, you will no longer have the strength to hold back the tears which are ready to flow, or to say to yourself: 'But perhaps this is not true'" [*OE*, pp. 78, 35]). The analogy to the experience of theater is made explicitly in this tableau representing Diderot in the act of reading: "Combien de fois ne me suis-je pas surpris, comme il est arrivé à des enfants qu'on avait menés au spectacle pour la première fois, criant: *Ne le croyez pas, il vous trompe. . . . Si vous allez là, vous êtes perdu*" ("How many times have I surprised myself by crying out—like children who are taken to the theater for the first time—'Don't believe him, he's trying to deceive you. . . . If you go there, you are lost'" [*OE*, p. 30]). Diderot is particularly interested in this moment of naïveté and credulity. In *Les Bijoux indiscrets*, "la perfection d'un spectacle" ("the perfection of a performance") is said to "consiste dans l'imitation si exacte d'une action, que le spectateur, trompé sans interruption, s'imagine assister à l'action même" ("consist in an imitation of an action so exact that the spectator, continually deceived, imagines that he is present at the action itself" [*OR*, p. 142]). The child seeing a play for the first time doesn't have to forget or imagine. In a sense, this child is like the marquis de Croismare, who doesn't know that he is in the presence of a fiction when he becomes the sympathetic spectator to the sufferings of Suzanne Simonin and tries to save her. However, in this case of *mystification*, as in the case of a child's naïveté, the reader or spectator is forced by a compelling theatrical illusion to pass from ignorance to knowledge. Diderot is interested here in precisely the opposite experience. What is important in the paradigmatic experience we are considering is the knowledge and understanding of the conditions of theater that make forgetting theater both possible and necessary.[25]

Diderot presents a comic version of this moment in *Jacques le fataliste*: as Jacques tells his master about the time he was attacked by thieves, he interrupts his story to ask: "What's wrong, Master? You are gritting your teeth, you are getting upset, as if you were in the presence of an enemy." The master explains: "I am there, in effect [J'y suis, en effet]; my sword is in hand, I rush upon your robbers and avenge you. . . . My poor Jacques, what will become of you? Your situation frightens me." Jacques tries to comfort his listener, insisting, "Reassure yourself, I am here [me voilà]," but the master seems to be somewhere else: "I wasn't thinking of that, I was there tomorrow [Je n'y pensais pas, j'étais à demain], next to you, at the doctor's, at the moment when you wake up, when they have asked you for money" (*OR*, pp. 572–73). Although the scene enacted here (which on the page is presented in the dialogic format of a play) might seem closer to a scene from a Marx Brothers movie than to Diderot's sentimental descriptions of the experience of reading Richardson, the master's forgetting of himself and the frame of fiction in hearing a moving story suggests what is at stake in Diderot's other descriptions of this moment.

As in conventional eighteenth-century descriptions of the power of fiction and dramatic illusion, the master seems to be transported to the scene of Jacques's story; describing himself in the present tense, he says "J'y suis," as if he were in the presence of the robbers. The master's "I am there" is answered by Jacques's ambiguous "me voilà" and for a moment there is a question of whether they can share a time and place. Like Diderot the reader and Diderot the spectator, like the child introduced into the alien space of the theater, the master ignores the fact that the spectacle moving him is out of his reach. Unable to interrupt the time and place of the story, he continues to prompt and narrate after the script has been put down and the performance suspended. The master's forgetting of the dramatized scene of fiction may parody experiences of an intense belief in illusion by displaying an unusually gullible or naive spectator, but Diderot is interested in what happens when a reader or spectator who knows better is reduced to the position of the child who cries out. The master's impulse to help Jacques by transporting himself to the scene of the crime points to what is impossible in the sudden desire to *ajouter un personnage réel à la scène.*

The experience of Jacques's master, like the experience of the child in the theater, like the experiences of Diderot the reader and spectator, involves the transports of sympathy. I mean by this both the imaginary transfer of places and persons that was expected to transport readers or spectators to the scene of fiction, and the more specific response to a scene of tragedy, danger, or suffering that not only leaves one *affligé* but calls upon one to come to the assistance of someone in distress. The first transport (which leads one to take the place of someone else) is what allows one momentarily to believe in the possibility of the second transport (in which one enters the place and time of the person in distress). Fried has analyzed what he calls Diderot's "pastoral" conception of painting, which manifests itself in the *Salons* as a fiction that would remove the beholder from his place before a painting by transporting him into the landscape of the scene. Fried cites various examples in which Diderot speaks of being able to enter a tableau. In the *Salon de 1767*, Diderot writes of a painting by Robert: "On s'oublie devant ce morceau ... c'est la plus forte magie de l'art. Ce n'est plus au Sallon ou dans un attelier qu'on est" ("One forgets oneself before this piece ... it is the strongest magic of art. One is no longer at the Salon or in a studio").[26] These descriptions utilize fictions of leisurely promenades and reveries that allow the spectator to pass into and out of the painted scenes (usually landscapes) almost imperceptibly. The experience of forgetting theater might be located on a continuum with

the forgetting Diderot dramatizes in these pastoral fictions of beholding; it is, however, more urgent and finally more disruptive.

The spectator who suddenly forgets theater in the transport of
sympathy that Diderot describes feels called upon to assist in a way
that forces him to come to terms with his role as an *assistant* in the
theater, as someone who "s'imagine assister à l'action même"
("imagines that he is present at the action itself"). I mean this in both
the French and English senses: in the moment of forgetting that
brings one to the limits of theatrical illusion, one must confront what
it means to *assister à un spectacle*. The desire to assist forces one to
trangress those limits—to cry out and address the characters or simply
to forget one's place and momentarily believe that one could add
oneself to the scene. In the forgetting of theater that takes place for the
actor, as in the self-forgetting of the enthusiast, Diderot focuses on the
moment of awakening: the gradual dawning which marks a dazed
return from the transport of metamorphosis, reverie, or enthusiasm.
When the spectator forgets theater he is forced to an abrupt
realization that he has forgotten himself. The master's realization that
he cannot reach the time or place in which Jacques was (and in the
dramatization of fiction *is*) assaulted suggests both the urgency and the
inevitable failure that must be inscribed in the spectator's forgetting of
theater.

Brought to a conviction of presence, the master discovers that he
cannot leave his place and enter the present of the scene Jacques
represents. His forgetting and subsequent realization mirror the
experience prescribed for the reader of *Jacques le fataliste*. In the novel,
Diderot appears to have written a book that would allow—even
compel—the reader to play the role in which he casts Richardson's
reader in the *Éloge*: "on prend, malgré qu'on en ait, un rôle dans tes
ouvrages, on se mêle à la conversation, on approuve, on blâme, on
admire, on s'irrite, on s'indigne" ("One takes, despite oneself, a role in
your works; one enters into the conversation, one approves, one
blames, one admires, one becomes irritated, one becomes indignant"
[*OE*, p. 30]). Yet the text turns out to be a Sternean subversion of this
Richardsonian model; the very dialogue with the reader that appears
to write the reader into the text finally must rule him out. It is when
the reader tries to enter into the conversation that he must discover
himself strangely absent. This is the experience prescribed for the
spectateur ignoré who tries to *ajouter un personnage réel à la scène*; this
is the experience of theater.

In an essay on Shakespeare, Stanley Cavell has described this scene
of theater: the characters on the stage are in the presence of the

audience but the audience cannot be in their presence. Since "we can no more confront a character in a play than we can confront any fictitious being" we cannot be present to the same characters that seem present to us. Cavell imagines a scene in which a naive spectator tries to rescue Desdemona from Othello and suggests that the most he could do would be to stop the performance of the play. He could stop the actors but he could never touch Othello, who would disappear, only to reappear "as near and as deaf as ever," when the actors picked up the thread of the performance.[27] This is the situation that Diderot's fantasy of the *spectacle domestique et réel* of *Le Fils naturel* seems designed to deny. It masks the fact that while one could interrupt the actors' performance, one could never add oneself to the scene of the drama.

Throughout his writing about the theater Diderot remains fascinated by the possibility of a *spectacle réel* with *personnages réels*. He repeatedly rehearses moments in which actors (or characters in the place and position of actors) forget themselves and in doing so seem to forget theater. Although in the arena of acting technique he rejects the conventional belief that the best actor is the one who becomes the character he plays, Diderot remains invested (even in the *Paradoxe*) in the idea of an actor who would annihilate himself, disappear so that the character could seem to appear in his place. He returns to a dream of theater in which the actors and the characters are the same, in which the characters are *personnages réels* rather than *personnages fictifs*. In this dream, theater would not represent absence, alienation, difference, and distance. Faced with such a real and domestic spectacle, or at least the overwhelmingly compelling illusion that the representation was true, the spectator might be able to forget theater: forget the inescapable roles of actor and *spectateur ignoré*.

However, it is precisely at this moment of forgetting that the spectator must remember that he is a *spectateur ignoré*: that he will always be unknown and ignored by characters who will never allow him to feel present. The most successful theatrical illusion must end in disillusionment by leading us to knock up against the stage's fourth wall, to discover ourselves *here* instead of *there*. The very illusions and conviction that move the spectator to the point where he thinks he could leave his place must finally remove him: put him in his place. I am suggesting that both the forgetting *and* the remembering of this position are crucial for Diderot. The spectator must forget theater in order to remember it. Indeed, the only way for the spectator to remember theater is to forget it; the moment of forgetting is what

forces the spectator to remember his place—which he might otherwise forget.

In suddenly responding to characters in a play as if they were
personnages réels we must recognize them as *personnages fictifs*. But
what happens when we recognize that the actors and the spectacle are
not "real," that we are faced with fictions? One effect is a demystify-
ing gesture in which Diderot acknowledges the conditions of his art,
acknowledges that his dramatic dialogues must lack the voice,
spectacle, immediacy, and presence that he (and his contemporaries)
have demanded of them. The remembering of theater that comes
with forgetting also serves to counteract the play's inevitable theatrical
address by leading us to recognize that the play must finally refuse to
admit our entry or presence within the borders of its time and space.
In ruling us out, however, these recognitions lead us to remember that
the boundaries of theater and fiction are in fact difficult to delineate.
If Diderot is preoccupied with the differences and similarities between
personnages réels and *personnages fictifs* in the playhouse, this is partly
because theater asks us to consider the problems we face in recognizing real and fictive characters outside of the playhouse. This is the
predicament we are left with at the end of the *Paradoxe sur le
comédien.*

I would like to close this chapter by returning to the story that the
second interlocutor tells about the Greek actor Paulus at the end of the
Paradoxe. As we saw, he tells the story about the actor who appears on
stage with the urn containing the ashes of his own son rather than the
urn of Orestes in order to imagine a situation in which great
sensibility and true feelings allowed a performance that was not a
"vaine représentation, une petite douleur de spectacle" ("vain representation, a little theatrical sorrow"). He does not explain whether the
audience knew that the "vrais gémissements" ("true lamentations")
that moved them were caused by (what the first interlocutor describes
as) "la vue d'un père désolé qui baignait de ses pleurs l'urne de son
propre fils" ("the sight of a despairing father who was bathing with
his tears the urn of his own son" [*OE,* p. 380]). What is remarkable
here is that Paulus is not playing just any scene of grief and mourning,
or even just any scene of Electra mourning. The second interlocutor
is describing the *Electra* of Sophocles. This means that Paulus is acting
the scene in which Electra only *thinks* that she holds the urn
containing the ashes of Orestes.

In the play, Orestes has returned home in disguise after having sent
a false account of his death; coming upon Electra, he presents her with

an urn and tells her that it contains her brother's ashes. After a long scene in which she expresses great despair and grief, he finally tells her that she has been deceived by an illusion, tricked by a stage prop and some playacting. The urn, he says, contains Orestes's ashes only in fiction: "it is not Orestes—except insofar as it has been contrived, by a tale only, to look like it."[28] During the entire scene, the audience knows that Electra is mistaking a representation for reality; like the marquis de Croismare or the child who does not understand that a play is a fiction, Electra is moved by a story or simulacrum that only looks like something real. From a privileged point of view, the audience witnesses a scene of theater which dramatizes the perhaps disturbing power of imitation, story telling, and playacting to move a credulous spectator.

The scene I have just described makes the scene of Paulus holding the urn of his son's ashes both charged and complex. At precisely the moment when the ashes in the urn are supposed to exist in illusion and fiction only, Paulus substitutes the real ashes of a real dead relative and transforms a "vaine représentation, une petite douleur de spectacle" into a *spectacle réel*. As he plays the character of someone who is moved by a representation, he replaces that representation with something real and thereby alters the character of his own represen-tation. If Paulus has forgotten theater it is not by losing himself and becoming his part but rather by somehow putting theater aside—precisely at the moment that what he is supposed to be enacting on stage is theater. Furthermore, although the first interlocutor's descrip-tion of "la vue d'un père désolé" leaves ambiguous exactly what the audience thinks it sees as it watches the scene, in *The Attic Nights* (the source the second interlocutor specifies for the story) Aulus Gellius explicitly notes that during this performance of *Electra* the audience does not know what Paulus has done: it does not know what he is doing before their eyes.

According to *The Attic Nights*, Paulus "took from the tomb the ashes and urn of his son, embraced them as if they were those of Orestes, and filled the whole place, not with the appearance and imitation of sorrow, but with genuine grief and unfeigned lamenta-tion." The passage concludes: "Therefore, while it seemed that a play was being acted, it was in fact real grief that was enacted."[29] Ironically, the moment that the spectators reassure themselves that the play is only a fiction (remind themselves, in case they forgot, that "tout ceci n'est qu'une comédie") is precisely the moment that reality has replaced fiction. What they take to be a *spectacle fictif* is in fact a *spectacle réel*. Unknown to the audience, Electra is right; Paulus makes her right. What everyone has taken to be contrived by a tale only to look like death turns out to be death.

This double scene appears at the end of the *Paradoxe* almost as if it were an afterthought, inserted after the enthusiastic monologues and reveries of the two characters and spoken as the last speech of the second interlocutor. The ways in which the situation I have been elaborating works to complicate the anecdote are barely acknowledged on the surface of the text; but the explicit references to both Sophocles's *Electra* and *The Attic Nights* suggest that Diderot meant for his reader to understand the depth and context of his allusions. Even for the reader who did not already understand the resonances of Paulus's double scene, Diderot provides the references needed to create a situation of dramatic irony in which the reader will understand what the characters appear to ignore. The reverberations of the scene must leave us with an afterthought as we close the pages of the *Paradoxe*: we are led to think about what it means that the audience of that performance of *Electra* could not tell the difference between a representation and real sentiment.

Unlike Electra, the spectators mistake something real for a fiction—although one can imagine that the cries of Paulus are so true that the spectators momentarily forget theater and move toward him (or Electra) in a transport of sympathy, only to remember that they are only watching a play. What we learn when we remember the stories of Electra and Paulus, however, is not that a play is only a fiction, even if it looks like something real; we learn that real sentiments may look like a representation. Indeed, real suffering, both inside and outside of the theater, must appear to us as a representation or a fiction. Other people may be *personnages réels* but they must represent themselves like *personnages fictifs*. This is why the *Paradoxe sur le comédien* is an epistemological investigation as much as treatise on aesthetics, dramatic convention, or acting technique.

Insofar as the *Paradoxe* is about acting, it is about hypocrisy: the deception of others through the imitation of the signs and symptoms of sentiments that are not really there. However, Diderot is not particularly worried about hypocrisy in the *Paradoxe*; in describing a semiotics of the passions he is more interested in the fact that even the most sincere people must represent their feelings than in the possibility that some people might act like actors and counterfeit feelings. Earlier in the dialogue, in making the point that the images of the passions presented in the theater are stylized caricatures subject to the rules of convention, the first interlocutor insists that sentiments can be communicated successfully to the audience only if they are represented according to the theater's unique semiotic code. He adds: "car il est impossible d'apprécier autrement ce qui se passe au dedans de nous" ("for it is impossible to appreciate otherwise what goes on within us"). As part of his debate about whether actors need to feel the sentiments they represent, he asks: "que nous importe en effet qu'ils sentent on qu'ils ne sentent pas, pourvu que nous l'ignorions?" ("what does it matter to us whether they feel or not, as long as we are unaware of it?" [*OE*, p. 358]).

Extended beyond a debate about conventions of representation and the experience of an audience, these comments describe the situation that the reader is called upon to remember at the end of the *Paradoxe*: since we are unaware of what other people feel, we can appreciate what takes place inside them only if they represent the exterior signs and symptoms of their sentiments. The danger in this situation is finally not that we might not believe other people, but that we might not believe in them. Diderot suggests that the real risk of theater might be the moment of forgetting in which we neglect to take a fiction for a real spectacle; yet theater also can teach us about the parallels between *personnages réels* and *personnages fictifs*. It is only by remembering theater, by remembering what separates all actors from both the characters they represent and the spectators who behold them, that we can act to add a real character to the scene.

FIVE

Rousseau and the State
of Theater

But pity, the arch passion in Rousseau is itself . . . inherently a fictional
process that transposes an actual situation into a world of appearance,
of drama and literary language: all pity is in essence theatrical.
Paul de Man, *Blindness and Insight*

The book that we refer to today as Rousseau's *Lettre à d'Alembert sur
les spectacles* usually is situated in the antitheatrical tradition, even if
defenders of the stage from d'Alembert to Jonas Barish have
considered it a belated and almost anachronistic contribution to that
tradition.[1] In this chapter I would like (at least temporarily) to
dislocate the *Lettre* from both the tradition of attacks on the stage and
the immediate occasion that prompted Rousseau to publish the book:
d'Alembert's proposal in the seventh volume of the *Encyclopédie* that
a theater be established in Geneva.[2] I will argue that although
Rousseau genuinely was concerned about the effects of a theater in
Geneva, and although much of his argument against the stage
reiterates the charges of Plato and later antitheatrical polemicists, we
blind ourselves to the full scope of Rousseau's indictment if we regard
the *Lettre* only as a particularly eloquent antitheatrical tract.

The original title of the book refers to d'Alembert's proposal to
establish a "théâtre de comédie" in Geneva, but the title that Rousseau
later used to refer to his text is the *Lettre à d'Alembert sur les
spectacles*—which I would insist on translating as the *Letter to
d'Alembert on Spectacles*. The title is *not*, as Rousseau's modern
American translator would suggest, the *Letter to M. d'Alembert on the
Theatre*.[3] The question of whether a "théâtre de comédie" should be
established in Geneva provides an occasion for Rousseau to reflect on
the character of *spectacles*—which include but by no means are limited
to dramatic representations performed by actors on a stage. Rousseau
is concerned not just with how Geneva should govern its spectacles
but with how spectacles govern our lives: how we are affected by the
theatrical relations enacted outside as well as inside the playhouse by

135

people who face each other as actors and spectators. I will suggest that the issue for Rousseau finally is not whether *a* theater should be established but whether theater (in its many manifestations) can be avoided at all.

The possibility that theatrical acts and relations are inescapable in Rousseau's view sets the stage for a consideration of Rousseau's own role in the *Lettre*, his own predicament in indicting actors and spectators. The original title page not only names Rousseau as author; it includes Rousseau's name in the title, which begins: "J. J. ROUSSEAU / CITOYEN DE GENEVE, / A M. D'ALEMBERT . . ." In announcing the completion of his book, Rousseau wrote to his publisher, "Non seulement vous pourrez me nommer, mais mon nom y sera et en fera même le titre" ("Not only may you name me, but my name will be in the title and indeed will be the title").[4] The subject of the book is identified with the subject of Rousseau from the very first line of the text. I do not mean to suggest that the text is strictly autobiographical; my point is that identity and identification are themselves key issues in the text. Not only does Rousseau's own involvement with the theatrical situations he is depicting come into play; Rousseau himself discusses theater in terms of an interplay between subjects. As a book about theater, the *Lettre* examines the conditions of projection, identification, and sympathy; it asks what it means to take the part of someone, to put oneself in someone else's place, to imagine that a story is about oneself. "Osons le dire sans détour," writes Rousseau in the *Lettre*, "qui de nous est assez sûr de lui pour supporter la représentation d'une pareille comédie sans être de moitié des tours qui s'y jouent. . . . Car s'intéresser pour quelqu'un, qu'est-ce autre chose que de se mettre à sa place?" ("Let us dare to say it directly: who among us is sure enough of himself to bear the performance of such a comedy without halfway taking part in the turns that are played out? . . . . For is being interested in someone anything other than putting oneself in his place?" [*L*, p. 159]). This chapter will consider Rousseau's interest in both actors and spectators. It will trace the risks and possibilities Rousseau sees in spectacles, in theatrical relations, and in writing about spectacles and theatrical relations.

The *Lettre à d'Alembert sur les spectacles* has been seen as a continuation of the reactionary crusade against civilization Rousseau began in his early discourses.[5] One could reverse this perspective, however, and see Rousseau's earlier writing—particularly the *Discours sur l'origine et les fondements de l'inégalité parmi les hommes*—as the beginning of a critique of theatricality: a critical investigation into the role of spectacles and theatrical relations in European culture. In the second

Discours, for example, when Rousseau asserts, "dans le véritable état de nature, l'Amour propre n'existe pas" ("in the true state of nature, vanity does not exist"), he goes on to describe "chaque homme en particulier se regardant lui-même comme le seul Spectateur qui l'observe, comme le seul être dans l'univers qui prenne intérêt à lui" ("each man regarding himself as the only spectator who observes him, as the only being in the universe who takes an interest in him" [*OC*, p. 219]). The state of nature seems untheatrical; it is in part defined by the absence of any consciousness of beholders.

As society develops, according to Rousseau, people become aware of the regard of others. They become conscious of others as both spectacles and spectators: "On s'accoutuma à s'assembler devant les Cabanes ou autour d'un grand Arbre: le chant et la danse ... devinrent l'amusement et plutôt l'occupation des hommes et des femmes oisifs et attroupés. Chacun commença à regarder les autres et à vouloir être regardé soi-même, et l'estime publique eut un prix" ("They became accustomed to assembling in front of the huts or around a large tree; song and dance ... became the amusement, or rather the occupation, of idle men and women gathered together in groups. Each one started to look at the others and to want to be looked at himself, and public esteem acquired a value" [*OC*, p. 169]). The invention of these performers, audiences, and displays of beauty and talent constitutes the first step toward inequality, according to Rousseau, and is soon followed by vanity, shame, contempt, and envy. Such an elevation of talents and personal qualities (over power and property, for example) is also seen to turn people into actors: "ces qualitiés étant les seules qui pouvoient attirer de la considération, il fallut bientôt les avoir ou les affecter; il fallut pour son avantage se montrer autre que ce qu'on étoit en effect. Etre et paroître devinrent deux choses tout à fait différentes" ("these qualities being the only ones which could attract consideration, it soon became necessary either to possess them or to affect them; it was necessary, for one's own advantage, to show oneself to be other than one in fact was. To be and to seem to be became two completely different things" [*OC*, p. 174]).

Rousseau's illustrations are carefully chosen to serve as both specific examples and more general emblems. Consequently, it is not so much the assembly of people singing and dancing for each other that is theatrical, although this is a literal instance of theater; what Rousseau is focusing on here is the exchange of regards, the awareness of others as beholders, that creates a theatrical consciousness. Rousseau's indictment of the acting and posing that develop in society is not limited to a denunciation of deception, hypocrisy, or false representation. People become actors—and this acting is problematic—from the moment they are aware that they must represent themselves for others. The "representative signs [signes représentatifs] of wealth" (*OC*, p. 175), for example, are not necessarily false; people become actors the moment they imagine what eighteenth-century English writers referred to as the eyes of the world. For Rousseau, there is as much danger in *se montrer* (showing oneself) as there is in *se montrer autre que ce qu'on est* (showing oneself to be other than one is). Those for whom "the gaze of the rest of the universe [les regards du reste de l'univers] counts for something, who are happy and content with themselves according to the testimony of others [le témoignage d'autrui] rather than their own" (*OC*, p. 193), seem to depend on those they imagine as eyewitnesses for their very being. Anticipating his own indictment of stage actors, as well as Sartre's critique of theatrical self-consciousness, Rousseau writes: "le Sauvage vit en lui-même; l'homme sociable, toujours hors de lui, ne sait vivre que dans l'opinion des autres; et c'est, pour ainsi dire, de leur seul jugement qu'il tire le sentiment de sa propre existence" ("the savage lives within himself; sociable man, always outside of himself, knows how to live only in the opinion of others; and it is, so to speak, only from their judgment that he derives the sentiment of his own existence" [*OC*, p. 193]). He concludes that a universal desire for reputation and distinction is responsible for what is best and worst in society. For better or for worse, however, the development of *amour-propre* and of the social relations that accompany it is seen as a theatrical problem.

Theater, then, in Rousseau's descriptions, represents the fall from the state of nature. The story of this fall and the rise of a society governed by *amour-propre* is told in part as if it were a story about the invention or establishment of theater. The rise of a theatrical perspective turns people into actors and encourages them to make spectacles of themselves; it also weakens the natural bonds between people by turning them into spectators. Rousseau describes in the second *Discours* how philosophy and reason isolate people and replace sympathy and commiseration with *amour-propre*: man is taught to say "at the sight of a suffering man: 'Perish if you wish; I am safe.' No longer do any dangers (except those that threaten all of society) trouble the tranquil sleep of the philosopher or pull him from his bed. One may cut the throat of his fellow man [son semblable] beneath his very window with impunity; he has only to cover his ears with his hands and argue with himself a little, to prevent nature, which revolts within him, from identifying with the man being murdered" (*OC*, p. 156).

This description of the ability to view someone suffering from a distance, through a frame, is throughout eighteenth-century aesthetics and moral philosophy a major figure for a theatrical perspective. Writers such as Hume, Smith, Du Bos, and Rousseau himself (in the *Lettre à d'Alembert*) tried to explain the paradox that audiences received pleasure from viewing representations of suffering in paintings or on the stage. As I have argued, Lucretius's description in *De Rerum Natura* of the pleasure of watching a shipwreck from a position of safety becomes a paradigm in the eighteenth century for the aesthetic experience of watching someone suffering from a position of distance and nonidentification.[6] Thus, in condemning the lesson of difference and indifference supposedly taught by philosophy, Rousseau is condemning a point of view that allows people to look at others from the position of an audience, through a distancing frame that is associated with the theater. Theater in its literal manifestation represents or figures the theatrical relations formed between self and others that Rousseau denounces in society. In Rousseau's view, society is theater and what goes on in the playhouse between actors and audience mirrors the more dangerous theater that society has become.

These are the terms in which Rousseau casts his critique of both theater and "social man" in the *Lettre à d'Alembert sur les spectacles*. If Geneva bears some resemblance to the more pleasant aspects of the state of nature in Rousseau's nostalgic and pastoral descriptions, this is partly because Rousseau highlights Geneva's untheatrical characteristics. Unlike the social and cosmopolitan citydwellers who seek reputation and the regard of others, the "true genius" Rousseau associates with Geneva and small towns "is unaware of the path of honors and fortune, and does not even think of looking for it; he compares himself to no one [il ne se compare à personne]" (*L*, p. 170). The Genevan seems to escape having the "relative self" Rousseau associates with *amour-propre*. "Imagine that as soon as vanity [amour-propre] is developed," writes Rousseau in the *Émile*, "le *moi* relatif se met en jeu sans cesse, et que jamais le jeune homme n'observe les autres sans revenir sur lui-même et se comparer avec eux" ("the relative self comes constantly into play, and the young man never observes others without coming back to himself and comparing himself to them" [*E*, p. 290]). Like the *homme sauvage*, the Genevan in Rousseau's portrait does not seem to depend on the regard of others for a sense of his own existence. His economic autonomy is analogous to the autonomy of his self: "all his resources are in himself alone" (*L*, p. 170).

Like the inhabitants of the state of nature, the inhabitants of Geneva seem to live in themselves more than in others. "Si nos habitudes naissent de nos propres sentiments dans la retraite," writes Rousseau, "elles naissent de l'opinion d'autrui dans la société. Quand on ne vit pas en soi, mais dans les autres, ce sont leurs jugements qui règlent tout" ("If our habits in a retired life arise from our own sentiments, in society they arise from the opinion of others. When one does not live within oneself, but in others, their judgments rule everything" [L, p. 176]). In large cities, according to Rousseau, this concern for the eyes of the world turns people into actors. "L'homme du monde est tout entier dans son masque" ("The man of the world is completely in his mask"), he writes in the *Émile*; "N'étant presque jamais en lui-même, il y est toujours étranger.... Ce qu'il est n'est rien, ce qu'il paraît est tout pour lui" ("Almost never in himself, he is always a stranger to himself.... What he is, is nothing; that which he seems is everything for him" [E, p. 271]). This dislocation and loss of self occurs in both men and women in Rousseau's view. In large cities, he writes in *La Nouvelle Héloïse*, "men become other than they are, and ... society gives them so to speak a being that is different from their own." Women in particular, he continues, "derive the only existence they care for from the regard of others [des regards d'autrui]. When approaching a lady at a gathering [assemblée], instead of the Parisian woman you think you see, you see only a simulacrum of the current fashion [un simulacre de la mode]" (NH, p. 251).[7]

Theater, in Rousseau's view, does more than mirror the theatrical representations and relations of cosmopolitan life. It reproduces these representations and relations outside as well as inside the playhouse. Theater is especially dangerous for women, according to Rousseau, because it plays on their already theatricalized character. Despite his condemnation of Parisian women who, he says, "derive the only existence they care for from the regard of others [des regards d'autrui]" (NH, p. 251), Rousseau insists in the *Émile* that "woman is specially made to please men" and that "a woman's conduct is subjugated to public opinion" (E, pp. 446, 473). In addition to using her arts to disguise her thoughts and desires, a woman (in Rousseau's terms) seems condemned to living outside of herself, in the regards and judgments of others. Like the actor who becomes "le jouet des spectateurs" ("the plaything of the spectators" [L, p. 187]), the little girl who plays with her doll "attend le moment d'être sa poupée elle-même" ("awaits the moment when she herself will be her doll" [E, p. 459]). Once on the stage, then, women seem unbearably theatrical as they double what Rousseau sees as their inherent dissimulation, *amour-propre*, and exhibitionism.

Actresses are singled out in the *Lettre à d'Alembert sur les spectacles* for an especially vitriolic attack; Rousseau condemns "un état dont l'unique objet est de se montrer en public, et qui pis est, de se montrer pour de l'argent" ("a state in which the sole object is to show oneself in public, and what is worse, to show oneself for money" [L, p. 195]). Yet this condemnation also extends to the women who expose themselves as spectators in the "exposition des dames et demoiselles parées tout de leur mieux et mises en étalage dans les loges comme sur le devant d'une boutique, en attendant les acheteurs" ("exhibition of married ladies and young girls dressed in their best and arranged in their boxes as in a shop window, waiting for purchasers" [L, p. 212]). According to Rousseau, women who enter the theater must enter theater; spectators become spectacles who are caught up in the "traffic de soi-même" ("traffic of the self" [L, p. 186]) that characterizes the actor's profession.[8]

This kind of theatricalization, Rousseau argues, would be the fate of women in Geneva if a theater were established. "Les femmes des Montagnons," he writes, "allant d'abord pour voir, et ensuite pour être vues, voudront être parées" ("The women [wives] of the Montagnons, going first to see, and then to be seen, would want to be elegantly dressed"); they would want to distinguish themselves and "se montrer au spectacle" (L, p. 173), which is to say, they would want to show themselves *en spectacle*, as spectacles. At this point, it seems, a woman already would be lost: "rechercher les regards des hommes c'est déjà s'en laisser corrompre.... toute femme qui se montre se déshonore" ("to seek men's looks is already to let oneself be corrupted by them.... every woman who shows herself dishonors herself" [L, p. 189]). To show oneself is to dishonor oneself. This seems to apply to men as well as women. Rousseau notes that "un ouvrier ne va point dans une assemblée se montrer en habit de travail; il faut prendre ses habits des dimanches" ("a working man does not go to a gathering to show himself in his work clothes; he must wear his Sunday best" [L, pp. 172–73). Rousseau is concerned about the economic and moral consequences in a Geneva suddenly preoccupied with clothing, ornament, display, appearance, distinction. What would be most dangerous, however, would be the mere desire of the relatively untheatrical Genevans to show themselves; making them spectators would threaten to transform them into spectacles and actors.

What is at stake in the *Lettre à d'Alembert sur les spectacles* is less the presence of a theater in Geneva than the possibility of Geneva as theater. Rousseau argues that d'Alembert's proposal to establish a "théâtre de comédie en Genève" would make a theater of Geneva. Theater would threaten to transform Geneva into Paris, to change it from a modern-day state of nature to a theatrical society in which not just the actors and actresses but all citizens would be condemned to exist in the regard of others. Theater would reproduce itself off the stage by drawing spectators into theatrical positions and by promoting the internalization in individual consciousnesses of the theatrical relations that in Rousseau's view characterize social life.

We saw that Rousseau condemned philosophy and reason for teaching a theatrical perspective that (in effect) promoted distance, indifference, and isolation. Theater is especially dangerous, according to Rousseau, because its business is to present and represent this theatrical perspective. It teaches people how to become spectators, how to act like spectators. "L'on croit s'assembler au spectacle, et c'est là que chacun s'isole" ("We think that we come together in the theater, but it is there that we isolate ourselves" [L, p. 134]) asserts Rousseau in a declaration that might stand for much of the argument of the *Lettre* in the way that the aphoristic "Man is born free, and everywhere he is in chains" has come to stand for the *Contrat social* (*OC*, p. 351). Both the *Contrat social* and the *Essai sur l'origine des langues* emphasize the importance of assemblies in social and political life.[9] Theater represents a perversion of the gatherings that brought people together in antiquity. Unlike those "assemblés en plein air" ("open air assemblies" [O, p. 496]), the spectacles of the playhouse "renferment tristement un petit nombre de gens dans un antre obscur" ("sadly close up a small number of people in a dark cavern"); there, the spectators are kept "craintifs et immobiles dans le silence et l'inaction" ("fearful and immobile in silence and inaction" [L, p. 224]).

The problem is not merely that spectators are powerless to act or that they are not called upon to act. Rousseau claims that theater teaches them how not to act. He asks how audiences are able to tolerate the tableaux of Greek tragedy, insisting that "les massacres des gladiateurs n'étaient pas si barbares que ces affreux spectacles. On voyoit couler du sang, il est vrai; mais on ne souilloit pas son imagination de crimes qui font frémir la nature" ("the massacres of the gladiators were not as barbarous as these frightful spectacles. One saw blood flow, it is true, but one did not soil one's imagination with crimes at which nature shudders" [L, p. 148]). One of the answers Rousseau suggests to this question is that "tout ce qu'on met en représentation au théâtre, on ne l'approche pas de nous, on l'éloigne" ("everything that is represented at the theater is not brought closer to us but rather placed at a distance" [L, p. 141]). Other eighteenth-century theoreticians of sympathy (such as Du Bos and Adam Smith) imagine a weak or secondary sympathy occurring in the minds and hearts of audiences. Rousseau claims that we are taught to respond in the theater with a kind of false sympathy, "a sterile pity" that is "transitory and vain" (L, p. 140) and somehow too pure and abstract to mean very much to us. Arguing against the defenders of the stage who evoke catharsis and speak of the moral and sentimental education of audiences, Rousseau insists that the theater teaches us how to replace real sympathy with a painless representation or imitation of sympathy. This occurs not so much through an aestheticization of other people's suffering as through a false sense that one has fulfilled one's responsibilities toward others by responding in the playhouse:

> En donnant des pleurs à ces fictions, nous avons satisfait à tous les droits de l'humanité, sans avoir plus rien à mettre du nôtre.... Au fond, quand un homme est allé admirer de belles actions dans des fables et pleurer des malheurs imaginaires, qu'a-t-on encore à exiger de lui? N'est-il pas content de lui-même? ... Ne s'est-il pas acquitté de tout ce qu'il doit à la vertu par l'hommage qu'il vient de lui rendre? Que voudroit-on qu'il fît de plus? ... il n'a point de rôle à jouer: il n'est pas comédien. (L, p. 141)

> In shedding our tears for these fictions, we have satisfied all the claims of humanity, without having to give any more of ourselves.... Finally, when a man has gone to admire fine actions in fables, and to weep over imaginary misfortunes, what more can one demand of him? ... Has he not acquitted himself of all he owes to virtue by the homage he has just rendered it? What more would one have him do? ... he has no role to play: he is not an actor.

Passages such as this one should make us aware of the inadequacy of merely assigning the *Lettre à d'Alembert* to a tradition of conservative antitheatrical polemics. In presenting a critique of theatricality (a critical investigation of what it means to face others as a spectator or a spectacle) Rousseau goes beyond the standard warnings about how plays arouse passions and incite their audiences to commit moral crimes. He offers a more radical analysis of the pathos, subjectivity, and sympathy that take place in the playhouse—an analysis that anticipates the critique Brecht would direct against the liberal, bourgeois theater he inherited from the eighteenth century.[10] Brecht, of course, thought there was too much identification and empathy in modern audiences, not too little. Yet he shared with Rousseau the conviction that the emotions exchanged and experienced in the playhouse served to release people from a responsibility for action and analysis. Both Brecht and Rousseau objected to the self-congratulatory sympathy that turns people into passive spectators both inside and outside of the theater. Action inside the playhouse seems to substitute for action in social and political life. Rousseau complains that the great sentiments celebrated in plays are relegated forever to the stage; virtue becomes "un jeu de théâtre" which is "bon pour amuser le public, mais qu'il y auroit de la folie à vouloir transporter sérieusement dans la société" ("a game of the theater . . . good for amusing the public, but which it would be madness to wish to see seriously transported into society" [L, p. 142]).

Furthermore, as if anticipating the Kantian tradition of disinterested and purposeless art (against which Brecht would oppose his didactic and political epic theater), Rousseau raises the question of utility: "Ces productions d'esprit . . . n'ont pour but que les applaudissements. . . . l'on n'y cherche point d'autre utilité" ("these productions of the mind . . . have no other aim but applause. . . . and one looks for no other utility in them" [L, p. 143]). Unlike Brecht, however, Rousseau is not interested in reforming or radicalizing the theater. The only theater Rousseau can imagine stands condemned for the failure of sympathy it institutionalizes. All it can teach (aside from the dissimulation and self-display exhibited by those who show themselves to the eyes of the world) is the false sympathy that allows people to think they have no role to play in the scenes and dramas around them. Paradoxically, this also turns the world to theater.

The Lettre à d'Alembert sur les spectacles indicts spectators for their ultimate failure of sympathy; it condemns the theatrical perspective that turns others into spectacles by substituting distance and isolation for the identification between semblables that is supposed to take place in the state of nature. In his analysis of these situations, Rousseau insists that the spectator has a role to play. But what would it mean to play a role, inside or outside the playhouse, and how would this role differ from the exhibitionism, imitation, posing, and living in others that Rousseau condemns in both actors and spectators? To answer these questions, we need to return to Rousseau's characterization of the actor. Following the standard accusations of the antitheatrical tradition, Rousseau charges the actor with counterfeiting, with appearing to be different than he really is, and deception (although he admits that while encouraging deception, the actor himself is not exactly "un trompeur" ["a deceiver"]). He calls attention to the shame of having to "faire aux yeux du public un rôle différent du vôtre" ("take on a role different from your own before the eyes of the public"), contrasting the actor with the orator who shows himself only "pour parler, et non pour se donner en spectacle" ("to speak, and not to make a spectacle of himself" [*L*, pp. 186–87]).

Rousseau also follows tradition in comparing the actor to a prostitute. However, the *traffic de soi-même* that disconcerts Rousseau the most is metaphysical rather than physical and commercial. The usual moral issues such as the deception or corruption of actors seem to concern Rousseau less than the loss of self that appears to take place in the actors themselves. The orator, claims Rousseau, "ne représente que lui-même, il ne fait que son propre rôle ... l'homme et le personnage étant le même être, il est à sa place" ("represents only himself, he acts his own role only ... the man and the character being the same, he is in his place"). The actor, in contrast, must "oublier enfin sa propre place à force de prendre celle d'autrui" ("finally forget his own place after having taken the place of someone else"); "représentant souvent un être chimérique," the actor "s'anéantit, pour ainsi dire, s'annule avec son héros" ("often representing a chimerical being," the actor "annihilates himself, so to speak, annuls himself in his hero"). For Rousseau, the actor's art amounts to an "oubli de l'homme" ("a forgetting of the man" [*L*, p. 186–87]).

What is at stake, then, is nothing less than the self-annihilation of the actor. Indeed, as we have seen, Rousseau's fears about the theater are not limited to professional actors. Rousseau also worries about self-forgetting and self-alienation in his characterizations of the theatrical aspects of women, social man, cosmopolitan life, and *amour-propre*. In the *Lettre*, he speaks of the "oubli d'eux-mêmes" ("forgetting of themselves" [*L*, p. 190]) that makes lovers vulnerable and he warns that if the Genevan attended the theater he would begin to "s'oublier soi-même et s'occuper d'objets étrangers" ("forget himself and occupy himself with foreign objects" [*L*, p. 168]). According to Rousseau, self-forgetting follows self-estrangement, trying to be other than one really is: "celui qui commence à se rendre étranger à lui-même ne tarde pas à s'oublier tout à fait" ("he who begins to be estranged from himself soon forgets himself completely" [*E*, p, 290]); and this self-estrangement is associated with leaving the self. The man of the world, for example, is reduced to nothing ("rien") because he leaves the self for a foreign state: "N'étant presque jamais en lui-même, il y est toujours étranger, et mal à son aise quand il est forcé d'y rentrer" ("Almost never existing within himself, he is always a stranger there, and ill at ease when forced to return" [*E*, p. 271]).

In all of these descriptions, Rousseau is preoccupied with the transport outside of the self that accompanies (or constitutes) self-forgetting. These characterizations go beyond Rousseau's descriptions of those who live in and for the opinion of others. Writing of those who practice imitation to "trick others [imposer aux autres] or to get applause for their talent," Rousseau asserts: "Imitation among us is based on the desire always to transport ourselves outside ourselves [se transporter toujours hors de soi]" (*E*, p. 99). His critique of *amour-propre* is based on the claim that social man is "always outside of himself [toujours hors de lui]"; the search for a reputation, according to Rousseau, "takes us almost always outside of ourselves [hors de nous-mêmes]" (*OC*, pp. 193, 189). In fact, following the *renvoi* of an endnote to the discussion of self-knowledge that begins the preface to the second *Discours*, one could argue that the hidden epigraph to the *Discours* is a passage from *L'Histoire naturelle de l'homme* in which Buffon asks why we "seek only to extend beyond ourselves, and exist outside ourselves [exister hors de nous]" (*OC*, p. 195).[11] A theatrical consciousness, whether on the stage or in society, seems to threaten the integrity of the self by taking people outside of themselves. The transport outside of the self that occurs in these acts of imitation, *amour-propre*, self-display, and representation seems to cause the actor to forget his own place and person, to leave himself behind.[12]

Rousseau's characterizations of the state and state of mind of the actor—in particular, his account of the self-annihilation caused by a transport outside of the self—present us with a paradox in Rousseau's conception of the roles of actor and spectator. Although spectators are condemned for lacking genuine sympathy, it appears that the actor is condemned precisely because he is sympathetic. The problem with the actor is that he exhibits and performs acts of sympathy; he almost embodies sympathy. According to Rousseau's characterizations, the actor forgets his own place and takes the place of someone else; he forgets his own identity in an act of identification that carries him outside of himself. These terms are precisely the terms with which Rousseau and his contemporaries defined sympathy. For moral philosophers, aestheticians, novelists, and protopsychologists in the eighteenth century, sympathy was an act of identification in which one left one's own place, part, and person and took the place and part of someone else; while representing to oneself the other's feelings, one was transported outside of the self: placed beyond or beside the self in a moment of self-forgetting.

Rousseau agrees that this is what happens to spectators who accept that they have a role to play when faced with a scene that demands their sympathy. In the second *Discours*, for example, he writes that commiseration is "a sentiment which puts us in the place of the one who suffers"; it depends on an act of identification, even in animals: "the commiseration will be that much more energetic as the observing animal [l'animal Spectateur] identifies itself with the suffering animal" (*OC*, p. 155). In the *Essai sur l'origine des langues*, Rousseau asks: "Comment nous laissons-nous émouvoir à la pitié?" ("How do we let ourselves be moved to pity?"), and he answers: "en nous transportant hors de nous-mêmes; en nous identifiant avec l'être souffrant" ("by transporting ourselves outside of ourselves, by identifying ourselves with the being who suffers" [*O*, p. 446]).

A similar description of pity occurs in the *Émile*: "comment nous laissons-nous émouvoir à la pitié, si ce n'est en nous transportant hors de nous, en nous identifiant avec l'animal souffrant, en quittant, pour ainsi dire, notre être pour prendre le sien?" ("how do we let ourselves be moved to pity, if not by transporting ourselves out of ourselves, by identifying with the suffering animal, by leaving our own being, so to speak, to take on its being?"). He continues: "Ainsi nul ne devient sensible que quand son imagination s'anime et commence à le transporter hors de lui" ("Thus one achieves sensibility only when his imagination is animated and starts to transport him outside of himself"). When we feel pity, writes Rousseau, we experience "cet état de force qui nous étend au délà de nous" ("that state of strength that extends us beyond ourselves" [*E*, pp. 261, 270]). Rousseau joined other theoreticians of sympathy in countering Hobbes's claim that sympathy was selfish rather than altruistic (since we imagine ourselves suffering, for example, not someone else) by insisting that we leave ourselves behind, so to speak, and become the other person.[13] In both the *Essai sur l'origine des langues* and the *Émile*, Rousseau writes: "Ce n'est pas dans nous, c'est dans lui que nous souffrons" ("It's not in ourselves but in him that we suffer" [*O*, p. 446; *E*, p. 261]). Thus, according to Rousseau's depictions of these parts, persons, and positions, while the orator might remain "in his place," the actor *and* the sympathetic spectator each must "oublier enfin sa propre place à force de prendre celle d'autrui" ("finally forget his own place after taking that of others" [*L*, p. 186]). Actors must act with sympathy and spectators should act like actors.

Rousseau's identification of acting and sympathy takes place within a long tradition of portraying the actor (and the author) as the epitome of sympathetic imagination.[14] Indeed, Rousseau's basic premise about the actor's art of sympathetic identification would not have been disputed by most actors or advocates of the stage in the first half of the eighteenth century. Diderot's argument in his *Paradoxe sur le comédien* that the best actor would not feel or become his part but rather coolly exhibit the exterior signs and symptoms of feelings was directed against prevalent theories of acting and poetic imagination that date back at least as far as the *Ion*.[15] Jonas Barish situates Rousseau in this context and remarks that Rousseau, in not rejecting the "sensibilist" or "emotionalist" view of acting as Diderot did, "is guilty of perpetuating an old confusion which others in his day were beginning finally to disentangle."[16] What interests me here, however, is that having accepted and elaborated contemporary beliefs about the experiences of sympathy and acting, Rousseau is in the position of condemning actors for possessing what he condemns spectators for lacking.

Theater is dangerous for Rousseau because it teaches people how to avoid sympathy: it completes the lesson of philosophy and reason by creating a theatrical perspective that inhibits acts of identification and fellow feeling, by substituting a simulacrum of sympathy for actual human interaction, and by promoting *amour-propre* among both actors and audiences. Theater is also dangerous for actors because in transporting them outside of themselves from their own place to the place of someone else, in making them forget themselves and take on the point of view of someone else, it threatens them with self-annihilation. However, as we have seen, this self-annihilation and transport out of the self feels remarkably similar to sympathy; indeed, the actor's role is to sympathize. This suggests that sympathy, too, may be dangerous; it too may threaten to annihilate the self. Rousseau's paradoxical portrayal of the actor should lead us to revise our understanding of Rousseau's indictment of theater and theatrical relations. To do this, we need to consider two questions: one concerns the opposition between sympathy and *amour-propre*; the other concerns Rousseau's sympathy with the actor.

We have seen that Rousseau's depictions of the state of nature suggest that the performances and self-displays of *amour-propre* and the theatrical perspective of philosophy and reason are partly responsible for the decline of sympathy and the fall from that primitive state into society. We are now in a position to see that Rousseau's representations of the primitive relations between self and other suggest that sympathy and *amour-propre* have disturbing similarities for him. According to Rousseau's analysis in the *Discours sur l'origine et les fondements de l'inégalité parmi les hommes*, the savage man is not afflicted with *amour-propre* since *amour-propre* has its source in "comparisons that he is not inclined to make." Regarding himself as his only spectator, and regarding his "semblables" or fellow beings as if they were "animals of another species," he can neither "appraise himself" nor "compare himself" (*OC*, p. 219). He cannot wish to distinguish himself in the eyes of other people because he imagines that he is alone. The *moi relatif* of *amour-propre* is set in play when he observes other people in order to "compare himself to them" (*E*, p. 291). Like the true genius that ignores reputation because it "compares itself to no one" (*L*, p. 170), savage man is untheatrical because he has no one with whom he can compare himself. Other people strike him as giants, not humans, suggests Rousseau in the *Essai sur l'origine des langues*: "Ils avoient l'idée d'un père, d'un fils, d'un frère, et non pas d'un homme. Leur cabane contenoit tous leurs semblables; un étranger, une bête, un monstre, étoient pour eux la même chose" ("They had the idea of a father, a son, a brother, but not of a man. Their hut contained all their fellow beings; a stranger, a beast, a monster, were for them the same thing" [*O*, p. 447]).

At the same time, however, Rousseau argues that pity cannot take place in this primitive condition. Sympathy or fellow feeling also depends on an act of comparison: a moment of identification in which one compares oneself to another and recognizes a *semblable* rather than a giant, a monster, or an animal of another species. After stating that pity depends on a transport out of the self in an act of identification, Rousseau adds, "How could I suffer when seeing another suffer, if I did not even know that he suffers, if I were unaware of what he and I have in common?" (*O*, p. 446). Sympathy is impossible without some kind of identification. In order to pity someone, we must see the person as our *semblable*, imagine the person as a reflection of ourselves rather than an other. "To become capable of sensibility and pity [devenir sensible et pitoyable]," writes Rousseau in the *Émile*, "the child must know that there are beings like himself [êtres semblables à lui] who suffer what he has suffered" (*E*, p. 261). What happens in the moment of comparison of self with other that teaches one that one is not alone?

In his dramatizations of the passage from the state of nature to society, Rousseau implies a sketchy chronology. At first, it seems, primitive people do not recognize each other as *semblables*; but then, with an act of comparison which identifies the other as someone with whom one shares something in common, comes a moment of imagination in which one transports oneself outside of oneself and identifies with the other. This moment of simultaneous imagination, comparison, recognition, transport, and identification does not so much allow sympathy as constitute it. However, this act of comparison in which one leaves oneself and enters into the sentiments of someone else, this moment of recognition that one is not alone in the world and thus not one's only spectator, is also the moment when *amour-propre* is made possible and inevitable. *Amour-propre* seems to follow sympathy in Rousseau's scheme since its theatrical relations threaten the apparently natural bonds of fellow feeling. Yet sympathy and *amour-propre* both are born in the moment the self compares itself with others. Each is structured by an act of identification through which one transports oneself to someone else's place, a comparison of the self with an other turned *semblable* in which one forgets oneself and imagines the point of view of the other. In this sense, both sympathy and *amour-propre* are inherently theatrical relations, structured by an exchange between a spectator and a spectacle, dependent on acts of acting. Rousseau's own terms suggest that the state of nature is always already theatrical.

It is not surprising, then, that it is sometimes difficult to tell the difference between sympathy and *amour-propre*. In an early version of the beginning of his *Confessions*, Rousseau speculates on the need to compare oneself with others in order to know both others and oneself; he worries, however, that such comparisons must be based on an imperfect knowledge of oneself. "On se fait la règle de tout" ("One makes oneself the measure of all things"), writes Rousseau, defining this dilemma as "la double illusion de l'amour-propre: soit en prêtant faussement à ceux que nous jugeons les motifs qui nous auraient fait agir comme eux à leur place; soit, dans cette supposition même, en nous abusant sur nos propres motifs, faute de savoir nous transporter assez dans une autre situation que celle où nous sommes" ("the double illusion of self-love: either in falsely ascribing to those we judge the motives which would have made us act like them in their place, or, in this very assumption, deceiving ourselves about our own motives, not knowing how to transport ourselves sufficiently into a situation different from our own" [*C*, p. 786]). At the moment when one is supposed to be entering into someone else's sentiments, one might be guilty of *amour-propre*, which here amounts to a double failure of sympathy: as Hobbes and Mandeville warned, one might only imagine oneself, not the other; and furthermore, one might even lack the sympathy and imagination to imagine oneself in a different situation. In an act of comparison one sees the other as a *semblable;* but what does it mean to look at the other and see a reflection of oneself? How does one know whether one sees oneself or the other in the mirror of comparison?

The breakdown of Rousseau's distinctions between sympathy and *amour-propre*, along with the breakdown of the temporal scheme in his dramatization of these relations, helps to account for (if not explain) the apparent contradiction in Rousseau's claims about the role of reflection: his assertion in the *Essai sur l'origine des langues* that pity depends on reflection ("He who has never reflected [réfléchi] can be neither merciful nor just, nor capable of pity" [*O*, p. 446]) and his insistence in the *Discours* that pity precedes "the use of all reflection," that it operates "without reflection," that reflection contributes to *amour-propre* (*OC*, pp. 154, 156).[17] What is at issue in both of Rousseau's claims about reflection is the moment of comparison that appears to constitute both pity and *amour-propre*. "La réflexion naît des idées comparées" ("Reflection comes from the comparison of ideas" [*O*, p. 446), writes Rousseau in the *Essai*, insisting that we must compare ourselves with others to recognize them as our *semblables*. Yet "la réflexion," which strengthens *amour-propre*, "turns man back on himself; it is what separates him from everything that disturbs and afflicts him" (*OC*, p. 156).

Comparison teaches one about one's difference from others; it also allows one to turn one's back on others because it turns one back on oneself. The double illusion of *amour-propre* turns one into a spectacle for others and a spectacle to oneself. The moment of comparison creates the double reflection through which one becomes both a spectator to one's *semblable* and a spectacle for one's *semblables* and oneself—although part of the vertigo of these double illusions is that one might be looking in the mirror of *amour-propre* precisely at the moment one thought one was looking in the mirror of sympathy. The theatrical structure of these relations creates mirror images of reflection: the act of comparison of the self with an other who appears as a *semblable* (that is, pity) and the act of comparison of the self with a *semblable* who appears as an other (that is, *amour-propre*). The reflection of sympathy is always in danger of being or becoming the reflection of *amour-propre* since sympathy and *amour-propre* appear as mirror images of each other.

In book 2 of the *Confessions*, Rousseau tells a story about a mirror that seems to mediate between the vertiginous terms we see set in play in his descriptions of sympathy and *amour-propre*. The mirror is at the center of a "lively and mute scene [scène vive et muette]" (*C*, p. 82) that is enacted by the young Rousseau and Mme Basile. Rousseau sets the stage for this scene by describing how he liked to watch Mme Basile secretly—"With an avid eye I devoured all that I could look at without being seen"—but, he adds, "je voyais quelquefois, par une sorte de sympathie, son fichu se renfler assez frequémment" ("I sometimes saw the lace on her bosom rise rather frequently, by a sort of sympathy"). This "dangereux spectacle," he continues, "achevait de me perdre, et quand j'étais prêt à céder à mon transport, elle m'addressait quelque mot ... qui me faisait rentrer en moi-même à l'instant" ("finally undid me, and just as I was ready to succumb to my transports, she spoke a word to me ... which instantly brought me back to myself"). Standing as an unseen spectator, Rousseau loses himself and leaves himself—he seems to be transported outside of himself—when faced with a dangerous spectacle of sympathy. This is the scenario in the scene with the mirror. Once again, Rousseau describes himself as an unseen spectator ("I entered unobserved"), this time before the sight of Mme Basile embroidering next to a window. Once again, he describes the spectacle taking him outside of himself: "Il régnait dans toute sa figure un charme ... qui me mit hors de moi" ("A charm prevailed throughout her figure ... which put me beside myself"). This time, however, a mirror unexpectedly transforms Rousseau from an unseen spectator to the spectacle of the scene: "il y avait à la cheminée une glace qui me trahit. Je ne sais quel effet ce transport fit sur elle" ("above the mantel there was a mirror which betrayed me. I do not know what effect that transport had on her" [C, pp. 80–81]).

What does Rousseau mean by *ce transport?* Is he referring to the transport that characterizes sympathy, the transport that took him outside of himself and made him lose himself when he witnessed the dangerous spectacle of her sympathy? Or is he referring to the transport that carried him out of himself and projected him into the mirror: the transport of his reflection? (In the *Lettre sur les aveugles*, Diderot reports this explanation from a blind man: "a mirror is a machine that places us in relief outside of ourselves.")[18] On this occasion, upon witnessing Rousseau's transport in the mirror, Mme Basile does not make him "rentrer en moi-même" ("come back to myself"). Instead, without saying a word, she motions him to her feet with a gesture that Rousseau describes as "un signe parti sans doute avant la réflexion" ("a sign given, no doubt, before any reflection"). There, writes Rousseau, "toute ma bêtise ne m'empêchait pas de juger qu'elle partageait mon embarras, peut-être mes désirs, et qu'elle était retenue par une honte semblable à la mienne" ("all my stupidity could not prevent me from determining that she shared my embarrassment, and perhaps my desires, and that she was held back by a shame similar to my own" [C, p. 81]). This is the effect of sympathy.

The sign she makes on seeing the reflection of his transport (or the reflection that is his transport) is made *avant la réflexion*; it allows Rousseau to see (or imagine that he sees) that she shares feelings that are *semblable* to his own. We do not know if Rousseau discovers his own reflection in the mirror, or if he can see Mme Basile's reflection at the moment she discovers his transport in the mirror; but we know that at this moment he sees Mme Basile as his reflection. Her sympathetic response *avant la réflexion*, the moment of transport and identification, occurs in the moment that Rousseau is mirrored. It occurs, as it were, in the mirror; and this moment of recognition turns Mme Basile into Rousseau's mirror—unless, of course, he suffers from the double illusion of *amour-propre* and only projects onto her his own feelings. However, whether or not Mme Basile mirrors Rousseau by becoming a spectacle of sympathy, a reflection of shared and analogous feelings, she mirrors Rousseau by becoming the unseen spectator to the spectacle of his transport out of himself.

The moment of identification between spectator and spectacle turns Rousseau into an actor and presents him with an image of himself as he is seen by an other. We can see, then, that the mirror and the mirroring that appear in this scene (both *avant la réflexion* and in the moment of reflection, comparison, and identification) themselves mirror the complex crossing of sympathy and *amour-propre* in Rousseau's thought. Within the retrospective reflection of the autobiographical account in which Rousseau presents an image of himself in order to receive the reader's sympathy, the mirror becomes a metaphor (through the *transport* of figurative language) for the double reflection that contains both sympathy and *amour-propre*.[19]

It is not surprising that the oscillation of Rousseau's oppositions between actor and spectator, *amour-propre* and sympathy, theatrical society and untheatrical state of nature, should lead us from Rousseau's polemic against theatricality to his autobiography. The *Lettre à d'Alembert sur les spectacles* (originally titled *J. J. Rousseau*) itself raises the question of Rousseau's own role in a critique of the theater: his ability to stand outside of the theater as a spectator, his sympathy and identification with the actor. Contemporary responses to the *Lettre* suggested that some of the terms of Rousseau's indictment could be turned against himself.[20] But Rousseau admits (in a footnote in which he acknowledges his love of "comédie," particularly Molière), "I have almost always written against my own interests" (*L*, p. 231). Rousseau's discussions of sympathy, *amour-propre*, and theater show us how complicated interest can be, especially the interest that one takes in someone else; Rousseau asks: "qui de nous est assez sûr de lui pour supporter la représentation d'une pareille comédie sans être de moitié des tours qui s'y jouent? ... Car s'intéresser pour quelqu'un, qu'est-ce autre chose que de se mettre à sa place?" ("who among us is sure enough of himself to bear the performance of such a comedy without halfway taking part in the turns that are played out? ... For is being interested in someone anything other than putting oneself in his place?" [L, p. 159]). The immediate context for Rousseau's questions is the alleged complicity of spectators who witness crimes portrayed on the stage; but we can see now that Rousseau's formulations evoke the act of identification and sympathy by which a spectator becomes an actor. What is Rousseau's interest in the Lettre? To what extent does he take the actor's part, imagine himself in the actor's place, find himself on the stage and thus guilty of the crimes he condemns?

Rousseau's questions about the complicity of putting oneself into someone else's place, and seeing oneself represented on the stage while watching a play, occur at the end of a long digression on Molière's Misanthrope. They help to situate Rousseau's reading of the Misanthrope within the context of his concern with sympathy and identification, especially his own sympathy and identification. Rousseau claims that despite Molière's decision to pander to the public and ridicule his noble protagonist, Alceste is essentially an autobiographical character: "Molière put such a large number of his own maxims into the mouth of Alceste that many have thought that he wanted to paint himself" (L, p. 152). But most critics have observed that it is Rousseau's reading of the play that is autobiographical. Accused of méchanceté for having rejected the society of the Encyclopedists and exiled himself in solitude, Rousseau clearly identifies with the misanthrope. His critique of Molière is a defense of both Alceste and himself.[21]

Rousseau's decision to take the part of Alceste, however, has its source in more than a coincidence of biographical details. Alceste represents (in his own and Rousseau's eyes at least) the most antitheatrical character of the French stage. If Tartuffe is the figure for the actor—in the eighteenth century he becomes the hypocrite hero of Le Paradoxe sur le comédien and Le Neveu de Rameau—then Alceste is a figure for the anti-actor. He claims to reject acting, hypocrisy, and a concern with the regard of his spectators. Of course Rousseau ignores or criticizes Molière's portrayal of Alceste's ultimate hypocrisy: the amour-propre of his honesty, his dependence on the opinion of others, the exhibitionism of his antitheatrical stance. Yet such blindness and denial further illustrate the extent of Rousseau's identification, as well as his need to use theater to defend himself against theater. Rousseau provides a self-portrait of himself as a sympathetic spectator to a play—he shows himself taking the part, person, and place of a character—but this demonstration of sympathy and identification serves to identify him with a dramatic character who rejects the theater. We see Rousseau move from spectator to actor but the transport that turns Alceste into a reflection of Jean-Jacques is meant to reveal Rousseau as a kind of anti-actor. The *Lettre*'s apparent acknowledgment of Rousseau's role as a sympathetic spectator in the theater seems to prescribe a specific reading of his autobiographical interest in actors.

Such a reading might seem necessary in light of Rousseau's resemblance to the actor condemned in the *Lettre à d'Alembert*. Barish rightly calls attention to Rousseau's "instability"—what Barish characterizes as "a craving for irresponsible metamorphosis, a theatrical penchant for allowing himself to be totally transfixed and transformed by the objects of his imagination." He quotes this notorious self-portrait of Rousseau: "In a word, a Proteus, a chameleon, a woman, are all beings who change less than I do."²² The *Confessions* are filled with what Rousseau calls "moments of inconceivable delirium in which I was no longer myself" (*C*, p. 164), moments in which Rousseau changes his identity, or converts, loses, forgets, or returns to himself. While riding in a coach, for example, embarrassed to identify himself as a "new convert," Rousseau suddenly says that he is an Englishman named M. Dudding (*C*, p. 288). In the same episode he speaks of the lack of confidence that "has almost always prevented me from being myself" and then describes his success in love in these terms: "I was no longer the same man" (*C*, pp. 291, 292). Later, after reforming, he writes, "I became another man, or rather I again became the man I had been before" (*C*, p. 301).

Rousseau's characterizations of himself and his acts within the *Lettre à d'Alembert sur les spectacles* also suggest an association between himself and the actor. The description of the actor who "représentant un être chimérique, s'anéantit" ("representing a chimerical being, annihilates himself"), recalls Rousseau's self-portrait in the preface: "En reprenant mon état naturel, je suis rentré dans le néant. . . . vous accueillerez mon ombre; car, pour moi, je ne suis plus" ("In returning to my natural state, I have returned to nothingness. . . . you will receive my shade; as for myself, I am no more" [*L*, pp. 187, 127]). Rousseau's characterization of the placelessness, mobility, and self-annihilation of actors also recalls this description of himself in the draft for the beginning of the *Confessions*: "Being nothing," he writes, "having no state of my own, I have known all states" (*C*, p. 788). The actor's self-annulment is described as "that forgetting of the man," but we have seen that Rousseau also declares in the *Lettre*, "I know then how to forget myself" (*L*, pp. 187, 230). The actor is condemned for his ability to "se passioner de sang-froid" ("become impassioned with sangfroid" [L, p. 186]) but in the first version of the preface to the *Lettre* (later excised) Rousseau writes, "je songe de sang-froid à ce qui m'enflammoit de colère" ("I think with sangfroid about what inflamed my anger").²³ Taken together, these verbal echoes and associations from the *Lettre* and Rousseau's explicitly autobiographical writing suggest that Rousseau does not remain a mere spectator to the theatrical acts condemned in the *Lettre*.

Furthermore, as Michael Fried has noted, Rousseau acknowledges the theatrical aspects of his own role as author of the *Lettre à d'Alembert sur les spectacles*.²⁴ Rousseau not only refers to a mountain covered with houses near Neufchâtel as "a rather aggreeable spectacle" (*L*, p. 170); he writes of his "repugnance in placing my fellow citizens on a stage [sur la scène]" (*L*, p. 197). From the outset of the text, Rousseau insists on the public status of the *Lettre* and the public audience that is destined to be its *destinataire*. For many of Rousseau's contemporaries, including Diderot, the form of the published letter provided a useful fiction with which to deny the public status of the published book and the author's stance before the eyes of the world. But Rousseau insists in the preface that he addresses "a whole people [tout un peuple]. I no longer speak to a few, but rather to the public. . . . Thus I had to change my style in order to make myself better understood by everyone [tout le monde]" (*L*, p. 126). Even in the body of the text, which is occasionally punctuated with an epistolary "Monsieur," Rousseau reminds d'Alembert, "although I address you, I write for the people" (*L*, p. 203).²⁵ Diderot, following the example of Shaftesbury, would have said: "although the public may read this text, I am addressing only you." Rousseau may imagine himself as an orator who inhabits a nontheatrical public space—just as he identified himself with a theatrical character who claims to reject theater—but he still insists on what eighteenth-century readers would have seen as the theatrical character of his book. Rousseau takes responsibility for placing his supposedly untheatrical Genevans on the stage. Despite his attempts to distance himself, Rousseau reminds us that he does not escape from the theatrical relations he deplores in the *Lettre*; this in turn may remind us of our role as spectators to the *Lettre sur les spectacles*.

One more act of identification on Rousseau's part might illuminate both Rousseau's ambivalence and the ambiguous status of theater in the *Lettre à d'Alembert sur les spectacles*. It is easy to see that Rousseau identified himself in the *Lettre* with Lycurgus, the famed legislator of Sparta who, writes Rousseau in the *Considérations sur le gouvernement de Pologne*, "undertook to establish a people who were already degraded by servitude and the vices which are its effects" (*OC*, p. 957).[26] In the *Confessions* Rousseau notes that Plutarch's *Lives* was a regular part of his childhood reading and that in his readings, "I would become one of the characters I imagined" (*C*, p. 43). As Rousseau sets out to reform a corrupt society and prevent Geneva from becoming like Paris rather than like Sparta, he again seems to imagine himself the legislator who created a state resembling the untheatrical state of nature described in the second *Discours*: a state where, according to Plutarch, the redistribution of property eliminated "all inequality and disparity," where wealth was "unenviable, since nobody could make any use or show of it," where the absence of private possessions prevented rivalry, where "all artificial enhancement of beauty" was forbidden, where women learned to "despise the opinion of the crowd," and where the citizens "did not attend either comedy or tragedy."[27] At the end of the *Lettre* Rousseau offers the "Lacedaemonian festivals [fêtes] as a model for those I would like to see among us" (*L*, p. 232), citing a specific example from Plutarch on his last pages. Clearly, Rousseau plays the role of the antitheatrical and (what we would anachronistically call) Puritan lawgiver who rejected a society of *amour-propre* and reformed his people.

However, if we return to Plutarch's accounts of Lycurgus in the *Moralia* and *Lives*, we discover that Lycurgus was attacked by wealthy citizens who were angry at their loss of privilege, and that one of them struck the Spartan leader and blinded him in one eye. According to the story, when Lycurgus showed his countrymen "his face besmeared with blood and his eye destroyed ... they were so filled with shame and sorrow at the sight" that they delivered his assailant to him "with sympathetic indignation."[28] Lycurgus is thus saved from those citizens angry about what Rousseau would have seen as his antitheatrical measures (laws which combat *amour-propre*) by losing half of his sight and simultaneously becoming a moving spectacle. In memory of his misfortune, Plutarch continues, Lycurgus "built a temple to Athena Optilitis, so called from 'optilus,' which is the local Doric word for *eye*."

We can see now that Rousseau writes the controversial *Lettre à d'Alembert sur les spectacles* while playing the part of a hero who built a temple to a newly styled goddess of eyes. What sort of spectacles does this temple represent? Plutarch notes in his *Lives* (although not in the *Sayings of Spartans*) that some writers "say that although Lycurgus was struck in the eye, his eye was not blinded, but he built the temple to the goddess as a thank-offering for its healing."[29] Thus, after being blinded in one eye and becoming a spectacle himself, Lycurgus builds a temple that commemorates either his loss of sight or the healing of his sight. The temple marks either blindness or a renewed sense of seeing, either punishment and censorship or the restoration of spectacles. Neither Plutarch nor Rousseau can resolve this ambiguity. The temple, then, must stand for blindness and sight at once. It is under this double sign of the temple of Athena Optilitis that Rousseau, posing as the priest of this undecidable altar to eyes, must write his *Lettre à d'Alembert sur les spectacles.*

If the oppositions between actor and spectator, *amour-propre* and sympathy, society and state of nature, all appear to break down; if Rousseau's representations of himself suggest that he identifies with the actor and is engaged in the *Lettre* in an autobiographical project; if Rousseau must identify with a character in a play to dramatize his rejection of theater; if Rousseau must acknowledge the theatrical aspects of his own text; then we must ask if theater (in Rousseau's view) can be avoided or escaped at all. If theater cannot be avoided, especially by merely refusing to build a "théâtre de comédie" in Geneva, then what type of theater or spectacle does Rousseau advocate in the *Lettre à d'Alembert sur les spectacles*? If he finally cannot propose to blind the spectators of Geneva, can he offer to heal their sight? Rousseau's antitheatrical polemic does indeed end by advocating spectacles. Can they escape—or defeat—the theatrical relations Rousseau deplores in his various critiques of theater and society?

"Quoi!" exclaims Rousseau in a famous passage toward the end of the *Lettre*, "ne faut-il donc aucun spectacle dans une république? Au contraire, il en faut beaucoup. . . . Mais quels seront enfin les objets de ces spectacles? qu'y montrera-t-on? Rien, si l'on veut. . . . donnez les spectateurs en spectacle; rendez-les acteurs eux-mêmes" ("Ought there to be no spectacles in a republic? On the contrary, there should be many. . . . But what will be the object of these spectacles? What will they show? Nothing, if you please. . . . make the spectators into the spectacle; let them be the actors themselves" [*L*, p. 224–25]). Rousseau proposes public *fêtes* as the proper spectacles for a republic. Modeled after athletic and military contests of the ancients, they would take place "in the open air" (*L*, p. 224), bringing the people together in assemblies rather than isolating them in the dark prison of the playhouse. In addition to proposing these public festivals, Rousseau recounts a childhood memory of a spontaneous *fête*: he recalls the "spectacle" (*L*, p. 232) of soldiers drunkenly dancing in the town square at night, spontaneously joined by their wives and children:

"Bientôt les fenêtres furent pleines de spectatrices qui donnoient un nouveau zèle aux acteurs: elles ne purent tenir longtemps à leurs fenêtres, elles descendirent. ... La danse fut suspendue. ... Il résulta de tout cela un attendrissement général" ("Soon the windows were filled with [female] spectators who gave the actors a new zeal: they could not long remain at their windows and they came down. ... The dance was suspended. ... The result of all this was a general feeling of being moved" [*L*, p. 233]). Rousseau implies that compared to such spectacles staged by and for the people themselves, a "théâtre de comédie" would seem superfluous as well as repugnant.

Various commentators (most importantly Jean Starobinski, Jean Duvignaud, Jacques Derrida, and Jonas Barish)[30] have rightly interpreted these scenes as the dream of the end of theater. The *fêtes* Rousseau describes, in particular the spectacle he recalls from his childhood, seem to use theater to defeat theater. Representation—which Rousseau deplored in political life as well as on the stage—is precluded as people play and stand for themselves only. The distance between spectators and actors seems to disappear as the spectacle moves outside of the playhouse and casts people as actors and spectators simultaneously; the female spectators in Rousseau's memory (who significantly are not the object of sight) leave the windows that frame the dance like a proscenium stage and join the actors. A private, isolating, theatrical spectacle is replaced by a public experience of universal sympathy as "chacun se voie et s'aime dans les autres" ("each sees and loves himself in the others" [*L*, p. 225]). Performance and *amour-propre* appear to have no place.

These festivals do not escape theater. The *fête* described in the fifth part of *La Nouvelle Héloïse*, for example, is presented as if it were a theatrical representation; Rousseau describes: "the veil of mist that the sun raises in the morning like the curtain in a theater in order to reveal to the eye such a charming spectacle: everything conspires to give it the air of a festival." However, unlike the spectacle of isolation, estrangement, inequality, and self-forgetting that takes place in the playhouse, in this theater, "everyone lives in the greatest familiarity; everyone is equal and no one forgets himself" (*NH*, pp. 591, 593). Rousseau seems to offer a vision of a transformed theater in which theatrical relations and spectacles are healed, as it were, redeemed by openness, transparency, immediacy, presence, reciprocity, communality, and universal sympathy. This vision, most critics seem to agree (whether they seek to endorse, demystify, or simply report Rousseau's view), is the alternative to theater posed by the *Lettre à d'Alembert sur les spectacles*.

I would like to suggest, however, that this utopian vision of an antitheatrical society of spectacle is finally *not* advocated by Rousseau. Rousseau proposes and praises such ideal festivals in general terms only; the description of the dance of the soldiers is presented as a dreamlike memory, not a proposal, and it is entirely contained in a lengthy footnote that places it outside of the text: as remote as the fictions of Sparta and the state of nature. What Rousseau does advocate as proper spectacles—and this is the only proposal he offers in detailed and specific terms—are "les bals entre de jeunes personnes à marier" ("balls for marriageable young people" [L, p. 226]). If we examine Rousseau's descriptions of these balls we can see that they are less utopian festivals of liberty than scenes of rigorously enforced theatricality.[31]

This "type" of "fêtes publiques" (L, p. 226) is structured around a dance strictly divided between actors and spectators. Only unmarried young people may perform in the spectacle; parents are expected to attend "pour veiller sur leurs enfants, pour être témoins de leurs grâces et de leur adresse, des applaudissements qu'ils auroient mérités, et jouir ainsi du plus doux spectacle qui puisse toucher un coeur paternel" ("to watch over their children, to be witnesses of their grace, their address, and the applause they merited, and thus to enjoy the sweetest spectacle that can touch a paternal heart" [L, p. 227]). Spectators watch over and witness this performance, sometimes moved to tears which themselves are "capable perhaps of drawing tears from a sensitive spectator" (L, p. 228). The young people on display, writes Rousseau, have no better place to "se voir avec plus de décence et de circonspection que dans une assemblée où les yeux du public, incessament ouverts sur elles, les forcent à la réserve, à la modestie, à s'observer avec le plus grand soin" ("see each other with more decency and circumspection than at an assembly where the eyes of the public, constantly open upon them, force them to be reserved and modest and to observe themselves with the greatest care" [L, p. 226]). Paradoxically, this reserve and modesty—what would otherwise pass as a lack of *amour-propre*, concern for the eyes of the world, and exhibitionism—is guaranteed by the relentlessly open eyes of the public. The young people are doubly aware of themselves as spectacles since they are forced to view and observe themselves by their awareness that they are being watched. If there is self-concealment here, it is maintained and necessitated by blatantly theatrical display and exposure. This public spectacle is also a competition: a young woman is to be selected as the queen of the ball and awarded "some public distinction" (L, p. 228) if she marries within a year.

Rousseau seems to sense that he is describing an ambiguous and liminal scene when he insists that married persons could be only spectators at the ball: "car à quelle fin honnête pourroit-elle se donner ainsi en montre au publique?" ("for to what honest end could they thus make shows of themselves in public?" [L, p. 228]). But what makes the public display of *unmarried* people honest—especially women, for whom, we are told, *se montrer* was equivalent to *se déshonorer*? How is this marriage market—which, Rousseau writes, will console young people "from being deprived of continual commerce" with each other (L, p. 229)—finally different from the traffic of women Rousseau describes taking place in the theater: "l'exposition des dames et demoiselles parées tout de leur mieux et mises en étalage dans les loges comme sur le devant d'une boutique, en attendant les acheteurs" ("the exhibition of married ladies and young girls dressed in their best and arranged in the boxes as in a shop window, waiting for purchasers" [L, p. 212])? Rousseau insists that the "adornment" of the young women will be "innocent" (L, p. 229), that the displays will "satisfy *amour-propre* without offending virtue" (L, p. 228), that dissembling will be precluded, that unsanctioned meetings between young people will be avoided, that the ball has a serious moral purpose (marriage: "the first and holiest of all the bonds of society"). But Rousseau's defense of "dancing and the gatherings [assemblées] it occasions" (L, p. 226) begins to sound like the defenses for the moral justification of theater that he scorns and attacks throughout the *Lettre à d'Alembert*.

Indeed, the ball represented by Rousseau has virtually all of the ingredients of the theater and theatrical society the *Lettre* is supposed to condemn: strictly defined and enforced divisions between actors and spectators, self-concealment caused by exposure before the eyes of the world, self-display, concern with the regard of others and the public, *amour-propre*, adornment, distinction, competition, inequality, performance, applause, a lack of spontaneity and freedom, and the offering of women *en spectacle* and *en montre au public* in order to procure husbands for them. This may be Geneva but it is certainly not the state of nature. In some ways the ball resembles the *fête* that Rousseau imagines (in the second *Discours*) marking the beginning of *amour-propre* and the transformation of the state of nature into society: "Chacun commença à regarder les autres et à vouloir être regardé soi-même, et l'estime publique eut un prix. Celui qui chantait ou dansait le mieux, le plus beau, le plus fort, le plus adroit, ou le plus éloquent, devint le plus consideré; et ce fut là le premier pas vers l'inégalité, et vers le vice en même temps" ("Each one began to look at the others and to want to be looked at himself, and public esteem acquired a value. The one who sang or danced the best, the handsomest, the strongest, the most skillful, or the most eloquent, received the most consideration; that was the first step toward inequality, and toward vice at the same time" [*OC*, pp. 169–70]).

Furthermore, Rousseau's "spectacles innocents"—both the outdoor military displays of soldiers and martial arts and the indoor ball, presided over by a magistrate—bear some resemblance to those spectacles that keep spectators "craintifs et immobiles dans le silence et l'inaction; qui n'offrent aux yeux que cloisons, que pointes de fer, que soldats, qu'affligeantes images de la servitude et de l'inégalité" ("fearful and immobile in silence and inaction; which offer to the eyes nothing but cells, spearheads, soldiers, and distressing images of servitude and inequality" [*L*, pp. 224–25]). The spectacles Rousseau presents seem to dramatize the return of the repressed; or perhaps we should say: at the same time he represents utopian festivals with the rhetoric of liberty, Rousseau presents a scenario for the return of repression.

In light of these *fêtes* we should reconsider Rousseau's representations of Geneva and Genevans. We are now in a position to appreciate a paradox in Rousseau's arguments opposing Paris and Geneva. Although Paris is presented as the epitome of theater and theatrical behavior, it is also presented as a city where actors hide from spectators: "everyone, easily concealing his conduct from the eyes of the public, shows himself only by his reputation." People make spectacles of themselves but deception takes place because everyone and everything is masked: "everyone is judged by appearances because no one has the leisure to examine anything." In contrast, in smaller towns, everything takes place before the eyes of the world; there, where individuals, "always in the public eye, are born censors of each other, and where it is easy for the police to inspect everyone, completely contrary maxims must be followed" (*L*, pp. 169–70). If Geneva avoids the theater of Paris, it does so because of a highly theatrical set of relations; the theater of masks and deception is avoided but only by a world of guaranteed theatrical exposure. Genevan women may not be the actresses that Parisian women have become, but they play the role of "severe observers! In our city they almost fulfill the function of censors" (*L*, pp. 208–9). Genevans, writes Rousseau proudly, are not reduced "to hiding our eyes for fear of horrifying ourselves"; like the citizens of ancient Rome, they are described as "surveillants les uns des autres" ("keeping watch over one another" [*L*, p. 209]).

The ball, then, where the relentless eyes of the public enforce both display and reserve, provides an almost ritualistic representation and enactment of the theatrical structure in which Genevans already act as spectators and spectacles for each other.³² The perfection of the proposed ball, claims Rousseau, would make the public festivals serve the goals of "policing and good morals" (L, p. 228). If there is transparency in these relations, it is the enforced exposure of state-controlled theatricality rather than the mutual sympathy of the utopian *fête*. Rousseau praises the absence of any division of work and play in Sparta, where "everything was pleasure and spectacle" (L, p. 231), but it is not so clear that the transformation of Geneva and Genevans into spectacles is entirely pleasurable. We witness in the ball a carefully staged display of the everyday surveillance with which Genevans play spectator and *censeur* to each other.

We are left, then, at the end of the *Lettre à d'Alembert sur les spectacles*, with an image of Geneva as theater. Geneva is theatrical, however, not only because its people are "born censors of each other" (L, p. 169). In addition to acting out the roles of spectator and spectacle, the mutual surveillance with which people observe and police each other depends on the theatrical consciousness of *amour-propre* in order to be effective. What is at stake here is what Rousseau calls in the *Lettre* "l'empire de l'opinion" ("the empire of opinion" [L, 138]): the power of public opinion to control people's manners and morals and consequently their actions.³³ We know that social man is compelled by *amour-propre* to imagine the regard and opinion of other people; aware of his place before other spectators beside himself, he must live "outside of himself . . . in the opinion of others." He is an actor: "it is, so to speak, from their judgment alone that he derives the sentiment of his existence" (OC, p. 193). The awareness of the regard of others is translated in society into a concern with the eyes of the public; and, according to Rousseau, a desire for reputation and distinction in the eyes of the public leads either to dissembling and corruption or to modesty, reserve, and moral behavior.

One result of *amour-propre* and a theatrical concern with the regard of those who face one as spectators is that public opinion will exert a powerful influence over people's behavior. Rousseau claims in the *Émile* that women are enslaved to public opinion but he suggests in the *Lettre à d'Alembert* and elsewhere that most people share this fate. Consequently, if people are governed by public opinion, then the best way to govern them is to control public opinion. According to Rousseau, rather than opposing *amour-propre* and people's subservience before the eyes of the world, government should seize the apparatus of public opinion. He asks, in the *Lettre à d'Alembert sur les spectacles*, "Par où le gouvernement peut-il donc avoir prise sur les moeurs?" ("By what means can the government get a hold on morals?"). He answers: "c'est par l'opinion publique. Si nos habitudes naissent de nos propres sentiments dans la retraite, elles naissent de l'opinion d'autrui dans la société. Quand on ne vit pas en soi, mais dans les autres, ce sont leurs jugements qui règlent tout" ("it is with public opinion. If in a retired life our habits arise from our own sentiments, in society they arise from the opinion of others. When one does not live within oneself, but in others, their judgments rule everything" [*L*, p. 176]). What is deplored in the second *Discours* (as well as in the *Lettre* itself) is here recommended to the state for exploitation. Only through this institutionalization of *amour-propre* can morals and manners be controlled. In Rousseau's view, it is the responsibility of government to play upon the theatrical character of people in society for its own ends. In discussing how a government can make use of *amour-propre*, Rousseau writes (in his *Projet de constitution pour la Corse*): "les arbitres de l'opinion d'un peuple le sont de ses actions. . . . lui montrer ce qu'il doit estimer, c'est lui dire ce qu'il doit faire" ("the arbiters of the opinion of a people are the arbiters of its actions. . . . to show it what it should value is to show it what it should do" [*OC*, p. 937]).

We can see now that Rousseau calls upon Genevans to prohibit the establishment of a theater in their city not because he rejects all forms of theatrical relations and all manifestations of *amour-propre*; rather, theater is rejected because it would rival the surveillance, policing, and manipulation of *amour-propre* that serve the state. Public opinion cannot be legislated, writes Rousseau in the chapter "De la censure" in the *Contrat social* (a chapter that refers the reader to the *Lettre à d'Alembert* for a more extensive discussion). "Just as the declaration of the general will is made by the law," he writes, "the declaration of public judgment is made by the censor. Public opinion is the type of law for which the censor is the minister." But *la censure* can only protect and maintain "morals by preventing opinions from being corrupted" (*OC*, pp. 458–59); it cannot establish either opinions or morals and manners. Consequently, *censeurs* would be engaged in a constant battle with actors for the control of public opinion. A theater in Geneva, warns Rousseau in the *Lettre*, would threaten to "change our maxims, or, if you please, our prejudices and our public opinions" (*L*, p. 181).

Actors and the theater they represent would stand as rivals to the ministers of public opinion: "il est aisé de prévoir que ces deux établissements ne sauroient subsister longtemps ensemble, et que la comédie tournera les censeurs en ridicule, ou que les censeurs feront chasser les comédiens" ("it is easy to foresee that these two institutions would not be able to exist together for long, and that the theater will make the censors look ridiculous, or the censors will drive out the actors" [L, p. 182]). The state cannot tolerate the theater because it needs theater for its own ends. If society is afflicted by a theatrical consciousness that subjugates individuals to the opinion of the public—that collective representative and representation of the others who stand as their spectators—then the state must use theater to promote its own ideology. In order to govern, the state must depend on theatrical relations, *amour-propre*, people who live in others rather than in themselves, *censeurs* who act as spectators to the spectacles of other people. Since it will not govern against the will of the people (the government, of course, is supposed to embody the general will) then the government must control the theatrical relations that determine public opinion.

If there is to be theater, then, in Rousseau's republic, it must belong to the state. The *spectacles* Rousseau proposes do not escape theater or defeat theater because they depend on theatrical relations. Indeed, the *fête* of the dance ball dramatizes the state of theater and theatricality that appears to prevail in Geneva at the end of the *Lettre à d'Alembert sur les spectacles*. This *fête* provides a reflection as well as a manifestation of the state that governs by theater. Ideally, of course, in Rousseau's terms, the government controls public opinion for the "good" of the people. In speaking of the legislator's use of "illusion and stage management" in Rousseau's state, Judith N. Shklar writes that festivals are necessary "to protect the public self against the alluring calls of the private self, of *amour-propre* and the false empire of opinion."[34] However, whether Rousseau's state represents the triumph of good *moeurs* over corruption or the marriage of the modern liberal police state and advertising, whether it results in a *moi commun* in which "chacun se donnant à tous ne se donne à personne" ("each in giving himself to all gives himself to no one" [OC, p. 361]) or in the annihilation of self that occurs when one is faced with the eyes of the state, it is finally a state of theatricality governed by theatrical relations. Rousseau must end the *Lettre à d'Alembert sur les spectacles* by insisting on the necessity of a society of spectacles. "Voilà, monsieur, les spectacles qu'il faut à des républiques" ("There, monsieur, are the spectacles necessary to republics" [L, p. 234]), writes Rousseau in the last paragraph of the *Lettre* after describing the dance of the Lacedaemonians. The *fêtes* Rousseau proposes are either military displays or spectacles in which representatives of authority exercise their role as *censeurs* who police the behavior of those under their surveillance. Both kinds of spectacle are finally representations (and performances) of the power of the state and the power of the theater that has established society in Geneva as well as in Paris.

The *Lettre à d'Alembert sur les spectacles* dramatizes the contradictions and paradoxes inherent in Rousseau's ambivalent attitude toward the theater: his critique and promotion of theatrical relations, his tenuous opposition between sympathy and *amour-propre*, his identification with the actor, his double sacrifice at the temple of blindness and the temple of sight. The *Lettre* repeatedly raises the question of Rousseau's own interest in the terms of theater, the role that he writes for himself in a society of spectators and spectacles. By the end of the *Lettre* Rousseau seems to try to identify himself with the point of view of the government as *censeur* and severe observer, just as in his writing about society he often plays (what Starobinski calls) "the role of observer."[35] Nowhere, however, is Rousseau's status as an actor and a spectacle more in question than in his explicitly autobiographical writings. I would like to end this chapter by briefly examining the theatrical aspects of Rousseau's stance in the *Confessions*. It is here, in negotiating a relation between self and other, that Rousseau must directly engage the problem of sympathy.

  The *Confessions* in particular, along with Rousseau's other autobiographical writing, both narrate and enact Rousseau's exhibitionism and his obsessive concern with public opinion and the eyes of the world. Like the young people at the ball who watch themselves with "les yeux du public, incessamment ouverts sur elles" ("the eyes of the public constantly open upon them"), Rousseau decides to "me montrer tout entier au public" ("show myself entirely to the public"). He continues, in book 2 of the *Confessions*, "il faut que rien de moi ne lui reste obscur ou caché; il faut que je me tienne incessamment sous ses yeux" ("nothing of myself must remain obscure or hidden from it; I must constantly stand before its eyes" [*C*, p. 64]). However, whereas this exposure before the incessant eyes of the public is supposed to force the young people "à la réserve, à la modestie" ("to be reserved and modest" [*L*, p. 226]), Rousseau vows to reveal himself "sans réserve" ("without reserve" [*C*, p. 790]); he wants to "rendre mon âme transparente aux yeux du lecteur ... à la lui montrer sous tous les points de vue, à l'eclairer par tous les jours" ("render my soul transparent to the eyes of the reader ... to show it to him from all points of view, to illuminate it with the light of day" [*C*, p. 198]). At the beginning of the *Confessions* he claims he will be able to address his sovereign judge and say, "j'ai dévoilé mon intérieur tel que tu l'as vu toi-même" ("I have unveiled my interior, just as you have seen it yourself" [C, p. 4]). Viewed in the context of Rousseau's representations of the terms and positions of theater, these promises to reveal himself before the eyes of the public suggest that the *Confessions* is an avowedly theatrical book. Rousseau claims, of course, to avoid all vestiges of masks, disguise, or dissimulation; he represents only himself, plays his role only. But what does it mean for Rousseau to *se donner en spectacle,* to present his self on the stage of the world through the act of writing?

To begin to answer this question, I would like to cite a rather unlikely passage from book 5 of the *Confessions* in which Rousseau tells the story of an accident:

> Je passai deux ou trois ans de cette façon entre la musique, les magistères, les projets, les voyages, flottant incessamment d'une chose à l'autre, cherchant à me fixer sans savoir à quoi, mais entraîné pourtant par degrés vers l'étude, voyant des gens de lettres, entendant parler de littérature, me mêlant quelquefois d'en parler moi-même, et prenant plutôt le jargon des livres que la connaissance de leur contenu. Dans mes voyages de Genève j'allais de temps en temps voir en passant mon ancien bon ami M. Simon, qui fomentait beaucoup mon émulation naissante par des nouvelles toutes fraîches de la république des lettres, tirées de Baillet ou de Colomiès. Je voyais aussi beaucoup à Chambéry un jacobin, professeur de physique, bonhomme de moine, dont j'ai oublié le nom, et qui faisait souvent de petites expériences qui m'amusaient extrêmement. Je voulus à son exemple faire de l'encre de sympathie. Pour cet effet, après avoir rempli une bouteille plus qu'à demi de chaux vive, d'orpiment et d'eau, je la bouchai bien. L'effervescence commença presque à l'instant très violemment. Je courus à la bouteille pour la déboucher, mais je n'y fus pas à temps; elle me sauta au visage comme une bombe. Je restai aveugle plus de six semaines, et j'appris ainsi à ne pas me mêler de physique experimentale sans en savoir les elements. (C, pp. 251–52)

I spent two or three years in this manner between music, alchemical potions, plans, and journeys, floating incessantly from one thing to another, seeking to fix myself without knowing to what, but nevertheless carried along by degrees toward study, seeing men of letters, listening to talk of literature, sometimes entering myself into the discussion, and acquiring rather the jargon of books than any knowledge of their content. In my journeys from Geneva, from time to time I went to see in passing my old friend M. Simon, who very much fostered my nascent ambition with fresh news from the republic of letters, drawn from Baillet or Colomiès. Also at Chambéry I often saw a Jacobin professor of physical chemistry, a good-natured friar whose name I have forgotten, and who often performed little experiments which greatly amused me. Following his example, I wanted to make sympathetic ink. To this end, after having filled a bottle more than half full with quicklime, sulphide of arsenic, and water, I corked it firmly. Almost instantaneously a very violent effervescence was produced. I ran to the bottle to uncork it but I did not get to it in time; it burst in my face like a bomb. I remained blinded for more than six weeks, and thus I learned not to meddle in experimental chemistry without knowing its elementary principles.

After becoming involved with literary people and the republic of letters, after learning "le jargon des livres," Rousseau decides to produce a kind of invisible ink. As he tries to create a writing that would blind its readers, his solution blows up like a bomb and he blinds himself—although, with or without the help of Athena Optilitis, his sight is eventually healed. We know that this incident really happened; yet is there more to Rousseau's narration of it (and its inclusion in the *Confessions*) than meets the eye? How can we understand, especially in the context of his autobiographical project, Rousseau's desire to make *l'encre de sympathie*, sympathetic ink? What would it mean for Rousseau to write in the ink of sympathy?[36]

Autobiography presupposes some degree of *amour-propre*—if not necessarily pride or vanity, at least an awareness of the regard of spectators. But it also depends on the possibility of sympathy: the presupposition that an author could tell other people what goes on inside him, that readers could put themselves in someone else's place. We have seen that this exchange of persons and places by which one could take someone else's part and know—or at least imagine—the thoughts and sentiments of someone else is the fundamental condition of sympathy for Rousseau, as well as his contemporaries. Autobiography, for Rousseau and others, presupposes at least the possibility of an act of sympathy in which the reader could enter into the author's sentiments. In the *Essai sur l'origine des langues*, Rousseau disputes the then common assumption that sight is the sense most able to "émouvoir le coeur et d'enflammer les passions" ("move the heart and inflame the passions"). He writes: "Supposez une situation de douleur parfaitement connue; en voyant la personne affligée vous serez difficilement ému jusqu'à pleurer: mais laissez-lui le temps de vous dire tout ce qu'elle sent, et bientôt vous allez fondre en larmes" ("Imagine a painful situation that is perfectly known; in seeing the afflicted person you would be moved to tears only with difficulty: but give him the time to tell you everything he feels, and soon you will burst into tears" [*O*, p. 419]). Rousseau expects hostile readers for his autobiographical writing but he still believes in the power of telling one's own story. In his *Confessions* he repeatedly calls on the reader to sympathize or to share his feelings: "Lecteur pitoyable, partagez mon affliction"; "qu'on se mette à ma place" ("Compassionate reader, share my affliction"; "put yourself in my place" [*C*, pp. 37, 304]).

If Rousseau addresses himself "à mes semblables" ("to my fellow beings"), however, he does so to declare, "je suis autre" ("I am other" [*C*, p. 3]). He offers himself and his book as a "pièce de comparaison" ("comparison piece" [*C*, p. 2]), but will the act of comparison set in play by the *Confessions* produce the identification of sympathy or the differentiation of *amour-propre*; will it reveal Rousseau as a *semblable* or an other? What is at stake is not Rousseau's uniqueness or similarity to others but rather the possibility of sympathy and (by implication) autobiography: the possibility that one person could know an other. We saw that Rousseau begins the *Confessions* (in an early version of the text) by addressing the interplay of sympathy and *amour-propre* involved in trying to know others. He describes the double illusion of *amour-propre*, which consists in either falsely assigning to others the motives which would have made us act like them in their place or misleading ourselves because we cannot transport ourselves to someone else's place. Whereas most people judge others according to their own felings, Rousseau insists that to know one's own heart one must "commencer par lire dans celui d'autrui" ("begin by reading in that of others" [*C*, p. 787]), and he offers himself as that other.

However, in the same pages Rousseau dwells on the epistemological problems of actually knowing someone else—and knowing that one knows them. Like Adam Smith, who insists in his *Theory of Moral Sentiments* that sympathy is based on an act of imagination in which we represent to ourselves an image of what we think the other person is feeling, Rousseau claims that our knowledge of others, our accounts and representations of them, are based on fantasy. "Des histoires, des vies, des portraits, des caractères," insists Rousseau, are only "romans ingénieux bâtis sur quelques actes extérieurs, . . . sur de subtiles conjectures. . . . On saisit les traits saillants d'un caractère, on les lie par des traits d'invention, et pourvu que le tout fasse une physionomie, qu'importe qu'elle ressemble?" ("Histories, lives, portraits, characters [are only] ingenious novels constructed upon a few exterior acts. . . . One seizes upon the salient traits of a character, one links them together with invented traits, and as long as the whole makes up a physiognomy, does it matter what it resembles?").

According to Rousseau, to know a character well one must know the "enchaînement d'affections secrètes" ("series of secret affections") that has shaped it. "Ce qui se voit," he writes, "n'est que la moindre partie de ce qui est; c'est l'effet apparent dont la cause interne est cachée et souvent tres compliquée. Chacun devine à sa manière et peint à sa fantaisie; il n'a pas peur qu'on confronte l'image au modèle" ("What can be seen, is only the least part of what is; it is the apparent effect of which the internal cause is hidden and often very complex. Each of us guesses in his own manner, and paints according to his fancy; he has no fear that the image may be confronted with the model"). Rousseau asserts that this original or interior model is effectively hidden from others: "comment nous ferait-on connaître ce modèle intérieur, que celui qui le peint dans un autre ne saurait voir, et que celui qui le voit en lui-même ne veut pas montrer" ("how can we be led to know this interior model; he who would paint it in another would not know how to see it, and he who saw it in himself would not want to show it" [C, p. 787]).

At the beginning of his autobiography, rather than dwelling on the possibility of self-knowledge, Rousseau must confront the problem of knowing others—the problem of being known by others. (The absence of these speculations from the final version of the *Confessions* suggests that these are problems that Rousseau must also repress in the beginning of his autobiography.) Such skeptical interrogations appear elsewhere in Rousseau's work. Rousseau's lengthy discussion of Socinianism at the beginning of the *Lettre à d'Alembert sur les spectacles* has religious, political, and polemical purposes, but it also seems designed to ask the questions: "comment peut-on juger de la foi d'autrui par conjecture? . . . Qui sait mieux que moi ce que je crois ou ne crois pas?" ("how can one judge the faith of others by conjecture? . . . Who knows better than I what I believe or do not believe?" [L, p. 128]). Such questions are not irrelevant in a discussion of theatrical and sympathetic relations. In the *Discours sur les sciences et les arts,* Rousseau writes: "Qu'il seroit doux de vivre parmi nous, si la contenance extérieure étoit toujours l'image des dispositions du coeur" ("How pleasant it would be to live among us if the exterior countenance were always the image of the dispositions of the heart"). In these well-known pages he bemoans the loss of our ability to see through each other ("la facilité de se pénétrer réciproquement") and the consequent insecurity and incertitude of not being able to read the hearts of others: "On n'ose plus paroître ce qu'on est. . . . On ne saura donc jamais bien à qui l'on a affaire" ("One no longer dares to appear

as one is. . . . Thus one can never know just who one is dealing with"
[*OC*, pp. 7–8]).

This problem applies to autobiography as well. "No one can write
the life of a man except himself," writes Rousseau in the variant
beginning of the *Confessions*, "mais en l'écrivant il la déguise; sous le
nom de sa vie, il fait son apologie; il se montre comme il veut être vu"
("but in writing it he disguises it; under the name of his life story, he
makes his apology; he shows himself as he wishes to be seen" [*C*, p.
787]). The problem, however, is not merely disguise or deception;
even in the best of circumstances, in Rousseau's view, the self is secret,
inaccessible, hidden. Rousseau makes it clear in his introduction to
autobiography in the draft of the *Confessions* that he could not believe
in the physiognomist's dream that the countenance could present an
image of the heart's dispositions and allow an observer to penetrate
into one's inner sentiments; of course even such an image would be a
representation as well, an external manifestation of what is hidden
below the surface.

Can the *Confessions*, then, present us with Rousseau's true, inner
self, or merely what Diderot calls (in speaking of actors) the exterior
signs and symptoms of the self? If our knowledge of others is only an
imagined representation based on our own feelings, if the selves of
other people are misrepresented at worst and secret at best, then how
can we read in the heart of another by reading his autobiographical
text? How can Rousseau show himself entirely to the public, put
himself incessantly under the eyes of the world, make his soul
transparent to the reader's eye? Rousseau vows to overcome the
distance and difference that blind people to each other, to replace the
misrepresentations caused by both self and other with an autobiography that will write the hidden self, lay bare what is secret and covered
up.

To accomplish this unprecedented task, he writes, he must create
a new language. For that which he has to say, writes Rousseau, he
must "inventer un langage aussi nouveau que mon projet: car quel
ton, quel style prendre pour débrouiller ce chaos immense de
sentiments si divers, si contradictoires" ("invent a language which is as
new as my project; for what tone, what style can one use to sort out
this immense chaos of such diverse and contradictory feelings?").
What sort of language would it take to expose the self rather than
disguise or hide it? Rousseau seems to want to invent a language for
his *Confessions* that would make sympathy possible, that would allow
the reader to see beyond or below an exterior surface to the hidden
meaning of the self. What sort of reading would one need to bring to

the language in which Rousseau writes "l'histoire la plus secrète de mon âme" ("the most secret history of my soul" [*C*, pp. 790–91])?

To understand the writing and reading that Rousseau seems to imagine for the *Confessions*, we need to return to the passage in book 5 which tells of Rousseau's attempt to make *l'encre de sympathie*. I have suggested why Rousseau might want to use the ink of sympathy in writing his autobiography—the text that would allow his readers to transcend the epistemological void that separates people and know his secret, inaccessible interior. At this point we should be more precise in defining the character of sympathetic ink: not simply disappearing ink or invisible ink, sympathetic ink is a kind of ink that disappears and becomes invisible but then becomes visible again when some catalyst with the proper chemical affinities is applied. When the solution (or in some cases heat) is applied to the page, the sympathy or affinity between the two substances brings the ink back to the surface, so to speak, revealing the hidden writing by making it visible again.

We know that Rousseau was trying to make this kind of ink because one of the variants of the *Confessions* identifies the text which was the source for Rousseau's overdetermined experiment: the *Récréations mathématiques et physiques* by Jacques Ozanam, published in 1722. Here, along with practical problems in arithmetic, geometry, music, optics, gnomonics, cosmography, mechanics, pyrotechnics, chemistry, physics, and a treatise on elementary clock making, one can find the recipe for sympathetic ink that Rousseau followed—although nowhere does it say to cork the bottle. Ozanam promises to teach the reader how to write letters with "a clear and transparent liquid" that can be read only under special circumstances. The *Encyclopédie* has a long entry on "Encre Sympathique" in which it describes how "on trace des caractères auxquels il n'y a qu'un moyen secret qui puisse donner une couleur autre que celle du papier" ("one traces characters which can be given a color other than that of the paper only by a secret process"). The article explains that this ink was "imaginé pour écrire avec plus de mystère et de sûreté" ("invented for the purpose of writing with more mystery and safety"); it continues: "Sur une écriture invisible, on met une écriture visible, et l'on fait disparaître l'écriture visible et fausse, et paraître l'invisible et vraie" ("Over an invisible writing one places a visible writing, and one makes the visible and false writing disappear, while making the invisible and true writing appear").[37]

By now the purpose of sympathetic ink should have become clear: an ink which is transparent disappears and is covered by a false and visible ink; then when *sympathy* is applied, when a sympathetic

reaction takes place, the false and visible ink disappears and the true
and invisible writing becomes legible. In other words, the text
becomes a palimpsest; underneath the text is a hidden, secret text
which is so transparent that it is invisible. Only a sympathetic reading
will reveal—bring to the surface—the real or true writing of the text.
It is no accident that Rousseau tries to make sympathetic ink after he
has been making "magistères" (prescriptions that are kept secret) and
after he has been meeting "gens de lettres" and learning to speak "le
jargon des livres." The *Encyclopédie* describes jargon as "an artificial
language upon which a few people agree so they can talk to each other
in company without being understood."[38] *Littré* defines it as a
"language of double entendres" and the *Oxford English Dictionary*
describes a method of writing or conversing by means of symbols or
ciphers which are meaningless unless one knows how to read them.
As a fabrication that would turn language into a secret cipher,
sympathetic ink is a literal version of the language Rousseau discovers
when he is initiated into the republic of letters and the jargon of
books. I am suggesting that Rousseau's unfortunate foray into a
professor's laboratory had more to do with his affinity for literature
and authorship than with an interest in science.[39]

More specifically, however, I am suggesting that we can see in
sympathetic ink a figure for the new style of writing that Rousseau felt
was required for his autobiographical project. We can see in this
language that would hide itself, revealing its true face only to the
reader capable of reproducing the meaning buried beneath its surface,
the new language Rousseau needed to invent for his *Confessions*. The
Confessions must be read as if it were written in sympathetic ink. In
book 3 Rousseau explains that he chose to absent himself from society
because even when present he misrepresented himself; he was certain,
he writes, to "m'y montrer non seulement à mon désavantage, mais
tout autre que je ne suis. Le parti que j'ai pris d'écrire et de me cacher
est précisément celui qui me convenait" ("show myself there not only
to my disadvantage but entirely other than I am. The decision I made
to write and to hide myself is precisely what suited me" [*C*, p. 129]).
Rousseau's autobiographical writing always puts him in the paradoxical position of revealing and concealing himself; he must write and
hide himself simultaneously.

My point is not merely that Rousseau is ambivalent about revealing
himself, that he would like to confess in an ink that would be legible
to sympathetic readers only. My point, rather, is that in writing his
autobiography Rousseau has no choice but to write and hide himself,
écrire et se cacher. Rousseau makes this clear in the introductory

meditation on autobiography and sympathy that lies buried beneath the revisions and erasures of the *Confessions*: he insists that representations of himself misrepresent him or disfigure him; the image that people see bears little resemblance to the model of which it is supposed to be a copy. Writing itself (especially autobiographical writing) covers even as it acts to uncover or discover. We might rephrase Rousseau's words and say: *écrire, c'est se cacher*, to write is to hide oneself. Only a reading that could bring to the surface what writing must hide could allow Rousseau to make himself transparent yet visible as well; only a reader who reacted with enough sympathy to enter into the secret feelings of other minds could help Rousseau to counteract the disguise implicit in all self-portraits and reveal himself. Rousseau's autobiography must be written in sympathetic ink if it is to expose as well as hide the self.

Indeed, for Rousseau, writing in which meaning is hidden offers the only language of revelation or confession. Acknowledging the need to interpret that which is screened rather than seen, it is the only language that can offer the self up to be deciphered. Sympathetic ink provides the language of autobiography because it stands as the only language capable of representing the self. In other words, sympathetic ink not only reveals how the self must be read; it is itself a figure for the self: that which cannot be figured, that which can only be figured.

For Rousseau, the self is hidden, invisible, covered over by exterior traits that mask its true character with a type of false representation. Inaccessible, unknown, buried beneath the surface, the self is itself a palimpsest that combines layers of characters and inscriptions—like the "crossed out, scrawled over, confused, indecipherable manuscripts" (*C*, p. 126) that Rousseau describes himself producing when he writes. At the end of the fourth book of the *Confessions*, where he speaks of painting himself as he is and rendering his soul transparent to the eyes of the reader, Rousseau explains that "toutes mes idées sont en images, les premiers traits qui se sont gravés dans ma tête y sont demeurés, et ceux qui s'y sont empreints dans la suite se sont plutôt combinés avec eux qu'ils ne les ont effacés" ("all my ideas are in images; the first features to engrave themselves in my head have remained there, and those which were imprinted afterward have combined with them rather than effaced them" [*C*, p. 198]). These figures of the self as a layered text with multiple impressions should preclude us from construing from the figure of sympathetic ink a naive model of the self in which a true inner self remains untouched beneath an external mask. The *Confessions* teaches us to read the self as a layering of double illusions which combine and overlap in continual self-eclipse—and which must be reproduced in the reactions and representations of other minds.

Furthermore, even if autobiography did aim to remove the layers of disguise and expose an inner self, Rousseau insists that the temporal stratification that turns the self into a palimpsest is inscribed within the process of autobiography itself. In the early introduction to the *Confessions*, Rousseau acknowledges the doubling aspect of his autobiography: "En me livrant à la fois au souvenir de l'impression reçue et au sentiment présent je peindrai doublement l'état de mon âme, au moment où l'événement m'est arrivé et au moment où je l'ai décrit; mon style ... fera lui-même partie de mon histoire" ("In devoting myself at once to the memory of the impression received and to the present feeling, I will paint the state of my soul doubly: at the moment when the event happened to me and at the moment when I described it; my style ... will itself form part of my story" [*C*, p. 791]). As a self-portrait, autobiography must double the self, add a layer of paint and impressions to the soul it seeks to reveal. If we are to read in the heart of an other, as Rousseau proposes, we must recognize that not only the text of the self but also the writing of the text of the self is the subject of autobiography. To read the *Confessions* we must see the role that its style or language plays. This two-faced and effacing language, hiding and revealing, representing and misrepresenting, is also the subject of the *Confessions*: the meaning as well as the means of confession.

This language of confession and, in particular, the figure of sympathetic ink suggest the possibility of an untheatrical autobiography: a book in which displaying oneself to the eyes of the world could still mean concealment, in which making oneself transparent might mean rendering oneself invisible. Despite the public stage of the book and the unveiling of autobiography, the language of confession itself might double the self's own layers of secrecy, unless a reader applied sympathy to the text and through an act of identification crossed the theatrical distance separating people and reproduced an image of the self. "C'est ici de mon portrait qu'il s'agit, et non pas d'un livre" ("I'm concerned here with my portrait and not with a book"), writes Rousseau in introducing his autobiography; "Je vais travailler pour ainsi dire dans la chambre obscure; il n'y faut point d'autre art que de suivre exactement les traits que j'y vois marqués" ("I shall work, so to speak, in a *camera obscura*; there the only art necessary is that of following exactly the traits which I see marked" [*C*, pp. 790–91]). Rousseau's figure of protophotographic realism introduces a set of lenses and mirrors into the process of autobiography: he will create his self-portrait in the dark, tracing the mirror image of a mirror image. To say that the work takes place in a *camera obscura* suggests that this self-portrait will reveal the self through a glass darkly, not face to face; it also reminds us that *amour-propre* cannot be ruled out of the acts of doubling, identification, and imagination that structure the mirroring act of sympathy. The self reproduced in autobiography must be both imaged and imagined: seen at several removes.

These figures of apparently untheatrical exposure might allow us to revise our view of the *fête* that Rousseau presents as a childhood memory at the end of the *Lettre à d'Alembert sur les spectacles*. Rousseau notes that the dance "sembleroit n'offrir rien de fort intéressant à voir" ("would seem to offer nothing very interesting to look at") but he insists that the scene was so moving that it caused "un attendrissement général que je ne saurois peindre" ("a general emotion that I could not paint" [*L*, pp. 232–33]). The dance, then, appeared to offer nothing to see and those who witnessed it had a reaction that could not be represented or at least visually depicted. Does this mean that there was literally nothing to see in the dance? Rousseau explains, "Je sens bien que ce spectacle dont je fus si touché seroit sans attraits pour mille autres; il faut des yeux faits pour le voir, et un coeur fait pour le sentir" ("I am well aware that this spectacle which touched me so much would be without any attraction for thousands of others; one must have eyes made to see it, and a heart made to feel it" [*L*, p. 233]). The spectacle would only be moving— indeed, it would only be visible—to those who knew how to see it, to those who had the eyes and heart necessary to view it with sympathy and be moved.

This dance can not be *mise en scène* like the spectacles of the Genevans; it is not even a spectacle unless one views it with a sympathetic reaction, with a sentiment and point of view capable of making it visible. Composed of soldiers "formant une longue bande qui serpentoit en cadence et sans confusion, avec mille tours et retours, mille espèces d'évolutions figurées" ("forming a long ribbon which wound around in cadence and without confusion, with a thousand turns and returns, a thousand kinds of figured evolutions" [*L*, p. 233]), the spectacle of the dance is like a text written in sympathetic ink— or a text written merely in *le jargon des livres*. As if composed of lines of turns and tropes, the figured evolutions of figures of speech both enfolding and unfolding meaning, the dance is like a text that is illegible unless it is interpreted: represented again in the reader's mind. If this is a spectacle of transparency for the characters involved, it is a spectacle which must be opaque to the reader or spectators, who must not see *through* the text if they are to see it at all. The text would appear to escape theatrical exposure by making itself invisible, by concealing itself in its own language. This means that the reader must enter the theater of the text. The spectacles that Rousseau imagines will liberate spectators from the "antre obscur" or dark cavern of the playhouse must be presented in his own work in "la chambre obscure"—the *camera obscura*—of reading.

SIX

Frankenstein, or Rousseau's Monster: Sympathy and Speculative Eyes

> A book is a dead man, a sort of mummy, embowelled and embalmed, but that once had flesh, and motion, and a boundless variety of determinations and actions. I am glad that I can, even upon these terms, converse with the dead, with the wise and the good of revolving centuries.
>
> William Godwin, *Fleetwood*

Rousseau's dream of an untheatrical autobiography, written in the figures and characters of a sympathetic ink that would reveal the self only to those who knew how to read it, finally is left in doubt. The utopian *fête* of mutual transparency and sympathy suggested in the *Lettre à d'Alembert sur les spectacles* is represented as forced and enforced theatrical exposure or as the idealized memory of a spectacle that would present *rien à voir* to the countless spectators who would regard it without sympathy. The attempt to write and to hide oneself, to inscribe oneself in exhibitionism using invisible ink, risks both overexposure and overconcealment. Indeed, the almost Sternean proliferation of Rousseau's autobiographical writings, accompanying his desperate attempts to find a literary executor who would convey his self-portrait to the supposedly less hostile reading public of the future, ends in the *Rêveries du promeneur solitaire.* There, in the autobiography Rousseau claims to write for himself, for which he doubles himself to play the roles of both writer and reader,[1] the biographical events that make Rousseau a hero of his own novel increasingly give way to densely figural descriptions of sympathetic transports transacted between himself and the landscape alone. All of this suggests that Rousseau looked to the possibility of representing himself before a sympathetic reader with increasing desire and doubt: desire, because his autobiographical project depended on sympathy; and doubt, because he could not trust sympathy. Given the apparent inevitability of hostile or uncomprehending readers, given the breakdown of sympathy in theatrical society, and given the secret language which structured and inscribed the self, Rousseau could not count on sympathetic readers or beholders for his *camera obscura* self-portrait. However, Rousseau could not trust sympathy because he feared its success as well as its failure.

I have traced the pattern of this ambivalence in my readings of Marivaux, Du Bos, and Diderot as well as Rousseau. Like other eighteenth-century observers of society and human nature, like other eighteenth-century theorists of an aesthetic of sentiment and sensibility, these authors often seem to depend on the powers of what many of their contemporaries assumed was an innate or natural sympathy. They seem to believe in both the need for and the possibility of a sympathetic transport that would allow readers and beholders of works of art or people in the world to exchange places, parts, and persons with the characters of others. However, this desire to transcend difference and distance, to cross the borders that turn people into both *spectateurs ignorés* and unknown actors, leads to two sets of problems.

First, the effects of sympathy often seem to be disconcerting. For Du Bos and Marivaux, sympathy is associated with acts and scenes of violence which picture the subjects of their spectacles as victims. Although these scenes are evoked to insist on the pity and compassion of readers and spectators who are moved or touched, they seem to generate only phantoms of passions that convert fellow feeling into aesthetic pleasure. Furthermore, this pleasure seems guilty since it often is occasioned by scenes of dangerous or transgressive eroticism; in the scenes I have discussed, actors become victims, and spectators are punished for both their voyeurism and their acts of sympathetic identification. For Diderot, sympathy seems to become a contagious disease which is dangerous for both victim and compassionate beholder. For Diderot and Marivaux, becoming the subject of a spectacle, the heroine or hero of a story, the object of sympathy, puts one in the position of victim; and to allow oneself to be moved by such a story or spectacle of suffering is to risk seduction and perhaps the punishment that seems to accompany erotic transgression. For both Diderot and Rousseau, these guilty transports also seem to represent a loss of self: a self-forgetting that threatens the concept of a stable identity and blurs the boundaries that define and differentiate both self and other.

Marivaux suggests in *La Vie de Marianne* that autobiography threatens to annihilate or victimize the self in turning it into the heroine or hero of a novel or the subject of a spectacle, although the doubling and replacement of Marianne's *récit* by the stories of

Varthon and Tervire suggest that the *dédoublement* of autobiography's self-representation might allow one to displace oneself and frame someone else in one's story. Rousseau enters the antitheatrical tradition to denounce actors for exhibiting the transport outside of self that he enacts throughout his life story; he condemns actors for possessing the acts of sympathetic imagination that he condemns spectators for lacking. Diderot, who appears to be anxious about the effects of sympathy on both actor and spectator, rejects the belief that actors should forget themselves in their roles—as if, like Rousseau, to exorcise the self-forgetting that characterizes some of his self-portraits as an artist; yet Diderot remains preoccupied with scenes in which either spectator or actor forget theater in a moment of sympathy that denies the inevitable partition that divides actors from both their parts and their audience. Indeed, all of the texts we have considered reveal the deeply ambivalent investment of their authors in acts and spectacles of sympathy: whether works of fiction or aesthetic theory or both, these texts seem compelled to deny, counteract, or warn the reader about the dangerous consequences of the sympathy that they advocate and even seek to elicit.

However, at the same time that the effects of sympathy seem too powerful for both actor and audience, both author and reader, sympathy has another disconcerting aspect: the age of sensibility must be played out in the age of skepticism. Both sympathy and skepticism address the question of whether one person could enter into the thoughts and sentiments of someone else. Indeed, one could read the hyperbolic claims made for the effects of sympathy in the eighteenth century as a response to the threat of skepticism. I have suggested that although Adam Smith bases his *Theory of Moral Sentiments* on the presumption of a universal need for sympathy, he describes a society in which sympathy seems unlikely and even impossible—not so much because people are disinclined to enter into sentiments or situations that are painful or distressing, but rather because (in Smith's view) people know the characters and sentiments of others only through representations they form in their imaginations of what they think others feel. We have seen that Du Bos, Marivaux, Diderot, and Rousseau are concerned with the representation, mimesis, and mediation that structure and even constitute acts of sympathy. Their investment in the analogies and parallels between moral sentiments and aesthetic experience comes less from an eighteenth-century interest in universal principles than from a sense that acts of sympathy depend on acts of reading and beholding.

One consequence of their recognition that sympathy must be acted

out in the realms of representation and interpretation is that Marivaux, Diderot, and Rousseau are aware of the threat of misrepresen-
tation and misinterpretation. This means that spectators might be
deceived by hypocrites: masters of a semiotics of the passions who
either on or off the stage know how to imitate the exterior signs and
symptoms of feelings and thus trick beholders into taking their
presentations of self at face value. It also means that the spectacles of
sincere people might be subject to misinterpretation by beholders who
misread or misconstrue appearances. The tableau of someone innocent or sincere might appear the same as the tableau of someone guilty
or deceptive.

However, for actors and spectators in scenes of sympathy, their
dependence on the appearances or representations they want to
penetrate or disregard leads to a greater threat than the possibility that
they might enter into the thoughts and sentiments of others in a
transport based on misreading. The real threat is that faced with the
impenetrable aspects of others, faced with the impossibility of knowing other people's sentiments except through acts of imagination,
sympathy itself might be impossible. In appearing before others, then,
one risks not only misunderstanding but also theatrical exposure
before unsympathetic spectators: the seemingly dangerous exposure of
theatricality. In reading or beholding the characters of others, one
risks not only being misled but also being placed in the position of
distance, difference, and isolation that sympathy is supposed to deny.
The investigations of sympathy conducted by Du Bos, Marivaux,
Diderot, and Rousseau—despite fears about the permeability of the
boundaries of the self—all confront the ineluctable barriers that
obstruct knowledge and place sympathy in the realm of fiction.

I have suggested that for the authors discussed in this book both the
success and the failure of sympathy present problems. In this chapter
I will consider another text that displays and examines the effects of
sympathy but which specifically focuses on the causes and effects of
sympathy's failure: Mary Shelley's *Frankenstein, or The Modern
Prometheus*. Rousseau once again will be at the center of this
investigation as I argue that Mary Shelley uses Rousseau's writings to
conduct a philosophical investigation of the failure of sympathy—a
reading of Rousseau that focuses on the epistemology and the rhetoric
of fellow feeling as it dramatizes questions about identification,
resemblance, likeness, difference, comparison, and the possibility of
transporting oneself into the thoughts and sentiments of an other.
Frankenstein represents both a continuation and an interpretation of
the types of issues and texts discussed in the preceding chapters. In

enacting a series of dialogues with, through, and about Rousseau, Mary Shelley reflects on eighteenth-century accounts of sympathy and displays her own ambivalent assessment of the moral and aesthetic sentiments that are at stake.

In the pages that follow, I will consider the figure of Rousseau in *Frankenstein*, beginning with the complex identifications at play as Mary Shelley uses Rousseau to act out and work through some of the key psychological issues that inform the novel. Rousseau was more than an intellectual influence for Mary Shelley; he represented a cluster of overdetermined and sometimes contradictory signs, associations, and preoccupations (many of which relate to her parents). After tracing the literary animation of Rousseau in the text of *Frankenstein*, I will argue that the novel's concern with sympathy must be understood in the context of Mary Shelley's reading of Rousseau. Finally, the interplay between the novel's famous family romance and its theory of sympathy will return us to the scene of theater and in particular to the primal scene.

There is considerable evidence that Rousseau was a formative influence in Mary Shelley's intellectual development and even in her personal life in the years leading up to and including the period in which she composed *Frankenstein*.[2] Rousseau was a major influence on (and was frequently mentioned in the writing of) Mary Shelley's parents, William Godwin and Mary Wollstonecraft. Wollstonecraft (who once claimed to "have always been half in love with" Rousseau) identified Rousseau as "the true Prometheus of sentiment" in her unfinished novel, *Maria, or The Wrongs of Woman*.[3] The author of *Frankenstein, or The Modern Prometheus* read or reread numerous works of Godwin, Wollstonecraft, and Rousseau in the year before she began her novel and during the months she was at work on it. Indeed, the novel was conceived and begun in Switzerland, where Mary Shelley was immersed in both the literal and the literary landscapes of Rousseau's life and work; during the summer of 1816, Byron and Percy Shelley took their now famous boat trip around Lake Geneva with a copy of *La Nouvelle Héloïse* in hand. Percy Shelley called Rousseau "the greatest man the world has produced since Milton" only six days before Mary Shelley recorded what is at least the first extant reference to *Frankenstein* in her journal.[4] It has been generally accepted that *Frankenstein* is deeply informed by Mary Shelley's reading of Milton.[5] I will argue that the figure of Rousseau is an even more pervasive and significant presence in the novel; we must read this figure if we are to read *Frankenstein*.

As a native of eighteenth-century Geneva, Victor Frankenstein is, as it were, a compatriot of Rousseau's. Frankenstein appears to present his narrative in English for the benefit of the English reader represented by Walton, although in one early version of the manuscript Mary Shelley has Walton praise Victor's eloquence when he speaks his native French;[6] the monster's narrative presumably has been translated from the French by either Frankenstein or Walton, just as the books that the monster reads have been translated from English, Latin, and German. Indeed, Mary Shelley goes out of her way to make French the monster's native language; in terms of verisimilitude, it seems more likely that he would have stumbled upon the cottage of a German-speaking rather than French-speaking family in the forest near Ingolstadt, and there is no reason why he and Victor couldn't have had their conversations in German. However, in a book preoccupied with absent or dead mothers, it seems significant that they would share a mother tongue—with both each other and the author who signed himself *Citoyen de Genève*.

It has been noted that Victor Frankenstein's descriptions of the sublime environs of Lake Geneva and the Alps resemble the landscapes of *La Nouvelle Héloïse* that so impressed the Shelleys and Byron in 1816.[7] *Frankenstein* also depicts another landscape that is closely associated with Rousseau: its picture of the state of nature in which the monster first discovers himself and eventually learns the arts and sciences of language and civilization. Walton first imagines the monster to be "a savage inhabitant of some undiscovered island" (*F*, p. 23); and indeed, the monster closely resembles the character of the *homme sauvage* that Rousseau created in his fiction of the state of nature. The monster's status as a noble (and sometimes not so noble) savage is the one indication of Rousseau in the text of *Frankenstein* that has received critical attention. Critics have recognized in the monster an Enlightenment noble savage whose early life in the forest (drinking at brooks, eating nuts and berries and not meat, sleeping under trees, encountering fire for the first time, acquiring language, and so on) conforms in both general outline and specific details to the life of Rousseau's savage.[8] Paul A. Cantor has presented the most extensive argument for the importance of Rousseau's second *Discours* (or at least the myth of origins it narrates) to *Frankenstein*. Arguing that Mary Shelley "drew upon Rousseau's conception of natural man" in portraying the monster, he claims that "at the same time as *Frankenstein* involves a retelling of *Paradise Lost*, it also undertakes an imaginative recreation of the *Second Discourse*, blending Milton and Rousseau."[9]

There are more signs of Rousseau's fiction of the state of nature in Mary Shelley's fiction. For example, the notes to the *Discours sur l'origine de l'inégalité* contain a long description of "monstres" taken from *L'Histoire des voyages*: one group of monsters, cites Rousseau, has "une ressemblance exacte avec l'homme, mais ils sont beaucoup plus gros, et de fort haute taille" ("have an exact resemblance to man, but they are much bigger and taller"). Like Frankenstein's monster, who looks like a human being despite being horribly ugly and "of a gigantic stature" (*F*, p. 52), these monsters eat fruit and nuts rather than meat. Just as Frankenstein's monster describes how he "found a fire which had been left by some wandering beggars" which "he knew not how to reproduce" (*F*, p. 100), this account describes the monsters finding fires abandoned by people and not knowing how to prolong them; Rousseau insists, however, that they could have figured out how to add wood if they desired—and indeed, Frankenstein's monster makes just this discovery. Rousseau notes that "on trouve dans la description de ces prétendus monstres des conformités frappantes avec l'espèce humaine" ("in the description of these supposed monsters we find striking similarities with the human species"), and he supposes that the so-called monsters were assumed not to be "hommes sauvages" only because they did not talk. He insists, however, that "quoique l'organe de la parole soit naturel à l'homme, la parole elle-même ne lui est pourtant pas naturelle, et qui connoissent jusqu'à quel point sa perfectibilité peut avoir élevé l'homme Civil au-dessus de son état originel?" ("although the organ of speech is natural to man, speech itself is not natural to him; and who knows how far his perfectibility may have raised civil man above his original state?" [*OC*, pp. 209–10]).

Frankenstein provides a detailed account of precisely this transition as the monster describes how he acquired language and the consequences of his elevation from his original state to so-called civil society. Rousseau's interest in this phenomenon has been noted by critics who have seen the monster as a version of the natural man Rousseau portrays in his *Discours*, but only Peter Brooks has suggested the relevance of Rousseau's *L'Essai sur l'origine des langues*.[10] I will argue that this essay figures significantly in *Frankenstein*. For the moment, however, I will simply note that it provides further textual evidence that Mary Shelley was using Rousseau's fictions to help her imagine what the monster calls "the original era of my being" (*F*, p. 98). For example, Rousseau describes how in "les premiers temps" ("the earliest times") the only language possessed by primitive people consisted in "le geste et quelques sons inarticulés" ("gestures and a few inarticulate sounds" [O, p. 445]). Frankenstein describes the monster in his first moments muttering "inarticulate sounds" (F, p. 57). The monster himself describes how in trying to imitate the "songs of the birds" he can make only "uncouth and inarticulate sounds"; he eventually observes Safie and the De Lacey family communicating through "signs" and finally understands the principle of language and then language itself (F, pp. 99, 112).

The monster also devotes considerable attention to the role of music in his first experiences with the expression of human emotion. He is "unable to bear these emotions" when he hears De Lacey's "sweet mournful air" (F, p. 103). This scene and other descriptions of the humans moving each other (and their hidden listener) by singing and playing the guitar recall Rousseau's unusual argument that "les vers, les chants, la parole, ont une origine commune" ("verse, song, and speech have a common origin"). For the monster, as for Rousseau's first humans, "les premiers discours furent les premières chansons" ("the first songs were the first speech" [O, p. 468]); his more or less simultaneous discovery of music, language, and then poetry provides a condensed tableau of the theories Rousseau outlines in the *Essai sur l'origine des langues*. The learning of language that is seen in the lessons and example of the young lovers Felix and Safie also follows Rousseau's hypothetical representation of "l'amour" inventing "la parole" (O, p. 416). Finally, the monster also dramatizes Rousseau's claim in the *Essai* that "un homme abandonné seul sur la face de la terre, à la merci du genre humain, devoit être un animal féroce"("a man abandoned alone on the face of the earth, at the mercy of humankind, had to be a ferocious animal" [O, p. 445]).

The monster is not the only character in *Frankenstein* who resembles a character from Rousseau's fictions. Both Alphonse and Victor Frankenstein evoke aspects of the plot and characters of *La Nouvelle Héloïse*.[11] However, even more significantly, Victor Frankenstein resembles Rousseau himself: in particular, the Rousseau of the *Rêveries du promeneur solitaire*. He twice describes his outings in a boat on Lake Geneva in language that often seems a translation of Rousseau's descriptions in the fifth *Promenade*. Rousseau writes:

> j'allais me jeter seul dans un bateau que je conduisais au milieu du lac quand l'eau était calme, et là, m'étendant tout de mon long dans le bateau les yeux tournés vers le ciel, je me laissais aller et dériver lentement au gré de l'eau, quelquefois pendant plusieurs heures, plongé dans milles rêveries confuses mais délicieuses ... (R, p. 67)

> I would go and throw myself into a boat all alone, which I would steer

into the middle of the lake when the water was calm, and there, stretching myself out at full length in the boat, my eyes turned up to the sky, I would let myself go and drift slowly with the current of the water, sometimes for several hours, plunged into a thousand confused but delicious reveries . . .

Frankenstein's autobiographical narrative reads: "I took the boat and passed many hours upon the water. Sometimes, with my sails set, I was carried by the wind, and sometimes, after rowing into the middle of the lake, I left the boat to pursue its own course and gave way to my own miserable reflections" (*F*, p. 87). Like the author of the *Rêveries du promeneur solitaire*, Frankenstein recounts how he "took refuge in the most perfect solitude." He continues: "I passed whole days on the lake alone in a little boat, watching the clouds and listening to the rippling of the waves, silent and listless" (*F*, p. 143). Later in the narrative he describes how he "stretched myself at the bottom of the boat"; the scene is not at all tranquil at this point yet he calls his reflections a "reverie" (*F*, p. 164).

Frankenstein's remorse and torturous guilt over Justine, who is fatally punished for the crime he considers his own fault, recall the remorse Rousseau expresses in the second book of the *Confessions* and the fourth *Promenade* for the unjust punishment of another servant girl, Marion. In addition, Frankenstein feels "loathing" for the "dissecting room and the slaughter-house" which furnish the "workshop of filthy creation" where he feels as if he has "mangled the living flesh of a human being"(*F*, pp. 53, 163), and pleasure in "serene sky and verdant field" and the "flowers of spring" and "summer" (*F*, p. 68) when he is able to forget his experiments; these descriptions may recall the third *Promenade* where Rousseau writes of the "appareil affreux" ("frightful apparatus") of an "amphithéâtre anatomique" ("anatomical amphitheater") with its "cadavres puants, de baveuses et livides chairs" ("stinking cadavers, livid and oozing flesh") and the power of "brillantes fleurs . . . ombrages frais . . . verdure" to "purifier mon imagination salié par tous ces hideux objets"("brilliant flowers . . . cool shades . . . verdure . . . to purify my imagination, soiled by all these hideous objects" [*R*, p. 97]). It is, of course, "natural philosophy" that leads to Victor's creation of that "hideous" object which eventually haunts his "disturbed imagination" (*F*, pp. 49, 57, 61).[12]

In addition to his similarities to Rousseau's literary persona, in his moments as Romantic poet turned madman and misanthrope, Victor also resembles the public persona of Rousseau that was current in the early nineteenth century among enlightened English readers who wished to claim him as a poet of nature while at the same time acknowledging the apparent insanity that caused a scandal during his residence in England. However, Victor is like Rousseau in a specific way that is of obsessive concern to Mary Shelley throughout the pages of *Frankenstein* (and probably throughout her life). Frankenstein is guilty of a crime that Rousseau was notorious for throughout Europe: he is a parent who abandons his child. Although Mary Shelley—like her mother—appreciated Rousseau in spite of his flaws, it is clear that for her one of the most salient aspects of Rousseau's life story was that he made orphans of the five infants born to him and Thérèse Levasseur.[13]

Rousseau includes a lengthy discussion of this part of his life story in the ninth *Promenade* of the *Rêveries*. "J'avais mis mes enfants aux Enfants-Trouvés," he writes; "c'en était assez pour m'avoir travesti en père dénaturé" ("I had put my children into the Foundling Home. . . . that was enough to get me misrepresented as an unnatural father" [*R*, p. 121]). Insisting that it would be "la chose du monde la plus incroyable que l'*Héloïse* et l'*Émile* fussent l'ouvrage d'un homme qui n'aimait pas les enfants" ("the most unbelievable thing in the world that the *Héloïse* and the *Émile* could be the works of a man who did not like children" [*R*, p. 123]), he tries to defend himself by claiming that if he had kept his children, Thérèse's family "en aurait fait des monstres" ("would have made monsters of them" [*R*, p. 122]). I suggest that Mary Shelley has Rousseau in mind as she tells the story of a parent who made his offspring a monster—precisely by abandoning him. The long biographical essay that she wrote on Rousseau in her volume *Eminent Literary and Scientific Men of France* for the *Cabinet Cyclopedia* reveals how much she associates Rousseau with this act, as she repeatedly turns and returns her attention to an examination and condemnation of the fact that "five of his children were thus sent to a receptacle where few survive." Mary Shelley is largely sympathetic to Rousseau throughout her recital of the controversial events of his life (taking Rousseau's side, for example, in his quarrel with Diderot and even with Hume), but she is relentlessly severe in denouncing him for having in regard to his children "failed in the plainest dictates of nature and conscience" (*CC*, p. 131).

Indeed, although she writes that it is "insulting the reader to dwell on the flagrancy of this act" (*CC*, p. 131), she dwells on it for two pages, justifying this digression from her narrative by insisting that it "was necessary to bring it so far forward as to show the evil effects of so bad a cause" and then vowing that "it is too painful to dwell further upon." However, she once again returns to "little children ... ruthlessly sacrificed" in the next paragraph, this time acknowledging her digression with a reminder to herself: "However, to go back to narrative" (*CC*, pp. 132–33); and then, as if irresistibly, she returns to the subject two pages later and then finally again in the conclusion to the essay.

Mary Shelley's condemnations of Rousseau were written about twenty years after she completed *Frankenstein* (although she began the project only six years after she revised her novel for its third edition);[14] yet the language and tone of the article are remarkably similar to the reproaches that the monster makes to the parent who has abandoned and orphaned him. "Our first duty is to render those to whom we gave birth, wise, virtuous, and happy," writes Mary Shelley in *Eminent Literary and Scientific Men*, adding that "Rousseau failed in this." Victor remarks that in his unique moment of compassion for the monster, "I felt what the duties of a creator towards his creature were, that I ought to render him happy before I complained of his wickedness" (*F*, p. 97). In his idealized tableau of his own childhood he recounts that his parents "fulfilled their duties toward me," emphasizing their "deep consciousness of what they owed toward the being to which they had given life" (*F*, p. 33). When the monster first confronts the man who proves what Mary Shelley says Rousseau's example proves—"that a father is not to be trusted for natural instincts towards his offspring" (*CC*, p. 131)—he speaks with the rhetoric of the literal author of his being: "you, my creator, detest and spurn me, thy creature, to whom thou art bound by ties only dissoluble by the annihilation of one of us. ... Do your duty towards me, and I will do mine towards you and the rest of mankind" (*F*, p. 95). However, like Rousseau, who "neglected the first duty of man by abandoning his children" (*CC*, p. 172), Victor abandons the monster; and the monster in turn is like Rousseau's children, who in Mary Shelley's imagination are "brutified by their situation, or depressed by the burden, ever weighing at the heart, that they have not inherited the commonest right of humanity, a parent's care" (*CC*, p. 131).

Like Mary Shelley's biography of Rousseau, *Frankenstein* tells the story of a man "full of genius and aspiration after virtue" who "failed in the plainest dictates of nature and conscience"; Mary Shelley might have said of Frankenstein's failure what she said of Rousseau's: "can we wonder that his after course was replete with sorrow?" (*CC*, pp. 131–32). In the same year that she read the *Rêveries* and the *Émile*, had her dream about a "hideous phantasm" and a "hideous corpse," and, unable to rid herself of "my hideous phantom" (*F*, p. xi), began to write the story of "a figure hideously deformed" (*F*, p. 115), Mary Shelley read in her mother's *Vindication of the Rights of Woman*: "A great proportion of the misery that wanders, in hideous forms, around the world, is allowed to rise from the negligence of parents."[15] Frankenstein's great failure in the novel—directly responsible for the monster's murderous rage as well as his misery—is his negligence as a parent. "No father could claim the gratitude of his child so completely as I should deserve theirs," he boasts as he imagines the "new species" that he plans to create after learning how to "animate the lifeless clay" (*F*, pp. 52–53); but Frankenstein misses the point that Mary Shelley found in her father's *Enquiry*: "Children are a sort of raw material put into our hands, a ductile and yielding substance, which, if we do not ultimately mould in conformity to our wishes, it is because we throw away the power committed to us, by the folly with which we are accustomed to exert it."[16]

In recent years several important readings of *Frankenstein* have demonstrated the novel's status as a "gothic psychodrama of [Mary Shelley's] family," a "phantasmagoria of the nursery" that is a deeply ambivalent account of a daughter's attitude toward the father who came close to disowning her and the mother who abandoned her at the moment of her birth.[17] I am suggesting that for Mary Shelley the figure of Rousseau was charged with all of the valences of this perverse family romance. I suggest in the Appendix that because of Mary Wollstonecraft's personal and public interest in Rousseau, Mary Shelley would have associated Rousseau with her mother. My point here is that Rousseau's abandonment of his children would have given Mary Shelley compelling psychological reason (consciously or unconsciously) to identify her mother with Rousseau. Like Rousseau, Mary Wollstonecraft was a genius who aspired after virtue and devoted herself to the education of children while abandoning her own offspring (albeit involuntarily). Consequently, in order to understand the family psychodrama that is enacted by the characters and phantoms of *Frankenstein*, we must understand how Mary Shelley uses Rousseau to triangulate, so to speak, her relation to her mother; we must understand the extent to which Victor plays the part of Rousseau in the pages of *Frankenstein* because in the series of identifications that are set in play in the novel, Rousseau often stands in for Mary Shelley's mother.

I want to suggest, however, that the *dramatis personae* of *Frankenstein*—its distribution of parts, persons, and roles—is still more complex and overdetermined. We have seen that in addition to the presence throughout the novel of various textual echoes of characters and ideas from Rousseau's works, the monster appears to be playing the role of the *homme sauvage* dramatized in the two *Discours* and the *Essai sur l'origine des langues*, while Victor, the genius who aspires after virtue yet commits the crime of abandoning his offspring, seems to be cast as Rousseau. I want to argue now that Mary Shelley's portrait of Rousseau in this most ambivalent of novels is in fact divided between Frankenstein and his monster. It has become a critical commonplace to observe that the monster is Frankenstein's "alterego" or "doppelgänger"—an "alternative Frankenstein."[18] I believe that part of what makes them doubles or more precisely two sides of the same person is their shared representation of the man who wrote *Rousseau juge de Jean-Jacques*, a series of dialogues created by the *dédoublement* of their autobiographical subject. It should not, therefore, contradict my assertion that Mary Shelley identifies Victor with Rousseau to assert now that the unnamed monster of the novel *is*, so to speak, Rousseau—or at least an allegorical version of him.

For example, for the same reasons that she repeatedly condemns Rousseau for abandoning and orphaning his children, Mary Shelley would have been very conscious of the fact that Rousseau himself was orphaned and abandoned by his mother. "His birth cost the life of his mother," she writes in her biography, "and was, he says, 'the first of his misfortunes' " (*CC*, p. 111). As this paraphrase and translation from the *Confessions* suggests, Rousseau was in this misfortune most like Mary Shelley herself; but as we have seen, of the many orphans in the novel the monster most explicitly dramatizes and laments this misfortune. "Un homme abandonné seul sur la face de la terre, à la merci du genre humain," Rousseau suggests in the *Essai sur l'origine des langues*, "devoit être un animal féroce" ("A man abandoned alone on the face of the earth, at the mercy of humankind, had to be a ferocious monster" [*O*, p. 445]); the monster is doubly abandoned and if his eloquent reproaches to Frankenstein suggest Mary Shelley's condemnation of Rousseau the parent, they also suggest her identification—through the monster—with the Rousseau whose mother died in giving him life.

Furthermore, Mary Shelley's portrayal of the abandoned monster specifically evokes Rousseau's role as outcast, exile, and wanderer—a public and literary persona of almost mythic proportions who was well known throughout Europe and, of course, dramatized in Rousseau's own versions of his life story.[19] We can read in the monster's eloquent lamentations and especially in the misfortunes of his life a dramatization of the conditions and sentiments that

Rousseau depicts in the *Rêveries*. Indeed, the monster acts out and at times seems to translate the striking first words of the first *Promenade*:

> Me voici donc seul sur la terre, n'ayant plus de frère, de prochain, d'ami, de société que moi-même. Le plus sociable et le plus aimant des humains en a été proscrit par un accord unanime. Ils ont cherché dans les raffinements de leur haine quel tourment pouvait être le plus cruel à mon âme sensible, et ils ont brisé violemment tous les liens qui m'attachaient à eux. (*R*, p. 3)

> Here I am, then, alone on the earth, without brother, neighbor, friend, or any society but myself. The most sociable and loving of human beings has been proscribed by a unanimous accord. They have sought, in the refinement of their hatred, the torment that would be the cruelest to my sensitive soul, and they have violently broken all the bonds which attached me to them.

The monster—who, we have seen, is like a savage man "abandonné seul sur la face de la terre, à la merci du genre humain," describes himself in similar terms. In his first confrontation with Frankenstein he laments, "must I be hated, who am miserable beyond all living things! Yet you, my creator, detest and spurn me . . . to whom thou art bound by ties only dissoluble by the annihilation of one of us." He continues: "Everywhere I see bliss, from which I alone am irrevocably excluded. I was benevolent and good . . . my soul glowed with love and humanity; but am I not alone, miserably alone?" Frankenstein's "fellow creatures," he says, "spurn and hate me. . . . If the multitude of mankind knew of my existence, they would do as you do, and arm themselves for my destruction" (*F*, pp. 95–96).

What seems paranoid or hyperbolic in Rousseau's autobiography is literally true in the life story of the monster. The monster seems to literalize the conditions that Rousseau describes with a figure of speech when he explains that despite his feelings of benevolence he has been taken for a monster: "Moi qui me sentais digne d'amour et d'estime . . . je me vis travesti tout d'un coup en un monstre affreux tel qu'il n'en exista jamais" ("I, who felt myself worthy of love and esteem . . . I saw myself suddenly misrepresented as a frightful monster, such as had never existed" [*R*, p. 108]). Like Frankenstein's monster, Rousseau tells the story of how he unexpectedly finds himself regarded as "un monstre" and "un assassin" (*R*, p. 4). Mary Shelley reproduces this image in her biography of Rousseau; she recounts how the "peasantry of Neufchâtel were taught to regard him as a monster; from execration they proceeded to personal attack; stones were thrown at him during his walks" (*CC*, p. 157). Mary Shelley also reproduces these images in her novel as she tells the story of a monster and a murderer—who is, by the way, "bruised by stones" when the peasants of a village "attack" him (*F*, p. 101).

The monster, then, might be seen as a literal translation of the figure of Rousseau represented in the *Rêveries*; another sign of this is contained in the beginning of the monster's autobiography in words that read as a translation or paraphrase of Rousseau's autobiography: "It is with considerable difficulty that I remember the original era of my being; all the events of that period appear confused and indistinct. A strange multiplicity of sensations seized me, and I saw, felt, heard, and smelt at the same time, and it was, indeed, a long time before I learned to distinguish between the operations of my various senses" (*F*, p. 98). This description of the first impressions of a being who awakens from the dead recalls the moment of awakening that Rousseau describes in the second *Promenade*: "Je naissais dans cet instant à la vie, et il me semblait que je remplissais de ma légère existence tous les objets que j'apercevais. Tout entier au moment présent je ne me souvenais de rien; je n'avais nulle notion distincte de mon individu, pas la moindre idée de ce qui venait de m'arriver; je ne savais ni qui j'étais ni où j'étais" ("At that instant I was born into life, and it seemed to me that with my frail existence I filled all the objects I perceived. Entirely in the present moment, I remembered nothing; I had no distinct notion of my individuality, nor the least idea of what had just happened to me; I knew neither who I was nor where I was" [*R*, p. 17]). The monster's experience is a literal version of the figurative awakening from death that Rousseau experiences after the accident that seems to kill him (and indeed is reported to have killed him by a premature obituary).[20] If the monster's awakening seems less pleasant, it may be because Mary Shelley grafted this description of gaining consciousness onto her condensed translation of Rousseau's description of the life of the *homme sauvage*; it is on the same page that Mary Shelley lists the activities that Rousseau ascribes to man in his natural state.[21]

As the monster gains consciousness, details of his early life also resemble the childhood Rousseau portrays in his autobiographies. We have seen that both narratives begin with the misfortune of losing the parent who gives the subject life. The monster's autobiography also resembles Rousseau's in its account of the reading that forms his sensibilities and idea of the world and constitutes his first education; of the three books that make up the monster's personal library, one of them—Plutarch's *Lives*—is singled out by Rousseau in the *Confessions* as having been "ma lecture favorite" ("my favorite reading" [*C*, p. 8]).

Rousseau writes of his preference for Plutarch in the *Rêveries*: "ce fut la première lecture de mon enfance, ce sera la derniére de ma vieillesse" ("it was my first reading in childhood, and it will be my last in old age" [*R*, p. 41]). In her biographical essay about Rousseau Mary Shelley devotes a long paragraph to a translation of Rousseau's account in the *Confessions* of his childhood reading and the influence on him of Plutarch, including his comment that "the pleasure I took in it cured me somewhat of my love for romances" (*CC*, p. 112). If the monster's reading list can be seen as an autobiographical gesture on Mary Shelley's part to her own reading lists, it also doubly refers to Rousseau—whose own reading list was included in a book she lists next to *Paradise Lost*, *The Sorrows of Young Werther*, and Plutarch's *Lives*.

However, in spite of these many echoes of language and plot, perhaps the most striking allusion to Rousseau's autobiography in the monster's life story is to be found in the fact that the monster has an autobiography. At the center of the novel we read the monster's confessions: insisting that even the guilty are allowed "to speak in their own defence," he insists on appearing before the being he calls "my creator" to present his life story (*F*, pp. 96, 95). I have suggested that Mary Shelley goes out of her way to make the monster speak French; but the monster speaks Rousseau's language in other senses as well. As Peter Brooks has written—in words that are reminiscent of descriptions of Rousseau—the monster is "a supreme rhetorician of his own situation, one who controls the antitheses and oxymorons that express the pathos of his existence."[22] We are continually reminded of the monster's eloquence, not just by the power of his language but by the commentaries on it included in the novel. Victor is at first "moved" (*F*, p. 139) in listening to the monster's autobiography; he later warns Walton: "He is eloquent and persuasive" (*F*, p. 198). When Walton meets the monster he is "touched by the expressions of his misery" until he recalls "what Frankenstein had said of his powers of eloquence and persuasion" (*F*, p. 209).

In Mary Wollstonecraft's book on the French Revolution (read or reread by Mary Shelley in 1814), man in "his savage state" is said to be "distinguished only by superiority of genius, prowess, and eloquence." "I say eloquence," Wollstonecraft adds, "for I believe, that in this state of society he is most eloquent, because most natural."[23] If the monster resembles natural man in his eloquence, however, he most resembles the author of the ideas that Wollstonecraft is borrowing. From Rousseau's first celebrity as an author (with his paradoxical *Discours sur les sciences et les arts*), he was noted by both advocates and detractors for his eloquence. Godwin writes of Rousseau in his *Enquiry* that "the term eloquence is perhaps more precisely descriptive of his mode of composition than that of any other writer that ever existed." An unsympathetic contemporary of Godwin's described "the glowing hues of impassioned eloquence" in Rousseau's writing; and Mary Shelley describes her husband as being "charmed by the passionate eloquence" of *La Nouvelle Héloïse* in her account of the summer spent "on the shores of Lake Geneva" in 1816.[24] Admired for its paradoxes and originality, Rousseau's eloquence was also considered suspect and he was sometimes accused of sophistry. Mary Shelley herself writes that he "defends himself by many baseless sophisms" (*CC*, p. 173), just as Frankenstein thinks that he had been "moved by the sophisms of the being I had created" (*F*, p. 159).

The monster understands his own investment in his powers of eloquence and persuasion; he realizes that his fate depends on his ability to move others through a recital of his autobiography. He delays his appeal to the De Laceys until he has confidence in his mastery of their language. When he finally confronts Frankenstein, he entreats him "to hear me ... Listen to my tale ... Listen to me ... listen to me ..." (*F*, pp. 95–96). Like Rousseau, he is not surprised by the hostility he meets with—"'I expected this reception,' said the demon" (*F*, p. 95)—yet like Rousseau he seems to possess a naive faith in the power of autobiography, in the effects of telling one's own story, as he reveals both his virtues and his crimes before the judgment of his creator. In the *Essai sur l'origine des langues*, arguing against the eighteenth-century truism that sight was the most powerful of the senses, Rousseau writes:

> lorsqu'il est question d'émouvoir le coeur et d'enflammer les passions, c'est tout autre chose. .... Supposez une situation de douleur parfaitement connue; en voyant la personne affligée vous serez difficilement ému jusqu'à pleurer: mais laissez-lui le temps de vous dire tout ce qu'elle sent, et bientôt vous allez fondre en larmes. Ce n'est qu'ainsi que les scènes de tragédie font leur effet. (*O*, p. 419)

> when the point is to move the heart and inflame the passions, it is another matter altogether. .... Imagine someone in a painful situation that is fully known; in seeing the afflicted person it would be difficult to be moved to tears: but give him the time to tell you everything he feels, and soon you will burst into tears. It is solely in this way that the scenes of a tragedy produce their effect.

The monster, of course, knows perfectly well that sight will not be adequate if the representation of his tragedy is to have any effect other than horror; it is for this reason that he first approaches the blind De Lacey. Asking Frankenstein, "How can I move thee?" and pleading, "Let your compassion be moved. . . . Listen to my tale" (*F*, p. 96), he places his hands over Frankenstein's eyes and seeks to move him through his story: "Thus I take from thee a sight which you abhor. Still thou canst listen to me and grant thy compassion. By the virtues that I once possessed, I demand this from you. Hear my tale" (*F*, p. 97). Like Rousseau, the monster puts his faith in autobiography, believing that everything depends on his ability to move the heart of his listener: to inflame his passions, to elicit his compassion. He understands that the story of his life depends on sympathy. This realization is at the center of the scene of his tragedy; I will suggest that it has its origins in a story that Rousseau tells about the origins of sympathy.

Frankenstein, I will argue, can be read as a parable about the failure of sympathy. From the outset of the novel the letters from Walton introduce a preoccupation with sympathy and fellow feeling. Noting in his letter to his sister that writing "is a poor medium for the communication of feeling," Walton writes: "I desire the company of a man who could sympathize with me, whose eyes would reply to mine" (*F*, p. 18). He complains about the lack of "interest and sympathy" in the master of the ship; he looks upon Frankenstein "with sympathy and compassion" (*F*, pp. 20, 25). By the end of Frankenstein's story he is almost overwhelmed with sympathy and compassion: "His eloquence is forcible and touching; nor can I hear him, when he relates a pathetic incident or endeavours to move the passions of pity or love, without tears" (*F*, p. 200).

Encouraged by "the sympathy which [Frankenstein] evinced to use the language of my heart," Walton tells Victor "of my desire of finding a friend, of my thirst for a more intimate sympathy with a fellow mind than had ever fallen to my lot" (*F*, pp. 26, 27). He laments, "I have longed for a friend; I have sought one who would sympathize with me and love me" (*F*, p. 201). The relatively large proportion of Walton's narrative devoted to these declarations of sentiment suggests Mary Shelley's interest in framing the stories of Frankenstein and the monster with the problem of sympathy; and indeed, her introduction of many of these passages in the revisions for the 1831 edition of the novel reveals her effort to make the problem of sympathy even more explicit, especially at the beginning of the text.[25]

Victor Frankenstein rebuffs Walton's plea for sympathy, describing himself as incapable of "new ties and fresh affection" (*F*, p. 201). His own narrative, however, often takes note of the presence or absence of sympathy: "Her sympathy was ours" (*F*, p. 37), he says of Elizabeth; and he notes that Clerval "had never sympathized in my tastes for natural science" yet still "sincerely sympathized in my feelings," expressing (for example) "his heartfelt sympathy" when William is killed and Victor "longed to console and sympathize with my loved and sorrowing friends" (*F*, pp. 66, 68, 71). He delays returning to Geneva after William's death because, he says, he feels "as if I had no right to claim their sympathies," and he later senses that he must check his "impatient thirst for sympathy" (*F*, pp. 142, 177). Frankenstein is disturbed when the woman who watches over him in prison seems "accustomed to see without sympathizing in sights of misery," and he notes that the "countenance" of Mr. Kirwin "expressed sympathy and compassion" (*F*, pp. 170, 171).

It is the monster, however, who is most concerned with sympathy in the course of the novel. Describing himself as "fashioned to be susceptible of love and sympathy" (*F*, p. 208), he displays all the characteristics of what was considered in the eighteenth century to be natural sympathy—even before he reads Goethe and learns about "sentiments and feelings, which had for their object something out of self" (*F*, p. 123). His account of his sentiments while watching the De Laceys reads like a citation from any of numerous eighteenth-century treatises on moral philosophy: "when they were unhappy, I felt depressed; when they rejoiced, I sympathized in their joys" (*F*, p. 107); and (like theoreticians of sympathy) extending his responses into the realm of aesthetic experience, the monster describes how he "sympathized with" the "beings concerning whom I read" (*F*, p. 123). Watching how the cottagers "sympathized with one another," he senses a desire to receive sympathy himself: "I required kindness and sympathy," he explains, noting that he hoped that the De Laceys "would compassionate me ... who solicited their compassion and friendship" (*F*, pp. 126, 125).

Of course the monster is unsuccessful. Finding himself "unsympathized with" and realizing that "none among the myriads of men that existed would pity or assist" him (*F*, p. 130), he seeks out Frankenstein and demands his "compassion." As we have seen, the monster tries to "move" his creator, to make Frankenstein "commiserate" him, pathetically trying to measure "the more moving part of my story" and persuade him with all the pathos his eloquence can convey (*F*, pp. 96, 111). Victor describes the "strange effect" of the monster's words: "I compassionated him and sometimes felt a wish to console him"; yet finally the effect of this compassion is not sympathy: "I could not sympathize with him" (*F*, p. 140). Walton's response at the end of the book is similar. Listening to the monster out of "curiosity and compassion," he is "at first touched by the expressions of his misery" (*F*, pp. 208–9); but the monster knows by this point not to expect sympathy. He says: "I seek not a fellow feeling in my misery. No sympathy may I ever find. ... in what should I seek for sympathy? I am content to suffer alone" (*F*, p. 209). By the end of the novel—the last word of which is "distance" (*F*, p. 211)—sympathy seems impossible.

It is a desire for sympathy that motivates the monster's demand that Frankenstein create another monster to be his companion. "You must create a female for me," he insists, "with whom I can live in the interchange of those sympathies necessary for my being" (*F*, p. 138). He insists that his "evil passions" will disappear when he meets "with sympathy" (*F*, p. 140). His plea, "Let me see that I excite the sympathy of some existing thing" (*F*, p. 139), recalls the pleas of Walton, yet in his wish for a companion who will satisfy his need for sympathy the monster also resembles Frankenstein himself. Indeed, it is precisely in creating a creature in the first place that Frankenstein seems to display the same interest in sympathy that is manifested by Walton and the monster. He describes his plan for "the creation of a human being" as a plan to "attempt the creation of a being like myself" (*F*, p. 52). This is the desire that torments both Walton and the monster, the desire that underwrites the pervasive preoccupation with sympathy in the novel: each character wishes for a fellow being, someone who is *like* himself. What they seek is not a friend or a companion but rather a *semblable*. It is not a coincidence that the only moment in which Frankenstein admits being moved and displays compassion in listening to the monster is during his plea for a being like himself.

Ironically, it is Frankenstein's creation of a being like himself that seems to cut him off from sympathy. It is after he creates the monster that he feels of his family and friends that he "had no right to claim their sympathies" (*F*, p. 142); and it is only after he destroys the companion monster that he feels "as if I belonged to a race of human beings like myself" (*F*, p. 162). After trying to create a being like himself, he feels separated from beings like himself; and he insists on denying the monster and Walton the sympathy and fellow feeling of beings like themselves. What has gone wrong? On the level of plot, we are told that the monster is of gigantic stature, that he is hideously disfigured, and that people are frightened when they see him. But does this mean that Frankenstein has failed in creating a being like himself? I suggest that the novel turns on this question.[26]

At the same time he imagines creating a being like himself, Frankenstein pictures himself as the father of a "new species" (F, p. 52). The question of whether Frankenstein is like the monster, whether the monster is like Frankenstein, is related to the question of whether Frankenstein and the monster are of the same species: whether they can regard each other as fellow creatures. When De Lacey assures the monster that he takes pleasure in being "in any way serviceable to a human creature," the monster responds: "You raise me from the dust by this kindness; and I trust that, by your aid, I shall not be driven from the society and sympathy of your fellow creatures" (F, p. 128). But the monster's identification of this patriarch with the father who literally raised him from the dust, as well as his reference to "your fellow creatures," suggests his apprehension that he will not be regarded as a "human creature." When he asks for a companion, he specifically requests a being "of the same species" (F, p. 137). The father of his species is indeed particularly concerned with such differences and likenesses. Throughout the novel he refers (and only occasionally in the context of the monster) to his "fellow creatures" (F, pp. 55, 141, 157, 163), his "fellow beings" (F, pp. 78, 176), his "fellow men" (F, p. 151), and "human beings like myself" (F, p. 162). It is this concern with the existence of fellow creatures—or more precisely, with the possibility of the existence of fellow creatures—that lies at the center of the novel's investigation of the conditions of sympathy.

I am suggesting that Mary Shelley's evident insistence on the language and the problem of sympathy in *Frankenstein* amounts to more than a gothic translation of a sentimental novel. She might have constructed the same plot around a monster who had read *The Sorrows of Young Werther* too many times and was frustrated in his desire for love and friendship. The question of sympathy in *Frankenstein* is also more specific than a Romantic meditation on the projection of self onto the landscape or the wish for a companionable form. Using terms and formulations that have their source in discussions of sympathy in eighteenth-century moral philosophy and aesthetics, Mary Shelley focuses on the epistemology and the rhetoric of fellow feeling—which, she shows, raise questions about identification, resemblance, likeness, difference, comparison, and the ability to transport oneself into someone else's thoughts and sentiments. I will argue, of course, that Rousseau is the theoretician of sympathy who most significantly informs Mary Shelley's investigation; but I would like to approach Rousseau through the two other figures who preside over the conception and composition of *Frankenstein*: Wollstonecraft and Godwin.

The first paragraph of the introduction to *A Vindication of the Rights of Woman* announces the author's interest in what she calls "the education of my fellow-creatures"; Wollstonecraft suggests that the "false system of education" that she deplores is based on books written by men who consider "females rather as women than human creatures." Women, she argues, have been "treated as kind of subordinate beings, and not as part of the human species." Singling out Rousseau, she insists that women are "one half of the human species," not "a fanciful kind of *half* being—one of Rousseau's wild chimeras." Wollstonecraft writes that she addresses men "as a fellow-creature" to "claim, in the name of my sex, some interest in their hearts"; and she continues, in an appeal that anticipates the monster's appropriation of Miltonic rhetoric, "I entreat them to assist to emancipate their companion, to make her a *help meet* for them!"[27]

Wollstonecraft suggests that by refusing to regard women as members of the same species, men not only deny women sympathy; they deprive themselves of the benefits of fellow feeling. In a long condemnation of Rousseau for making Sophie the slave of love as well as the slave of Émile, she cites Adam Smith's *Theory of Moral Sentiments*: "'The charm of life,' says a grave philosopher, 'is sympathy; nothing pleases us more than to observe in other men a fellow-feeling with all the emotions of our breast.'"[28] Smith argues that fellow feeling is possible only through the imaginative transport and identification that constitute an act of sympathy, the interchange of parts and persons that allows one to represent in one's imagination the thoughts and sentiments of someone else; but, as Wollstonecraft (following Smith) insists, this identification will only be possible if we recognize an other as a fellow creature, as a member of the same species. We can experience fellow feeling only with those whom we recognize as fellow creatures.

Mary Shelley's story about the denial of sympathy, fellow feeling, and fellow creatures seems to draw upon Wollstonecraft's critique of the ideology of sexual difference. In this context we can also see Mary Shelley continuing the analysis her mother dramatizes in the fictional counterpart of her *Vindication: Maria, or The Wrongs of Woman*, where a feminist critique is extended to include a class analysis. The unfinished novel in which Wollstonecraft inscribed Rousseau as Prometheus clearly provided a model for the narrative of *Franken-*

stein: the story about the protagonist named in the title contains within it the autobiographical narrative of someone who tells a life story that is remarkably similar to the monster's.[29] Jemima, Maria's attendant, is orphaned immediately after her birth; like the monster, she receives her literary and moral education while observing a household in which she is unseen and unheard (in her case because of her rank).[30] Jemima describes herself in her early life as "an egg dropped on the sand; a pauper by nature, hunted from family to family, who belonged to nobody." "I was despised from my birth," she recounts, "I had not even the chance of being considered as a fellow creature." Like *The Rights of Woman*, *The Wrongs of Woman* emphasizes the predicament of not being viewed as a fellow creature: Jemima is mistreated by one family because "they had been accustomed to view me as a creature of another species"; she asks Maria, who is said to be the first person to treat her "like a fellow-creature," "Who ever acknowledged me to be a fellow-creature?"[31]

Describing her life after being cast out from the household where she gained literacy and refined her sensibilities, Jemima says: "To be cut off from human converse, now that I had been taught to relish it, was to wander a ghost among the living." Without "any companions to alleviate" her existence "by sympathy," she becomes embittered and she even, by her account, acts like "a monster."[32] Like Frankenstein's monster, who is also in a sense a ghost among the living, Jemima is an orphan and an outcast who is denied sympathy and fellow feeling because she is regarded as a creature of another species. As she does with Rousseau's autobiographical narrative, Mary Shelley literalizes what is figurative in her mother's text, creating a sort of allegory about a monster who really is (or seems to be) a creature of another species. This translation from Wollstonecraft supports the interpretation advanced by Sandra Gilbert and Susan Gubar that *Frankenstein*, as a mock rendition of *Paradise Lost*, casts the monster in "the part of Eve," "a female in disguise," a "creature of the second sex."[33] However, if we recognize *Frankenstein* as an allegory about the status of women as creatures of a different species, we must also recognize how Mary Shelley inscribes herself in a literary and philosophical dialogue with her mother about the possibility of fellow feeling. We should recognize further that this dialogue includes the literary and philosophical reflections on this subject by her father.

Godwin's *Caleb Williams* (read or reread by Mary Shelley, along with *The Wrongs of Woman*, in 1814) also tells the story of "a solitary being cut off from the expectation of sympathy" who is accused of being "a monster"; he is told, he reports, that "it would be

an abuse of words to consider me in the light of a human creature"
(*CW*, pp. 247, 249). Unjustly persecuted as a criminal throughout the
narrative, he is considered "a monster of depravity" and the "oppro-
brium of the human species" (*CW*, p. 174). Even the woman whose
family provided "an enviable resting-place for me, who ... had
scarcely dared to look for sympathy and kindness in the countenance
of a human being," comes to consider him "a monster, and not a man"
(*CW*, pp. 292, 300). Describing himself as completely "cut off from the
whole human species," Williams recounts an existence in which he is
deprived of fellow feeling: "Sympathy, the magnetic virtue, the
hidden essence of our life, was extinct" (*CW*, pp. 303, 308). Once
again, we see the rhetoric of sympathy representing a being who is
denied fellow feeling and cut off from the human species as a monster
and not a man. The psychologically and dramatically intense dialectical struggle between a master and a servant and a hunter and the
hunted in *Caleb Williams* has been recognized as a model for
Frankenstein—which, of course, was dedicated to the author of *Caleb
Williams*. I am suggesting that (along with Wollstonecraft's novel)
Godwin's novel also provided Mary Shelley with a vocabulary for
thinking about sympathy.[34]

Furthermore, like *The Wrongs of Woman* (which addresses in
fiction many of the issues discussed in *A Vindication of the Rights of
Woman*), in its relation to *An Enquiry Concerning Political Justice*
Godwin's first fiction also provides a model for a philosophical novel.
In the same year in which she read *Caleb Williams* and *The Wrongs of
Woman*, Mary Shelley also read her father's *Enquiry*—including,
presumably, the chapter entitled "Of Self-Love and Benevolence."
There, following Smith, Rousseau, and a tradition of eighteenth-
century moral philosophy, Godwin writes: "We find by observation
that we are surrounded by beings of the same nature as ourselves.
They have the same senses, are susceptible of the same pleasures and
pains. . . . We are able in imagination to go out of ourselves, and
become impartial spectators of the system of which we are a part."[35]
Writing in the context of a discussion of our ability to counter the
delusions of self-love with the perspective and points of view of others,
Godwin relates the imaginative transport of sympathy to the perception that other beings are like ourselves. Earlier in the *Enquiry*, in
discussing "man in his original state"—and specifically, the origins of
language—Godwin writes that the act of "comparison, or the
coupling together of two ideas and the perception of resemblances and
differences,"[36] constituted the first step following the existence of
mind and the capacity for abstraction.

Godwin does not explicitly relate the perception of resemblance that leads us to see others as beings like ourselves (allowing an imaginative transport that takes us outside of ourselves) to the perception of resemblance that occurs to man in his original state and allows the invention of language. These two moments of observation are explicitly juxtaposed, however, in a text that, I believe, is behind Godwin's speculations: Rousseau's *Essai sur l'origine des langues*. Whether or not Godwin was drawing on Rousseau in these particular passages is finally not relevant here, for we have seen that *Frankenstein* appears to draw on Mary Shelley's own study of Rousseau's *Essai sur l'origine des langues*. I have suggested that in her efforts to write a philosophical novel of her own, Mary Shelley is working through Godwin's and Wollstonecraft's inquiries into the effects of the failure of sympathy and the recognition of others as fellow creatures with fellow feelings that sympathy seems to depend on. What I want to argue now is that in her attempt to carry on her parents' philosophical and literary investigations, Mary Shelley (like her parents) found Rousseau to offer compelling formulations about the perception of resemblance, the recognition of fellow creatures, and the transport of sympathy.

In the *Essai sur l'origine des langues*, Rousseau describes the first activation of pity by the transport of imagination and identification. "La pitié, bien que naturelle au coeur de l'homme, resteroit éternellement inactive sans l'imagination qui la met en jeu. Comment nous laissons-nous émouvoir à la pitié? En nous transportant hors de nous-mêmes, en nous identifiant avec l'être souffrant" ("Pity, although natural to the heart of man, would remain forever inactive unless it were set in play by imagination. How are we moved to pity? By transporting ourselves outside of ourselves, by identifying ourselves with the being who suffers"). This act of identification which accompanies imagination and reflection is, according to Rousseau, a precondition of fellow feeling: "Comment souffrirais-je en voyant souffrir un autre, si je ne sais même qu'il souffre, si j'ignore ce qu'il y a de commun entre lui et moi? ... La réflexion naît des idées comparées" ("How could I suffer when seeing another suffer, if I do not even know that he suffers, if I do not know what we have in common? ... Reflection comes from the comparison of ideas").

Without this act of comparison man is "seul au milieu du genre humain" ("alone in the midst of humankind"); without the ability to perceive resemblances and understand what he shares in common with another, he is in his most primitive state:

Appliquez ces idées aux premiers hommes, vous verrez la raison de
leur barbarie. N'ayant jamais rien vu que ce qui étoit autour d'eux, cela
même ils ne le connaissaient pas; ils ne se connaissaient pas eux-mêmes.
Ils avaient l'idée d'un père, d'un fils, d'un frère, et non pas d'un
homme. Leur cabane contenait tous leurs semblables; un étranger, une
bête, un monstre, étaient pour eux la même chose: hors eux et leur
famille, l'univers entier ne leur étoit rien. (*O*, pp. 445–47)

Apply these ideas to the first men, and you will see the reason for their
barbarity. Never having seen anything but what was around them,
they did not know even that; they did not know themselves. They had
the idea of a father, a son, a brother, but not that of a man. Their hut
contained all their fellow beings; a stranger, a beast, a monster, were
for them the same thing: outside of themselves and their family, the
whole universe was nothing to them.

Without the ability to compare himself to others and recognize them
as fellow creatures, as beings like himself, primitive man cannot look
on anyone outside of his immediate family with sympathy. Where he
should see a *semblable*, he sees an other who appears to him as a
stranger, a beast, a monster.

I believe that in this tableau of primitive man we can see the story
of Mary Shelley's monster. Looked on without fellow feeling, he is
considered to be a creature of another species: a monster, anything but
a *semblable*. Alone among humankind, seeking refuge from "the
barbarity of man," he comes across the cabin of a family where he
discovers the ideas of "father," "sister," "brother," and "son" (*F*, pp.
102, 107). (Neither Rousseau nor Mary Shelley imagines a family with
the idea of "mother.") These ideas coincide with the origin of the
monster's acquisition of language and sympathy; but he will learn that
they do not include him in their reference. In this sense the De Lacey
family resembles the Frankenstein household as Victor describes it in
his account of his youth: "My life had hitherto been remarkably
secluded and domestic, and this had given me invincible repugnance
to new countenances," he says; "I believed myself totally unfitted for
the company of strangers." Yet Victor decides to "enter the world and
take my station among other human beings" (*F*, p. 44). Neither the
Frankenstein nor the De Lacey family, however, will recognize the
monster as another human being, as a man. Paradoxically, it is the
homme sauvage embodied by the monster who experiences the
transport and identification of sympathy, while the civilized family
(who know only the ideas of "father," "sister," "brother," and "son"
that exist in their secluded and domestic life) display repugnance to

the "stranger" (*F*, p. 127)—this is De Lacey's term—who enters their cottage in the shape of a monster. They act as if he is a beast; their idea of "man" does not include the creature Frankenstein created to be a human being.[37]

Mary Shelley's dramatization of this tableau from the *Essai sur l'origine des langues* also seems to be informed by the "Entretien sur les romans" that serves as the second preface to *La Nouvelle Héloïse*. In Rousseau's dialogue between the characters N. and R., N. insists that a novel should present not a mere "portrait" of a particular individual but rather "un tableau d'imagination" in which "toute figure humaine doit avoir les traits communs à l'homme" ("every human figure should have the features common to man"); to his claim that the characters of *La Nouvelle Héloïse* are not "dans la nature," R. responds that both men and characters can differ. He asks: "Qui est-ce qui ose assigner des bornes précises à la nature, et dire: 'Voilà jusqu'où l'homme peut aller et pas au-delà'?" ("Who dares assign precise boundaries to nature and say: this is as far as man should go, and no further?"). R. then counters: "Avec ce beau raisonnement, les monstres inouïs, les géants, les pygmées, les chimères de toute espèce, . . . tout serait defiguré; nous n'aurions plus de modèl commun. Je le répète, dans les tableaux de l'humanité, chacun doit reconnaître l'homme" ("With this fine reasoning, unheard of monsters, giants, pygmies, chimeras of all kinds, . . . all would be disfigured; we would no longer have any common model. I repeat, in the tableaux of humanity, everyone should recognize man" [*NH*, p. 738]).

The issue in *Frankenstein* is not whether its characters can be found in nature (although Percy Shelley's preface makes claims for "the truth of the elementary principles of human nature" [*F*, p. xiii]); the novel, after all, is about the transgression of the borders of nature. The problem dramatized in the novel is how, in spite of disfiguration, one can recognize man in the tableaux of humanity; how one can delineate among the figures in the tableaux the human figure with the characteristics that are common to a man; how one can draw precise borders between a man and a monster. Frankenstein is obsessed with "the tremendous secrets of the human frame" (*F*, p. 53). Hoping to "banish disease from the human frame," he makes a special study of "the structure of the human frame" (*F*, pp. 40, 50). But after he succeeds in his project it is difficult for him to "delineate" (*F*, p. 56) the creature he meant to create in his own image. When the monster pleads for a companion he tells Frankenstein, "The picture I present to you is peaceful and human" (*F*, p. 139), but no one in the novel will regard his picture as human or recognize the figure of a human in his frame.

He forms in his "imagination" what he describes as "a thousand pictures of presenting myself" (*F*, p. 109); he hopes to move De Lacey "by my representations," and he eagerly notes when Frankenstein for a moment seems "moved by my representations" (*F*, pp. 131, 140). However, the monster meets with no one who will pardon his "outward form," and he ends the novel ready to "consume to ashes this miserable frame" (*F*, pp. 209–10). The frame that forms the pictures he presents and represents is not recognized as the frame of a human; the traits of his disfigured figure seem to have more in common with an unheard of monster or a giant than a man.[38]

This predicament is more fully explained in a remarkable tableau contained in the *Essai sur l'origine des langues*. In arguing that the first language was figurative, Rousseau offers this example:

> Un homme sauvage en rencontrant d'autres se sera d'abord effrayé. Sa frayeur lui aura fait voir ces hommes plus grands et plus forts que lui-même; il leur aura donné le nom de *géants*. Après beaucoup d'expériences, il aura reconnu que ces prétendus géants n'étant ni plus grands ni plus forts que lui, leur stature ne convenait point à l'idée d'abord attachée au mot de géant. Il inventera donc un autre nom commun à eux et à lui, tel par example que le nom d'*homme*, et laissera celui de *géant* à l'objet faux qui l'avait frappé devant son illusion. Voilà comment le mot figuré naît avant le mot propre, lorsque la passion nous fascine les yeux, et que la première idée qu'elle nous offre n'est pas celle de la vérité. (*O*, p. 425)

> A primitive man, coming upon others, will at first be frightened. His fear will have made him see these men as bigger and stronger than himself; he will have given them the name of *giants*. After many experiences, he will have recognized that these supposed giants are neither bigger nor stronger than himself, that their stature did not at all fit with the idea first attached to the word "giant." Thus he will invent another name, common to himself and them, such as for example the name *man*, and will leave that of *giant* to the false object which had struck him during his illusion. This is how the figurative word comes into being before the literal, when passion fascinates our eyes, and when the first idea it presents to us is not the true one.

I have quoted this well-known passage at length because I believe that it represents an emblem for the monster's condition in Mary Shelley's novel. An *homme sauvage* who wanders the forests like man in the state of nature, the monster is in fact a giant. He is first described by

Walton (who also calls him a "savage") as "a being which had the shape of a man, but apparently of gigantic stature" (*F*, p. 23). Frankenstein recounts his decision to "make the being of a gigantic stature, that is to say, about eight feet in height, and proportionately large" (*F*, p. 52); when he first sees him again in the Alps he recognizes the monster first by "its gigantic stature" (*F*, p. 73). The monster himself calls his "stature gigantic" (*F*, p. 123). In pursuing his creature, Frankenstein reports the testimony of frightened eyewitnesses who described seeing a "gigantic monster" (*F*, p. 196).[39]

The point of Rousseau's allegory about sympathy is that the giant that frightens the man is not literally a giant; "giant" is only a *mot figuré* for "man" in this story: a metaphor born in mistake. Frankenstein's monster according to the plot of Mary Shelley's story appears to be literally a giant. But how do we know that Frankenstein and the others are not also making a mistake in failing (or refusing) to recognize in his frame the figure of a man? Rousseau describes the first apparition of another man in the form of a giant as an "illusion" (*O*, p. 425). Walton refers to the "appearance" of "a being which had the shape of a man, but apparently of gigantic stature" as an "apparition" (*F*, p. 23)—and in Mary Shelley's earlier version of this passage, he refers to an "optical delusion."[40] How do we know that Frankenstein really failed in his attempt to create a "human being," a "being like myself" (*F*, p. 52); can we be sure (regardless of the monster's actual size) that Frankenstein and the others are not operating under an illusion when they fail to recognize the monster as a fellow creature? Frankenstein tells how "none could behold" the young Elizabeth "without looking on her as of a distinct species" (*F*, p. 34)—a perspective which he represents as a sign of admiration but which Wollstonecraft represents as a mistake which denies one half of the species the status of human creatures.

What is at stake in the story of the monster, however, is more than the error of not recognizing an other as a *semblable*: a fellow creature who shares the common name of *man*. The monster in Mary Shelley's novel is denied that status of a fellow creature because—unlike the *homme sauvage* in Rousseau's story—Frankenstein never realizes that *monster*, like *giant*, is only a trope. He never realizes that the appellation "gigantic monster" is only a figure for a man: a figure of a man. Frankenstein, in short, is not a good reader. In his account of his childhood he remarks that when his mother presented Elizabeth to him as a "gift" that he "interpreted her words literally and looked upon Elizabeth as mine" (*F*, p. 35). He makes the same error in reading when he interprets the monster literally, rather than as a figure. When the monster represents himself to De Lacey by saying that people who see him "behold only a detestable monster . . . where they ought to see a feeling and kind friend," De Lacey interprets these words figuratively and suggests that the monster "undeceive them" (*F*, p. 128). *Monster* here is recognized as a figure, just as it is when Elizabeth says, "men appear to me as monsters," or when Justine says, "I almost began to think that I was the monster that he said I was," or when Frankenstein is told that the body of Clerval seemed to have been "placed, as it were, by some fiend across your path" (*F*, pp. 88, 83, 171).

No one will recognize an "as it were" framing the figure of the monster that Frankenstein repeatedly calls a "fiend" (*F*, p. 95); the monster cannot "undeceive" man from his "illusion," the "optical delusion" that blinds him to his error in reading. Frankenstein insists on taking the monster literally—even though the monster is continually presented to him as a figure, even though his own narrative repeatedly represents the monster as a figure. When Frankenstein sees the monster for the first time after the creation scene and its subsequent nightmare, just after watching "the lightnings playing on the summit of Mont Blanc in the most beautiful figures," he relates that he "perceived in the gloom a figure which stole from behind a clump of trees near me," and after he recognizes the creature as "the filthy demon to whom I had given life," he says, "the figure passed me quickly" (*F*, p. 73). When he sees the monster again, he says, "I suddenly beheld the figure of a man, at some distance" (*F*, p. 94).

Frankenstein beholds the figure of a man at some distance, just as in the next chapter the monster recounts: "I saw the figure of a man at a distance" (*F*, p. 102). The monster beholds the figure of a man and recognizes him as a man, even if what he expects from him is only "the barbarity of man" (*F*, p. 102). Frankenstein, however, does not understand that the figure he sees is a figure. The monster may be "a figure the most hideous and abhorred" (*F*, p. 187); even to himself he may be "a figure hideously deformed" who wishes people could "overlook the deformity of my figure" (*F*, pp. 115, 108). Yet however disfigured, he is represented as a figure; and because people cannot or will not recognize him as a figure, because they overlook the figure that he forms, they cannot recognize him as the figure of a man. Blinded to his figurative status, they deny the nameless monster a *nom propre*.

Rousseau suggests that only sympathy, only the perception of resemblance that reveals what one has in common with others, will allow one to recognize others as fellow creatures rather than as monsters or giants or beasts or strangers; only the recognition of fellow feeling can save people from monsters: save them from turning others into monsters, save them from becoming monsters. Mary Shelley's monster offers this moral for his story when he suggests that had he been granted sympathy and fellow feeling, had he been acknowledged as a fellow creature, he would not have acted like a monster. Yet at the same time *Frankenstein* also suggests that people might regard the monster as a monster precisely because they perceive his resemblance; they might refuse to recognize him as a man, a human creature, precisely because they apprehend the extent to which this monster *is* the figure of a man. To understand this we need to ask what is so monstrous about the creature Frankenstein sets out to make in his own image as a human being like himself. We need to recognize that the monster is not a figure only because he is a trope substituted for the proper name of *man*. He is also a figure in the sense that he stands as a simile: he is in fact a being *like* his creator—and it is this likeness that makes him so monstrous.

I am suggesting that what is so horrible about Frankenstein's experiment is that it is too successful. He might have been happier if he had created an unheard-of monster, a chimera in which he could not recognize the traits of man; but he has instead created "a being which had the shape of a man" (*F*, p. 23). Writing of "the possibility of shaping a life in one's own image" and describing the monster as "a figure for autobiography as such," Barbara Johnson argues: "the desire for resemblance, the desire to create a being like oneself—which is the autobiographical desire par excellence—is also the *central* transgression in Mary Shelley's novel."[41] The punishment for this transgression is that Frankenstein ends up creating a being who is both similar to and unlike himself, a being who is caught in what Peter Brooks calls (referring to the principles of language acquired by the monster) the "play of sameness and difference."[42] The monster's predicament in this story of failed sympathy and misreading is perhaps best summed up in his account of his own trouble identifying with the characters in his reading: "I found myself similar yet at the same time strangely unlike to the beings concerning whom I read" (*F*, p. 123). In perceiving his resemblance and difference, the monster glimpses his uncanny threat to the system of human signifiers, to the figures that stand as similes for men, but he does not understand that it is his sameness that is most threatening.

The monster reproaches his creator for not, like the God he reads about in Milton, making him "after his own image"; he tells Frankenstein: "My form is a filthy type of yours, more horrid even from the very resemblance" (*F*, p. 125). What is so horrid is precisely the resemblance, precisely the likeness that makes him a type of his creator. He becomes convinced, he says, that "I was in reality the monster that I am" (*F*, p. 108) when he sees the image of himself reflected in the mirror of a pool; but what he sees—what Frankenstein sees—is the monstrosity of resemblance, the likeness that proves something in common between his figure and a man. When Frankenstein speaks toward the end of the novel of planning to destroy the monster, he speaks of putting "an end to the existence of the monstrous image which I had endued with the mockery of a soul still more monstrous" (*F*, p. 174). What is so monstrous, however, is the image itself, the reproduction of himself that presents a simile of a man in its likeness. In creating a being like himself, a type of himself that is like yet strangely unlike him, Frankenstein has created a monstrous image that is most horrid in its resemblance, a figure that is monstrous precisely because it is a figure.

Behind Mary Shelley's dramatization of the creation of monstrous images there is also a scene from William Godwin's third novel, *Fleetwood*. Toward the end of the novel, wrongly convinced of his wife's infidelity in a plot borrowed from *Othello*, Fleetwood procures life-size wax models of his wife and the man he imagines is her lover. He recounts how he brings a "miniature of my wife" to a "celebrated modeller in wax" and instructs him to "make a likeness, as exact as he could, of the size of life" which he then dresses in a "complete suit of my wife's clothes." For the lieutenant he believes is having an affair with his wife, writes Fleetwood, "I fixed upon a terrible and monstrous figure of a fiend, which I found in the magazine of my artist." After he dresses this figure in a lieutenant's uniform, Fleetwood conducts in his room an insane ceremony, complete with props and music. He places himself, he relates, "my eyes fixed," as the spectator to a tableau vivant in which he eventually can no longer "distinguish fiction from reality." He describes how he "gazed at the figure" of his wife, thinking "it was, and it was not" her; as a valet "who ever executed his orders literally" guards the door, Fleetwood beholds "the figures before me" and he raves at them using "all the tropes that imagination ever supplied to the tongue of man" until finally he tears his wife's clothes "from off the figure that represented her" and "struck the figures vehemently . . . till they were broken to pieces."[43]

Like Fleetwood, Frankenstein sets out to make a likeness of the size of life; as an "artist" (*F*, p. xi), he makes a figure that is supposed to represent a human being. However, the only creation that comes out of this artist's magazine turns out to be literally *a terrible and monstrous figure of a fiend*. (Among the first names that Frankenstein calls his creation, after he recognizes what he first calls "the figure of a man," are "Abhorred monster" and "Fiend" [*F*, pp. 94–95].) Fleetwood, in a flurry of tropes, loses the ability to distinguish between fiction and reality, figures and human creatures. Frankenstein's mistake is more complicated: as in the Pygmalion story that both he and Fleetwood perversely repeat, his figure really does come to life; but this means that it is both more difficult and more crucial for him to recognize that he has created a figure, that his monstrous figure of a fiend is in fact a likeness—a fiction for himself.

Fleetwood in his madness finally strikes his figures "till they are broken to pieces." Frankenstein, who fails to destroy the "monstrous image" (*F*, p. 174) of the male fiend he has created from various pieces, does destroy his female figure; he says: "I thought with a sensation of madness on my promise of creating another like to him, and trembling with passion, tore to pieces the thing on which I was engaged" (*F*, p. 159). What drives him mad is the thought of another likeness—a creature like to the figure he created to be like to himself. (It is no coincidence that before he enters the room to pick up the pieces of the second monster that "lay scattered on the floor," Frankenstein recounts, "I paused to collect myself" [*F*, p. 163].) *Fleetwood* and *Frankenstein* suggest that it may be both mad and monstrous to create likenesses: fictions and figures in one's own image that will act out scenes from one's life. This, as Johnson suggests, is also the madness of autobiography; Mary Shelley's novel, which readers have considered to be as painfully and uncontrollably autobiographical as a dream, reveals why the monstrous image of likeness must be destroyed or disowned or denied.

In *Fleetwood*, a character named Macneil (who is locally renowned for having been a friend of Rousseau) claims that there is "a principle in the heart of man, which demands the society of his like. He that has no such society, is in a state but one degree removed from insanity." Asserting a universal need for sympathy and fellow feeling, Macneil insists: "If there is any thing in human form that does not feel these wants, that thing is not to be counted in the file for a man; the form it bears is a deception, and the legend, Man, which you read in its front, is a lie."[44] Frankenstein rejects the society of his like; he denies fellow feeling to the being he created to be like himself by refusing him both his own sympathy and the sympathy the monster seeks in the society of his like.[45] Paradoxically, in denying the monster sympathy, in refusing to recognize in his figure the traits common to man, Frankenstein makes a lie of the legend that names him as *Man*. In the terms of Macneil and Rousseau, by misreading the figure of a man as a monster, by persisting in an illusion rather than granting him the name of man, Frankenstein turns his own form into a deception and forfeits his own legend of *Man*. In other words, he turns himself into a monster. The monstrous image of the monster is in this sense an exact likeness of Frankenstein.

This speech about sympathy and the society of one's like by the friend of Rousseau (in terms that recall the texts of Rousseau we have been reading, as well as accusations about Rousseau's insanity and preference for solitude over society) returns us to the tableaux about figures and sympathy in the *Essai sur l'origine des langues*. There Rousseau tells stories about the origins of figurative language and the origins of sympathy and shows the relation between them. The story of the origin of language is a parable about sympathy that demonstrates the likeness of sympathy and similes: sympathy depends on the syntax of a simile, the perception of resemblance or likeness that allows a transport from one term to another. Sympathy, in Rousseau's terms, would prevent one from turning others into monsters because it would allow one to recognize them as similes in a double sense: the *monster* stops being a monster when it is recognized as a figure for *man*, and it is recognized as a man when it is acknowledged to be a being like oneself. Sympathy would allow one to stop regarding others as figures by bringing one to recognize them as figures; but to do so one must recognize others as similes, likenesses, fellow creatures in a society of one's like.

Horrified by the uncanny likeness of what is other to him, repelled by the monstrous image of resemblance, tormented by the fiendish figures of his own artistic workshop, Frankenstein must deny sympathy and fellow feeling because they present and represent a mirror of likeness. In these terms sympathy itself must seem monstrous to him. Indeed, the thought that provokes Frankenstein to tear to pieces the creature who is supposed to be like the creature he made to be like himself—the companion of the same species who will let the monster see that he excites "the sympathy of some existing thing" (*F*, p. 139)—is his fantasy that "one of the first results of those sympathies for which the demon thirsted would be children, and a race of devils would be propogated upon the earth" (*F*, p. 158). In the science fiction of the novel one can imagine Frankenstein's fears of a race of monsters. However, he specifically images and imagines these monsters as the results of sympathy. Sympathy may be a euphemism for sexual relations here, but in the network of associations and analogies of the novel sexual union can be seen as a physical instance of sympathy. It is no coincidence that Frankenstein looks with equal horror on the idea of his own marriage to the fellow creature whose sympathy was always his; he says: "To me the idea of an immediate union with my Elizabeth was one of horror and dismay" (F, p. 145).

Of course Frankenstein once looked on Elizabeth as if she were of another species; and part of his horror at the likeness of the female monster may be the uncanny combination of likeness and difference that has caused the male monster himself to be read as a figure for *woman* rather than *man*.[46] Yet Frankenstein's fear of sexual union, like his fear of sympathy, seems to be related to the threat of likeness rather than difference. Readers have noticed the shadow of incest cast throughout the pages of *Frankenstein*, a novel written in the form of letters from a brother to his sister; this was apparently disconcerting enough to cause Mary Shelley to change Elizabeth from Victor's cousin to an adopted orphan when she revised the novel for the third edition.[47] Indeed, this reading is first offered by Frankenstein's father, who speaks to his son about the woman called "my more than sister" (F, p. 35) and suggests: "You, perhaps, regard her as your sister, without any wish that she might become your wife" (F, p. 144)—a possibility that Elizabeth herself addresses when she says: "as brother and sister often entertain a lively affection toward each other without desiring a more intimate union, may not such also be our case?" (F, p. 178). Furthermore, the sympathy that the monster seeks in an intimate union with a fellow creature would be literally incestuous since as offspring of the same parent the monster and his female companion in effect would be brother and sister.

Sympathy, then, seems incestuous. In *Frankenstein*, as in *La Religieuse*, both sympathy and incest seem to be associated with the fear of too much sameness and not enough difference.[48] Sexual union would embody the monstrous likeness that makes sympathy so threatening; it must therefore be regarded by Frankenstein with horror and dismay. In destroying the similar yet strangely unlike female monster, he destroys the possibility of sympathy for the monster and ultimately for himself since the destruction of the creature—which he says almost makes him feel as if "I had mangled the living flesh of a human being" (F, p. 163)—leads directly to the murder of Elizabeth by the monster on Frankenstein's wedding night. Frankenstein thus simultaneously destroys (one is tempted to say *murders*) sympathy, incest, sexual union, and monstrous likeness.

In describing the scene of Elizabeth's death, Frankenstein suddenly shifts into a present tense and says: "Everywhere I turn I see the same figure—her bloodless arms and relaxed form flung by the murderer on its bridal bier" (*F*, p. 186). This is the only time in his narrative that Frankenstein uses "figure" to refer to someone other than the monster; just two paragraphs later he describes the image of the monster at the window as "a figure the most hideous and abhorred" (*F*, p. 187). The association between these two figures is furthered by Frankenstein's strange use of the possessive pronoun "its"; ostensibly he shifts in midsentence from "her" to "its" because he is speaking of the "figure" or "form" of Elizabeth, because "she" is now a corpse. Yet the juxtaposition of "the murderer" (that is, the monster) and "*its* bridal bier" causes a moment of confusion, as if the figure of the monster and the figure of Elizabeth have merged for a moment into the same figure.

In the context of the novel this fusion or confusion makes sense; both Elizabeth and the monster are figures for sameness, figures for the sympathy that Frankenstein destroys when he murders the female monster meant to be his double's bride in his symbolic and overdetermined destruction of monstrous likeness. Elizabeth and the monster are the same figure: they are figures of the same, figures for the same. In refusing sympathy, Frankenstein is like the reader described by Roland Barthes who is condemned to read the same story everywhere because he does not reread.[49] Condemned to repeat rather than remember the error of reading that both determines and is determined by his failure of sympathy, Frankenstein must see the same figure everywhere he turns. Everywhere he turns he must see the monstrous figure of a monster.

Like Marivaux, Diderot, and Rousseau, Mary Shelley presents an ambivalent view of sympathy. Her revisionary dramatization of Rousseau's parables about sympathy suggests the dangerous effects of both sympathy and a lack of sympathy: the failure to recognize others as fellow creatures with fellow feeling turns both oneself and others into monsters, while sympathy itself seems to result in monstrous forms of reproduction—both the monstrous images and figures of likeness that reflect horrid resemblance and the horrifying sexuality that seems like incest in its union of too much sameness and not enough difference. After reading *Les Effets surprenants de la sympathie*, *La Vie de Marianne*, and *La Religieuse*, we should not be surprised to discover in the scene of sympathy a scene of dangerous or at least ambivalent eroticism. I would like to conclude my reading of *Frankenstein* with a consideration of this scene; as our readings of Du Bos, Marivaux, Diderot, and Rousseau suggest, it is a scene that should be regarded from the perspective of the theatrical relations that structure scenes of sympathy.

The central and in some ways the paradigmatic scene of sympathy in *Frankenstein*—the scene of the origins of the monster's sympathy—is represented as a scene of theater. Mary Shelley seems to adopt the theatrical model of sympathy she has inherited from eighteenth-century aesthetics and moral philosophy by placing the monster as an unseen, sympathetic spectator to the *tableau de famille* of the De Laceys. As he looks through "a small chink" in the wall of his hovel, "a small and almost imperceptible chink through which the eye could just penetrate," the monster is "unseen and unknown" (*F*, pp. 102–3, 115)—which is to say that he assumes precisely the position of Diderot's ideal "spectateur ignoré" who watches the "spectacle domestique et réel" of another French family "sans être vu" (*OE*, pp. 78, 369).[50] Indeed, as he watches the *drame bourgeois* and *tragédie larmoyante* of the De Lacey family, the monster plays the role of the ideal sympathetic spectator in a theater.

In this position the monster witnesses musical performances and has his first aesthetic experiences; he witnesses the cottagers as they (in his words) "exhibited" respect or "performed" acts of affection and sympathy which, he says, "moved me sensibly" (*F*, p. 106); and in the transport of sympathy through which one takes someone else's part and person, he feels what they feel: "when they were unhappy, I felt depressed; when they rejoiced, I sympathized in their joys" (*F*, p. 107). Finally, moved by the sentiments that they exhibit, the monster experiences "a desire to become an actor in the busy scene where so many admirable qualities were called forth and displayed" (*F*, p. 122)—in Diderot's formulation, a desire to "ajouter un personnage réel à la scène" ("add a real character to the scene" [*OE*, p. 78]).

As Diderot suggests, this ideal aesthetic and sympathetic response must finally be frustrated. After watching the cottagers the monster may find ways to "assist their labours" (*F*, p. 106), but he can only *assister à* this *tableau de famille* as a *témoin ignoré*; he can no more become an actor in the scene of the De Lacey's family drama than the moved spectator in the theater can help the actors or enter the scene on stage. Like De Lacey, the actors in this scene must be blind to him or else the play will come to an end. The monster's attempts to move De Lacey by his own "representations" are doomed to fail and he is left with only the "horrible scene of the preceding day ... forever acting before my eyes" (*F*, p. 131). The monster's experience as sympathetic spectator seems to dramatize Diderot's parable about the limits of sympathy; Diderot also suggests that this is a lesson which must be forever acting before the eyes of readers and spectators.

We have seen that if the scene of theater must end in the failure of sympathy, this is also because of the epistemological limits that define one's ability to enter into the thoughts and feelings of someone else. When the monster acknowledges the hopelessness of his desire to live with humans "in the interchange of kindness" and pity since "the human senses are insurmountable barriers to our union" (*F*, p. 138), he is referring to humans' revulsion at the aspect of a being whom they will not recognize as a fellow creature; but this barrier does not apply to him alone. Victor Frankenstein says at one point, "I saw an unsurmountable barrier placed between me and my fellow men" (*F*, p. 151). He later looks upon the sea as "an insuperable barrier between me and my fellow creatures" (*F*, pp. 161–62). On the next day he says that he feels again "as if I belonged to a race of human beings" (*F*, p. 162) but the novel suggests that there are insurmountable barriers even between humans, even between beings of the same species. Justine Moritz is condemned to die because misleading appearances (which turn upon the presence of a picture) are misconstrued and misinterpreted by witnesses and spectators.

Justine is a victim of misinterpretation because she is a victim of the limits of the human senses. Frankenstein describes Justine's "appearance," her "countenance," and her "look" as she is "gazed on and execrated by thousands"; she pleads: "I hope the character I have always borne will incline my judges to a favourable interpretation where any circumstance appears doubtful or suspicious" (*F*, pp. 78–79). However, the aspects of her appearance and public character and even Elizabeth's testimony about "what I know of her character" are contradicted by the "evidence," and her guilt seems to be "proved" by the "picture" (*F*, pp. 81, 78–79); her spectators and judges can know her inner character only by its outward appearances—a predicament even temporarily (and in this case inappropriately) brought home to Elizabeth when she hears that Justine has confessed. Justine has been framed by the monster's manipulation of a picture; the portrait of a woman he places in the folds of her dress convicts her because it stands for a secret motive; since the inner sentiment that would prove her innocence cannot be known, she is condemned by the pictures and appearances by which and through which the world construes her inner motives and judges her.

This, of course, is the monster's predicament throughout the novel. He also wants to appear as "the most amiable and benevolent of human creatures" (*F*, p. 81) (Elizabeth's description of Justine) yet becomes a victim of misinterpretation and misleading appearances. At the end of the novel, in response to Walton's claim, "It is not pity that you feel," he acknowledges that no explanation or defense will prevent his actions and feelings—indeed, in this case his very sympathy—from being misinterpreted: "Yet such must be the impression conveyed to you by what appears to be the purport of my actions." He has resigned himself to the impossibility of sympathy: "Yet I seek not a fellow feeling in my misery. No sympathy will I ever find" (*F*, p. 209). Sympathy appears to be impossible because both impressions and expressions will be misconstrued; and the imaginative transport that might convey his beholder across the epistemological void that separates even fellow beings, carrying him beyond or across the purport of appearances, will be blocked by the insurmountable barrier of the human senses. Like Rousseau's parable about the origins of language and sympathy, the meeting of these two creatures is a scene of misreading in which the sense of a human is misinterpreted.

The theatrical conditions of sympathy, then, seem to dictate sympathy's failure, either by leading sympathy to the limits where it must discover its own impossibility, or by underlining its epistemological barriers. The theater of sympathy must depend on representations: representations presented to the beholder that will deny the beholder's presence unless counteracted by the imaginary transport of sympathy and identification; and representations imagined by the beholder that might be misrepresentations or at best mere fantasies. Furthermore, even the idealized sympathy with which the monster watches the De Lacey family drama in the position of Diderot's *spectateur ignoré* itself suggests a voyeurism that might give the theatrical scene of sympathy a more sinister aspect.

We have seen that Du Bos, Marivaux, and to some extent Rousseau at moments anticipate Freud's suggestion that the sympathy experienced in watching spectacles of suffering might be interpreted as a reaction formation against a secret sadistic pleasure—or as a masochistic identification with the role of victim.[51] Diderot's versions of these scenes in *La Religieuse* depict a dangerously contagious eroticism in the experience of sympathy. However, it is in Marivaux's dramatizations of the theater of sympathy that we saw the most explicit characterizations of these scenes as scenes of violence or dangerous eroticism. In particular, we saw the frequent repetition of what I called a primal scene scenario, a set of spectator-spectacle relations that infuse the scene of sympathy with a sense of anxious or ambivalent sexuality. We saw that *Frankenstein* relates the effects of sympathy to a problematic sexuality; in these contexts we need to speculate about what it means that Mary Shelley also casts her central scene of sympathy not only as a scene of theater but specifically as a primal scene.[52]

As he secretly looks through the chink in the wall at his adopted family, gaining an education in "the difference of sexes, and the birth and growth of children ... and all the various relationships which bind one human being to another in mutual bonds" (*F*, p. 115), the monster acts out a remarkably explicit primal scene scenario. In addition to this family drama (which includes the romance of the young lovers, Felix and Safie) the monster has a literary primal scene when he discovers the journal kept by Frankenstein which tells the story of "the four months that preceded my creation" and his "accursed origin" (*F*, p. 124). These experiences both raise and help to answer the questions that present themselves to him in the form of spectacle and speculation: "Who was I? What was I? Whence did I come?" (*F*, p. 123).

Readers have remarked the preoccupation with primal scenes that is acted out in the pages of *Frankenstein*.[53] In the most extensive account of the novel's "primal scene imagery" to date, Marc A. Rubenstein argues that "the spirit of primal scene observation penetrates into the very structure of the novel," and he offers a psychoanalytic interpretation of the novel's obsession with origins, exploration, and investigation in terms of Mary Shelley's "search for the mother."[54] Gilbert and Gubar emphasize the ways in which Mary Shelley's "birth myth" is projected onto the "myth of origins" represented in *Paradise Lost*—to which we could now add Rousseau's myths about the origins of society, language, sympathy, and the self. Rousseau's status as a composite figure representing both an abandoning parent and an abandoned child, as well as his associations with Mary Shelley's mother, also demonstrate how deeply Rousseau is implicated in the novel's primal scenes.

Rubenstein argues persuasively that the monster's primal scenes can be specifically related to Mary Shelley's investigations of her own origins. In particular, he reads the monster's discovery of the journal of his creation as a screen for Mary Shelley's reading of her parent's love letters.[55] Without disputing this interpretation, I would note that it is not necessary to conjecture about Mary Shelley's knowledge of the then unpublished letters between Godwin and Wollstonecraft when we know for certain that she read the letters Wollstonecraft wrote to Gilbert Imlay (the father of Wollstonecraft's first child)—letters that

Godwin rather scandalously published in his edition of Wollstone-craft's *Posthumous Works*.[56] Furthermore, and perhaps more impor-tantly, Mary Shelley read in Godwin's *Memoirs* of Wollstonecraft a detailed and graphic account of her own birth: what she might have called, in the words the monster uses to refer to his origin, the "disgusting circumstances" (*F*, p. 124) of her delivery on her mother's death bed. Godwin provides a clinical description of the "extraction of the placenta ... in pieces,"[57] just as Frankenstein presumably de-scribes how he created his progeny from "pieces" of the dead.[58]

Godwin's *Memoir* also indicates that the monster's reading of *The Sorrows of Young Werther* dramatizes a primal scene scenario. Narra-ting the story of someone who tries to kill herself because of unrequited love, he calls Wollstonecraft "a female Werter."[59] In his introduction to her letters to Imlay, Godwin claims that "they bear a striking resemblance to the celebrated romance of Werter."[60] Thus the monster's reading of Goethe's epistolary novel represents more than his education in sensibility; the romance of Werther can be seen to stand in for Wollstonecraft's letters. The monster's reading of his parent's memoir must also allude to Mary Shelley's experience reading her mother's posthumously published novel. Gilbert and Gubar have suggested that in *Maria, or The Wrongs of Woman* Wollstonecraft would have seemed to be reaching "from beyond the grave ... toward a daughter."[61] Indeed, the novel tells the story of a daughter whose mother died nine days after her birth (Mary Wollstonecraft died eleven days after her daughter's birth) and it contains what is written to be a posthumous letter from a mother to an "abandoned daughter."[62] We can see, then, that all of the texts the monster reads—his parent's memoir, the romance of Werther, Milton's myth of origins and original parents, and the book of Plutarch that alludes to the reading of a child whose mother died after giving him life—in some sense replicate or allude to the scenes of reading that appear to constitute Mary Shelley's primal scenes.

There are still more ways, however, in which the primal scenes of *Frankenstein* can be traced to primal scenes involving the texts of Godwin and Wollstonecraft. I have suggested that while she was composing *Frankenstein* Mary Shelley was thinking of what is arguably the strangest and most interesting chapter in *Fleetwood*: the scene with the wax figures. This scene takes on another level of significance if we recognize that it placed her in a particularly complex primal scene scenario in relation to both her father's text and his marriage. *Fleetwood* tells the story of a man who becomes obsessed with jealous fantasies about his wife's relationship with another man;

if we remark that Fleetwood's wife's name is Mary, and that her supposed lover is a lieutenant, we can read in Fleetwood's mad fiction-making the tableau vivant of William Godwin creating a fiction that retrospectively torments him with fantasies about Mary Wollstonecraft's affair with Gilbert Imlay—a man who was known as a captain.[63]

Fleetwood's bizarre inclusion in his tableau vivant of a "cradle, and a chest of child-bed linen"[64] (apparently representing Mary's pregnancy) makes the scene correspond even more closely to Godwin's situation in publishing Wollstonecraft's letters to Captain Imlay, many of which are about their illegitimate infant—as well as Godwin's situation in making up a fiction about a man who fantasizes that his wife Mary is having a child after an affair with an officer. One could read in the scene with the wax figures Godwin's portrait of himself as a (retrospectively) jealous and obsessed spectator to a tableau vivant that turns life into fiction and threatens to turn fiction into life.[65] The confusion of fiction and reality is compounded by the apparent intersection of the story line of *Fleetwood* with the proposed story line of *Maria*: the account of Fleetwood's court proceedings indicting Mary for adultery evokes Maria's trial for adultery (as if imagined from the husband's point of view).[66]

I am not arguing that Mary Shelley necessarily would have been consciously aware of this relation between *Fleetwood* and her father's somewhat daring edition of Wollstonecraft's letters to Captain Imlay—the publication of which led to one anti-Jacobin journal to cross reference "Mary Wollstonecraft" with the entry "Prostitution" in its index.[67] (Mary Shelley did read both books in 1815, the year before she began *Frankenstein*.) I do believe that the voyeuristic scene that Fleetwood stages to dramatize his fantasy about Mary's love affair with an officer and the child of their illicit union must have had some resonance with the fantasies in which the author of *Frankenstein* became a spectator to an imagined primal scene—either the one that produced her sister Fanny or the one that produced her. Furthermore, reading *Fleetwood* in 1815, Mary Shelley might have been alerted to biographical and autobiographical interpretations by the novel's uncanny evocation of its author's rage at another Mary: the daughter who recently had incurred her father's wrath by entering into an illicit affair with the young Percy Shelley and becoming pregnant. (Borrowing a relationship from the plot of *La Nouvelle Héloïse*, *Fleetwood* emphasizes Mary's role as a kind of daughter to the intimidating husband who was a friend and peer of her father.)[68]

Godwin's novel, then, offers a multiple and overdetermined primal scene: it represents a tableau of Mary Wollstonecraft and Imlay and the child they created; it constitutes a tableau of Godwin picturing that scene; it represents a tableau of Godwin picturing himself as a beholder of the scene; it offers a reflection of the primal scene Mary Shelley might have imagined, as well as a dramatization of someone fantasizing and beholding that scene; and finally, it offers what we might call a reverse primal scene in which the father is pictured watching the illicit sexual scene enacted by the daughter and her lover. In evoking, picturing, and combining these scenes, *Fleetwood's* decription of the tableau vivant of the wax figures makes explicit the vertiginously *theatrical* relations enacted in the primal scenes that are behind the primal scenes of *Frankenstein*. This situation is further compounded (in a way that makes Mary Shelley's position as a reader and spectator of the fictions of her father even more relevant to her first novel) by the fact that Godwin's first novel is also obsessed with primal scenes.

I do not have space here to present a complete reading of *Caleb Williams*; but it is not difficult to see that the novel is in one sense about a child who is punished for having witnessed a primal scene. Williams sums up the sad story of his life when he asks the rhetorical question, "Have I not been employed from my infancy in gratifying an insatiable curiosity?" (*CW*, p. 185). He puts this another way when he says in the first pages of his life story: "The spring of action which, perhaps more than any other, characterised the whole train of my life, was curiosity" (*CW*, p. 4). At the age of eighteen (Mary Shelley was seventeen when she read *Caleb Williams* in 1814) Williams enters the service of Mr. Falkland, whom he describes as a kind of father figure, and almost immediately develops an obsessive curiosity about him. "I determined to place myself as a watch upon my patron," he says, explaining his resolution to "spy upon Mr. Falkland"; he adds: "The more impenetrable Mr. Falkland was determined to be, the more uncontrollable was my curiosity" (*CW*, pp. 107–8).

Williams finds this "study" an "ample field for speculation and conjecture" (*CW*, p. 6), but his curiosity and speculation get him into trouble in a climactic scene that excites his curiosity even further and provokes the wrath of his patron. Williams writes:

> I went to a closet or small apartment which was separated from the library by a narrow gallery that was lighted by a small window near the roof. . . . As I opened the door, I heard at the same instant a deep groan expressive of intolerable anguish. The sound of the door in opening seemed to alarm the person within; I heard the lid of a trunk hastily shut, and the noise as of fastening a lock. . . . (*CW*, p. 7)

Williams's master is enraged with this intrusion and threatens him: "You set yourself as a spy upon my actions. . . . Do you think you shall watch my privacies with impunity?" This "extraordinary scene" (*CW*, p. 8)—the language and details of which read as a scarcely transfigured screen memory of a childhood intrusion into the parental bedroom—is the originary trauma that leads to Williams's misfortunes. It arouses his curiosity even more and convinces him that Mr. Falkland is guilty of some crime, and it leads to accusations of his own guilt which are followed by imprisonment, punishment, and years of persecution.

However, the real punishment begins after Mr. Falkland unexpectedly discovers Williams in the act of prying into the trunk that occasioned the "original" primal scene. (Williams describes this as "an act so monstrous" and can account for it only in terms of an "unexplained and involuntary sympathy" and a "kind of instant insanity," and he defends himself by saying, "My offence had merely been a mistaken thirst of knowledge" [*CW*, p. 133].) This reversal of positions inaugurates the punishment that will pursue Williams for the rest of his narrative: from that moment on, he becomes a spectacle for Mr. Falkland: "All my actions observed; all my gestures marked. I could move neither to the right nor the left, but the eye of my keeper was upon me. He watched me; and his vigilance was a sickness to my heart" (*CW*, p. 143). He begins a desperate flight to escape the eyes of Mr. Falkland and the various surrogates and spies who are sent to seek him out, see through disguises that would have impressed Moll Flanders, and expose him to the world.[69]

Caleb Williams suggests that the punishment for beholding the spectacle of a primal scene (or relentlessly imagining one) is to be cast in the role of a criminal actor in a guilty spectacle. Like Defoe's *Roxana* (which I see as a model for Godwin's first novel), *Caleb Williams* dramatizes a struggle between a parent and child about theatricality; the relentless spectator finds himself an unwilling spectacle and cannot escape the eyes of relentless spectators.[70] This reversal of the roles of spectator and spectacle seems to be a punishment for observing the primal scene—the only consolation of which might be the sort of displacement of responsibility that we can see in the dream of Freud's "wolf man" that *he* is the one being watched.[71]

One could speculate about how Mary Shelley might have consciously or unconsciously responded to Williams's or William's dramatization of primal scene anxiety: whether (as in her experience reading her mother's fiction) she would have found an uncanny proleptic message in a novel written by her parent before she was born; or whether, despite her evident preoccupation with primal scenes, she might have preferred not to focus on such a story. We must recognize, however, that Mary Shelley's first novel tells virtually the same story about a struggle concerning the theatrical positions enacted in the primal scene. Even more than *Caleb Williams* (which is named in Mary Shelley's dedication of her novel to her father) *Frankenstein* explores the theatrical dynamics of the primal scene from multiple points of view, as if it were both compulsively repeating Godwin's scenario and dramatizing its own relation to the tableaux of his figures and fiction.

From the outset, *Frankenstein* emphasizes the curiosity of both Walton and Victor in terms that evoke primal scene speculation.[72] Walton (whose dangerous acts of exploration Rubenstein relates to primal scene observation)[73] speaks of his "curiosity" and his drive for "the acquisition of knowledge" (*F*, p. 26). Frankenstein, of course, shares with Caleb Williams a compulsion to investigate causes; he says: "The world was to me a secret which I desired to divine. Curiosity, earnest research to learn the hidden laws of nature, gladness akin to rapture, as they were unfolded to me, are among the earliest sensations I can remember" (*F*, p. 36). There are many references to Frankenstein's "curiosity," his "eager desire to learn," his fascination with "secrets," his "fervent longing to penetrate the secrets of nature," his desire to "penetrate into the recesses of nature and show how she works in her hiding-places," and, of course, the obsession with "the deepest mysteries of creation" which leads him to discover "the cause of generation and life" (*F*, pp. 40, 37, 39, 47, 51). It is no accident that he describes the "acquirement of knowledge" as "dangerous" or that after his fantasies are realized he feels "as if I had been guilty of a crime" (*F*, pp. 52, 55).

Paradoxically, however, at virtually the moment he arrives at the primal scene of creation, Frankenstein finds that his position as spectator to the primal scene has been reversed. The first sign that a "spark of life" has been infused into the creature is the opening of an eye; Victor observes: "I saw the dull yellow eye of the creature open" (*F*, p. 56). He emphasizes his horror at the sight of these "watery eyes," which he finds upon him once again after going to sleep and dreaming of his fiancée and his dead mother (in another allusion to the scene of Mary Shelley's birth). He describes the moment of his trauma: "by the dim and yellow light of the moon, as it forced its way through the window shutters, I beheld the wretch—the miserable monster whom I had created. He held up the curtain of the bed; and his eyes, if eyes they may be called, were fixed on me" (*F*, p. 57). As the curtain opens to reveal the yellow eyes which force entry like the yellow light forcing its way through the shutters, Victor experiences the trauma of a primal scene as viewed from the perspective of the parent. As he lies in bed embracing and kissing his wife-to-be in a dream, turning her into a "dead mother," he is interrupted by the creature "whom I had created" who pulls open the theatrical curtain and with ubiquitous eyes fixes him as a spectacle.

This scene obviously parallels the "account of the origin of the story" that Mary Shelley provides in the 1831 introduction to *Frankenstein* in which she describes first imagining "the pale student of unhallowed arts"—"the artist"—awakening in the night: "behold, the horrid thing stands at his bedside, opening his curtains and looking on him with yellow, watery, but speculative eyes"; at this point in her waking dream, Mary Shelley recounts, "I opened mine in terror" to see "the closed shutters with the moonlight struggling through" (*F*, pp. x–xi). Thus the primal scene of Frankenstein and the monster is apparently the primal scene of the novel; or to put it another way, the novel apparently has its primal scene in a fantasy of a primal scene. Mary Shelley recalls (in a memory that James Rieger claims she invented)[74] that Polidori's entry in the ghost story contest concerned "a skull-headed lady who was so punished for peeping through a key-hole—what to see I forget: something very shocking and wrong of course" (*F*, p. ix); her own ghost story has its origins (at least in this account) in a primal scene viewed from the perspective of the person who is seen through the keyhole. Of course, Frankenstein himself has been peeping through the keyhole of nature; but the punishment for his peeping is to find himself confronted by the "speculative eyes" of his offspring.[75]

Once the monster opens his speculative eyes on this primal scene he becomes obsessed with repeating it: first benevolently in witnessing the family romance of the De Laceys, then sympathetically in reading the primal scene of creation in *Paradise Lost*, then traumatically in reading about the disgusting circumstances of his creation in Frankenstein's journal, and finally most obsessively in becoming the relentless spectator of the creator he saw when he opened his eyes for the first time. Indeed, we can read in the monster's insistence that Frankenstein create another monster not only the desire for a fellow being with whom to share sympathy but also the desire to witness a reenactment of the primal scene that gave him life. He tells Frankenstein that he will watch this new scene of creation: "Depart to your home and commence your labours," he commands; "I shall watch their progress with unutterable anxiety" (*F*, p. 141). Frankenstein feels a corresponding anxiety, and his decision to interrupt violently the "labours" of giving life to another creature is immediately prompted by his sudden realization that his first offspring is secretly watching: "on looking up, I saw by the light of the moon the demon at the casement. A ghastly grin wrinkled his lips as he gazed on me, where I sat fulfilling the task which he had alloted to me." It is at this moment that Frankenstein, "trembling with passion, tore to pieces the thing on which I was engaged," vowing "never to resume my labours" (*F*, p. 159).

Caught in the act of procreation by the offspring whose speculative eyes watch him through the window, Frankenstein once again finds himself at the center of a primal scene, cast as the spectacle rather than the spectator who tried to penetrate secret recesses and hiding places. He vows never to repeat this scene of creation; but he is cast as a character in a story that repeatedly collapses the moment of birth and the moment of sexual union, and the monster responds to his vow by vowing: "I shall be with you on your wedding-night" (*F*, p. 161). These words become a source of great anxiety for Frankenstein, who is haunted by the specter of the monster beholding him. He describes himself as surrounded by darkness that was "penetrated by no light but the glimmer of two eyes that glared upon me. Sometimes they were the expressive eyes of Henry, languishing in death, the dark orbs nearly covered by the lids and the long black lashes that fringed them; sometimes it was the watery, clouded eyes of the monster, as I first saw them in my chamber at Ingolstadt" (*F*, p. 174). As he returns to Geneva to marry Elizabeth, Frankenstein is tormented by this recurrent vision of both past and future primal scenes.

The scene of creation and procreation that obsesses both parent and child is finally repeated as the monster keeps his promise to intrude on Frankenstein's wedding night. Frankenstein is "anxious and watchful" after arriving at the "amphitheatre of the mountains" (*F*, pp. 184–85) where he and Elizabeth are to spend their honeymoon; but, he says, "the monster had blinded me to his real intentions" (*F*, p. 182), and he is surprised to find that he is again the spectacle in the theater of a primal scene that once more unites sexual union, birth, and death. Discovering the "figure" of Elizabeth "flung by the murderer on its bridal bier"—"Could I behold this and live?" he asks—Frankenstein looks up to see this vision: "The windows of the room had before been darkened, and I felt a kind of panic on seeing the pale yellow light of the moon illuminate the chamber. The shutters had been thrown back, and with a sensation of horror not to be described I saw at the open window a figure the most hideous and abhorred" (*F*, pp. 186–87). Once again we can recognize all of the ingredients that formulated the primal scenes of the monster and the novel: the window, the yellow light of the moon entering the shutters, the marriage bed which has become a bridal bier—like the marriage beds of Victor's dream and Mary Shelley's birth—and of course the watching face of the monster. Frankenstein has imagined that the monster "had determined to consummate his crimes" (*F*, p. 179) by killing him, but he has blinded himself to the character of both the consummation and the crime at the center of a scene in which a father "embrace[s]" the corpse of the dead wife whose body bears "the murderous mark" (*F*, p. 186) of the intrusive offspring.

The details of the window and especially Frankenstein's "pistol" (*F*, p. 187) recall the props and setting of the primal scene confrontations that take place in *Caleb Williams*;[76] but I have been suggesting that this entire series of primal scenes in *Frankenstein* is inscribed under the sign, as it were, of Godwin's first novel. Whereas the father's novel tells the story of a child whose "father" turns him into a spectacle as punishment for his primal scene speculation, the child's novel tells the story of a "father" who is punished for *his* primal scene curiosity by the relentlessly speculative eyes of the child. In the child's version of this scene, both father and child seem responsible for the death of the wife/mother—who is completely absent and effaced in the father's novel.[77]

Mary Shelley incorporates both *Caleb Williams* and her reading of *Caleb Williams* into the text of *Frankenstein* as she dramatizes a child who beholds a primal scene that includes and reflects the tableau of the father beholding a primal scene; we saw the same vertiginous doubling in her incorporation of the wax figures scene from *Fleetwood*. Father and child (that is, Godwin and Mary Shelley, and Frankenstein and the monster) seem united in a bond of mutual obsession with a primal scene that becomes both the scene of the crime and the scene of punishment: the amphitheater in which a desperate struggle over the roles of spectator and spectacle takes place between parent and child. We can see in *Frankenstein*'s relation to *Caleb Williams* a *mise en abîme* of primal scene identification in which the transport of sympathy seems directed at the spectators rather than the actors in the scene.

We could speculate also that part of the guilt of primal scene observation comes from identification, the act of sympathy through which the spectator imaginatively plays a part in the scene; Williams ascribes the "act so monstrous" by which he pries into Mr. Falkland's trunk and thus plays the parent's role in the primal scene in terms of "unexplained and involuntary sympathy" (*CW*, p. 133). The reverse primal scene we have been tracing is in this sense a punishment for sympathy: the observing child's act of identification imaginatively transforms him or her from a spectator to an actor in the scene. In Mary Shelley's case, this would have been compounded by Godwin's position as a Fleetwood-like jealous spectator to the tableau of Mary Wollstonecraft Godwin becoming a lover and a mother. Imagining the tableau of a primal scene representing her parents, Mary Shelley finds herself identified with the figure of "Mary."

At the center of the primal scene in *Frankenstein* is a spectator peeping through a keyhole to see a shocking sight: the sight of speculative eyes that punish sympathy and speculation by presenting the mirror image that turns the spectator into a spectacle. This is the vision represented by the monster. The most horrifying aspect of his figure is not his deformity as much as the speculative eyes that represent vision itself. At the end of the novel, in describing a "scene" which he doubts he has "the power to detail," a "form which I cannot find words to describe," Walton writes of the sight of the monster: "Never did I behold a vision so horrible as his face. . . . I shut my eyes involuntarily" (*F*, p.207). The vision that the monster forces one to behold, the vision that makes Walton close his eyes and back away from representation, is *vision*: not only seeing and sight but that which is seen.

In *Phèdre*, another fiction obsessed with sight, secrets, and both figurative and literal monsters, Thésée calls Hippolyte a "Monstre" immediately after asking him, "oses-tu bien te montrer devant moi?" ("do you dare show yourself before me?").[78] The apposition of *monstre* and *montrer* suggests on an etymological level a relation that is demonstrated on a thematic level throughout the play: that which is shown—what should be kept secret and hidden—is monstrous. *Frankenstein* also plays upon these senses. One aspect of what is most monstrous about the monster is his appearance as a figure of what is *montré*. The vision the monster represents is also a vision of the monstrosity of *showing*. *Frankenstein* demonstrates the danger of sight, both seeing and being seen; it displays how vision and speculation can show one to be showing as well as looking. But in the vision of the surrealistically metonymic eyes that haunt its pages, the novel also suggests that vision itself is frightening.

At the end of *Frankenstein*, the monster vows to Walton: "I leave you, and in you the last of humankind whom these eyes will ever behold" (*F*, p. 211). He may promise that his eyes will behold humans no more, but Mary Shelley knows that such vision is not easily forgotten or escaped. As she says of the "hideous phantasm" that she saw "with shut eyes, but acute mental vision," "I could not so easily get rid of my hideous phantom; still it haunted me" (*F*, p. xxi). What is so hideous about the monster is his embodiment of *phantasma*: the monstrous image of that which is made visible, shown, presented to the eye, brought to light. This is the monstrous figure that will not disappear when one shuts one's eyes, or one's book.

Appendix
Mary Shelley and Rousseau

I argue in chapter six that the character of Rousseau is present throughout the narrative of *Frankenstein*, both in the portrayals of Victor and the monster and in the novel's theoretical investigation of the problem of sympathy. Although my argument for this literary animation and philosophical dialogue is based primarily on textual evidence, it is logical to ask what Mary Shelley might have known of Rousseau—not only what she read or might have read before and during the composition of *Frankenstein*, but also to what extent the figure of Rousseau was a presence in both her education and her life. Although I do not want to suggest that the argument I have made in chapter six can be "proved" by circumstantial or biographical "evidence," there are many reasons (in addition to the textual echoes and allusions I have described) to believe that Mary Shelley was aware of Rousseau both from reading his works and from reading her parents' works, that she would have associated Rousseau to some extent with her mother, and that she was intensely engaged with Rousseau's work at the moment she began her first novel.

In 1815, the year before she began to write *Frankenstein*, Mary Shelley read Rousseau's *Confessions*, *Émile*, and *La Nouvelle Héloïse*.[1] (Percy Shelley read the *Rêveries*.) During the same year Mary Shelley read *Fleetwood* and the *Posthumous Works* of Wollstonecraft, as well as the three books that constitute the monster's education: *Paradise Lost*, Plutarch's *Lives*, and *The Sorrows of Young Werther*. She continued to read Rousseau throughout the period in which she wrote her first novel, noting on specific days in her journal the *Rêveries* and *Émile* in 1816 and *La Nouvelle Héloïse* and the *Confessions et Lettres de Rousseau* in 1817. (We know that the Shelleys were still carrying Rousseau around with them in 1818 since they had trouble with a customs agent when "Rousseau, Voltaire, etc." were discovered among their possessions.)[2] Since Mary Shelley lost the box of her early writings— what Percy Shelley calls the "productions of her mind before our intercourse"—and since her journal for 14 May 1815 to 20 July 1816 also has disappeared, we do not have a record of any of Rousseau's works Mary Shelley might have read before she left her father's house or, more important, in the two months immediately preceding the composition of *Frankenstein*. When the journal resumes, however, she is reading Rousseau, often on the same days that she is writing what she calls "my story"—for example: "August 1: Write, and read 'Reveries' of Rousseau."³

We do know that during the months for which the journal is missing and in which the Shelleys, Byron, and Polidori had the ghost story contest that inspired *Frankenstein*, Rousseau must have been on Mary Shelley's mind.⁴ She describes (in a letter dated 1 June 1816) walking around Geneva and visiting "a small obelisk" which was "erected to the glory of Rousseau."⁵ It was during the month of June that Byron and Percy Shelley took their now famous boat trip around Lake Geneva "with Rousseau in hand," as Byron wrote on 23 June, "to see his scenery—according to his delineation in his Heloise now before me."⁶ Percy Shelley wrote to Peacock that the trip was "delightful, but most especially, because then I first knew the divine beauty of Rousseau's imagination, as it exhibits itself in Julie"; he recounts how he and Byron traced the steps of Julie and Saint-Preux (already shrines and tourist attractions) and even came close to accidentally drowning "precisely in the spot where Julie and her lover were nearly overset."⁷

If Mary Shelley did not join in this literary excursion, she surely participated in the poets' conversations about Rousseau—whom Percy Shelley (writing to Hogg on 18 July) described as "in my mind the greatest man the world has produced since Milton."⁸ Some years later, when she wrote the notes for the poems her late husband wrote in 1816, the salient piece of information that Mary Shelley recalled for the reader was that the poet read "The Nouvelle Heloise for the first time . . . on the very spot where the scenes are laid"; she adds that "there was something in the character of Saint Preux . . . that coincided with Shelley's own disposition."⁹ Indeed, having herself read Rousseau's novel in 1815, she might have thought of herself as a Julie who did elope with the engaging young *philosophe* her father had unsuspectingly welcomed into his house. Furthermore, as Mary Shelley recalls in her 1831 introduction to *Frankenstein*, Byron "was writing the third canto of *Childe Harold*" during the summer in which she began her novel (*F*, p. viii). (She records Byron's poem on her list of books read in both 1816 and 1817.) Canto three devotes five stanzas to a poetically condensed yet extensive portrayal of Rousseau, and Byron's notes to the poem reveal that he also associated Rousseau with

that summer: a particularly long note contains citations from the
Confessions and *La Nouvelle Héloïse* and describes the "voyage round
the lake of Geneva."[10] Byron himself would later be called a
"patrician Rousseau."[11]

Jacques Voisine suggests that the Shelleys and Byron would have
read the article on Rousseau that Hazlitt published in *The Examiner*
in April of 1816 in which he compares Rousseau to Wordsworth and
concludes that "we see no other difference between them, than that
the one wrote in prose and the other in poetry."[12] It would not be until
several years later that Hazlitt would call Rousseau "another Prometheus," just as Mary Wollstonecraft named him "the true Prometheus
of sentiment."[13] My point, however, is that the author of *The Modern
Prometheus* began her novel in the context of the growing reappropriation and rehabilitation of Rousseau by a new generation of
Romantic writers.[14] Furthermore, I suggest that whereas Percy
Shelley makes much of his discovery of Rousseau during this period,
Mary Shelley would have had uninterrupted access, as it were, to a
"tradition" of reading Rousseau—in short, to the Rousseau of her
parents. She appears to have grown up with a library that included the
complete *Oeuvres* of Rousseau; but she also would have encountered
Rousseau in the most famous works of Wollstonecraft and Godwin
(whose writings she was reading and rereading, along with works of
Rousseau, shortly before and during the composition of *Frankenstein*).[15]

Godwin specifies "the works of Rousseau" as a major influence on
his *Enquiry Concerning Political Justice*; as he himself notes, he
"frequently quote[s] Rousseau in the course of this work."[16] Anti-
Jacobin critics blamed both Godwin and Rousseau for having written
highly influential books that supposedly encouraged the excesses of
revolutionary terror.[17] Godwin was interested in more than Rousseau's political writings, however. He appears to have worked
intermittently on translating parts of the *Confessions*.[18] In the second
volume of *Fleetwood*, the novel Godwin published in 1804, the
narrator seeks out the acquaintance of a man named Macneil who
"was supposed particularly to have possessed the confidence of the
celebrated Jean Jacques Rousseau, who had been some years an
inhabitant of the banks of the Windermere."[19] Macneil becomes
Fleetwood's best friend and during conversations about "the character
of Rousseau" he provides a sympathetic portrait of "a man of exquisite
sensibility," explaining if not defending Rousseau's notorious behavior
while exiled in England.[20]

It seems appropriate that Macneil should claim intimacy with

Rousseau; his story in some respects resembles the plot of *Julie, ou La Nouvelle Héloïse*: like Wolmar, he has married a young woman who had been seduced by one of her instructors and he now lives in seclusion and domestic harmony. The character of Wolmar is also evoked in the novel in the portrait of Fleetwood's only other intimate friend, M. Ruffigny. The paternal and white-haired Ruffigny often speaks of the *moeurs* and republican virtues of his native Switzerland and he reproaches the young Fleetwood for living an immoral life (like Saint-Preux) in cosmopolitan Paris and London. Godwin's second novel, *St. Leon*, also draws on the Rousseau of sensibility in describing domestic scenes that have been identified with both *La Nouvelle Héloïse* and Mary Wollstonecraft.[21]

It is in Mary Wollstonecraft's works that Mary Shelley would have discovered the most complex and ambiguous representation of Rousseau. If *A Vindication of the Rights of Woman* is acutely critical of Rousseau, specifically the *Émile*, the extent of this critique often casts the book in the form of an ongoing dialogue with him. Wollstonecraft's condemnation includes sympathetic (if somewhat ironic) gestures of accommodation: "But all Rousseau's errors in reasoning," she writes, "arose from sensibility, and sensibility to their charms women are very ready to forgive! . . . peace to his manes! I war not with his ashes, but with his opinions. I war only with the sensibility that led him to degrade woman by making her the slave of love."[22] It is likely that in her almost obsessive search for her mother—what was by necessity a search conducted through textual research[23]—Mary Shelley would have read the pieces her mother wrote on Rouseau for the *Analytical Review*, reviewing editions of his works and on one occasion defending him in personal terms: "It is impossible to puruse his simple descriptions without loving the man in spite of the weaknesses of character that he himself depicts."[24]

Wollstonecraft's first novel, *Mary, A Fiction*, published in 1788 and read or reread by Mary Shelley in 1814, takes its epigraph from Rousseau: "L'exercice des plus sublimes vertus élève et nourrit le génie" ("The exercise of the most sublime virtues fosters and nourishes genius"); although it specifies in its Advertisement that the "Heroine of this Fiction" is not "a * Sophie" (the asterisk names "Rousseau" at the bottom of the page).[25] Wollstonecraft dramatizes a double moment of reading Rousseau in *Maria, or The Wrongs of Woman*, the unfinished novel of Mary Wollstonecraft that Godwin published in her *Posthumous Works* in 1798. While wrongly imprisoned in a private madhouse, Maria is loaned a book by a man who is a fellow inmate. The book is "Rousseau's *Héloïse*"; the narrator explains that Maria "had read this work long since; but now it seemed to open a new world to her—the only world worth inhabiting."[26] She imagines the man with whom she will enter into first a secret correspondence and then an illicit love affair as "the personification of Saint Preux" and she feels justified in attributing "all St. Preux's sentiments and feelings" to the owner of the book when she finds inscribed "on the margin of an impassioned letter, written in the well-known hand—'Rousseau alone, the true Prometheus of senti-ment, possessed the fire of genius necessary to pourtray the passion, the truth of which goes so directly to the heart.' "[27]

My point in detailing Wollstonecraft's evident engagement with Rousseau is not merely to suggest that Mary Shelley would have read in her mother's works recommendations, so to speak, of Rousseau's works. I want to suggest that Mary Shelley had reason to associate Rousseau with her mother. (In chapter six I argue that Mary Shelley's intense interest in the figure of her mother and her intensive engagement with the figure of Rousseau not only exist side by side in the pages of *Frankenstein* but are in many ways inseparable.) She may have read the note that Wollstonecraft sent to Godwin toward the beginning of their relationship: "I send you the last volume of 'Heloise,' because if you have it not, you may chance to wish for it. You may perceive by this remark that I do not give you credit for as much philosophy as our friend."[28] (Indeed, perhaps Mary Shelley read this volume; she might have found in it an inscription from her mother to her father.) She did read the letter that her mother wrote to Gilbert Imlay about their newly born daughter, Fanny: describing an outing to a "*fête*" in revolutionary Paris, Wollstonecraft writes: "to honor J. J. Rousseau, I intend to give her a sash, the first she has ever had round her—and why not?—for I have always been half in love with him."[29] In addition to reading Wollstonecraft's public and private comments about "loving" Rousseau, Mary Shelley also read in her father's *Memoirs of the Author of A Vindication of the Rights of Woman* that her mother was in love with Henry Fuseli. In addition to being an artist, Fuseli was the author of *Remarks on the Writings and Conduct of Rousseau* (a book included in the inventory of Godwin's library), and in a somewhat condescending portrait of him Godwin goes on at some length about Fuseli's worship of "Jean Jacques Rousseau."[30]

Based on this circumstantial evidence, then, it seems clear that Mary Shelley would have learned about the importance of Rousseau early in her education, at the very least from her study of the writings of her parents; that she would have participated in the general

Romantic appropriation of Rousseau; and, more specifically, that
during the months in which she conceived and began to write
Frankenstein she was immersed in the literary as well as the literal
landscapes of Rousseau's life and work. It seems certain—indeed, it
would be strange to doubt—that just as Percy Shelley and Byron had
intense experiences with Rousseau's writing which became specifically
and identifiably and explicitly translated into the texts they were
writing at the time, as well as inscribed in memories of those times
and texts, Mary Shelley began to write her first novel in the context of
a similarly intense engagement with Rousseau. Critics have recognized that *Frankenstein* is deeply informed by Mary Shelley's reading
of Milton.[31] Percy Shelley (who himself would cast Rousseau as a
character in "The Triumph of Life") called Rousseau "the greatest
man the world has produced since Milton" only six days before Mary
Shelley recorded what is at least the first extant reference to
Frankenstein in her journal.[32] There are biographical, psychological,
literary, and philosophical indications that Rousseau is inscribed in the
margins and the characters of Mary Shelley's first novel more than any
other author except Wollstonecraft and Godwin. Mary Shelley's
overdetermined acts of reading (of Rousseau, Wollstonecraft, and
Godwin; of her parents' reading of Rousseau; and of the biographical
and autobiographical texts of Rousseau, Wollstonecraft, Godwin, and
herself) are also signs of the surprising effects of sympathy.

Notes

ABBREVIATIONS

C   Jean-Jacques Rousseau, *Les Confessions*, ed. Jacques Voisine (Paris: Garnier Frères, 1964).

CC   Mary Shelley, "Rousseau," in *Eminent Literary and Scientific Men of France*, 2 vols., *The Cabinet Cyclopedia Conducted by the Rev. Dionysius Lardner* (London: Longman, Orme, Brown, Green, and Longmans, 1838–39).

CW   William Godwin, *Things as They Are, or The Adventures of Caleb Williams*, ed. David McCracken (New York: Norton, 1977).

E   Rousseau, *Émile, ou De l'éducation*, ed. François and Pierre Richard (Paris: Garnier Fréres, 1964).

F   Mary Shelley, *Frankenstein, or The Modern Prometheus* (New York: New American Library, 1965).

L   Rousseau, *Lettre à M. d'Alembert sur les spectacles*, in *Du contrat social et autres oeuvres politiques* (Paris: Garnier Frères, 1975).

NH   Rousseau, *Julie, ou La Nouvelle Héloïse*, ed. René Pomeau (Paris: Garnier Frères, 1960).

O   Rousseau, *Essai sur l'origine des langues*, in vol. 2 of *Oeuvres complètes*, ed. V. D. Musset-Pathay, 25 vols. (Paris: P. Dupont, 1823–26).

OC   Rousseau, *Oeuvres complètes*, vol. 3, ed. François Bouchardy *et al.*, 4 vols. (Paris: Gallimard, 1959–69).

OE   Denis Diderot, *Oeuvres esthétiques*, ed. Paul Vernière (Paris: Garnier Frères, 1968).

OJ   Marivaux, *Oeuvres de jeunesse*, ed. Frédéric Deloffre (Paris: Gallimard, 1972).

OR   Diderot, *Oeuvres romanesques*, ed. Henri Bénac (Paris: Garnier Frères, 1960).

R   Rousseau, *Les Rêveries du promeneur solitaire*, ed. Henri Roddier (Paris: Garnier, 1960).

RC   L'Abbé Du Bos, *Réflexions critiques sur la poésie et sur la peinture*, 4th ed. (Paris: Pierre-Jean Marette, 1740).

VM   Marivaux, *La Vie de Marianne*, ed. Frédéric Deloffre (Paris: Garnier Frères, 1963).

INTRODUCTION

1. *The Figure of Theater: Shaftesbury, Defoe, Adam Smith, and George Eliot* (New York: Columbia University Press, 1986).

2. For discussions of sympathy and related words and concepts, see Geoffroy Atkinson, *The Sentimental Revolution: French Writers of 1690–1740*, ed. Abraham C. Keller (Seattle: University of Washington Press, 1965), pp. 62–98; Atkinson and Keller, *Prelude to the Enlightenment: French Literature, 1690–1740* (Seattle: University of Washington Press, 1970), p. 26; R. F. Brissenden, *Virtue in Distress: Studies in the Novel of Sentiment from Richardson to Sade* (London: Macmillan, 1974), pp. 11–55; Northrop Frye, "Towards Defining an Age of Sensibility," *Eighteenth-Century English Literature*, ed. James L. Clifford (Oxford: Oxford University Press, 1959), pp. 311–18; G. S. Rousseau, "Nerves, Spirits, and Fibres: Towards Defining the Origins of Sensibility," *Studies in the Eighteenth Century, III: Papers presented at the Third David Nichol Smith Memorial Seminar, Canberra, 1973* (Toronto: University of Toronto Press, 1976), pp. 137–57; John S. Spink, "'Sentiment,' 'Sensible,' 'Sensibilité': Les mots, les idées, d'après les 'moralistes' français et britanniques du début du dix-huitième siècle," *Zagadnienia Rodzajów Literackich* 20 (1977): 33–48, and "Marivaux: The 'Mechanism of the Passions' and the 'Metaphysics of Sentiment,'" *Modern Language Review* 73 (1978): 278–90. Also relevant here are the articles in the *Encyclopédie* on "Compassion," "Émouvoir," "Expression," "Pathétique," "Physionomie," "Pitié," "Sentiment," and "Sympathie."

3. Adam Smith, *The Theory of Moral Sentiments*, ed. D. D. Raphael and A. L. Macfie (Oxford: Clarendon Press, 1976), p. 10.

4. Smith, *The Theory of Moral Sentiments*, p. 9.

5. For a more extensive discussion of this passage in the context of a reading of the theatrical dynamics of *The Theory of Moral Sentiments*, see my chapter on Smith in *The Figure of Theater*, pp. 167–92. For a related discussion, see Jean-Christophe Agnew, *Worlds Apart: The Market and the Theater in Anglo-American Thought, 1550–1750* (Cambridge: Cambridge University Press, 1986), pp. 176–88. I would like to add here that in the course of running up various intellectual debts to Agnew, I have had the benefit of reading his "From Prayer to Performance: The Market and the Theater in Anglo-American Thought, 1600–1900," (Ph.D. diss., Harvard University, 1977), which includes relevant discussions of the problem of theatricality in the French tradition.

6. I borrow the phrase "blurred genres" from Clifford Geertz, "Blurred Genres: The Refiguration of Social Thought," *The American Scholar* 29 (1980): 165–79.

CHAPTER ONE

1. Marivaux, *Les Aventures de *** ou les Effets surprenants de la sympathie*, in *OJ*. Critics have long noted Marivaux's debt to Cervantes's *Persiles and Sigismunda*, as well as general resemblances to the picaresque and romance

traditions. See, for example, Jean Fleury, *Marivaux et le marivaudage* (Paris: Plon, 1881), p. 17; E. J. H. Greene, *Marivaux* (Toronto: University of Toronto Press, 1965), p. 9; Oscar A. Haac, *Marivaux* (New York: Twayne Publishers, 1973), pp. 22–24; and Martin Turnell, *The Rise of the French Novel* (New York: New Directions, 1978), pp. 35–36.

2. See Introduction, n. 2, for references to discussions of the meanings of *sympathie*.

3. While *Les Effets surprenants de la sympathie* had been condemned to relative obscurity until recent years, mentioned at most in passing in surveys of Marivaux's early years as a writer, the "Avis au lecteur" was almost completely forgotten until Frédéric Deloffre published a summary of it with extensive citations in "Premières idées de Marivaux sur l'art du roman," *L'Esprit créateur* 1 (1961): 178–83. Deloffre included (and commented on) the complete text of the "Avis" in the 1972 *Oeuvres de jeunesse*. In arguing for the importance of Marivaux's preface, I will be arguing against the attitudes represented by the particular characterization of E. J. H. Greene, who writes, "The repetitious thirty page *Avis au lecteur* which he wrote for *Les Effets* has the curious aggressive character of a preface by an eager beginner who is unsure of himself" (*Marivaux*, p. 12), and the general claim of F. C. Green, who writes that "not until 1728 do we come across any important reference to the novel" ("The Eighteenth-Century French Critic and the Contemporary Novel," *Modern Language Review* 23 [1928]: 174). For discussions of the "Avis au lecteur," see Henri Coulet, *Marivaux romancier: Essai sur l'esprit et le coeur dans les romans de Marivaux* (Paris: A. Colin, 1975), pp. 102–3; David Coward, *Marivaux: La Vie de Marianne and Le Paysan parvenu* (London: Grant and Cutler, 1982), pp. 10–12; Deloffre, "De Marianne à Jacob: Les deux sexes du roman chez Marivaux," *L'Information littéraire* 11 (1959): 186–87; Haac, "Theories of Literary Criticism and Marivaux," *Studies on Voltaire and the Eighteenth Century* 88 (1972): 722–34; Ronald C. Rosbottom, *Marivaux's Novels: Theme and Function in Early Eighteenth-Century Narrative* (Rutherford, N.J.: Fairleigh Dickinson University Press, 1974), p. 58; English Showalter, *The Evolution of the French Novel, 1691–1782* (Princeton, N.J.: Princeton University Press, 1972), p. 45; Ioan Williams, *The Idea of the Novel in Europe, 1660–1800* (London: Macmillan, 1979), pp. 141–42, 165. General discussions of *Les Effets surprenants de la sympathie*—which sometimes amount to little more than attempts to summarize the narrative's impossibly convoluted plot—can be found in Marcel Arland, *Marivaux* (Paris: Gallimard, 1950), pp. 23–28; Coulet, *Marivaux romancier*, pp. 92–103, 306–9, 369–80; Coulet and Michel Gilot, *Marivaux: Un humanisme expérimental* (Paris: Larousse, 1973), pp. 157–92; Deloffre, *Marivaux et le marivaudage* (Paris: A. Colin, 1967), pp. 85–90; Deloffre, *La Nouvelle en France à l'âge classique* (Paris: Didier, 1968), pp. 68–69; Fleury, *Marivaux et le marivaudage*, pp. 13–18; Greene, *Marivaux*, p. 186; Haac, *Marivaux*, pp. 22–24; Ruth Kirby Jamieson, *Marivaux: A Study in Sensibility* (New York: King's Crown Press, 1941), pp. 28–33; Rosbottom, *Marivaux's Novels*, pp. 57–62; J. S. Spink,

"Marivaux: The 'Mechanism of the Passions' and the 'Metaphysics of Sentiment,'" *Modern Language Review* 73 (1978): 278; Philip Stewart, *Imitation and Illusion in the French Memoir-Novel, 1770–1750: The Art of Make-Believe* (New Haven, Conn.: Yale University Press, 1969), pp. 156–57; Turnell, *The Rise of the French Novel*, pp. 35–36.

4. See Georges May, *Le Dilemme du roman au XVIIIe siècle: Étude sur les rapports du roman et de la critique (1715–1761)* (New Haven, Conn.: Yale University Press, 1963). May writes: "Le rapprochement des attaques contre le roman au XVIIIe siècle avec celles dirigées contre le théâtre au XVIIe et reprises plus d'une fois au XVIIIe n'est pas donc un simple jeu d'esprit, mais répond au contraire à une realité historique certaine. De plus, ce rapprochement semble être la meilleure, sinon la seule manière, de comprendre certains des aspects particuliers de l'attaque contre le roman" (p. 29). Marivaux's defense both of novels in general and of *Les Effets surprenants de la sympathie* in particular also can be seen in the contexts of the quarrel between the ancients and the moderns and the transition from the rules and reason of seventeenth-century classicism to the pre-Romantic ideals of sensibility and sentiment. See Coward, *Marivaux*, p. 12; Lionel Gossman, "Literature and Society in the Early Enlightenment: The Case of Marivaux," *MLN* 82 (1967): 308–9; Haac, "Theories of Literary Criticism and Marivaux," p. 722; Rosbottom, *Marivaux's Novels*, p. 58; A. Lombard, *La Querelle des anciens et des modernes: L'Abbé Du Bos* (Neuchâtel: Attinger Frères, 1908); Rémy G. Saisselin, *The Rule of Reason and the Rules of the Heart: A Philosophical Dictionary of Classical French Criticism, Critics, and Aesthetic Issues* (Cleveland: The Press of Case Western Reserve University, 1970), pp. 5–15, 176–81; Wladyslaw Folkierski, *Entre le classicisme et le romantisme: Étude sur l'esthétique et les esthéticiens du XVIIIe siècle* (Paris: Librairie Ancienne Honoré Champion, 1925), pp. 135–69; Spink, *French Free Thought from Gassendi to Voltaire* (London: The Athlone Press, 1960), pp. 203–5.

5. For relevant discussions of Du Bos and aesthetic theory, see Ernst Cassirer, *The Philosophy of the Enlightenment*, trans. Fritz C. A. Koelln and James P. Pettegrove (Princeton, N.J.: Princeton University Press, 1951), pp. 275–360, esp. pp. 302–31, 323–25; Robert Finch, *The Sixth Sense* (Toronto: University of Toronto Press, 1966), pp. 81–87; Folkierski, *Entre le classicisme et le romantisme*, pp. 135–69; Michael Fried, *Absorption and Theatricality: Painting and Beholder in the Age of Diderot* (Berkeley and Los Angeles: University of California Press, 1979), pp. 73–74, 92–93, 204–5; Marion Hobson, *The Object of Art: The Theory of Illusion in Eighteenth-Century France* (Cambridge: Cambridge University Press, 1982), pp. 38–42; Charlotte Hogsett, "Jean-Baptiste Dubos on Art as Illusion," *Studies on Voltaire and the Eighteenth Century* 73 (1970): 147–64; N. Jonsard, "L'Abbé Du Bos et l'Italie," *Revue de littérature comparée* 37 (1963): 177–201; Lombard, *L'Abbé Dubos, un initiateur de la pensée moderne (1670–1742)* (Paris: Librairie Hachette, 1913), and *La Querelle des anciens et des modernes*; Basil Munteano, "L'Abbé Du Bos: Esthéticien de la persuasion passionnelle," *Revue de*

littérature comparée 30 (1956): 318–50, and "Les Premises rhétoriques du système de l'abbé Du Bos," *Rivista di letterature moderne e comparate* 10 (1957): 5–30; Saisselin, *The Rule of Reason*, pp. 20–24, 263–266, and "Ut Pictura Poesis: Dubos to Diderot," *Journal of Aesthetics and Art Criticism* 20 (1961): 145–56.

6. Although critics have noted the place of the "Avis au lecteur" in the aesthetic debates of the early eighteenth century, Du Bos and Marivaux are hardly ever mentioned together. Coulet notes that Marivaux, in his "Avis au lecteur," "interprète Aristote dans le sens où l'interprètera l'abbé Du Bos dès l'année suivante" and concludes, "c'est le seul point où l'on puisse déceler dans *Les Effets surprenants* une influence des fréquentations parisiennes de Marivaux, si du moins il y a influence, car Marivaux n'avait ici qu'à suivre son propre tempérament" (*Marivaux romancier*, p. 103n). I am arguing that both the "Avis" and the narrative, and especially the "Avis" and the narrative considered together, indicate Marivaux's deep involvement and investment in the aesthetic arguments that Du Bos presents in the *Réflexions critiques*. Jamieson also mentions Marivaux's participation in the salon society of Fontenelle, La Motte, and Mme de Lambert (*Marivaux*, pp. 13–15), as does Coward (*Marivaux*, p. 12). Daniel Mornet briefly relates the two in discussing the concept of *je ne sais quoi* (*French Thought in the Eighteenth Century*, trans. Lawrence M. Levin [n.p.: Archon Books, 1969], p. 194). Rosbottom mentions Du Bos in speaking of Marivaux's role in the quarrel of the ancients and the moderns and notes that *Les Effets surprenants de la sympathie* was officially approved for publication by Fontenelle (*Marivaux's Novels*, pp. 24, 58). See also Haac, "Theories of Literary Criticism," p. 711; and Spink, "'Sentiment,' 'Sensible,' 'Sensibilité': Les mots, les idées, d'après les 'moralistes' français et britanniques du début du dix-huitième siècle," *Zagadnienia Rodzajów Literackich* 20 (1977): 44. See also James F. Jones, Jr., "Du Bos and Rousseau: A Question of Influence," *Studies on Voltaire and the Eighteenth Century* 127 (1974): 231–41; and Enzo Caramaschi, "Du Bos and Voltaire," *Studies on Voltaire and the Eighteenth Century* 10 (1959): 113–236.

7. Jean Rousset, *Forme et signification: Essais sur les formes littéraires de Corneille à Claudel* (Paris: Librairie José Corti, 1973), pp. 50, 64. For a response to Rousset, see Walter Ince, "L'Unité du double registre chez Marivaux," *Les Chemins actuels de la critique*, ed. Georges Poulet (Paris: Plon, 1967), pp. 131–44. My specific focus on questions of theatricality in novels and discussions about acting and the institution of the theater, as well as limits of space, have precluded consideration of Marivaux's plays. It goes without saying, however, that Marivaux spent his career thinking about theater. For other discussions of the role of theater or theatrical relations in Marivaux's fiction, see Peter Brooks, *The Novel of Wordliness: Crébillon, Marivaux, Laclos, Stendhal* (Princeton, N.J.: Princeton University Press, 1969), pp. 94–144, 29–35; René Girard, "Marivaudage and Hypocrisy," *American Society Legion of Honor Magazine* 34 (1963): 163–74; Gossman, "Literature and Society," pp. 306–33; Philip Koch, "On Marivaux's Expression 'se donner la comédie,'"

Romanic Review 56 (1965): 22–29; Henri Lafon, "'Voir sans être vu': Un cliché, un fantasme," *Poetique* 29 (1977): 50–60; Lubbé Levin, "Masque et Identité dans *Le Paysan parvenu*," *Studies on Voltaire and the Eighteenth Century* 79 (1970): 177–92; Nancy K. Miller, *The Heroine's Text: Readings in the French and English Novel 1722–1782* (New York: Columbia University Press, 1980), pp. 21–36; Rosbottom, *Marivaux's Novels*, pp. 40–47, 93–170; William S. Rogers, "Marivaux: The Mirror and the Mask," *L'Esprit Créateur* 1 (1961): 166–77; Harold Schaad, *Le Thème de l'être et du paraître dans l'oeuvre de Marivaux* (Zurich: J. Druck, 1969); Stewart, *Le Masque et la parole: Le langage de l'amour au XVIIIe siècle* (Paris: J. Corti, 1973).

8. For discussions of the role of women and the "feminine" in Marivaux's fiction, see Brooks, *The Novel of Worldliness*, pp. 132–33; Deloffre, "De Marianne à Jacob," pp. 186–87; Greene, *Marivaux*, p. 186; Jamieson, *Marivaux: A Study in Sensibility*; Kathy Luthi, *Les Femmes dans l'oeuvre de Marivaux* (Bienne: Editions du Chandelier, 1943); May, *Le Dilemme du roman*, pp. 204–45; Miller, *The Heroine's Text*; Leo Spitzer, "A Propos de la *Vie de Marianne* (Lettre à M. Georges Poulet)," *Romanic Review* 44 (1953): 122; Stewart, *Le Masque et la parole*, pp. 24–43.

9. For discussions of Du Bos and the question of rules, see esp. Folkierski, *Entre le classicisme et le romantisme*, pp. 135–69; Saisselin, *The Rule of Reason*, pp. 176–81, 263–66.

10. In "L'Abbé Du Bos: Esthéticien de la persuasion passionnelle," Munteano places the demand that works of art move their audience in the context of classical and seventeenth-century rhetoric. He writes: "Du coup, les *Réflexions* deviennent l'instrument de la crise immémoriale que l'alternative *instruire-émouvoir*, autant dire *raison-coeur*, fait peser, dès l'antiquité, sur la conscience de l'homme" (p. 331). Speaking of "l'antique *movere* des rhéteurs," he summarizes Du Bos's position: "l'art est fait, essentiellement, pour *toucher*, pour *attendrir*, pour *remuer l'âme*, bref, pour *émouvoir* . . ." (p. 343). For more background, see Donald Sellstrom, "Rhetoric and the Poetics of French Classicism," *French Review* 34 (1960–61): 425–31; and Hugh M. Davidson, *Audience, Words, and Art: Studies in Seventeenth-Century French Rhetoric* (Columbus: Ohio State University Press, 1965). In *The Philosophy of the Enlightenment*, Cassirer describes Du Bos's theory of art as "an aesthetics of 'pathos.' . . . The value of a scene in painting or in poetry lies in the pathos of its images, not in its verisimilitude. . . . The mere intensity of the effect is looked upon as its valid aesthetic standard, and the degree of emotion decides its value. Poetry and painting aim only to please and to move, and know no higher goal" (pp. 324–25).

11. See Aristotle, *Poetics*, 4:1448b, in *Rhetoric and Poetics of Aristotle*, trans. W. Rhys Roberts and Ingram Bywater (New York: Modern Library, 1954). See also Coulet, *Marivaux romancier*, pp. 102–3; and Haac, "Theories of Literary Criticism," p. 713.

12. For discussions of *ut pictura poesis*, see Rensselaer W. Lee, *Ut Pictura Poesis: The Humanistic Theory of Painting* (New York: W. W. Norton, 1967);

William G. Howard, "Ut Pictura Poesis," *PMLA* 24 (1909): 40–123; Saisselin, "Ut Pictura Poesis," pp. 145–56, and *The Rule of Reason*, pp. 216–24; Cicely Davis, "Ut Pictura Poesis," *MLR* 30 (1935): 159–69; Hogsett, "Jean-Baptiste Dubos," pp. 159–60.

13. For more on the role of "portraits" in Marivaux's fiction, see Brooks, *The Novel of Worldliness*, pp. 103–41, 44–82; Coulet, *Marivaux romancier*, pp. 285–342, esp. pp. 317–25; and Stewart, "Marianne's Snapshot Album: Instances of Dramatic Stasis in Narrative," *Modern Language Studies* 15 (1985): 281–88.

14. Henry Home, Lord Kames, *Elements of Criticism*, 3d. ed., 2 vols. (Edinburgh, 1765), 1:84.

15. Smith writes: "As we have no immediate experience of what other men feel, we can form no idea of the manner in which they are affected, but by conceiving what we ourselves should feel in the like situation. Though our brother is upon the rack, as long as we ourselves are at ease, our senses will never inform us of what he suffers. They never did, and never can, carry us beyond our own person, and it is by the imagination only that we can form any conception of what are his sensations. Neither can that faculty help us to this any other way, than by representing to us what would be our own, if we were in his case. . . . By the imagination we place ourselves in his situation" (*The Theory of Moral Sentiments*, ed. D. D. Raphael and A. L. Macfie [Oxford: Clarendon Press, 1976], p. 9). See my chapter on Smith in *The Figure of Theater: Shaftesbury, Defoe, Adam Smith, and George Eliot* (New York: Columbia University Press, 1986), pp. 167–92.

16. Shakespeare, *The Tempest*, 1.2.5–6, 27.

17. See T. Lucreti Cari, *De Rerum Natura*, ed. H. A. J. Munro (Cambridge: Deighton Bell and Co., 1866), 1:78. Munro's version of the lines Du Bos translates is: "It is sweet, when on the great sea the winds trouble its waters, to behold from land another's deep distress; not that it is a pleasure and delight that they should be afflicted, but because it is sweet to see from what evils you are yourself exempt" (3:28). See my discussion of George Eliot's use of these sources and tropes in *The Figure of Theater*, pp. 207–10.

18. Marivaux, *Journaux et Oeuvres diverses*, ed. Deloffre and Michel Gilot (Paris: Garnier, 1969), p. 12.

19. Noting that Du Bos "does not hesitate to place the impression we gain from the contemplation of a painting or from listening to a tragedy immediately alongside of those other emotions which we feel, for instance, at the execution of a criminal or at gladiatorial combats and bullfights," Cassirer worries that in Du Bos's system "the work of art threatens to become a mere spectacle" (*The Philosophy of Enlightenment*, pp. 323–24). See Michel Foucault's discussion, "The Spectacle of the Scaffold," in *Discipline and Punish: The Birth of the Prison*, trans. Alan Sheridan (New York: Vintage, 1979), pp. 32–69.

20. For a comprehensive survey of the antitheatrical tradition, see Jonas Barish, *The Antitheatrical Prejudice* (Berkeley and Los Angeles: University of

California Press, 1981). See also chapter 5, "Rousseau and the State of Theater."

21. Other critics have noted this discrepancy. For example, Coward writes, "In his 'Avis au Lecteur,' [Marivaux] makes out a case for fiction which is curiously at odds with the tale he tells" (*Marivaux*, p. 10). Williams, who describes the "Avis" as "a daring progressive statement" that "provides the basis for a whole new approach to criticism and composition of the novel," writes that this "progressive theory, however, is unmatched in Marivaux's practice" (*The Idea of the Novel*, pp. 141–42). I am suggesting that the relation between "Avis" and narrative should be understood in a different way.

22. See Fried, *Absorption and Theatricality*, esp. pp. 7–70. See also Lafon, "Voir sans être vu"; and Jamieson, *Marivaux*, p. 41.

23. See Mornet, *French Thought in the Eighteenth Century*, p. 194; and Saisselin, *The Rule of Reason*, pp. 115–18.

24. The scene of someone suddenly stumbling into a room and interpreting a spectacle becomes a trope in nineteenth-century novels by authors such as Eliot and James. See *The Figure of Theater*, pp. 230–40.

25. In "The Sexual Theories of Children," Freud discusses what he calls the "sadistic view of coition" adopted by children who "become witnesses of sexual intercourse." In this view the primal scene is interpreted as "an act of violence." According to Freud, "if the child discovers spots of blood in his mother's bed or on her underclothes, he regards it as a confirmation of his view. It proves to him that his father has made another similar assault on his mother during the night.... Much of the otherwise inexplicable 'horror of blood' shown by neurotics finds its explanation from this connection. Once again, however, the child's mistake contains a fragment of truth. For in certain familiar circumstances a trace of blood is in fact judged as a sign that sexual intercourse has been begun" (*The Standard Edition of the Complete Psychological Works of Sigmund Freud*, ed. and trans. James Strachey, 24 vols. [London: Hogarth Press, 1953–74], 9:220–22). Psychoanalysis would suggest that it is no coincidence that a novel about scenes of sympathy (or in the case of Du Bos, a treatise about the effects of sympathy) would repeatedly return to scenes of violence—or that, as in the scene with Mériante confronting the bloody sheets of Parménie's bed, the scene of sympathy and the scene of violence or suffering should be the same scene. In "Instincts and Their Vicissitudes," Freud discusses sympathy in the context of the "reversal of an instinct into its opposite" (specifically in regard to the pairs "sadism-masochism" and "scopophilia-exhibitionism"). Freud notes that "once feeling pains has become a masochistic aim, the sadistic aim of *causing* pains can arise also, retrogressively; for while these pains are being inflicted on other people, they are enjoyed masochistically by the subject through his identification of himself with the suffering object." He continues: "I may add that feelings of pity cannot be described as a result of a transformation of instinct occurring in sadism, but necessitate the notion of a *reaction-formation* against that

instinct" (*Standard Edition*, 14:127–29). See also Jean Laplanche's discussion of this text in *Vie et Mort en Psychanalyse* (Paris: Flammarion, 1970), pp. 145–73.

In a provocative and relevant discussion of both Freud and Laplanche, Leo Bersani writes, "we might ask to what extent the fantasy-identifications outlined by Freud are crucial to *all* sympathetic responses to suffering. Ironically enough, Sade's sadism is consistent with the theories of benevolent sympathy which he scornfully rejects. For what Sade rejects is not the mechanism of sympathetic projection assumed by theories of benevolence, but rather the pious view that we are stirred by *virtuous* identifications with others. Virtue is irrelevant to the agitation induced by the suffering of others. It is the identification itself—that is, a fantasmic introjection of the other—which appears to be intrinsically sexual. . . . a reading of Laplanche's reading of Freud may suggest to us that 'sympathy' always includes a trace of sexual pleasure, and that this pleasure is, inescapably, masochistic. If this is the case, there is a certain risk in all sympathetic projections: the pleasure that accompanies them promotes a secret attachment to scenes of suffering or violence" ("Representation and Its Discontents," *Allegory and Representation: Selected Papers from the English Institute, 1979–1980*, ed. Stephen J. Greenblatt [Baltimore: Johns Hopkins University Press, 1981], pp. 149–50).

For other discussions of the primal scene, see "From the History of an Infantile Neurosis," *Standard Edition*, 17:7–122. See also *Three Essays on the Theory of Sexuality, Standard Edition*, 7:125–43, and "The Sexual Theories of Children," *Standard Edition*, 9:205–26. See also Laplanche and J. Pontalis, "Fantasme originaire, fantasme des origines, origines du fantasme," *Les Temps modernes* 215 (1964): 1833–68; "Scientific Proceedings Panel Reports: The Pathogenicity of the Primal Scene," reported by Richard A. Isay, *Journal of the American Psychoanalytical Association* 26 (1978): 131–42; Aaron H. Esman, "The Primal Scene: A Review and a Reconsideration," *Psychoanalytic Study of the Child* 28 (1973): 49–81; Henry Edelheit, "Mythopoiesis and the Primal Scene," *Psychoanalytic Study of Society* 5 (1972): 212–33. Chapter two and chapter six also will address some of these questions.

CHAPTER TWO

1. For some other discussions of *La Vie de Marianne*, see Frédéric Deloffre's introduction to the Garnier edition, *VM*, pp. i–lxxxv; Peter Brooks, *The Novel of Worldliness: Crébillon, Marivaux, Laclos, Stendhal* (Princeton, N.J.: Princeton University Press, 1969), pp. 94–141; Henri Coulet, *Marivaux romancier: Essai sur l'esprit et le coeur dans les romans de Marivaux* (Paris: A. Colin, 1975), pp. 285–342; Deloffre, *Marivaux et le marivaudage* (Paris: A. Colin, 1967), and "De Marianne à Jacob: Les deux sexes du roman chez Marivaux," *L'Information littéraire* 11 (1959): 185–92; Jean Fabre, "Intention et structure dans les romans de Marivaux," *Zagadnienia Rodzajów Literackich* 3 (1960): 5–25; René Girard, "Marivaudage and Hypocrisy," *American Society Legion of Honor Magazine* 34 (1963): 163–74; Lionel Gossman, "Literature

and Society in the Early Enlightenment: The Case of Marivaux," *MLN* 82 (1967): 306–33; Oscar A. Haac, *Marivaux* (New York: Twayne, 1973), pp. 69–70; Ruth Kirby Jamieson, *Marivaux: A Study in Sensibility* (New York: King's Crown Press, 1941); Nancy K. Miller, *The Heroine's Text: Readings in the French and English Novel, 1722–1782* (New York: Columbia University Press, 1980), pp. 21–36; Georges Poulet, *Études sur le temps humain, II: La Distance intérieure* (Paris: Plon, 1952), pp. 1–34; Jean Rousset, "Comment insérer le présent dans le récit: L'exemple de Marivaux," *Littérature* 5 (1972): 3–10; Ronald C. Rosbottom, *Marivaux's Novels: Theme and Function in Early Eighteenth-Century Narrative* (Rutherford, N.J.: Fairleigh Dickinson University Press, 1974), pp. 93–170; Claude Roy, *Lire Marivaux* (Neuchâtel: Editions de la Baconnière, 1947); Leo Spitzer, "A Propros de la *Vie de Marianne* (Lettre à M. Georges Poulet)," *Romanic Review* 44 (1953): 102–26; Martin Turnell, *The Rise of the French Novel* (New York: New Directions, 1978), pp. 37–55; Arnold Weinstein, *Fictions of the Self: 1550–1880* (Princeton, N.J.: Princeton University Press, 1981), pp. 100–114; Ioan Williams, *The Idea of the Novel in Europe, 1660–1800* (London: The Macmillan Press, 1979), pp. 162–74.

2. See Georges May, *Le Dilemme du roman au XVIIIe siècle: Étude sur les rapports du roman et de la critique (1715–1761)* (New Haven, Conn.: Yale University Press, 1963); Deloffre, *La Nouvelle en France à l'âge classique* (Paris: Didier, 1968). Marion Hobson refers to "the crudely held view" in the eighteenth century that "the novel was an upstart genre without literary pedigree" (*The Object of Art: The Theory of Illusion in Eighteenth-Century France* [Cambridge: Cambridge University Press, 1982], p. 85); in other words, the novel was seen very much as Marianne is seen.

3. Jean Laplanche and J.-B. Pontalis, "Fantasy and the Origins of Sexuality," *International Journal of Psycho-analysis* 49 (1968): 11. (This is a translation of "Fantasme originaire, fantaisie des origines, origine des fantasmes," *Les Temps modernes* 215 [1964]: 1833–68.) I am grateful to my colleague Cathy Caruth for bringing this article to my attention. For other references concerning the primal scene, see chapter 1 n. 25 and chapter 6.

4. See *VM*, pp. vii–xi. See also E. J. H. Greene, *Marivaux* (Toronto: University of Toronto Press, 1965), p. 186; and Rosbottom, *Marivaux's Novels*, pp. 94–95.

5. Marivaux, *Journaux et oeuvres diverses*, ed. Deloffre and Michel Gilot (Paris: Garnier, 1969), p. 12.

6. The famous scene in which M. de Climal tries to seduce Marianne by appealing to her vanity may recall the scene in *Roxana* (1726) in which the prince comes to Roxana's Parisian home and seduces her with gifts and a mirror. M. de Climal tells Marianne: "allez vous regarder dans le miroir, et voyez si ce linge est trop beau pour votre visage" (*VM*, p. 39); Roxana recounts: "He stood up, and taking me by the Hand, led me to a large Looking-Glass . . . ; Look there, Madam, *said he*; Is it fit that face, pointing to my Figure in the Glass, should go back to *Poictou?*" (Daniel Defoe,

Roxana, The Fortunate Mistress, ed. Jane Jack [Oxford: Oxford University Press, 1969], pp. 59–60). She repeats this experience in front of another "Peir-Glass" in her "best Suit of Cloaths" several pages later and is "all on fire with the Sight" (pp. 71, 73). Compare Marianne's comment: "j'essayai mon habit le plus modestement qu'il me fut possible, devant un petit miroir ingrat qui ne me rendait que la moitié de ma figure; et ce que j'en voyais me paraissait bien piquant" (*VM*, pp. 49–50). See my discussion of theatricality and *Roxana* in *The Figure of Theater: Shaftesbury, Defoe, Adam Smith, and George Eliot* (New York: Columbia University Press, 1986), pp. 131–55. See also Marivaux's famous account of a young woman in front of a mirror in the first number of *Le Spectateur français* in *Journaux et oeuvres diverses*, p. 118.

7. Miller, *The Heroine's Text*, p. 25. For references to discussions of the role of theater in Marivaux's fiction, see chapter 1 n. 6.

8. See Freud's discussion of fetishism in *Three Essays on Sexuality* (*The Standard Edition of the Complete Psychological Works of Sigmund Freud*, ed. and trans. James Strachey, 24 vols. [London: Hogarth Press, 1953–74], 7:153–55). In Freud's view, it would make sense that Marianne's scene of exhibitionism in front of Valville in the church would be followed by the incident with her foot. Freud writes: "In a number of cases of foot-fetishism, it has been possible to show that the scopophilic instinct, seeking to reach its object (originally the genitals) from underneath, was brought to a halt in its pathway by prohibition and repression. For that reason it became attached to a fetish in the form of a foot or a shoe, the female genitals (in accordance with the expectations of childhood) being imagined as male ones" (p. 155 n. 2). Freud relates fetishism to the imagined castration of women in "Fetishism" (*Standard Edition*, 21:149–57). See also "Splitting of the Ego in the Process of Defence" (*Standard Edition*, 23:275–78) and *Introductory Lectures on Psycho-Analysis* (*Standard Edition*, 16:348–49).

9. *VM*, pp. 65, 67, 72, 78, 91, 100.

10. For another discussion of this situation, see *The Figure of Theater*, pp. 231–40.

11. Jamieson writes: "As M. Trahard has pointed out, Marivaux anticipates the talent of Greuze and Diderot in constructing *tableaux* of sensibility, scenes of filial devotion, death-bed scenes, scenes of forgiveness and farewell. Such scenes, rare in the plays, are calculated to touch the reader and to allow him to indulge in one of the chief pleasures of the sensitive heart, a generous enjoyment of the sorrows of others" (*Marivaux: A Study in Sensibility*, p. 41). Brooks comments that the "pathetic tableau which Mlle de Tervire arranges to promote the reconcilation of Mme Dursan and her estranged son should have appealed to that lover of Greuze, Diderot" (*The Novel of Worldliness*, p. 138). See also Philip Stewart, "Marianne's Snapshot Album: Instances of Dramatic Stasis in Narrative," *Modern Language Studies* 15 (1985): 281–88; and Michael Fried's discussions of Diderot and Greuze in *Absorption and Theatricality: Painting and Beholder in the Age of Diderot* (Berkeley and Los Angeles: University of California Press, 1979).

12. Sylvère Lotringer identifies Varthon and Tervire as doubles of Marianne in "Le Roman impossible," *Poétique* 3 (1970): 317–18.

13. This relation is discussed at greater length in chapter 3 "*La Religieuse*: Sympathy and Seduction."

14. See chapter 4, "Forgetting Theater."

15. See definitions of "miroir" and "mirer" in *Le Petit Robert* (Paris: Le Robert, 1984), pp. 1206–7.

16. See Fried, *Absorption and Theatricality*. See also Henri Lafon, "'Voir sans être vu': Un Cliché, un fantasme," *Poétique* 29 (1977): 50–60.

17. For more on Marivaux and Mme de Lambert, see Jamieson, *Marivaux: A Study in Sensibility*. For more on sympathy and related concepts, see Geoffroy Atkinson, *The Sentimental Revolution: French Writers of 1690-1740*, ed. Abraham C. Keller (Seattle: University of Washington Press, 1965), pp. 62–98; John S. Spink, "'Sentiment,' 'Sensible,' 'Sensibilité': Les mots, les idées, d'après les 'moralistes' français et britanniques du début du dix-huitième siècle," *Zagadnienia Rodzajów Literackich* 20 (1977): 33–48.

18. See Lafon's discussion of the motif of "la belle endormie" in "'Voir sans être vu,'" p. 51.

19. See May, *Le Dilemme du roman;* Hobson, *The Object of Art*, pp. 81–138; Vivienne Mylne, *The Eighteenth-Century Novel: Techniques of Illusion* (Cambridge: Cambridge University Press, 1965); Stewart, *Imitation and Illusion in the French Memoir-Novel, 1700–1750: The Art of Make-Believe* (New Haven, Conn.: Yale University Press, 1969); A. J. Tieje, "A Peculiar Phase of the Theory of Realism in Pre-Richardsonian Fiction," *PMLA* 28 (1913): 213–52.

20. For discussions of the figure of Hermes, see Jean-Christophe Agnew, "The Threshold of Exchange: Speculations on the Market," *Radical History Review* 21 (1979): 101 and *Worlds Apart: The Market and the Theater in Anglo-American Thought, 1550–1750* (Cambridge: Cambridge University Press, 1986), pp. 20–21; Norman O. Brown, *Hermes the Thief* (Madison: University of Wisconsin Press, 1947).

21. *Dictionnaire de l'Académie françoise* (Paris, 1694); *Dictionnaire de l'Académie françoise* (Paris, 1718); *Dictionnaire de l'Académie françoise* (Paris, 1740). In the section, "Le Vocabulaire," in *Marivaux et le marivaudage*, Deloffre cites "accident" as a *terme de philosophie*. He offers this definition from Furetière's *Dictionnaire universel* (La Haye: P. Husson, 1972): "Proprieté accidentelle, ce qui survient à la substance et ne lui est pas essentiel" and notes that "définitions analogues" appear in the *Dictionnaire de l'Académie Françoise*, 1694, 1718, and 1740, as well as Pierre Richelet's *Nouveau Dictionnaire François* (Rouen: Vaultier, 1719) (*Marivaux et le marivaudage*, p. 314). See Michel Foucault, *Les Mots et les choses* (Paris: Gallimard, 1966), pp. 113–14.

22. See Aristotle, *The Metaphysics*, trans. Hugh Tredennick, 2 vols. (London: William Heinemann, 1933), 1:147–207; esp. 165–73. For the early publication history of the *Logique*, see the introduction by P. Roubinet to the

reprint of the 1683 (fifth) edition of [Antoine Arnauld and Pierre Nicole], *La Logique ou l'Art de penser* (Lille: Librairie René Girad, 1964), unpaginated.

23. *Logique*, pp. 48, 71, 67. See Louis Marin, *La Critique du discours: Sur la "Logique de Port-Royal" et les "Pensées" de Pascal* (Paris: Les Editions de Minuit, 1975). See also Foucault, *Les Mots et les choses*, pp. 92–136. For another view of Marivaux's theories about language and their relation to the works of Port-Royal, see Coulet, *Marivaux romancier*, pp. 269–83. Coulet notes that it is "invraisemblable" that Marivaux did not read the Port-Royal *Logique* and *Grammaire* (p. 271n). Basil Munteano also discusses the relevance of Arnauld and Nicole to early eighteenth-century aesthetics in "Les Premises rhétoriques du système de l'abbé Du Bos," *Rivista de litterature moderne e comparate* 10 (1957): 322–33. See also Deloffre's discussions of Marivaux's views of language in *Marivaux et le marivaudage*, esp. pp. 144–47, 207–16, 252–55. Marivaux's "Pensées sur différents sujets," which contains the brief "Sur la clarté de discours" and "Sur la pensée sublime," appear in *Journaux et oeuvres diverses*, pp. 52–72.

24. *Logique*, p. 372.

25. Ibid., pp. 379.

26. Ibid., pp. 368–69.

27. In *Marivaux romancier*, Coulet presents a different view of the problems of exterior signs, equivocation, the representation of the self, and interpretation in Marivaux's work (pp. 285–342).

28. Antoine Arnauld and Claude Lancelot, *Grammaire générale et raisonnée de Port-Royal* (Geneva: Slatkine Reprints, 1980), pp. 48–49.

29. *Encyclopédie, ou Dictionnaire raisonné des sciences, des arts, et des métiers* (Paris, 1751), 1:70. For more on Du Marsais's sources and innovations, see Gunvor Sahlin, *César Chesneau Du Marsais et son rôle dans l'évolution de la grammaire générale* (Paris: Presses Universitaires de France, 1928).

30. *Le Grand Vocabulaire françois* (Paris, 1767). The entry reads: "en termes de Grammaire, se dit d'une propriété qui pour être attachée au mot, ne lui est pas essentielle. Par exemple, le mot *ours* dans sa signification propre, désigne un animal féroce: voilà sa destination. Je me servirai cependant de ce mot par figure, et je dirai d'un homme qu'il est un ours, pour faire entendre qu'il vit hors de la société. Cette signification nouvelle sera un *accident*."

CHAPTER THREE

1. Grimm refers to the "horrible complot" in the "Préface-Annexe" to the novel (*OR*, p. 848). For accounts of the plot, the "Préface-Annexe," the correspondence with the marquis de Croismare, and the genesis and evolution of the manuscript of the novel, see Herbert Dieckmann, "The *Préface-Annexe* of *La Religieuse*," *Diderot Studies* 2 (1952): 21–40; Marion Hobson, *The Object of Art: The Theory of Illusion in Eighteenth-Century France* (Cambridge: Cambridge University Press, 1982), pp. 98–102; Georges May, *Diderot et La Religieuse* (New Haven, Conn.: Yale University Press, 1954), pp. 35–46; Vivienne Mylne, "Truth and Illusion in the *Préface-annexe*

to Diderot's *La Religieuse*," *Modern Language Review* 57 (1962): 320–56; Arthur M. Wilson, *Diderot* (New York: Oxford University Press, 1972), pp. 382–91. See also Jean Catrysse, *Diderot et la mystification* (Paris: A. G. Nizet, 1970), and Philip Stewart, *Imitation and Illusion in the French Memoir-Novel, 1700–1750: The Art of Make-Believe* (New Haven, Conn.: Yale University Press, 1969). The historical basis and background of *La Religieuse* are discussed in Pierre de Gorsse, *La Religieuse de Diderot: A-t-elle existé?* (Toulouse: Imprimerie Fournie, 1968); Jacques Proust, "Recherches nouvelles sur *La Religieuse*," *Diderot Studies* 6 (1964): 197–214; and May's authoritative studies: *Diderot et La Religieuse; Quatre visages de Denis Diderot* (Paris: Boivin, 1951), pp. 38–44; "Quelques nouveaux eclaircissements sur la mystification du Marquis de Croismare," *Essays on Diderot and the Enlightenment in Honor of Otis Fellows*, ed. John Pappas (Geneva: Droz, 1974), pp. 182–97; "Une certaine Madame Madin," *Literature and History in the Age of Ideas: Essays on the French Enlightenment Presented to George R. Havens*, ed. Charles G. S. Williams (Columbus: Ohio State Press, 1975), pp. 255–71. See also Jean Parrish's introduction to and critical edition of the original manuscript of the novel, presented with textual variants, published in *Studies on Voltaire and the Eighteenth Century* 22 (1963). For some other discussions of the novel not specifically cited here, see Beatrice Fink, "Des mets et des mots de Suzanne," *Diderot, Digression and Dispersion: A Bicentennial Tribute*, ed. Jack Undank and Herbert Josephs (Lexington, Ky.: French Forum Publishers, 1984), pp. 98–105; Susan Hayward, " 'Res Brutae' and Diderot's Nun, Suzanne Simonin," *Diderot Studies* 20 (1981): 109–23; Mylne, *Diderot et la Religieuse* (London: Grant and Cutler, 1981); P. Trahard, *Les Maîtres de la sensibilité française au XVIIIe siècle*, 4 vols. (Paris: Boivin, 1931–33), 2:168–72.

2. See Vernière's introduction to the *Éloge de Richardson* in OE, pp. 23–27; and Diderot's letters to Sophie Volland of 20 October 1760, 17 September 1761, 28 September 1761, and 16 September 1762 in *Correspondance*, ed. Georges Roth, 16 vols. (Paris: Editions de Minuit, 1955–70), 3:173–74, 306, 317–21, 4:151–53. For some discussions of Diderot and Richardson, see Jacques Chouillet, *La Formation des idées esthétiques de Diderot* (Paris: Presses Universitaires de France, 1973), pp. 508–9; Rita Goldberg, *Sex and Enlightenment: Women in Richardson and Diderot* (Cambridge: Cambridge University Press, 1984), pp. 128–45; Catrysse, *Diderot et la mystification*, pp. 142–45; June Sigler Siegel, "Grandeur-Intimacy, the Dramatist's Dilemma," *Diderot Studies* 4 (1963): 247–60.

3. See Dieckmann's well-known discussion of these lines in "Diderot et son lecteur," *Cinq leçons sur Diderot* (Geneva: Droz, 1959), pp. 17–39. For more on the role of dialogue in Diderot's work, see James Creech, "Diderot and the Pleasure of the Other: Friends, Readers, and Posterity," *Eighteenth-Century Studies* 11 (1978): 439–56; Joan DeJean, "Insertions and Interventions in *Le Neveu de Rameau*," *Eighteenth-Century Studies* 19 (1976): 511–22; Herbert Josephs, *Diderot's Dialogue of Language and Gesture* (Columbus: Ohio State University Press, 1969); Christie V. McDonald, *The Dialogue of*

Writing: Essays in Eighteenth-Century French Literature (Waterloo: Wilfrid Laurier University Press, 1984); Maurice Roelens, "Le Dialogue philosophique, genre impossible," *Cahiers de l'Association Internationale d'Études Françaises* 24 (1972): 43–58; Carol Sherman, "In Defense of the Dialogue: Diderot, Shaftesbury, and Galiani," *Romance Notes* 15 (1973): 268–73, and *Diderot and the Art of Dialogue* (Geneva: Droz, 1976); Jean Starobinski, "Diderot et la parole des autres," *Critique* 296 (1972): 3–33. See also Daniel Brewer, "The Philosophical Dialogue and the Forcing of Truth," *MLN* 98 (1983): 1234–47.

4. See Richardson's prefaces to *Pamela* in *Pamela, or Virtue Rewarded* (New York: New American Library, 1980), pp. 21–44.

5. In *Framed Narratives: Diderot's Genealogy of the Beholder* (Minneapolis: University of Minnesota Press, 1985), Jay Caplan writes: "In this sentimental novel [*La Religieuse*], as well as in Sade later on, the fundamental narrative bond is between virile figures (regardless of their gender): a 'man' is invited to share with a member of his own rhetorical gender in the pleasures of making a female figure suffer and of occasionally suffering with her" (p. 55). See Eve Kosofsky Sedgwick, *Between Men: English Literature and Male Homosocial Desire* (New York: Columbia University Press, 1985).

6. For other considerations of the problem of sympathy and seduction in *La Religieuse*, see Hobson, *The Object of Art*, pp. 98–102; and especially, Herbert Josephs, "Diderot's *La Religieuse*: Libertinism and the Dark Cave of the Soul," *MLN* 91 (1976): 734–55. For a useful discussion of the conception of the artist as seducer in Diderot and other authors, see Alice Laborde, *L'Esthétique circéenne* (Paris: A. G. Nizet, 1969), pp. 37–49. She writes: "Diderot est le représentant le plus authentique du mouvement circéen et, sans le savoir, l'un des défenseurs les plus éloquents" (p. 37). See also Laborde, *Diderot et l'amour* (Saratoga: Anma Libri, 1979), pp. 92–101; and Ronald Grimsley, "L'Ambiguïté dans l'oeuvre romanesque de Diderot," *Cahiers de l'Association Internationale des Études Françaises* 13 (1961): 225–36; and for relevant discussions of the question of seduction in various nineteenth- and twentieth-century narratives, see Ross Chambers, *Story and Situation: Narrative Seduction and the Power of Fiction* (Minneapolis: University of Minnesota Press, 1984).

7. For a comparison of Diderot and Marivaux, see Janet Whatley, "Nun's Stories: Marivaux and Diderot," *Diderot Studies* 20 (1981): 299–319.

8. For other comments about the similarities between these two mother superiors, see Josephs, "Diderot's *La Religieuse*," p. 746; Elisabeth de Fontenay, *Diderot: Reason and Resonance*, trans. Jeffrey Mehlman (New York: George Braziller, 1982), pp. 142–43; Roger Lewinter, *Diderot: ou, Les Mots de l'absence: Essai sur la forme de l'oeuvre* (Paris: Editions Champs Libre, 1976), pp. 78–79.

9. *Encyclopédie, ou Dictionnaire raisonné des sciences, des arts et des métiers* (Neufchastel, 1765), 15:735–40, 8:889. For a discussion of the article, "Jouissance," see Leo Spitzer, *Linguistics and Literary History* (Princeton, N.J.: Princeton University Press, 1948), pp. 137–46.

10. Spitzer, *Linguistics and Literary History*, p. 149.

11. *Le Petit Robert* (Paris: Le Robert, 1984), pp. 376–77. See Goldberg's discussion, "Female Sexuality as a Disease," in *Sex and Enlightenment*, pp. 153–62. Raymond Jean notes that Diderot "présente volontiers la crise sexuelle comme épileptiforme," particularly in "Sur les femmes" ("Le Sadisme de Diderot," *Critique* 188 [1963]: 47–48).

12. For a discussion of Suzanne as a self-conscious artist, see Robert J. Ellrich, "The Rhetoric of *La Religieuse* and Eighteenth-Century Forensic Rhetoric," *Diderot Studies* 3 (1961): 131–34, 143–49.

13. See chapter 1, "The Surprising Effects of Sympathy." Laborde notes Suzanne's status as a victim in the novel (*L'Esthétique circéenne*, p. 70). For discussions of Diderot and Sade or sadism, see Creech, *Diderot: Thresholds of Representation* (Columbus: Ohio State University Press, 1986), pp. 168–79; Giorgio Cerrutti, "Le Paradoxe sur le comédien et le paradoxe sur le libertin, Diderot et Sade," *Revue des sciences humaines*, fasc. 146 (1972): 235–51; Josephs, "Diderot's *La Religieuse*," pp. 738, 752–53; Caplan, *Framed Narratives*, p. 55; Jean, "Le Sadisme de Diderot," pp. 33–50.

14. See chapter 4, "Forgetting Theater."

15. *Encylopédie*, 30:554; my emphasis. See Laborde, *L'Esthétique circéenne*, pp. 37–49.

16. *Encyclopédie*, 32:220.

17. In "Diderot's *La Religieuse*," Josephs writes of a "psychic fluidity that is itself erotic" in the novel; he continues, "The condition and qualities of characters seem to fuse and separate as if the prevalent undercurrent of eroticism that crosses Suzanne's novel blurred the boundaries of the self" (pp. 748–49).

18. See, for example, Spitzer's account of reading the seduction scene between the mother superior and Suzanne: "Anyone, when reading this description must experience a slight shudder of repulsion" (p. 178n). However, Spitzer, who claims in this essay to have "allowed myself to attempt to penetrate to the soul not only of the author but of the man" (p. 135), does not confine his repulsion to the description of homosexuality; the "shudder," he continues, "is surely not alone due to the perversity of the Mother Superior. We feel that the glance of the author himself lingers unduly on the 'charmes' of the young nun, as he savours her Greuze-like décolleté ('à deminue'). There is some undigested, unrefined, unassuaged sensuality in Diderot that allows him to abuse the privilege of an author. And if we think that we get this impression of Diderot's enjoyment through the words of the nun herself, we must realize that this creature of Diderot's is made to appear conscious of her own seductive powers; that she has been infected by her creator's sensuality" (pp. 178–79n). Although Spitzer's comments could be read as a defense against contagion, they point to something that both Suzanne and Diderot are worried about.

19. Josephs writes: "Suzanne discovers the evil of sexuality in the perverted form of lesbianism, a perversion which serves, however, in the

novel as a thin veil for that which is proclaimed as essentially accursed and condemned in any form" ("Diderot's *La Religieuse*," p. 747). For other comments on homosexuality in the novel, see Lester Crocker, *Diderot's Chaotic Order* (Princeton, N.J.: Princeton University Press, 1974), pp. 88–90; De Fontenay, *Diderot*, pp. 137–40; Otis Fellows,"Diderot's *Supplément* as Pendant for *La Religieuse*," *Literature and History in the Age of Ideas: Essays on the French Enlightenment Presented to George R. Havens*, ed. Charles G. S. Williams (Columbus: Ohio State University Press, 1975), pp. 239–40; Goldberg, *Sex and Enlightenment*; May, *Diderot et La Religieuse*, pp. 98–146. See also Jean, "Le Sadisme de Diderot"; and Aram Vartanian, "Erotisme et philosophie chez Diderot," *Cahiers de l'Association Internationale des Études Françaises* 13 (1961): 367–90.

20. Peter Brooks, *Reading for the Plot: Design and Intention in Narrative* (New York: Alfred A. Knopf, 1984), p. 308.

21. Chouillet, in discussing Diderot's description of a Fragonard painting, writes: "l'attrait du même par le même, qui est censé definir l'homosexualité, ne serait qu'une forme dérivée de l'amour incestueux" (*Diderot, poète de l'énergie* [Paris: Presses Universitaires de France, 1984], p. 216). See also Caplan, *Framed Narratives*, p. 57. For more on the question of incest elsewhere in Diderot's work, see Creech, *Thresholds of Representation*, pp. 82–96; and Jeffrey Mehlman, *Cataract: A Study in Diderot* (Middletown, Conn.: Wesleyan University Press, 1979), pp. 34–35.

22. In his discussion of *La Religieuse*, Chouillet notes that out of 65,577 words in the novel, "regroupés en 7,769 formes," including 2,098 occurrences of "je," there is a high number of "les termes ayants une connotation familiale ou domestique et qui font partie de la vie conventuelle: 'supérieure' (228), 'mère' (150), 'soeur' (115), 'soeurs' (57)" (p. 212).

23. See May, *Diderot et la Religieuse*, pp. 142–54. See also de Gorsse, *La Religieuse*, p. 20; Lewinter, *Diderot*, pp. 73–74; and other historial accounts cited in note 1.

CHAPTER FOUR

1. See Michael Fried, *Absorption and Theatricality: Painting and Beholder in the Age of Diderot* (Berkeley and Los Angeles: University of California Press, 1979). (It should be clear that I find Fried's discussions of the problem of the painting-beholder relationship in eighteenth-century French art, particularly as seen in the dramatic theory and art criticism of Diderot, to be very important to an understanding of all of the authors discussed in this book—not only Diderot.) For discussions of Diderot's dramatic theory not specifically noted here, see Roland Barthes, "Diderot, Brecht, Eisenstein," *Image Music Text*, trans. Stephen Heath (New York: Hill and Wang, 1977), pp. 67–78; Michael D. Cartwright, "Diderot critique d'art et le problème de l'expression," *Diderot Studies* 13 (1969): 236–46; Giorgio Cerrutti, "Le paradoxe sur le comédien et le paradoxe sur le libertin, Diderot et Sade," *Revue des sciences humaines*, fasc. 146 (1972): 235–51; Jacques Chouillet, *La*

Formation des idées esthétiques de Diderot (Paris: Presses Universitaires de France, 1973), pp. 418–89; Hans Robert Jauss, *Aesthetic Experience and Literary Hermeneutics*, trans. Michael Shaw (Minneapolis: University of Minnesota Press, 1982), pp. 172–88; Roger Kempf, *Diderot et le roman, ou Le Démon de la présence* (Paris: Editions du Seuil, 1964), pp. 58–92; Robert Niklaus, "Diderot et Rousseau pour et contre le théâtre," *Diderot Studies* 4 (1963): 153–89, and "La Portée des théories dramatiques de Diderot et de ses réalisations théâtrales," *Romantic Review* 54 (1963): 6–19; Pierre Saint-Amand, *Diderot, le labyrinthe de la relation* (Paris: J. Vrin, 1984), pp. 97–101; P. Trahard, *Les Maîtres de la sensibilité française au XVIIIe siècle*, 4 vols. (Paris: Boivin, 1931–1933), 2:186–214. For some general discussions of Diderot's aesthetics, see Annie Becq, *Genèse de l'esthétique française moderne: De la raison classique à l'imagination créatrice 1680–1814*, 2 vols. (Pisa: Pacini, 1984), 2:534–43; Lester Crocker, *Two Diderot Studies: Ethics and Esthetics* (Baltimore: Johns Hopkins University Press, 1952), pp. 49–114; Herbert Dieckmann, *Cinq leçons sur Diderot* (Geneva: Droz, 1959), pp. 97–126; David Funt, "Diderot and the Esthetics of the Enlightenment," *Diderot Studies* 11 (1968); Wladyslaw Folkierski, *Entre le classicisme et le romantisme: Étude sur l'esthétique et les esthéticiens du XVIIIe siècle* (Paris: Librairie Ancienne Honoré Champion, 1925). For a relevant discussion of Diderot, Condillac, and "the theaters of perception," see Suzanne Gearhart, *The Open Boundary of History and Fiction: A Critical Approach to the French Enlightenment* (Princeton, N.J.: Princeton University Press, 1984), pp. 161–99.

2. Diderot's description of himself watching the performance of *Le Fils naturel* from a corner, "sans être vu," appears in the "Histoire véritable de la Pièce," the narrative frame that precedes the published text of the play; this crucial part of the fiction of *Le Fils naturel* and the *Entretiens sur Le Fils naturel* does not appear in the Garnier edition of the *Oeuvres esthétiques*. See Diderot, *Oeuvres complètes*, 25 vols. to date (Paris: Hermann, 1975–), 10:17. See Diderot's advice to Mlle Jodin: "Si, quand vous êtes sur le théâtre, vous ne croyez pas être seule, tout est perdu"; "Que le théâtre n'ait pour vous ni fond ni devant, que ce soit rigoureusement un lieu où et d'où personne ne vous voie. Il faut avoir le courage quelquefois de tourner le dos au spectateur; il ne faut jamais se souvenir de lui" (*Correspondance*, ed. Georges Roth, 16 vols. [Paris: Editions de Minuit, 1957], 6:168, 240). For other texts on the theater, see Diderot's letter to Mme Riccoboni of 18 November 1758 (*Correspondance*, 2:86–103); and the original version of the *Paradoxe, Observations sur une brochure intitulée Garrick ou Les Acteurs Anglais*, in *Oeuvres complètes*, ed. J. Assézat and Maurice Tourneux, 20 vols. (Paris: Garnier, 1875–77), 8:343–59.

3. Anthony Ashley Cooper, Earl of Shaftesbury, *Characteristics of Men, Manners, Opinions, Times, etc.*, ed. John M. Robertson, 3 vols. (Gloucester, Mass.: Peter Smith, 1963), 1:131.

4. See my book, *The Figure of Theater: Shaftesbury, Defoe, Adam Smith, and George Eliot* (New York: Columbia University Press, 1986), pp. 9–70.

5. Aristotle, *Poetics*, chap. 24, 1460a, trans. W. Rhys Roberts (New York: Modern Library, 1954), p. 258.

6. For an account of the typically strange and ambiguous publication history of the *Paradoxe*, see Vernière, *OE*, pp. 291–98. Critics often have raised the question of whether one should or could attempt to reconcile Diderot's early and late writing on the theater; see, for example, Yvon Belaval, *L'Esthétique sans paradoxe de Diderot* (Paris: Gallimard, 1950); Douglas Bonneville, "Diderot's Artist: Puppet and Poet," *Literature and History in the Age of Ideas: Essays on the French Enlightenment Presented to George R. Havens*, ed. Charles G. S. Williams (Columbus: Ohio State University Press, 1975), pp. 245–52; Fried, *Absorption and Theatricality*, pp. 220–21; Monique Moser-Verrey, "De la prédication au persiflage: Image et action dans le théâtre et la dramaturgie de Diderot," *Stanford French Review* 8 (1984):309–20; James Creech, *Diderot: Thresholds of Representation* (Columbus: Ohio State University Press, 1986), p. 84; Philippe Lacoue-Labarthe, "Diderot, le paradoxe et la mimesis," *Poétique* 43 (1980): 271.

7. For discussions of the *Paradoxe*, see Crocker, *Diderot's Chaotic Order* (Princeton, N.J.: Princeton University Press, 1974), pp. 56–59; Ross Chambers, *L'Ange et l'automate: Variations sur le mythe de l'actrice de Nerval à Proust*, Archives des lettres modernes, no. 128 (Paris: Lettres Modernes, 1971), pp. 6–11, 53–54; François Dagognet, *Écriture et iconographie* (Paris: J. Vrin, 1973), pp. 149–258; Jean Duvignaud, *L'Acteur* (Paris: Gallimard, 1965), pp. 25–26; 259–63; Alan J. Freer, "Talma and Diderot's Paradox on Acting," *Diderot Studies* 8 (1966): 23–76; Peter France, *Rhetoric and Truth in France* (Oxford: Oxford University Press, 1972), pp. 214–17; Gearhart, *The Open Boundary of History and Fiction*, pp. 190–99; Lionel Gossman and Elizabeth MacArthur, "Diderot's Displaced *Paradoxe*," *Diderot, Digression and Dispersion: A Bicentennial Tribute*, ed. Jack Undank and Herbert Josephs (Lexington, Ky.: French Forum, 1984), pp. 106–20; Marion Hobson, "*Le Paradoxe sur le comédien* est un paradoxe," *Poétique* 4 (1973): 320–39; "Sensibilité et spectacle: Le contexte médical du *Paradoxe sur le comédien* de Diderot," *Revue de métaphysique et de morale* 82 (1977): 147–64; and *The Object of Art: The Theory of Illusion in Eighteenth-Century France* (Cambridge: Cambridge University Press, 1982), pp. 139–208; Alice Laborde, *L'Esthétique circéenne* (Paris: A. G. Nizet, 1969), pp. 37–49; Roger Lewinter, *Diderot: ou, Les mots de l'absence: Essai sur la forme de l'oeuvre* (Paris: Editions de Champs Libre, 1976), pp. 237–41; Richard Sennett, *The Fall of Public Man: On the Social Psychology of Capitalism* (New York: Vintage, 1978), pp. 110–15; Carol Sherman, *Diderot and the Art of Dialogue* (Geneva: Droz, 1976), pp. 63–78. Discussions of the sources of the *Paradoxe* include Chouillet, "Une Source anglaise du *Paradoxe*," *Dix-huitième siècle* 2 (1970): 207–26; Lucette Pérol, "Diderot, les tragiques grecs et le p. Brumoy," *Studies on Voltaire and the Eighteenth Century* 154 (1976): 1593–1616; Patrick Tort, *L'Origine du Paradoxe sur le comédien: La partition intérieure* (Paris: J. Vrin, 1980).

For discussions of the *Entretiens* and the *Discours*, see Fried, *Absorption and Theatricality*, esp. pp. 71–105; Peter Brooks, *The Melodramatic Imagination: Balzac, Henry James, Melodrama, and the Mode of Excess* (New Haven, Conn.: Yale University Press, 1976), pp. 64–68, 82–85; Jay Caplan, *Framed Narratives: Diderot's Genealogy of the Beholder* (Minneapolis: University of Minnesota Press, 1985), pp. 15–18, 29–39; Creech, *Diderot*, pp. 62–96; Crocker, *Diderot's Chaotic Order*, pp. 63–66, 211–14; France, *Rhetoric and Truth in France*, pp. 211–17; Hobson, *The Object of Art*, and "Notes pour les *Entretiens sur le 'Fils naturel'*," *Revue d'histoire littéraire de la France* 74 (1974): 203–13; Raymond Joly, *Deux études sur la préhistoire du réalisme* (Quebec: Laval University Press, 1969), pp. 19–118; Sherman, *Diderot and the Art of Dialogue*, pp. 55–63; Peter Szondi, "*Tableau* and *Coup de Théâtre*: On the Social Psychology of Diderot's Bourgeois Tragedy," *New Literary History* 11 (1980): 323–43.

8. See chapter 5, "Rousseau and the State of Theater."

9. Shaftesbury, *Characteristics*, 1:131. For discussions of the question of the actor's loss of self or alienation, see Jonas Barish, *The Antitheatrical Prejudice* (Berkeley and Los Angeles: University of California Press, 1981), pp. 256–94; Caplan, *Framed Narratives*, pp. 68, 89–91; Andrea Calzolari, "Les Interprétations du paradoxe et les paradoxes de l'interprétation," *Interpréter Diderot aujourd'hui*, ed. E. de Fontenay et J. Proust (n.p.: Le Sycomore, 1984), pp. 117–29; Dieckmann, "Le Thème de l'acteur dans la pensée de Diderot," *Cahiers de l'Association Internationale des Études Françaises* 13 (1961): 157–72; Gossman and MacArthur, "Diderot's Displaced Paradoxe," pp. 112, 114–19; Hobson, "Sensibilité et spectacle," pp. 162–64; Herbert Josephs, *Diderot's Dialogue of Language and Gesture* (Columbus: Ohio State University Press, 1969), pp. 91–98; Lacoue-Labarthe, "Diderot," pp. 276–79. Also relevant are Jacques Proust, "Diderot et la physiognomie," *Cahiers de l'Association Internationale des Études Françaises* 13 (1961): 317–29; Aram Vartanian, "Diderot's Rhetoric of Paradox, or the Conscious Automaton Observed," *Eighteenth-Century Studies* 14 (1981): 379–405; W. J. Bate, "The Sympathetic Imagination in Eighteenth-Century Criticism," *ELH* 12 (1945): 144–64; Earl R. Wasserman, "The Sympathetic Imagination in Eighteenth-Century Theories of Acting," *Journal of English and Germanic Philology* 46 (1947): 264–72; Chambers, *L'Ange et l'automate*, pp. 31–53.

10. See Bénac's introduction, *OR*, p. 874.

11. See Proust, "Diderot et la physiognomie."

12. For a brief discussion of the tension between narrative and similes, see my "Similes and Delay," *Modern Critical Views: Homer*, ed. Harold Bloom (New York: Chelsea House, 1986).

13. See Shaftesbury, *Letter Concerning Enthusiasm* and *The Moralists*, in *Characteristics*, 1:5–39, 2:1–153.

14. See "Enthousiasme" and "Génie" in the *Encyclopédie* (Paris, 1755), 5:719–22; and (Paris, 1757), 7:582–84. The article "Génie" also appears in *OE*, pp. 9–17. See Belaval, *L'Esthétique sans paradoxe de Diderot*, pp. 150–61; and

Hans Molbjerg, *Aspects de l'esthétique de Diderot* (Copenhagen: J. H. Schultz Forlag, 1964), pp. 87–116.

15. See "Sur le génie," *OE*, pp. 19–20. See also Dieckmann, "Diderot's Conception of Genius," *Journal of the History of Ideas* (1941): 151–82.

16. Few critics have discussed the strange narrative form and structure of the *Paradoxe*. Peter France sees the ending as a lapse in a generally perfunctory narrative strategy: "Diderot has not bothered to dress up the next page or two in this way, although he returns to dialogue at the end of the work. In general, the use of dialogue in the *Paradoxe* is about as perfunctory as the use of allegory in the *Promenade du sceptique*. It is a hastily assumed disguise rather than something integral to Diderot's thought" (p. 216). For attempts to make sense of the eruption of narrative at the end of the dialogue, see Sherman, *Diderot and the Art of Dialogue*, pp. 68–71; Belaval, *L'Esthétique sans paradoxe de Diderot*, pp. 207–9; and Lacoue-Labarthe, "Diderot," pp. 267–70.

17. See chapter 1, "The Surprising Effects of Sympathy."

18. In a letter to Sophie Volland dated 1 November 1760, Diderot describes a production of *Le Père de famille* in Marseille. Citing from an account in a "gazette," he writes: "Entre autre[s] chose[s] qu'on y dit et qui me font plaisir, c'est qu'à peine la première scène est-elle jouée, qu'on croit être en famille et qu'on oublie qu'on est devant un théâtre. Ce ne sont plus des tréteaux, c'est une maison particulière" (*Correspondance*, 3:280).

19. *Encyclopédie, ou Dictionnaire raisonné des sciences, des arts et des métiers* (Neufchastel, 1765), 12:430.

20. See *Discours, OE*, pp. 234–42.

21. Diderot, *Oeuvres complètes* (Paris, 1975–), 10:16.

22. For comments on this imagined production of *Le Fils naturel* and its ritualistic aspects, see Creech, *Diderot*, pp. 94–95; Caplan, *Framed Narratives*, pp. 33–35; Lewinter, *Diderot*, p. 25; Jeffrey Mehlman, *Cataract: A Study in Diderot* (Middletown, Conn.: Wesleyan University Press, 1979), pp. 33–35; Jack Undank, *Diderot: Inside, Outside, and In-Between* (Madison, Wisc.: Coda Press, 1979), p. 95. For general discussions of Diderot and the theater and acting companies of his time, see Jean de Beer, "Diderot et la Comédie-Française," *Europe* 405–6 (1963): 220–26; Adrienne D. Hytier, "Diderot et Molière," *Diderot Studies* 8 (1966): 77–103; P.-B. Marquet, "Diderot et le théâtre au XVIIIe siècle," *Europe* 69 (1951): 115–28. See also Maurice Descotes, *Le Public de théâtre et son histoire* (Paris: Presses Universitaires de France, 1964). Discussions of Diderot's plays include Caplan, *Framed Narratives*; Creech, *Diderot*, pp. 82–96; Dieckmann, "Zu einigen Motiven in *Le Fils naturel*" and "Diderot und Goldini," *Diderot und die Aufklärung: Aufsätze zur europäischen Literatur des 18. Jahrhunderts* (Stuttgart: J. B. Metzler, 1972), pp. 158–68; 169–95; Aimé Guedj, "Les Drames de Diderot," *Diderot Studies* 14 (1971): 15–95; Lewinter, "L'Exaltation de la vertu dans le théâtre de Diderot," *Diderot Studies* 8 (1966): 119–69, and *Diderot*, pp. 21–32, 33–47; Blandine McLaughlin, "A New Look at Diderot's *Le Fils naturel*,"

Diderot Studies 10 (1968): 109–19; Barbara G. Mittman, "Ambiguity and Unresolved Conflict in Diderot's Theatre," *Eighteenth-Century Studies* 5 (1971–72): 270–93; Moser-Verrey, "De la prédication," pp. 309–20; John Pappas, "D'Alembert et *le Fils naturel,*" *Essays on Diderot and the Enlightenment in Honor of Otis Fellows,* ed. Pappas (Geneva: Droz, 1974), 246–55; Proust, "Le Paradoxe du *Fils naturel,*" *Diderot Studies* 4 (1963): 209–20; Undank, *Diderot,* pp. 95–109.

23. Caplan writes: "pathos relies on an elliptical rhetoric: and the actor playing Lysimond comes on like a human ellipsis, a figure that summarizes and elides the pathetic movement of the play. . . . his very presence speaks to his beholders and to himself of Lysimond's absence and of their own mortality" (*Framed Narratives,* p. 70). Creech describes the scene: "Death then intervenes in such a fashion that this 'father' becomes an actor. With the intrusion of an audience, the 'salon' becomes a theater; with the intrusion of a real actor, one is no longer 'à sa place,' and the whole range of representation's effects slices its way into the field of familial closure" (*Diderot,* p. 94). See also Moser-Verrey's description of Lysimond as a "signe vide" and her account of the transformation of the father into an actor ("De la prédication," pp. 318–19).

24. See Chouillet, *La Formation,* pp. 494–95.

25. In *Les Bijoux indiscrets,* Diderot presents the example of a "nouveau débarqué d'Angote, qui n'ait jamais entendu parler de spectacles, mais qui ne manque ni de sens ni d'usage." Mirzoza proposes leading him to the theater under the pretense that he will witness a real-life drama between the prince and his son: "je le mène dans une loge grillée, d'où il voit le théâtre qu'il prend pour le palais du sultan. Croyez-vous que, malgré tout le sérieux que j'affecterais, l'illusion de cet homme durât un instant? Ne conviendrez-vous pas, au contraire, qu'à la démarche empesée des acteurs, à la bizarrerie de leurs vêtements, à l'extravagance de leurs gestes, à l'emphase d'un langage singulier, rimé, cadencé, et a mille autres dissonances qui le frapperont, il doit, m'éclater au nez dès la première scène et me déclarer ou que je me joue de lui, ou que le prince et toute sa cour extravaguent?" (*OR,* pp. 144–45). For Diderot, an ideal theatrical performance would fool the spectator who had never been to the theater—or reduce the more conscious spectator to a state of naïveté through a moment of forgetting.

Although the "nouveau embarqué" is a familiar trope in the eighteenth century, Diderot may have in mind this tableau of Shaftesbury's from the *Essay on the Freedom of Wit and Humour*: "If a native of Ethiopia were on a sudden transported into Europe, and placed either at Paris or Venice at a time of carnival, when the general face of mankind was disguised, and almost every creature wore a mask, 'tis probable he would for some time be at a stand, before he discovered the cheat; not imagining that a whole people could be so fantastical as upon agreement, at an appointed time, to transform themselves by a variety of habits, and make it a solemn practice to impose upon one another, by this universal confusion of characters and persons." Shaftesbury goes on to complicate the situation further: "However, should it so happen that in the transport of ridicule, our Ethiopian, having his head still running upon masks, and knowing nothing of the fair complexion and common dress of the Europeans, should upon the sight of a natural face and habit, laugh just as heartily as before, would not he in turn become ridiculous, by carrying the jest too far; when by a silly presumption he took nature for mere art, and mistook perhaps a man of sobriety and sense for one of those ridiculous mummers?" (*Characteristics*, 1:57). The fact that the "nouveau embarqúe" in the *Bijoux indiscrets* would not mistake a theatrical performance for reality demonstrates the breakdown in verisimiltude in the theater. Diderot suggests that it is the people who are accustomed to the falseness of the theater who are ridiculous. However, as I will suggest, Diderot is also interested in these liminal moments of confusion when the barriers between nature and art become blurred.

26. *Salon de 1767*, cited in Fried, *Absorption and Theatricality*, p. 130.

27. Stanley Cavell, *Must We Mean What We Say?* (New York: Scribners, 1969), p. 330.

28. Sophocles, *Electra*, trans. J. H. Kells (Cambridge: Cambridge University Press, 1973), p. 197.

29. *The Attic Nights of Aulus Gellius*, trans. John C. Rolfe, 3 vols. (Cambridge, Mass.: Harvard University Press, 1960), 2:37. In "Diderot, les tragiques grecs et le p. Brumoy," Pérol argues that Diderot's source for the story of Paulus was Brumoy's *Théâtre des Grecs*. Although it seems likely that Diderot read the *Théâtre des Grecs* (which contains translations of various Greek tragedies, including *Electra*), Pérol does not present any evidence that Diderot would not also have known the text of *The Attic Nights*. Belaval writes of Diderot's education: "Il y reçoit une si solide instruction, qu'il restera un des meilleurs latinistes et hellénistes de son temps" (*L'Esthétique sans paradoxe*, p. 16). For useful discussions of Diderot's knowledge of and involvement with classical texts, see Raymond Trousson's articles, "Le Théâtre tragique grec au siècle des lumières," *Studies on Voltaire and the Eighteenth Century* 154 (1976): 2113–36; "Diderot et l'Antiquité grecque," *Diderot Studies* 6 (1964):215-45; and "Diderot et Homère," *Diderot Studies* 8 (1966): 185–216. Brumoy's French version reads: "un certain Polus qui faisoit le rôle d'Electre, pour se pénétrer mieux de l'esprit de son personnage, tira du tombeau d'un fils qu'il avoit perdu, l'urne qui contenoit ses cendres, & l'embrassant sur le théâtre, comme si c'eût été l'urne d'Oreste, il remplit toute l'assemblée, non-pas d'une simple émotion de douleur bien imitée, mais de cris & de pleurs véritables." See *Le Théâtre des Grecs, par le R. P. Brumoy, de la compagnie de Jésus*, 3 vols. (Paris: Rollin, 1730), 1:198. See also Jean Seznec, *Essais sur Diderot et l'Antiquité* (Oxford: The Clarendon Press, 1957).

CHAPTER FIVE

1. See d'Alembert's response to Rousseau, *Lettre à M. Rousseau, Citoyen de Genève*, which, along with Marmontel's rebuttal of Rousseau, *Apologie du Théâtre ou Analyse de la Lettre de Rousseau, Citoyen de Genève, à d'Alembert*,

au sujet des spectacles, is included in *Oeuvres complètes de J. J. Rousseau*, ed. V. D. Musset-Pathay, 25 vols. (Paris: Du Pont, 1823–26), 2:199–384, and in Jonas Barish, *The Antitheatrical Prejudice* (Berkeley and Los Angeles: University of California Press, 1981), pp. 256–94. Parts of my discussion of Rousseau are written in dialogue with Barish's provocative and helpful chapter on the *Lettre à d'Alembert*. For other discussions of Rousseau's place in the antitheatrical tradition and his attitude toward acting and theater, see M. Barras, *The Stage Controversy in France from Corneille to Rousseau* (New York: Institute for French Studies, 1933); Louis Bourquin, "La Controverse sur la comédie au XVIIIe siècle et *La Lettre à d'Alembert sur les spectacles*," *Revue d'histoire littéraire de la France* 26 (1919): 43–86, 556–76; 27 (1920): 548–70; 28 (1921): 549–74; Amal Banerjee, "Rousseau's Concept of Theatre," *British Journal of Aesthetics* 17 (1977): 171–77; Benjamin R. Barber, "Rousseau and the Paradoxes of the Dramatic Imagination," *Daedalus* 107 (1978): 79–92; Michèle Mat-Hasquin, "Théâtre de Jean-Jacques Rousseau: La Genèse d'une vision du monde," *Etudes sur le XVIIIe siècle* 5 (1978): 85–99; Margaret Mary Moffat, *Rousseau et la querelle du théâtre au XVIIIe siècle* (Paris: Bocard, 1930); Jacques Vier, "Jean-Jacques Rousseau et le théâtre," *La Table Ronde* 176 (1962): 43–49; Bernard Waisbord, "Rousseau et le théâtre," *Europe* 391–92 (1961): 108–20; Amilda A. Pons, *Jean-Jacques Rousseau et le théâtre* (Geneva: Jullien, 1909).

2. D'Alembert's article, "Genève," appeared in December of 1757; Rousseau published the *Lettre* in 1758. To the chagrin of Voltaire (who, as Rousseau suspected, was behind d'Alembert's proposal) the *Lettre* was remarkably efficacious: it helped to prevent the establishment of a permanent theater in Geneva until 1782. A theater established in 1766 apparently burned down in 1768 while Genevans looked on. See M. Fuchs, introduction to Rousseau, *Lettre à Mr. d'Alembert sur les spectacles*, ed. M. Fuchs (Lille: Giard, 1948), p. xlv. See also Michel Lavany, introduction to Rousseau, *Lettre à M. d'Alembert sur son article Genève* (Paris: Garnier-Flammarion, 1967), pp. 16–37.

3. A facsimile of the original title page appears at the beginning of the fifth volume of the *Correspondance complète*, ed. R. A. Leigh, 45 vols. (Geneva: Institut et Musée Voltaire, 1965–86). For Rousseau's subsequent references to the *Lettre*, see the brief introduction to *De l'imitation théâtrale* in *Oeuvres complètes* (1824), 2:386; and *C*, p. 585. Allan Bloom acknowledges in the notes to his generally meticulous translation that "theatre" is not an adequate translation of the French "spectacle"; yet despite his decision to translate "moeurs" as "morals [manners]" throughout the text, he chooses to render "spectacle" as "theatre" (or sometimes "entertainment"). My reading of the *Lettre* will suggest that such a reduction or delimitation of this key term blinds the reader to the full scope of Rousseau's critique and argument. See Bloom, trans., *Politics and the Arts: Letter to M. d'Alembert on the Theatre* (Ithaca, N.Y.: Cornell University Press, 1960). My text for the *Lettre* is the one contained in *Du Contrat social et autres oeuvres politiques* (Paris: Garnier Frères, 1957).

4. Rousseau, *Correspondance complète*, 5:70.

5. See Barras, *The Stage Controversy*, p. 258.

6. See chapter 1, "The Surprising Effects of Sympathy," and *The Figure of Theater: Shaftesbury, Defoe, Adam Smith, and George Eliot* (New York: Columbia University Press, 1986), pp. 208–9, 218.

7. For a discussion of Rousseau's view of the theater of cosmopolitan life, see Richard Sennett, *The Fall of Public Man: On the Social Psychology of Capitalism* (New York: Vintage, 1978), pp. 115–22.

8. For discussions of Rousseau's attitude toward women, see Richard A. Brooks, "Rousseau's Antifeminism in the *Lettre à d'Alembert* and *Émile*," in *The Age of Ideas: Essays on the French Enlightenment Presented to George R. Havens*, ed. Charles G. S. Williams (Columbus: Ohio State University Press, 1975), pp. 209–27; Ron Christenson, "The Political Theory of Male Chauvinism: Jean-Jacques Rousseau's Paradigm," *Midwest Quarterly: A Journal of Contemporary Thought* 13 (1972): 291–99; Ruth Graham, "Rousseau's Sexism Revolutionized," in *Women in the Eighteenth Century and Other Essays*, ed. Paul Fritz and Richard Marten (Toronto: Hakkert, 1976), pp. 127–39; Peggy Kamuf de Magnin, "Rousseau's Politics of Visibility," *Diacritics* (1975): 51–56; Carol Pateman, "The Disorder of Women," *Ethics* 91 (1980): 20–34; Joel Schwartz, *The Sexual Politics of Jean-Jacques Rousseau* (Chicago: University of Chicago Press, 1984); David Williams, "The Politics of Feminism in the French Enlightenment," in *The Varied Pattern: Studies in the Eighteenth Century*, ed. Peter Hughes and David Williams (Toronto: Hakkert, 1971), pp. 333–52; Victor B. Wexler, "'Made for Man's Delight': Rousseau as Antifeminist," *American Historical Review* 81 (1976): 266–91. Also relevant is Ross Chambers, *L'Ange et l'automate: Variations sur le mythe de l'actrice de Nerval à Proust*, Archives des lettres modernes, no. 128 (Paris: Lettres Modernes, 1971).

9. See *OC*, pp. 430–31, and *O*, pp. 495–97.

10. Banerjee also makes this connection in "Rousseau's Concept of Theater," p. 176. See also Walter Benjamin, "What is Epic Theater?" in *Illuminations*, trans. Harry Zohn (New York: Schocken, 1969), 147–54.

11. See Buffon, *Histoire naturelle de l'homme, Oeuvres* (Paris: La Société des Publications Illustrées, 1834), p. 157.

12. See Lionel Trilling, *Sincerity and Authenticity* (Cambridge, Mass.: Harvard University Press, 1972), pp. 53–80; Henri Peyre, *Literature and Sincerity* (New Haven, Conn.: Yale University Press, 1963), pp. 79–110; Marshall Brown, *The Politics of Authenticity: Radical Individualism and the Emergence of Modern Society* (New York: Atheneum, 1970), pp. 75–159; Judith N. Shklar, *Men and Citizens: A Study of Rousseau's Social Theory* (Cambridge: Cambridge University Press, 1969); and Sennett, *The Fall of Public Man*.

13. See *The Figure of Theater*, pp. 178–79.

14. For discussions of the relation between theories of sympathy and theories of acting in the eighteenth century, see W. J. Bate, "The Sympathetic

Imagination in Eighteenth-Century Criticism," *ELH* 12 (1945): 144–64 and
Earl R. Wasserman, "The Sympathetic Imagination in Eighteenth-Century
Theories of Acting," *Journal of English and Germanic Philology* 46 (1947):
264–72. Jacques Derrida discusses the problem of pity in Rousseau in *De la
grammatologie* (Paris: Editions de Minuit, 1967), esp. pp. 245–72; see also Paul
de Man, "The Rhetoric of Blindness: Jacques Derrida's Reading of Rous-
seau," in *Blindness and Insight: Essays in the Rhetoric of Contemporary
Criticism*, pp. 102–41; and Barish, *The Antitheatrical Prejudice*, pp. 269–71.
Addressing the readings of Derrida and especially de Man, Suzanne
Gearhart discusses pity, theater, theatricality, and the *Lettre à d'Alembert* in
*The Open Boundary of History and Fiction: A Critical Approach to the French
Enlightenment* (Princeton, N.J.: Princeton University Press, 1984), pp. 261–84.
Patrick Coleman discusses pity and identification in the context of the *Lettre*
in *Rousseau's Political Imagination: Rule and Representation in the Lettre à
d'Alembert* (Geneva: Librairie Droz, 1984), pp. 50–74. For more on sympathy
and identification, see Banerjee, "Rousseau's Concept of Theatre," pp.
173–74; Marian Hobson, *The Object of Art: The Theory of Illusion in
Eighteenth-Century France* (Cambridge: Cambridge University Press, 1982),
pp. 180–87; and chapter 4, "Forgetting Theater."

   15. For Plato, the poet is "out of his senses . . . in a state of
unconsciousness" while the rhapsodist, who is called a "Proteus" and a
"deceiver," is asked by Socrates: "Are you not carried out of yourself?" (*The
Dialogues of Plato*, trans. B. Jowett, 2 vols. [New York: Random House,
1982], 1:289, 296). It was a commonplace among seventeenth-century French
theoreticians of acting to demand "an abdication of the self" on the part of
the actor. Actors, wrote Scudéry in the 1639 *Apologie du théâtre*, must "se
métamorphosent, aux personnages qu'ils représentent" (cited by Henry
Phillips, *The Theatre and its Critics in Seventeenth-Century France* [Oxford:
Oxford University Press, 1980], p. 185). Barish cites a spokesman for
Port-Royal who condemned the playwright because he "se passione jusqu'à
sortir de lui-même pour entrer dans le sentiment des personnes qu'il
représente" (*The Antitheatrical Prejudice*, p. 273). Well into the eighteenth
century, both friend and enemy of the theater agreed that the dramatic
imagination was a sympathetic imagination. "The player of true spirit . . .
awakened by sensibility, is no longer himself, when he assumes his
character," wrote John Hill in the 1755 version of *The Actor*, a loose
translation of Sainte-Albine's 1747 *Le Comédien*, which, when loosely
translated back into French in 1769 as *Garrick, ou les acteurs anglais* by
Sticotti, provoked the review which later became Diderot's *Paradoxe* (John
Hill, *The Actor; or, A Treatise on the Art of Playing* [1755; reprint New York:
Benjamin Blom, 1972], p. 110). One year after Rousseau's *Lettre à d'Alembert*
appeared, John Wilkes wrote in *A General View of the Stage* that an actor
should "make a temporary renunciation of himself" and "forget, if possible,
his own identity" (cited in Wasserman, "The Sympathetic Imagination,"
p. 276).

16. Barish, *The Antitheatrical Prejudice*, p. 276.

17. See Derrida, *De la grammatologie*, pp. 243–72.

18. Denis Diderot, *Lettre sur les aveugles à l'usage de ceux qui voient*, in *Oeuvres philosophiques*, ed. Paul Vernière (Paris: Garnier, 1964), p. 85.

19. For another interpretation of this scene, see Jean Starobinski, "Jean-Jacques Rousseau et le peril de la réflexion," *L'Oeil vivant* (Paris: Gallimard, 1968), pp. 93–188.

20. For example, both d'Alembert and Marmontel noted that Rousseau's condemnation of actors would apply to writers as well: "L'art de faire illusion," writes Marmontel, "est-il plus de l'essence du comédien, que de l'essence du poéte, du musicien, du peintre, etc.?" (*Apologie du Théâtre*, p. 348; d'Alembert, *Lettre à M. J. J. Rousseau*, p. 228). See Barish, *The Antitheatrical Prejudice*, p. 272.

21. Jacques Voisine writes in his notes to the *Confessions*: "La critique du *Misanthrope* dans la *Lettre à d'Alembert* . . . met en effet en scène Grimm-Philinte, Mme d'Épinay-Célimène, et Rousseau est naturellement Alceste" (*C*, p. 585). Rousseau discusses the events in his life at the time of the composition of the *Lettre* in book 10 of the *Confessions*. See also William H. Blanchard, *Rousseau and the Spirit of Revolt: A Psychological Study* (Ann Arbor: University of Michigan Press, 1967), pp. 104–25; and Lester G. Crocker, *Jean-Jacques Rousseau: The Prophetic Voice (1758–1778)* (New York: Macmillan, 1973), pp. 1–18. For a discussion of the significance of Molière in the *Lettre*, see Coleman, *Rousseau's Political Imagination*, pp. 155–86.

22. Barish, *The Antitheatrical Prejudice*, p. 259. See Rousseau, *Oeuvres complètes* (1824), 10:63.

23. *Lettre à Mr. d'Alembert sur les spectacles*, ed. Fuchs, p. 188. For an account of Rousseau's composition of the different drafts of the preface to the *Lettre*, see Anatole Feugère, "Pourquoi Rousseau a remanié la préface de la 'Lettre à d'Alembert,' " *Annales de la Société Jean-Jacques Rousseau* 20 (1931): 127–62.

24. Michael Fried, *Absorption and Theatricality: Painting and Beholder in the Age of Diderot* (Berkeley and Los Angeles: University of California Press, 1980), pp. 170–71.

25. See Werner Bahner, "Le mot et les notions de 'peuple' dans l'oeuvre de Rousseau," *Studies on Voltaire and the Eighteenth Century* 55 (1967): 113–27.

26. Voisine notes that "un cahier d'extraits de lectures du jeune Rousseau, conservé à Neuchâtel, contient 56 citations de Plutarque" (*C*, p. 9) and refers the reader to the "Quatrième Promenade" of the *Rêveries*, which begins: "Dans le petit nombre de livres que je lis quelquefois encore, Plutarque est celui qui m'attache et me profite le plus. Ce fut la première lecture de mon enfance, ce sera la dernière de ma vieillese" (*R*, p. 41). See also Georges Pire, "Du Bon Plutarque au Citoyen de Genève," *Revue de littérature comparée* 32 (1958):510–47.

27. Plutarch, *Sayings of Spartans*, in *Moralia*, trans. Frank Cole Babbitt, 14

vols. (New York: William Heinemann, 1931), 3:355, 357, 361, 365, 363; *The Ancient Customs of the Spartans*, in *Moralia*, 3:441.

28. Plutarch, *Lives*, trans. Bernadotte Perrin, 11 vols. (Cambridge, Mass.: Harvard University Press, 1967), 1:235.

29. *Lives*, 1:237.

30. See Starobinski, *Jean-Jacques Rousseau: La Transparance et l'obstacle* (Paris: Gallimard, 1971), esp. pp. 116–21; Jean Duvignaud, *Sociologie du théâtre: Essai sur les ombres collectives* (Paris: Presses Universitaires de France, 1965), pp. 341–51, and *Fêtes et civilisations* (Geneva: Librairie Weber, 1973), pp. 120–26; Derrida, *De la grammatologie*, pp. 428–41; Barish, *The Antitheatrical Prejudice*, pp. 289–94. For other discussions of the *fêtes* in the *Lettre à d'Alembert*, see Fried, *Absorption and Theatricality*, pp. 167–71; Chambers, *La Comédie au château: Contribution à la poétique du théâtre* (Paris: Librairie José Corti, 1971), pp. 24–25, 171–72; Coleman, *Rousseau's Political Imagination*, pp. 143–53; and Paule Monique Vernes, *La Ville, la fête, la democratie: Rousseau et les illusions de la communauté* (Paris: Payot, 1978). On the problem of representation in Rousseau's works, see Barish, *The Antitheatrical Prejudice*, pp. 290–91, and esp. Derrida, *De la grammatologie*; see also Richard Fralin, *Rousseau and Representation: A Study of the Development of His Concept of Political Institutions* (New York: Columbia University Press, 1978); Hanna Fenichel Pitkin, *The Concept of Representation* (Berkeley and Los Angeles: University of California Press, 1967). Starobinski, of course, has discussed the role of transparency in Rousseau's concept of the *fête* extensively, and parts of my discussion are meant to be in dialogue with *La Transparence et l'obstacle*.

31. Fried refers to "the impositions of strict spectacular controls over the activities of the engaged and married couples" in his comments about the ambiguity of gender in Rousseau's description of the ball (*Absorption and Theatricality*, p. 170).

32. For a relevant discussion of ritualistic theater that is both a representation *and* an enactment of state power, see Clifford Geertz, *Negara: The Theatre State in Nineteenth-Century Bali* (Princeton, N.J.: Princeton University Press, 1980). Relevant to the history of the French theater is Timothy C. Murray, "Richelieu's Theater: The Mirror of a Prince," *Renaissance Drama*, n.s. 8 (1977): 275–98. For related discussions of the English scene, see Stephen Orgel, *The Illusion of Power: Political Theater in the English Renaissance* (Berkeley and Los Angeles: University of California Press, 1975); Stephen Greenblatt, "Invisible Bullets: Renaissance Authority and Its Subversion," *Glyph* 8 (1981): 40–61; and Christopher Pye, "The Sovereign, the Theater, and the Kingdome of Darknesse: Hobbes and the Spectacle of Power," *Representations* 8 (1984): 85–106.

33. See Crocker, "Rousseau et l' 'opinion,' " *Studies on Voltaire and the Eighteenth Century* 55 (1967): 395–415; and Judith N. Shklar, *Men and Citizens*, pp. 75–126. Bloom's introduction to his translation of the *Lettre* aims to argue Rousseau's case for censorship of the arts (*Politics and the Arts*, pp. xi–xxxiv). For other discussions of Rousseau's political beliefs, see Louis Althusser, *Montesquieu, Rousseau, Marx: Politics and History*, trans. Ben

Brewster (London: Verso, 1982), pp. 113–60; Maurice Cranston and Richard
S. Peters, eds., *Hobbes and Rousseau: A Collection of Critical Essays* (New
York: Anchor, 1972); Ronald Grimsley, *The Philosophy of Rousseau* (London:
Oxford University Press, 1973); David Cameron, *The Social Thought of
Rousseau and Burke: A Comparative Study* (London: Weidenfeld and Nicol-
son, 1973); and *Political Theory* 6 (1978) (a special issue devoted to Rousseau).

34. Shklar, *Men and Citizens*, pp. 157–58.

35. Starobinski, *Jean-Jacques Rousseau*, p. 16.

36. One could argue that it is no accident that Rousseau's account of his
petites expériences occurs in book 5, even if on the surface it appears to be
related to its context only by the slightest threads of chronology. Book 5
begins with the story of another accident: the attempted suicide of Claude
Anet. Anet, the companion of Mme de Warens, the woman who acts the part
of "maman" for Rousseau, is an older man who is described as a "sort of
guardian" and a father figure. He is a botanist and he introduces Rousseau
to the work Rousseau claims he was born for. Anet is also described as
Rousseau's rival for Mme de Warens's affections and his death occurs shortly
after Rousseau's sexual initiation by the woman Rousseau calls "maman."
Rousseau logically experiences this affair as "incest." We don't need to know
that Rousseau gets into trouble by asking if he will inherit Anet's old clothes
to see the family romance fall into place. After taking the place of his father
figure, committing incest with his mother figure, and perhaps causing the
death of his father figure, Rousseau has an accident in the laboratory
(previously Anet's realm) and blinds himself. We can understand now the
logic of his exaggeration about the severity of his wounds. In the following
paragraph, he reflects on his inability to think of Mme de Warens as "mère"
and "maîtresse" at the same time. In this context it is probably not accidental
that book 5 mentions an older, more experienced musician who "lost his
eyes" and recounts the death of the man who was a second father to
Rousseau, his Uncle Bernard.

37. *Encyclopédie, ou Dictionnaire raisonné des sciences, des arts, et des métiers*
(Paris, 1755), 5:634; Jacques Ozanam, *Récréations mathématiques et physiques*
(Paris: Charles-Antoine Jombert, 1750), 3:222–24.

38. *Encyclopédie* (Neufchastel, 1765), 8:461.

39. In reference to the psychoanalytic reading suggested in note 36, we
should observe that Ozanam calls one type of invisible ink "l'Impreignation
de Saturne." Of course, Saturn or Kronos (who lends his name to this
"liqueur claire et transparente" [p. 224] which seems to be capable of
impregnating) is known for having usurped his father by castrating him and
then for having been castrated and usurped by *his* son, Zeus.

CHAPTER SIX

1. Contrasting his enterprise to that of Montaigne, Rousseau writes: "je
n'écris mes rêveries que pour moi. Si dans mes plus vieux jours aux
approches du départ, je reste, comme je l'espère, dans la même disposition où

je suis, leur lecture me rappellera la douceur que je goûte à les écrire, et faisant renaître ainsi pour moi le temps passé, doublera pour ainsi dire mon existence" (*R*, p. 11).

2. See Appendix.

3. [Mary Wollstonecraft], *Posthumous Works of the Author of a Vindication of the Rights of Woman*, 4 vols. (1798; reprint New York: Garland Publishing, 1974), 1:42–43.

4. *Mary Shelley's Journal*, ed. Frederick L. Jones (Norman: University of Oklahoma Press, 1944), p. 53. All further references to Mary Shelley's reading will be based on this journal. Although the entries and the lists of books read contained in this journal are invaluable, it is important to keep in mind that the lists are not always complete or consistent with the books noted in the actual entries of the journals (see Jones's preface, p. xiv); the absence of a title from the journal obviously does not mean that Mary Shelley did *not* read a particular book; nor do the lists indicate whether Mary Shelley was rereading a book or reading it for the first time. Percy Shelley refers to Rousseau in a letter to Hogg on 18 July. (See *The Letters of Percy Bysshe Shelley*, ed. Jones [Oxford: The Clarendon Press, 1964], 1:494.) The first entry that reads "write my story" appears in Mary Shelley's entry for 24 July (*Journal*, p. 53). For more information, see Appendix.

5. See, for example, Joyce Carol Oates, "Frankenstein's Fallen Angel," *Critical Inquiry* 10 (1984): 543–54; Margaret Homans, "Bearing Demons: Frankenstein's Circumvention of the Maternal," in *Bearing the Word: Language and Female Experience in Nineteenth-Century Women's Writing* (Chicago: University of Chicago Press, 1986), pp. 104–6, 114–15; Sandra Gilbert and Susan Gubar, "Horror's Twin: Mary Shelley's Monstrous Eve," in *The Madwoman in the Attic: The Woman Writer and the Nineteenth-Century Literary Imagination* (New Haven, Conn.: Yale University Press, 1979); and Harold Bloom, "Afterword" to *Frankenstein, or The Modern Prometheus* (New York: New American Library, 1965), pp. 212–23. I have used this text, which is based on the 1831 (third) edition, throughout this chapter. I also have utilized James Rieger's reprint of the 1818 text with textual variants. See Mary Wollstonecraft Shelley, *Frankenstein, or The Modern Prometheus (The 1818 Text)* (Indianapolis: The Bobbs-Merrill Company, 1974).

6. At one point, in writing in corrections on the book she presented to Mrs. Thomas in 1823, Mary Shelley inserted the bracketed phrase in this passage: "when he speaks, [in his native language which is French], although his words are culled with the choicest art, yet they flow with rapidity and unparalleled eloquence." See *Frankenstein or The Modern Prometheus (The 1818 Text)*, p. 22, and Rieger's "Note on the Text," pp. xliii–xlv. The phrase does not appear in the 1831 edition. In both the 1818 and the 1831 texts, Walton writes: "the stranger addressed me in English, although with a foreign accent" (p. 18 [1818]; p. 23 [1831]).

7. Jean de Palacio, *Mary Shelley dans son oeuvre: Contribution aux études shelleyennes* (Paris: Editions Klincksieck, 1969), p. 378. A few critics have

detected traces of Rousseau's works in Mary Shelley's novel. De Palacio hears echoes of Rousseau in the praises of Swiss liberty and "republican institutions" spoken by Elizabeth and Justine (pp. 186–87). Burton R. Pollin suggests that Safie, the young woman whose lessons provide a model and a means of education for the monster, might be named after Sophie of the *Émile*; and he notes that the Pygmalion myth which ironically informs the plot of *Frankenstein* might have been suggested to Mary Shelley by her reading in the summer of 1816 of Mme de Genlis's "Pygmalion et Galatée"—a play that announces itself as a companion piece to Rousseau's "Pygmalion" ("Philosophical and Literary Sources of *Frankenstein*," *Comparative Literature* 17 [1965]: 100). Peter Dale Scott notes also: "In Safie, *Frankenstein* proffers an androgynously balanced corrective to Rousseau's docile, domestic, and affectionate Sophie, a figure reproved by Mary Wollstonecraft." He adds: "On an ideological level, then, one might say that 'The Modern Prometheus' is a pendant to *Emile* and *La Nouvelle Héloïse"* (*"Vital Artifice: Mary, Percy, and the Psychopolitical Integrity of* Frankenstein," in *The Endurance of* Frankenstein: *Essays on Mary Shelley's Novel*, ed. George Levine and U.C. Knoepflmacher [Berkeley and Los Angeles: University of California Press, 1979], p. 174). The "Avertissement de l'Auteur sur Galatée" begins: "Cette pièce fut composée pour être jouée en société, à la suite du Pygmalion de Rousseau." See [Mme de Genlis], "Pygmalion et Galatée, ou La Statue Animée Depuis Vingt-Quatre Heures," in *Nouveaux Contes Moraux, et Nouvelles Historiques*, 6 vols. (Paris, 1825), 16:236.

8. For example, Pollin notes, "We might mention in passing the considerable admixture of the primitivistic doctrines of the Rousseau of the two *Discours"* ("Philosophical and Literary Sources," p. 100). De Palacio juxtaposes the monster's account, "I ate some berries which I found hanging on the trees or lying on the ground. I slaked my thirst at the brook, and then lying down, was overcome with sleep" (*F*, p. 98), with this account from the second *Discours*: "Je le vois se rassasiant sous un chêne, se désaltérant au premier Ruisseau, trouvant son lit au pied du même arbre qui lui a fourni son repas" (*OC*, p. 135; quoted in de Palacio, *Mary Shelley*, p. 210). See also Peter Brooks, " 'Godlike Science/Unhallowed Arts': Language, Nature, and Monstrosity," in *The Endurance of Frankenstein*, p. 209; Martin Tropp, *Mary Shelley's Monster* (Boston: Houghton Mifflin Company, 1976), p. 71; Christopher Small, *Mary Shelley's Frankenstein: Tracing the Myth* (Pittsburgh: University of Pittsburgh Press, 1972), p. 62; Radu Florescu, *In Search of Frankenstein* (Boston: New York Graphic Society, 1975), pp. 179–80; and John A. Dussinger, "Kinship and Guilt in Mary Shelley's *Frankenstein*," *Studies in the Novel* 8 (1976): 39–40. Lowry Nelson, Jr., suggests that the "monster's account of his awakening consciousness and his education is Mrs. Shelley's version of her father William Godwin's notions derived from Rousseau" ("Night Thoughts on the Gothic Novel," *Yale Review* 52 [1963]: 246). It might be said that the monster's exposure to Volney's *Ruins of Empires*, which Felix reads to Safie (*F*, pp. 113–14), constitutes an indirect

exposure to the ideas of Rousseau. See M. Volney, *Les Ruines, ou Méditations sur les révolutions des empires* (Paris, 1792).

9. Cantor continues: "The monster as originally created corresponds to natural man; his fall is his fatal attraction to civil society; and his attempt to join the ranks of social men leads to his misery" (*Creature and Creator: Myth-making and English Romanticism* [Cambridge: Cambridge University Press, 1984], pp. 119–20). Cantor's persuasive account of the novel takes place in the context of an argument about the influence of Rousseau's *Second Discourse* as a Romantic myth of creation—an influence, he rightly claims, that was "so pervasive in the late eighteenth century that we need not show that individual Romantics had read it in order to claim that it shaped their thinking about human nature" (pp. 4–5).

10. Brooks, " 'Godlike Science, Unhallowed Arts,' " p. 209. In an article I became acquainted with after writing this chapter, Daniel Cottom mentions in passing that an aspect of the "representational crisis that produces Frankenstein's monster and the novel of which he is the image . . . may be related to Rousseau's suggestion that the idea of gigantism signifies a distortion of perception caused by man's fear of others" ("*Frankenstein* and the Monster of Representation," *Sub-stance* 28 [1980]: 61). He is referring to an "analysis" suggested in a passage in the *Essai*, which will be discussed in detail later in this chapter. The *Essai sur l'origine des langues*, published posthumously, appears in editions of Rousseau's *Oeuvres* after 1781. It was published in the third volume of the *Oeuvres posthumes de Jean-Jacques Rousseau, ou Recueil de pièces manuscrites pour servir de supplément aux éditions publiées pendant sa vie* (Geneva, 1781–83) and it appears in subsequent *Oeuvres complètes*, sometimes with the essays on music, sometimes under the category of "Mélanges." The July, 1782 edition of *A New Review* reviews the posthumous writings for an English audience (2:12–24). (See Edward Duffy, *Rousseau in England: The Context of Shelley's Critique of the Enlightenment* [Berkeley and Los Angeles: University of California Press, 1979], pp. 46–47). Rousseau refers to the *Essai sur l'origine des langues* by name in book 11 of the *Confessions* (*C*, p. 662).

11. Details and characters of *La Nouvelle Héloïse* can be seen throughout Mary Shelley's novel. The venerable Alphonse Frankenstein, who marries a younger woman and continually recalls the overenthusiastic Victor to reason and duty, resembles M. de Wolmar. In addition, one could read the waking nightmare that (according to the Introduction) gave Mary Shelley the idea for her story, together with the companion nightmare that Victor has in which the image of Elizabeth is replaced by the image of his dead mother, as a reworking of the nightmare in which Saint-Preux sees Julie's mother on her deathbed and then sees "Julie à sa place." "I could not so easily get rid of my hideous phantom," writes Mary Shelley, "still it haunted me" (*F*, p. xi), just as Saint-Preux describes how his dream leaves him "environné de fantômes." One might also juxtapose the dreamed and figuratively painted tableau of Julie on her knees by her mother's death bed—"cette scène que vous m'avez

autrefois dépeinte," writes Saint-Preux—with the actual painting of Elizabeth "kneeling by the coffin of her dead father" (F, p. 75) that hangs over the mantelpiece in the Frankenstein library. (These images, of course, hang over the literary phantasmagoria through which Mary Shelley perpetually kneels by the mother's deathbed on which she was born.) One can imagine Mary Shelley's reaction to this deathbed scene, in which the dying mother says to her daughter: "il faut remplir son sort . . . Dieu est juste . . . tu seras mère à ton tour" (NH, pp. 603–4).

12. See the list of the activities of "l'homme" in the first lines of the Émile: "Il bouleverse tout, il défigure tout, il aime la difformité, les monstres; il ne veut rien tel que l'a fait la nature, pas même homme" (E, p. 5). At this point I might add that Walton's decision to keep a journal to record the autobiography of the man he wishes to regard as a "fellow mind" and his exclamation, "with what interest and sympathy shall I read it in some future day!" (F, pp. 27, 29), evoke Rousseau's comment about the future of the autobiographical manuscript of the Rêveries: "leur lecture me rappellera la douceur que je goûte à les écrire, et faisant renaître ainsi pour moi le temps passé, doublera pour ainsi dire mon existence" (R, p. 11).

13. Rousseau discusses his decision to send his children to the "Enfants-Trouvés" in the seventh and eighth books of the Confessions (pp. 404–5 and 423–24). In the twelfth book, he refers to the "aveu public" (p. 702) he included out of remorse in the first book of the Émile. For his discussion in the Rêveries, see below. See Maurice Cranston, Jean-Jacques: The Early Life and Work of Jean-Jacques Rousseau 1712–1754 (New York: Norton, 1983), p. 244.

14. Mary Shelley writes in a letter to Leigh Hunt in 1837, "I am now writing French Lives" (The Letters of Mary W. Shelley, ed. Jones, 2 vols. [Norman: University of Oklahoma Press, 1944], 2:122).

15. Wollstonecraft, A Vindication of the Rights of Woman, ed. Carol H. Poston (New York: Norton, 1975), p. 154.

16. William Godwin, Enquiry Concerning Political Justice and Its Influence on Modern Morals and Happiness (Harmondsworth: Penguin Books, 1985), p. 112. At the end of Caleb Williams, Williams says to Mr. Falkland, who, in a perverse way, has been a father figure to him: "You took me up a raw and inexperienced boy, capable of being moulded to any form you pleased" (CW, p. 282).

17. Gilbert and Gubar, The Madwoman in the Attic, p. 223; Ellen Moers, "Female Gothic," in The Endurance of Frankenstein, p. 87. In recent years, several articles, especially those informed by feminist and/or psychoanalytic criticism, have helped to illuminate this aspect of the novel. In addition to Gilbert and Gubar, Moers, and Homans, see Mary Poovey, The Proper Lady and the Woman Writer: Ideology as Style in the Words of Mary Wollstonecraft, Mary Shelley, and Jane Austen (Chicago: University of Chicago Press, 1984); Marc Rubenstein, " 'My Accursed Origin': The Search for the Mother in Frankenstein," Studies in Romanticism 15 (1976): 165–94; U. C. Knoepflma-

cher, "Thoughts on the Aggression of Daughters," in *The Endurance of Frankenstein*, pp. 88–119; Mary Jacobus, "Is There a Woman in This Text?" *New Literary History* 14 (1982): 117–41; William Veeder, "The Negative Oedipus: Father, *Frankenstein*, and the Shelleys," *Critical Inquiry* 12 (1986): 365–90; Barbara Johnson, "My Monster/My Self," *Diacritics* 12 (1982): 2–10. See also Gordon D. Hirsch, "The Monster Was a Lady: On the Psychology of Mary Shelley's *Frankenstein*," *Hartford Studies in Literature* 8 (1976): 116–53; Susan Harris Smith, "*Frankenstein*: Mary Shelley's Psychic Divisiveness," *Women and Literature* 5 (1977): 42–53; J. M. Hill, "*Frankenstein* and the Physiognomy of Desire," *American Imago* 32 (1975): 332–58; Morton Kaplan, "Fantasy of Paternity and the Doppelgänger: Mary Shelley's *Frankenstein*," in Morton Kaplan and Robert Kloss, *The Unspoken Motive: A Guide to Psychoanalytic Literary Criticism* (New York: The Free Press, 1973), pp. 119–45; and Paul Sherwin, "*Frankenstein*: Creation as Catastrophe," *PMLA* 96 (1981): 883–903.

18. Robert Kiely, *The Romantic Novel in England* (Cambridge, Mass.: Harvard University Press, 1972), p. 170; Muriel Spark, *Child of Light: A Reassessment of Mary Wollstonecraft Shelley* (Hadleigh, Essex: Tower Bridge Publications Limited, 1951), pp. 137, 134. See also Nelson, "Night Thoughts," p. 244; Kaplan, "Fantasy of Paternity," pp. 135–45; Gerhard Joseph, "Frankenstein's Dream: The Child as Father of the Monster," *Hartford Studies in Literature* 8 (1976): 105; R. E. Foust, "Monstrous Image: Theory of Fantasy Antagonists," *Genre* 13 (1980): 444–45; and Masao Miyoshi, *The Divided Self: A Perspective on the Literature of the Victorians* (New York: New York University Press, 1969), pp. 79–89.

19. Consider this portrait from a book called *Extracts from the Diary of a Lover of Literature*: "Expelled at a tender age from those domestic habitudes which mitigate the natural fierceness of man; a sort of outcast from his family, his country, and almost from his species; a wild and needy adventurer, cursed with a fastidious delicacy, and exposed to that scorn and contumely and insolent neglect, which the pride of genius most impatiently endures; he contracted a distempered sensibility, which forms the distinguishing feature of his character . . . . Upon [mankind] he pours out, in consuming fire, the vials of his wrath, while he arrays in all the glowing hues of impassioned eloquence, romantic modes of being . . ." ([Thomas Green], *Extracts from The Diary of a Lover of Literature* [Ipswich, 1810], p. 72). I cite this passage at length because it reads almost word for word as a description of Frankenstein's monster; indeed it is not a bad plot summary of the monster's autobiographical narrative. Thomas Green, the author, published his *Diary* in 1810, six years before Mary Shelley dreamed of her monster; what makes its uncanny applicability to the monster less surprising is that Green is summarizing the life and character of Rousseau.

It is not important whether or not Mary Shelley read Green's description (although there is reason to believe she might have). This and other passages from the *Diary* appeared in *Quarterly Review* 4 (1810): 155–56. The Godwin household would have had some reason to pay attention to Green's *Diary*: Green's *Examination of the Leading Principles of the New System of Morals* (1798) was, according to Godwin's most recent biographer, "the most able and serious reply" to the *Enquiry Concerning Political Justice* (Peter H. Marshall, *William Godwin* [New Haven, Conn.: Yale University Press, 1984], p. 220). In addition to the discussion of Rousseau, Green's *Diary* contains reviews of both "Godwin's Memoirs of Mrs. Woolstonecraft" [sic] (p. 81) and Godwin's second novel, *St. Leon*. Green writes of Godwin: "I flatter myself with having been instrumental in a little humanizing him; but the volcanic and blasphemous spirit still peeps, occasionally, through a flimsy disguise" (p. 209). Various critics have argued that Mary Shelley paid close attention to the reception of her parents' works, especially by the "opposition" (see, for example, Lee Sterrenburg, "Mary Shelley's Monster: Politics and Psyche in *Frankenstein*," in *The Endurance of Frankenstein*, pp. 143–71). Mary Shelley's own account of Rousseau, although more sympathetic, describes Rousseau in similar terms. For example, he acquires "a taste for the romantic, and a precocious knowledge of the language of passion and sentiment" and later becomes an "exile and wanderer" who "could not tell where to take up his abode" (*CC*, pp. 112, 162). Compare Frankenstein's remark that had he known about the monster's plans for revenge, "I would rather have banished myself forever from my native country and wandered a friendless outcast over the earth" (*F*, p. 182).

20. See Henri Roddier's Introduction to *R*, pp. xliv–xlvi.

21. See note 8, above.

22. Brooks, " 'Godlike Science/Unhallowed Arts,' " pp. 206–7.

23. [Wollstonecraft], *An Historical and Moral View of the Origin and Progress of the French Revolution; and the Effect it has Produced in Europe* (London, 1794), p. 485.

24. Godwin, *Enquiry*, p. 497n. See Green, *Diary*, p. 72. See *The Poetical Works of Percy Bysshe Shelley*, p. 496. D'Alembert's response to the *Lettre à d'Alembert sur les spectacles* refers (in an ironic and somewhat bitter apostrophe to Rousseau) to "l'éloquence & la chaleur de votre style" (*Lettre à M. Rousseau, Citoyen de Genève*, in *Oeuvres de M. Rousseau de Genève. Nouvelle Édition* [Neuchâtel, 1764], p. 275). Duffy notes that the *Monthly Review* [5 (August 1751): 237] responded to the English translation of the *Discours sur les sciences et les arts* with praise for this " 'complete master of the declamatory art' and similar contempt for his sophistical opinions"; and the *Quarterly Review* [11 (April 1814): 174] wrote of passages in *La Nouvelle Héloïse* that "astonish by their eloquence" (*Rousseau in England*, pp. 9, 56).

25. See Rieger's "Collation of the Texts of 1818 and 1831," *The 1818 Text*, pp. 230–59, particularly for the pages relating to Walton. Nelson notes that through Walton's letters "the major theme of 'sympathy' is established, as is the documentary and 'sincere' mode which helps to domesticate the strange events" ("Night Thoughts," p. 243).

26. Kiely writes that "Mary Shelley's definition of a monster is precisely

that being to which nothing corresponds, the product of a genius who tried to exercise its will without reference to other beings"; although he calls the monster Frankenstein's "alter-ego," he suggests that the monster finds "no true resemblance, no reciprocation." I would like to hold this question open, at least long enough to pose it as a question. On the question of sympathy, Kiely notes that "through human sympathy" Frankenstein's crime "might have been avoided or redeemed" (*The Romantic Novel*, pp. 171, 170, 167). Cantor writes: "In depicting the monster's sympathetic reaching out for human beings, Mary Shelley draws upon another trait of natural man in Rousseau's view, his compassion . . . . From the beginning, the monster experiences fellow feeling for all living creatures. . . . One can compare his situation to that of the savages brought to Europe whom Rousseau discusses in the *Second Discourse*. His situation is even worse, since the people who meet the monster will not even acknowledge his common humanity" (*Creature and Creator*, pp. 124–25). Poovey writes that the monster "cannot enter the human community it longs to join, and it cannot earn the sympathy it can all too vividly imagine" (*The Proper Lady*, p. 128).

27. Wollstonecraft, *Vindication*, pp. 7–8, 22, 39, 150.

28. Ibid., p. 90. For a discussion of Smith's theory of sympathy in *The Theory of Moral Sentiments*, see my chapter, "Adam Smith and the Theatricality of Moral Sentiments," in *The Figure of Theater: Shaftesbury, Defoe, Adam Smith, and George Eliot* (New York: Columbia University Press, 1986), pp. 167–92.

29. Janet M. Todd also makes this point, along with a discussion of other similarities between *Frankenstein* and *The Wrongs of Woman*, in "Frankenstein's Daughter: Mary Shelley and Mary Wollstonecraft," *Women and Literature* 4 (1976): 18–27.

30. In an account that anticipates the monster's educational experiences watching the De Laceys, Jemima remarks that she had "the advantages of hearing discussions, from which, in the common course of life, women are excluded. You may easily imagine that it was only by degrees that I could comprehend some of the subjects they investigated, or acquire from their reasoning what might be termed a moral sense. But my fondness for reading increased . . ." (Wollstonecraft, *The Wrongs of Woman*, in *Posthumous Works* 1: 104–5). See Gilbert and Gubar, *The Madwoman in the Attic*, p. 246.

31. Wollstonecraft, *Posthumous Works*, 1:90, 93, 76, 127.

32. Ibid., 1:109; 91; 119.

33. Gilbert and Gubar, *The Madwoman in the Attic*, pp. 247, 237, 235. See also Poovey, *The Proper Lady*, p. 128; Homans, *Bearing the Word*, pp. 105–6; and Hirsch, "The Monster Was a Lady."

34. See Bloom, Afterword, p. 216; Spark, *Child of Light*, p. 136. The dedication reads: "To William Godwin, Author of Political Justice, Caleb Williams, etc. These Volumes Are respectfully inscribed By The Author" (Rieger, *The 1818 Text*, p. 5). In Godwin's novel, *Fleetwood*, the narrator describes his "impatient thirst for friendship" in terms of sympathy and

species. A few pages before recounting his meeting with Macneil—who knew Rousseau—he writes: "If the lash inflicted on me, will, being inflicted on another, be attended with a similar effect, I then know that there is a being of the same species or genus with myself. But, if there is a being who feels the blow under which I flinch, in whom my sensations are by a kind of necessity echoed and repeated, that being is a part of myself. Every reasoning and sensitive creature seems intuitively to require . . . this sort of sympathy" (*Fleetwood, or the New Man of Feeling*, 3 vols. [1805; reprint New York: Garland Publishing, 1979] 2:148–49).

35. Godwin, *Enquiry*, p. 381. See note 28, above.

36. Ibid., pp. 157, 159.

37. In this discussion I have been informed by Paul de Man's readings of Rousseau in *Allegories of Reading: Figural Language in Rousseau, Nietzsche, Rilke, and Proust* (New Haven, Conn.: Yale University Press, 1979). See also Jacques Derrida's readings of the question of pity and related issues in the *Essai sur l'origine des langues* in *De la grammatologie* (Paris: Editions de Minuit, 1967). I might note at this point that in discussing the idea of "man" in Rousseau's and Mary Shelley's texts, I have consciously retained the masculine category rather than substituting the more universal "human." Any discordance with the gender of *Frankenstein's* author or the screened gender of the monster is part of the meaning and irony of the novel; it is at the center of the critique Mary Shelley presents of the "idea of *man*" through the story of the monster.

38. It is no coincidence that everyone assumes that the motive for William's murder was "a very valuable miniature" of Frankenstein's mother or that Frankenstein remarks that "a sense of mortal agony crept over my frame" after he beholds another "picture of my mother" and "a miniature of William" (*F*, pp. 70, 75). The monster is enraged when he sees the miniature William possesses and imagines the "portrait of a most lovely woman" (*F*, p. 136) regarding him; he uses the portrait to frame Justine after he imagines her beholding him. The novel is concerned with the pictures that people present and represent to each other within human frames. It is also worth noting that this scene contains many of the ingredients of the scene from *Les Effets surprenants de la sympathie* in which Frédélingue discovers Parménie sleeping in a garden next to a miniature and experiences pangs of jealousy (see chapter 1).

39. In another context, de Man notes: "The actual word 'giant,' as we know it from every day usage, presupposes the word 'man' and is not the metaphorical figure that Rousseau, for lack of an existing word, has to call 'giant.' Rousseau's 'giant' would be more like some mythological monster; one could think of Goliath, or of Polyphemos (leaving aside the temptation to develop the implications of Odysseus' strategy in giving his name to Polyphemos as no-man)" (153 n. 2). For a different treatment of questions of figures and literalization in *Frankenstein*, see Homans, *Bearing the Word*, esp. pp. 109–11.

40. Rieger, *The 1818 Text*, p. 18.

41. Johnson, "My Monster/My Self," pp. 3–4. Cottom mentions the ideas that the monster "images the monstrous nature of representation" and is "a figure for the text" ("The Monster of Representation," pp. 60, 63) but takes his discussion in different directions than those taken here.

42. Brooks, " 'Godlike Science/Unhallowed Arts,' " p. 218. See also Brooks's use of this category in his reading of *Absalom, Absalom!* in *Reading for the Plot: Design and Intention in Narrative* (New York: Knopf, 1984), pp. 286–312.

43. Godwin, *Fleetwood*, 3:247–51.

44. Ibid., 2:198–99.

45. Frances Ferguson writes in a different context of *Frankenstein* that "it figures the Gothic reversal of the sublime dream of self-affirmation, the fear that the presence of other people is totally invasive and erosive of the self" ("The Nuclear Sublime," *Diacritics* 14 [1984]: 8). See also Poovey's reading of the novel as a critique of romantic egotism (*The Proper Lady*, pp. 114–42).

46. See notes 33 and 37, above.

47. On the question of incest, see Knoepflmacher, "The Aggression of Daughters"; Veeder, "The Negative Oedipus"; Joseph, "Frankenstein's Dream," pp. 102–3; Kaplan, "The Fantasy of Paternity," pp. 132–34.

48. Homans writes: "The demon's promise to be present at the wedding night suggests that there is something monstrous about Frankenstein's sexuality. A solipsist's sexuality is monstrous because his desire is for his own envisionings rather than for somebody else, some other body" (*Bearing the Word*, p. 104). My chapter 3, "*La Religieuse*: Sympathy and Seduction," also discusses the problem of sexuality, incest, and sameness.

49. Barthes writes: "la relecture est ici proposée d'emblée, car elle seule sauve le texte de la répétition (ceux qui négligent de relire s'obligent à lire partout la même histoire)" (*S/Z* [Paris: Editions du Seuil, 1970], p. 22).

50. Diderot, *Oeuvres complètes*, 25 vols. (Paris: Herman, 1975–), 10:17. Against my interests perhaps, I should note that Jones is surely wrong in glossing the reference to the "Tableau de famille" in Mary Shelley's journal entry of 4 August 1816 as "A play by Denis Diderot, translated 'by a lady' as *The Family Picture*" (*Journal*, p. 55). (Neither a translation nor a work by the name of *The Family Picture* is mentioned in the journal in any case.) Although Diderot's plays and his writings about his plays concern both tableaux and families, Diderot never wrote a play with that name. The *Salon de 1767* does contain a brief section with a subheading, "Un Tableau de Famille" in the discussion of L'Épicié but I doubt this is what Mary Shelley was referring to; see *Oeuvres complètes*, ed. J. Assézzat and Maurice Tourneaux (Paris: Garnier, 1875–77), 11:292–94. There is a pamphlet from the French Revolution that the Shelleys might have come across in their wide-ranging reading about this subject: *Le Tableau de Famille. Fragment de l'Histoire de France.* (It bears neither author nor place of publication on its title page—only "L'an de la Liberté O"; it is collated in vol. 15 of *French Revolution Tracts* contained in the Sterling Memorial Library of Yale

University.) For an indication of the extent of the Shelleys' interest in the Revolution, see Sterrenburg, "Mary Shelley's Monster," and Ronald Paulson, *Representations of Revolution (1789–1820)* (New Haven, Conn.: Yale University Press, 1983), pp. 239–47. All this being said, I can add that Mary Shelley apparently had access to Diderot's works: Percy Shelley wrote a letter on 24 December 1812 ordering "Les Ouvres [sic] de Diderot"; on both 17 December 1812 and 15 February 1813 he wrote letters ordering the *Encyclopédie*—"a book," he says in the February 15th letter, "which I am desirous, very desirous of possessing" (*Letters of Percy Bysshe Shelley*, 1:345, 342, 354).

51. See chapter 1 and Sigmund Freud, "Instincts and Their Vicissitudes," *General Psychological Theory: Papers on Metapsychology* (New York: Collier, 1978), pp. 83–103, esp. p. 93. See also Jean Laplanche, *Vie et Mort en Psychanalyse* (Paris: Flammarion, 1970), pp. 145–73; and Leo Bersani, "Representation and its Discontents," *Allegory and Representation: Selected Papers from the English Institute, 1979–1980*, ed. Stephen J. Greenblatt (Baltimore: Johns Hopkins University Press, 1981), pp. 145–62, esp. pp. 149–50. (See chapter 1, note 25.)

52. Following Freud, I am concerned here with the power of the primal scene as a fantasy, whether or not an actual event really took place. Freud's most famous and extensive discussion of the primal scene is, of course, the "wolf-man" case history, "From the History of an Infantile Neurosis" in *The Standard Edition of the Complete Psychological Works of Sigmund Freud*, ed. and trans. James Strachey, 24 vols. (London: Hogarth Press, 1953–74), 17:7–122. (I was tempted to title the last section of this chapter, "Frankenstein Meets the Wolf-Man.") See also *Three Essays on the Theory of Sexuality* (*Standard Edition*, 7:125–43) and "The Sexual Theories of Children" (*Standard Edition*, 9:205–26). For other discussions of the primal scene, see J. Laplanche and J. Pontalis, "Fantasme originaire, fantasme des origines, origines du fantasme," *Les Temps modernes* 215 (1964): 1833–68; "Scientific Proceedings Panel Reports: The Pathogenicity of the Primal Scene," reported by Richard A. Isay, *Journal of the American Psychoanalytical Association* 26 (1978): 131–42; Aaron H. Esman, "The Primal Scene: A Review and a Reconsideration," *Psychoanalytic Study of the Child* 28 (1973):49–81; Henry Edelheit, "Mythopoiesis and the Primal Scene," *Psychoanalytic Study of Society* 5 (1972): 212–33. Esman, citing Greenacre, notes that "the scary ogres that people children's fantasies and children's literature are representations of the primal scene with the sexual images of the parents fused into frightening or awe-inspiring figures" (p. 65). Edelheit notes that the image of the "bound Prometheus" is "built upon a widely recurring pattern which I call the primal scene schema" (p. 212). (See also Edelheit, "Crucifixion Fantasies and their Relation to the Primal Scene," *Summaries of Scientific Proceedings* 4 [1970]: 19–21.) I am grateful to Dr. Seymour Handler for conversations about psychoanalytic theories of the primal scene, *Frankenstein*, and related questions.

53. In addition to Rubenstein, "'My Accursed Origin,'" see Johnson, "My

Monster/My Self," p. 7; Hirsch, "The Monster Was a Lady," p. 125; Kaplan, "Fantasy of Paternity," pp. 125–26.

54. Rubenstein, "'My Accursed Origin,'" p. 165.

55. See ibid. pp. 170–71.

56. Mary Shelley refers to these letters in a letter she wrote to Percy Shelley on 2 October 1817: "come and see your sweet babes and the little Commodore [Allegra or Alba] who is lively and an uncommonly interesting child—I never see her without thinking of the expressions in my Mother's letters concerning Fanny" (*The Letters of Mary W. Shelley*, ed. Jones, 2 vols. [Norman: University of Oklahoma Press, 1944], 1:39).

57. *Memoirs*, p. 176. See also Gilbert and Gubar, *The Madwoman in the Attic*, p. 244.

58. Frankenstein describes how he "collected bones from charnel-houses" and how "the dissecting room and the slaughter-house furnished many of my materials" (*F*, p. 53); when he destroys the female monster, he says he "tore to pieces the thing on which I was engaged" (*F*, p. 159).

59. *Memoirs*, p. 112.

60. Wollstonecraft, *Posthumous Works*, 3:5.

61. Gilbert and Gubar, *The Madwoman in the Attic*, p. 246.

62. Wollstonecraft, *Posthumous Works*, 1:132.

63. The title page of the 1797 (London) edition of Gilbert Imlay's *Topographical Description of the Western Territory of North America* describes the author as "A Captain in the American Army during the War" (reprinted in "Series in American Studies" [Johnson Reprint Corporation, 1968], p. v).

64. Godwin, *Fleetwood*, 3:248.

65. B. J. Tysdahl writes of Godwin's publication of his wife's letters to Imlay that "twentieth-century readers may speculate on the psychological undercurrents in Godwin's mind that enabled him to luxuriate in the idea of his wife being so happy with another man." As I read the *Memoirs*, Godwin is demonstrating Wollstonecraft's unhappiness in detailing her love for (her obsession with) Imlay: for example, her suicide attempts. Tysdahl goes on to suggest, "It was only when Godwin had recovered from the loss of Mary Wollstonecraft and had himself experienced another kind of marriage that he could return to some of the problems that he touched in writing his first wife's biography. *Fleetwood* (1805) is a study in a husband's strange mixture of insecurity and aggression" (*William Godwin as Novelist* [London: Athlone, 1981], pp. 79–80).

66. See Wollstonecraft, *Posthumous Works*, 2:159–61. Of course "Mary" was also the name Mary Wollstonecraft used to represent a version of herself in the autobiographical fiction of her first novel, *Mary, A Fiction*.

67. Ralph M. Wardle, *Mary Wollstonecraft: A Critical Biography* (Lawrence: University of Kansas Press, 1951), p. 318; see also pp. 317–30.

68. As I mentioned earlier, Alphonse Frankenstein marries the young daughter of his best friend. Mary Shelley later wrote of her "excessive and romantic attachment to my father" (*Letters*, 2:88). For more on the theme of

father/daughter incest in Mary Shelley's works, including Mary Shelley's attitude toward her father, see Veeder, "The Negative Oedipus," and Knoepflmacher, "The Aggression of Daughters."

69. Caleb Williams's adventures often resemble those of Moll Flanders. He falls in with a gang of rogues, and becomes a master of deceit, disguise, and impersonation. At one point he disguises himself as a beggar (*CW*, p. 233); at another he disguises himself as a Jew: "By the talent of mimicry, which I had hitherto had recourse, I could copy their pronunciation of the English language. . . . one of my cares was to discolour my complexion . . . when my metamorphosis was finished, I could not upon the strictest examination conceive, that any one could have traced out the person of Caleb Williams in this new disguise" (*CW*, pp. 254-55).

70. Roxana is pursued by her daughter in a relentless chase which begins when her daughter sees her dancing in an immodest dress in what amounts to a spectacular primal scene scenario. For relevant readings of *Moll Flanders* and *Roxana*, see *The Figure of Theater*.

71. Freud, "From the History of An Infantile Neurosis," *Standard Edition*, 17:29-47.

72. David Seed notes, "Like Frankenstein, Caleb Williams is driven by curiosity to discover what is the secret of his employer, Mr. Falkland," although he claims that "there is no explicit allusion to this novel in *Frankenstein*" ("'Frankenstein'—Parable of [*sic*] Spectacle?" *Criticism: A Quarterly Journal for Literature and the Arts* 24 [1982]: 337-38).

73. Rubenstein, "'My Accursed Origin,'" p. 174.

74. James Rieger describes the "received history" of the ghost story contest as "an almost total fabrication." See his "Dr. Polidori and the Genesis of *Frankenstein*," appendix to *The Mutiny Within: The Heresies of Percy Bysshe Shelley* (New York: George Braziller, 1967), pp. 237-47.

75. At this point we might recall another waking nightmare brought about by the ghost story contest that also informs the primal scenes of *Frankenstein*: according to the now well-known story recounted by Polidori, Byron's recital of the lines about Geraldine from Coleridge's *Christabel* caused Percy Shelley to scream and run out of the room; he explained that looking at his wife while hearing the lines, he "suddenly thought of a woman he had heard of who had eyes instead of nipples." See *The Diary of Dr. John William Polidori*, ed. W. M. Rossetti (London: Elkin Mathews, 1911), pp. 128-29. For comments on this episode, see Rubenstein, "'My Accursed Origin,'" pp. 184-85, and Homans, *Bearing the Word*, p. 109.

76. Williams notes that the room in which he spies Mr. Falkland with the trunk is lit "by a small window near the roof" (*CW*, p. 7). When he is caught in the "private apartment" with the trunk, Mr. Falkland puts a loaded pistol to Williams's head but then throws it out the window (*CW*, pp. 131-32).

77. Critics have read in Frankenstein's scientific achievement a repression of the primal scene: the repression of sexual union as the origin of human beings and especially the repression of the mother. See Rubenstein, "'My

Accursed Origin,'" p. 177; Jacobus, "Is There a Woman in this Text?" p. 131; Knoepflmacher, "The Aggression of Daughters," p. 105; Kiely, *The Romantic Novel*, p. 164; Homans, *Bearing the Word*, pp. 101–4. Another parental text behind the primal scenes that conflate the wedding night and the death of the mother in *Frankenstein* may be the suicide note that Wollstonecraft sent to Imlay after her return from Scandinavia—published as Letter 69 in Godwin's edition of her *Posthumous Works*. Wollstonecraft, who already had survived a suicide attempt, writes: "Let my wrongs sleep with me! Soon, very soon shall I be at peace. . . . I go to find comfort, and my only fear is, that my poor body will be insulted by an endeavour to recall my hated existence. . . . Should your sensibility ever awake, remorse will find its way to your heart; and in the midst of sensual pleasure, I shall appear before you, the victim of your deviation from rectitude" (*Posthumous Works*, 4:11–12). The monster, who has been "called . . . into being" by Frankenstein, whose existence has been recalled from the dead, ends the novel with a vow of suicide: "My spirit will sleep in peace . . ." (*F*, p. 211). I hear in the monster's vow to Frankenstein, "I shall be with you on your wedding-night"—the sentence that haunts Frankenstein—an echo of Wollstonecraft's vow to appear before Imlay when he is "in the midst of sensual pleasure." It is perhaps not a coincidence that after he destroys the female monster and hears the monster's promise to appear at the consummation of his marriage, Frankenstein receives a letter from Clerval, about which he says: "This letter in a degree recalled me to life" (*F*, pp. 161–62).

78. Racine, *Phèdre*, act 4, sc. 2, ll. 10–11. Of course incest also figures prominently in Racine's play.

APPENDIX

1. *Mary Shelley's Journal*, ed. Frederick L. Jones (Norman: University of Oklahoma Press, 1944), pp. 47–50. All further references to Mary Shelley's reading will be based on this journal. Although the entries and the lists of books read contained in this journal are invaluable, it is important to keep in mind that the lists are not always complete or consistent with the books noted in the actual entries of the journals (see Jones, p. xiv); the absence of a title from the journal obviously does not mean that Mary Shelley did *not* read a particular book; nor do the lists indicate whether Mary Shelley was rereading a book or reading it for the first time.

2. *Journal*, p. 94. The entry is written by Percy Shelley on 26 March 1818. See also *The Letters of Percy Bysshe Shelley*, ed. Roger Ingpen (London: G. Bell, 1914), 2:590.

3. *Journal*, pp. 5, 55. Jones notes the loss of the journal on p. 50 n. 1.

4. In her account of the ghost story contest in the 1831 Introduction to *Frankenstein*, Mary Shelley seems to repress the presence of her stepsister, Jane (or Clare) Clairmont.

5. *The Letters of Mary W. Shelley*, ed. Jones, 2 vols. (Norman: University of Oklahoma Press, 1944), 1:12. She writes: "Here a small obelisk is erected

to the glory of Rousseau, and here (such is the mutability of human life) the magistrates, the successors of those who exiled him from his native country, were shot by the populace during that revolution which his writings mainly contributed to mature, and which, notwithstanding the temporary bloodshed and injustice with which it was polluted, has produced enduring benefits to mankind."

6. *Byron's Letters and Journals*, ed. Leslie A. Marchand (Cambridge, Mass.: Harvard University Press, 1976), 5:81. See also the letter of 27 June to John Murray: "I have traversed all Rousseau's ground—with the Heloise before me—& am struck to a degree with the force and accuracy of his descriptions—& the beauty of their reality" (5:82).

7. *The Letters of Percy Bysshe Shelley*, ed. Jones 2 vols. (Oxford: The Clarendon Press, 1964), 1:480, 486.

8. Ibid., 1:494.

9. *The Poetical Works of Percy Bysshe Shelley*, ed. Edward Dowden (London: Macmillan, 1900), p. 496. See Percy Shelley's 1811 letter to Hogg about Harriet Shelley: "I am not jealous, I perfectly understand the beauty of Rousseau's sentiment; yet Harriet is *not* an Heloisa, even were I a St. Preux,—but I am not jealous" (*Letters of Percy Bysshe Shelley*, 1:140). See also Voisine, *Jean-Jacques Rousseau en Angleterre à l'époque romantique: Les Ecrits autobiographiques et la légende* (Paris: Librairie Marcel Didier, 1956), p. 281.

10. *Byron*, ed. Jerome J. McGann (Oxford: Oxford University Press, 1986), pp. 142–45. See stanzas 77 to 81. P. D. Fleck argues that Mary Shelley "was profoundly affected by her reading with Shelley during the summer of 1816 of the third canto of *Childe Harold*" ("Mary Shelley's Notes to Shelley's Poems and *Frankenstein*," *Studies in Romanticism* 6 [1967]: 245).

11. Cited in Edward Duffy, *Rousseau in England: The Context of Shelley's Critique of the Enlightenment* (Berkeley and Los Angeles: University of California Press, 1979), p. 74.

12. William Hazlitt, "The Round Table" (No. 36), *The Examiner* (14 April 1816), p. 238.

13. In "Mr. Northcote's Conversations," originally published in 1826 and 1827 and revised in 1830, Hazlitt writes: "Rousseau was the first who held the torch (lighted at the never-dying fire in his own bosom) to the hidden chambers of the mind of man—like another Prometheus, breathed into his nostrils the breath of a new and intellectual life, enraging the Gods of the earth, and made him feel what is due to himself and his fellows" (*The Collected Works of William Hazlitt*, ed. A. R. Waller and Arnold Glover [London: J. M. Dent, 1903], p. 424).

14. In addition to Voisine and Duffy, see Irving Babbit, *Rousseau and Romanticism* (Austin: University of Texas Press, 1977); Henri Roddier, *J.-J. Rousseau en Angleterre au XVIIIe siècle: L'oeuvre et l'homme* (Paris: Boivin & Cie [1949?]; Henri Peyre, *Shelley et La France* (Paris: Librairie E. Droz, 1935). I have not attempted to cite or summarize the many critical

works devoted to particular Romantic poets (especially Percy Shelley) and Rousseau.

15. See Voisine, *Rousseau en Angleterre*, p. 262; G. D. Kelley, "Godwin, Wollstonecraft, and Rousseau," *Women and Literature* 3 (1975): 21–26. Entry 633 of the catalogue of Godwin's library includes: "Rousseau, (J.J.) ses Oeuvres. 17 vol. Londres 1782-86/ Remarks on the Writings and Conduct of Rousseau, 1767/ Anecdotes of his Life, 1798 3 vol." The "Catalogue of the Curious Library of that Very Eminent and Distinguished Author, William Godwin, Esq.," used for the auction conducted by Sotheby and Son on 17 June 1836, is reprinted in *Sales Catalogues of Libraries of Eminent Persons*, ed. A. N. L. Munby (London: Mansell with Sotheby Parke-Bernet Publications, 1973), 8:307. The *Remarks* are by Fuseli and the *Anecdotes* appears to be a translation of Corancez. Voisine speculates that although the *Oeuvres* of Rousseau are said to list London as the place of publication, they are "vraisemblement édités par Cazin, qui a donné entre ces deux dates sous la mensongère indication 'a Londres' dix-neuf volumes de Rousseau" (p. 182). (See also J. H. Warner, "Bibliography of XVIIIth-Century Editions of Rousseau with Notes on the Early Diffusion of His Writings," *Philological Quarterly* 13 [1934]: 225–47.) Although we do not know exactly when Godwin acquired his works of Rousseau, it seems more than likely that they were part of his library before Mary Shelley was born. Describing the evolution of his ideas in the 1793 preface to his *Enquiry Concerning Political Justice*, Godwin notes that approximately "twelve years" earlier (he is not precise in his dates) "the works of Rousseau" "fell into his hands"—in other words, around 1781, or about when his edition of the *Oeuvres* began to be published (*Enquiry Concerning Political Justice and Its Influence on Modern Morals and Happiness* [Harmondsworth: Penguin Books, 1985], p. 69.) It is also possible that some of these books belonged to Wollstonecraft before her death and thus were in the house while Mary Shelley was growing up.

16. Godwin, *Enquiry*, pp. 69, 496.

17. For a brief discussion of Godwin's relation to Rousseau as seen in the *Enquiry*, see Isaac Kramnick's Introduction to the *Enquiry*, esp. pp. 16–24. Lee Sterrenburg argues that Mary Shelley was responding to and drawing upon anti-Jacobin attacks on both her parents and the *philosophes* associated with the French Revolution ("Mary Shelley's Monster: Politics and Psyche in *Frankenstein*," in *The Endurance of Frankenstein: Essays on Mary Shelley's Novel*, ed. George Levine and U. C. Knoepflmacher [Berkeley and Los Angeles: University of California Press, 1979], pp. 143–71). See also Ronald Paulson's account of the analogies at play between the Revolution, the creation of the monster, and the birth of Mary Shelley herself in *Representations of Revolution (1789–1820)* (New Haven, Conn.: Yale University Press, 1983), pp. 239–47. Burke's polemics in his *Reflections on the Revolution in France* and elsewhere also are relevant here. Coleridge, an ambivalent reader of Godwin, draws on Godwin and Rousseau together for a critique of property in the sixth of his lectures on politics and religion. See *Lectures 1795*

On Politics and Religion, in *The Collected Works of Samuel Taylor Coleridge*, ed. Lewis Patton and Peter Mann, 13 vols. (Princeton, N.J.: Princeton University Press, 1971–81), 1:214–29.

18. See Kelley, "Godwin, Wollstonecraft, and Rousseau," p. 24.

19. William Godwin, *Fleetwood, or the New Man of Feeling*, 3 vols. (1805; reprint New York: Garland Publishing, 1979) 2:155.

20. Ibid., 2:179–80. See B. J. Tysdahl, *William Godwin as Novelist* (London: Athlone, 1981), p. 81.

21. For information about the importance of Rousseau for Godwin and Wollstonecraft (as well as Percy Shelley, Byron, and to some extent Mary Shelley), see Voisine, *Rousseau en Angleterre*, pp. 167–85, 261–319; see also pp. 21–26. For more on the relation of *Fleetwood* to Rousseau (as well as Mackenzie) see Tysdahl, *Godwin as Novelist*, pp. 100–101.

22. Mary Wollstonecraft, *A Vindication of the Rights of Woman*, ed. Carol H. Poston (New York: Norton, 1975), pp. 90–91. Compare Godwin: "Rousseau, notwithstanding his great genius, was full of weakness and prejudice. His *Émile* deserves perhaps, upon the whole, to be regarded as one of the principal reservoirs of philosophical truth as yet existing in the world; though with a perpetual mixture of absurdity and mistake" (*Enquiry*, p. 497).

23. Sandra M. Gilbert and Susan Gubar write: "Endlessly studying her mother's works and her father's, Mary Shelley may be said to have 'read' her family. . . . she studied her parents' writings, alone or together with Shelley, like a scholarly detective seeking clues to the significance of some cryptic text" ("Horror's Twin: Mary Shelley's Monstrous Eve," in *The Madwoman in the Attic: The Woman Writer and the Nineteenth-Century Literary Imagination* [New Haven, Conn.: Yale University Press, 1979], p. 223.) See also Marc A. Rubenstein, " 'My Accursed Origin': The Search for the Mother in *Frankenstein*," *Studies in Romanticism* 15 (1976): 165–94.

24. *Analytical Review* 11 (1791): 528. See also *Analytical Review* 9 (1791): 182–83; and *Analytical Review* 6 (1790): 385–91. On the attribution of these and other articles to Mary Wollstonecraft, see Voisine, *Rousseau en Angleterre*, pp. 118–21, 169, and Ralph M. Wardle, *Mary Wollstonecraft: A Critical Biography* (Lawrence: University of Kansas Press, 1951), pp. 131–32. Wollstonecraft also refers to Rousseau in *A Vindication of the Rights of Men in A Letter to the Right Honourable Edmund Burke; Occasioned by his Reflections on the Revolution in France* (London, 1790). On 24 March 1787, Wollstonecraft wrote to her sister Everina: "I am now reading Rousseau's *Emile*, and love his paradoxes. He chuses a *common* capacity to educate— and gives as a reason, that a genius will educate itself—however he wanders into that *chimerical* world in which I have too often [wand]ered— and draws the usual conclusions that all is vanity and vexation of spirit. He was a strange inconsistent unhappy clever creature—yet he possessed an uncommon portion of sensibility and penetration" (*Collected Letters of Mary Wollstonecraft*, ed. Wardle [Ithaca, N.Y.: Cornell University Press, 1979], p. 145).

25. [Wollstonecraft,] *Mary, A Fiction* (1788; reprint New York: Garland Publishing, 1974), title page; p. 1.

26. [Wollstonecraft], *Posthumous Works of the Author of a Vindication of the Rights of Woman*, 4 vols. (1798; reprint New York: Garland Publishing, 1974), 1:42. Mary Poovey suggests another reading of Wollstonecraft's relation to the novel of sensibility in *The Proper Lady and the Woman Writer: Ideology as Style in the Works of Mary Wollstonecraft, Mary Shelley, and Jane Austen* (Chicago: University of Chicago Press, 1984), pp. 114–42.

27. [Wollstonecraft], *The Wrongs of Woman*, in *Posthumous Works*, 1:42–43.

28. Letter of 1 July 1796, *Collected Letters of Mary Wollstonecraft*, p. 331. Rubenstein argues that Mary Shelley would have read the unpublished correspondence between Wollstonecraft and Godwin ("'My Accursed Origin,'" pp. 170–71).

29. Wollstonecraft, Letter 23, *Posthumous Works*, 3:59. Mary Shelley refers to her mother's letters about Fanny in a letter she wrote to Percy Shelley on 2 October 1817: "come and see your sweet babes and the little Commodore [Allegra or Alba] who is lively and an uncommonly interesting child—I never see her without thinking of the expressions in my Mother's letters concerning Fanny" (*The Letters of Mary W. Shelley*, 1:39).

30. William Godwin, *Memoirs of the Author of a Vindication of the Rights of Woman* (1798; reprint New York: Garland Publishing, 1974), p. 88. See [Henry Fuseli], *Remarks on the Writings and Conduct of J. J. Rousseau* (London, 1767). See also note 15 above.

31. See Chapter 6, note 5.

32. Percy Shelley writes to Hogg on 18 July; the first appearance of the phrase "write my story" occurs in Mary Shelley's entry for 24 July (*Journal*, p. 53).

Index